MARTHA GRAHAM DANCE COMPANY 100 YEARS

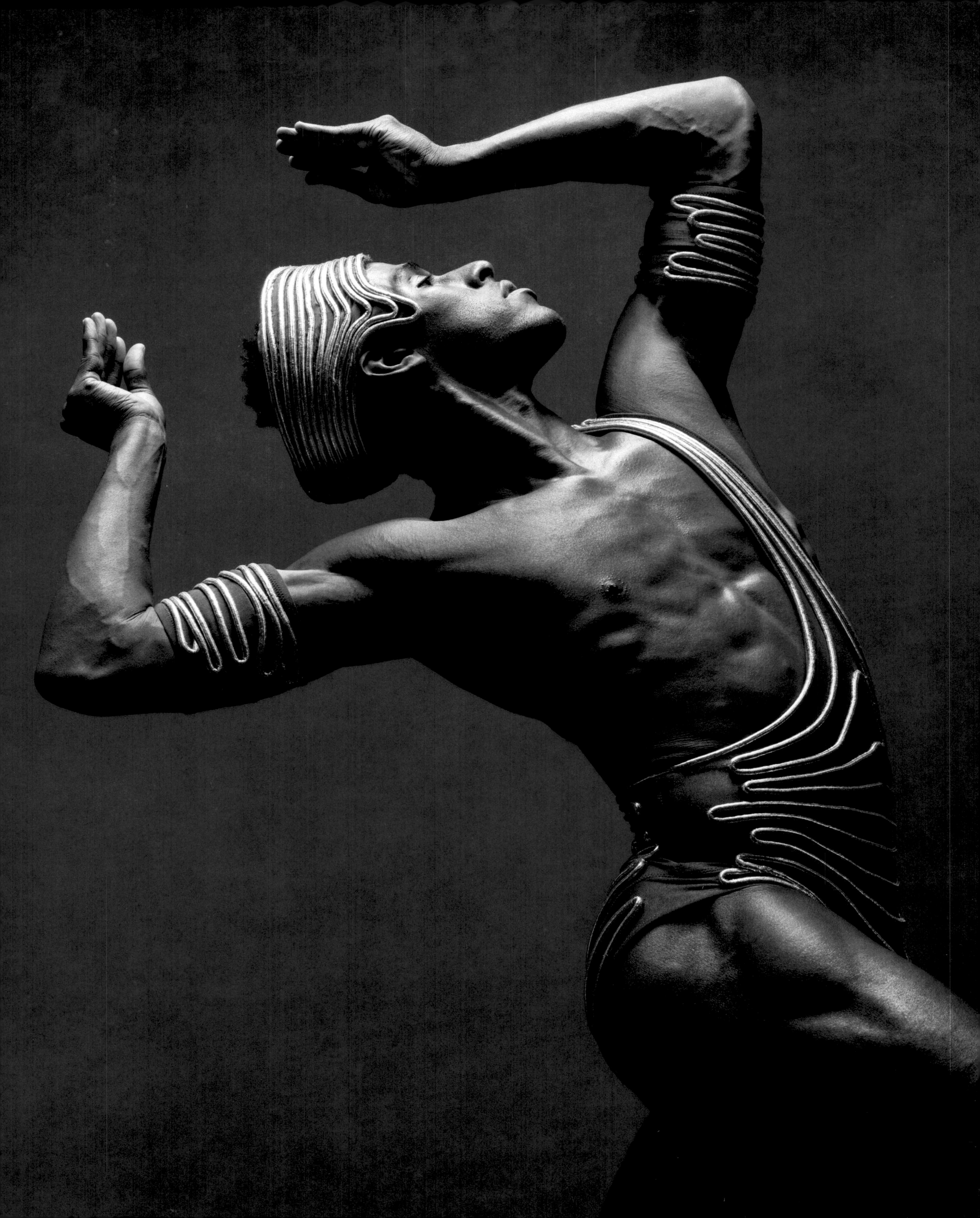

MARTHA GRAHAM DANCE COMPANY 100 YEARS

Ken Browar and Deborah Ory

NYC DANCE PROJECT

Introduction by Janet Eilber

Text by Peter Sparling

All Choreography by Martha Graham

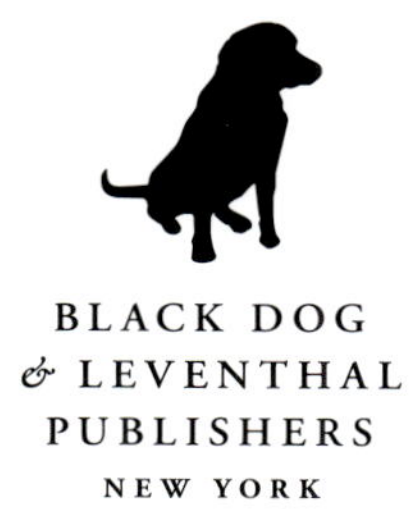

BLACK DOG
& LEVENTHAL
PUBLISHERS
NEW YORK

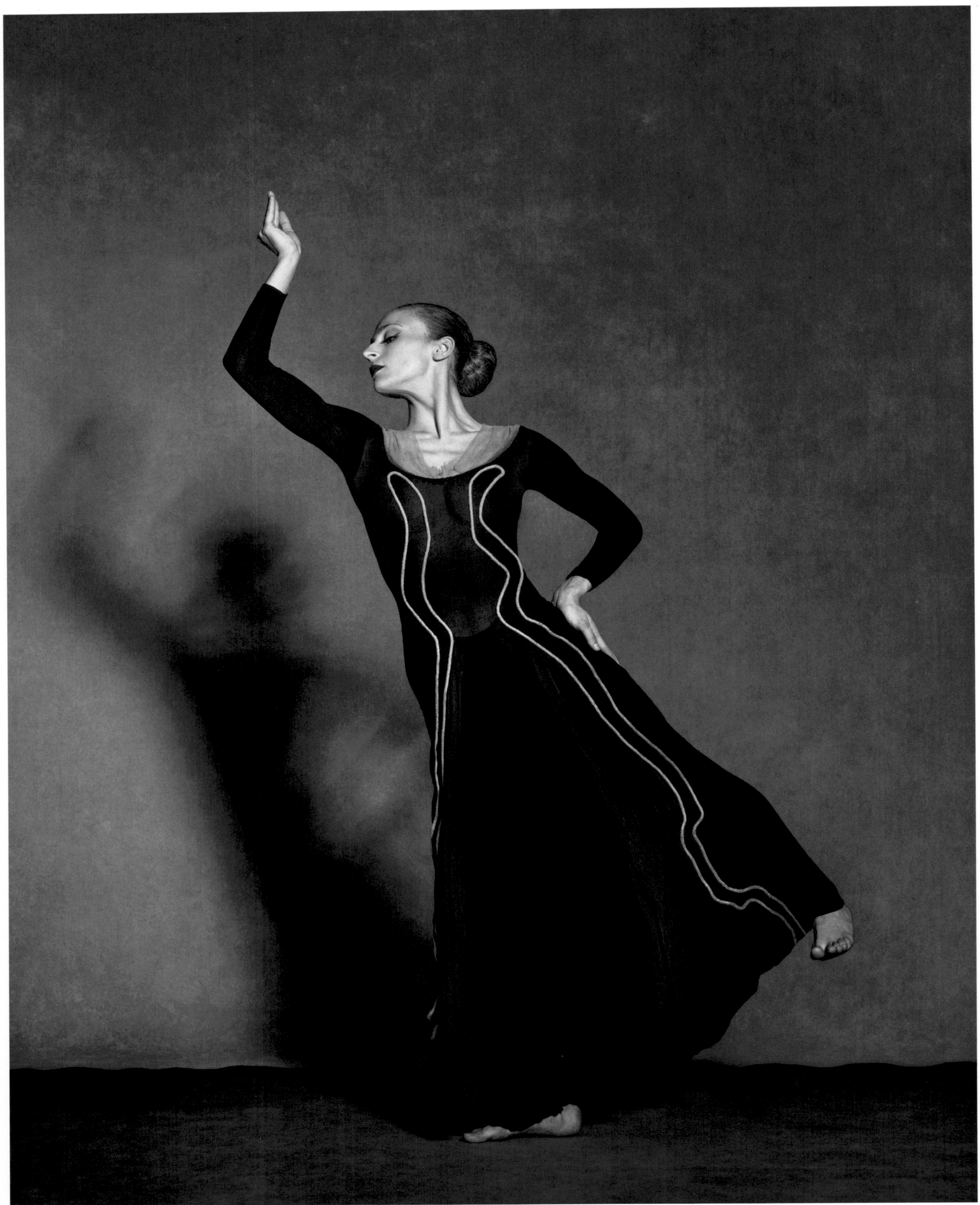

Marzia Memoli in vintage costume. Previous: Lloyd Knight dancing in *Andromache's Lament*. Costume by Halston.

The body says what words cannot.

—MARTHA GRAHAM

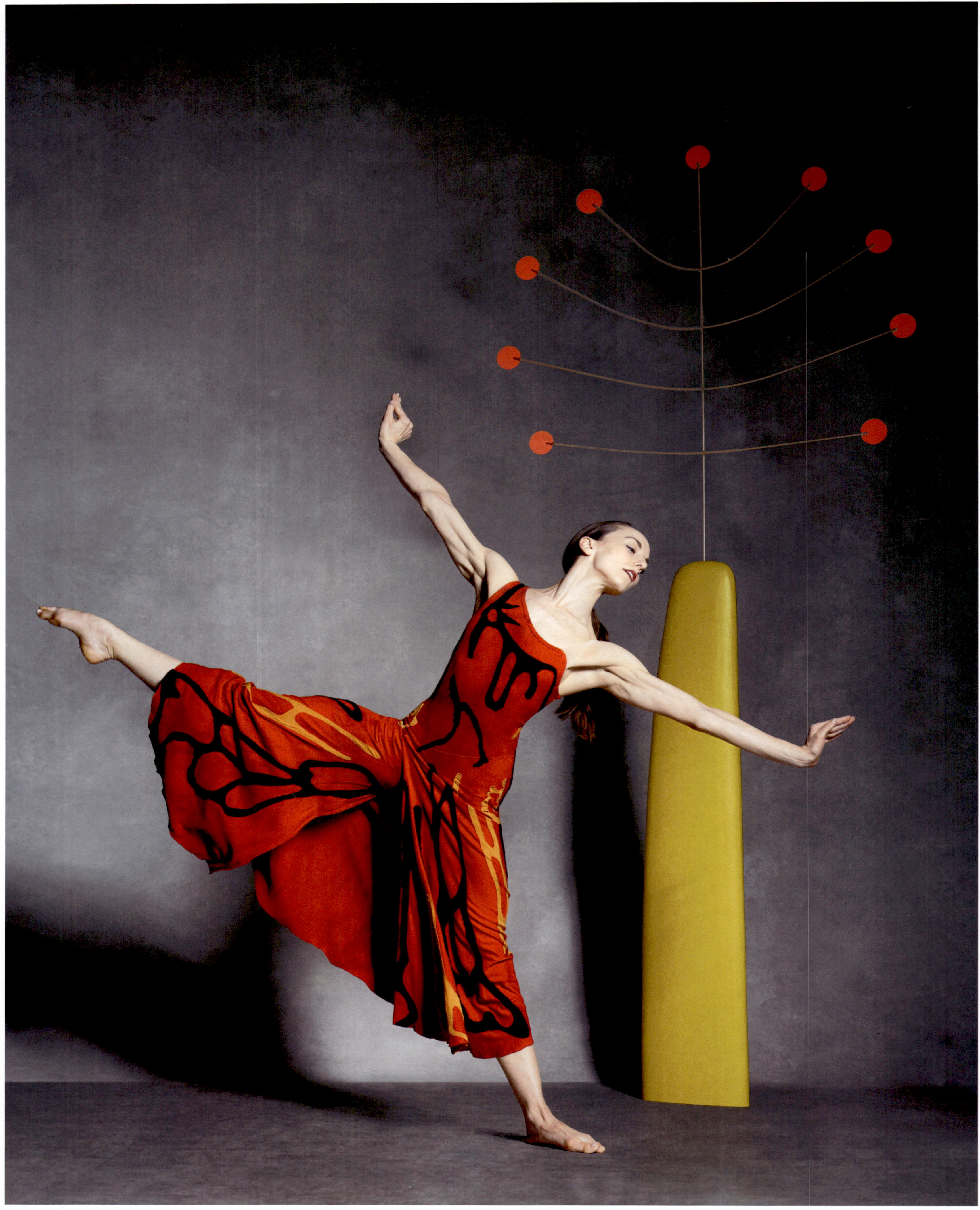

Anne Souder dancing in *Dark Meadow*.

Contents

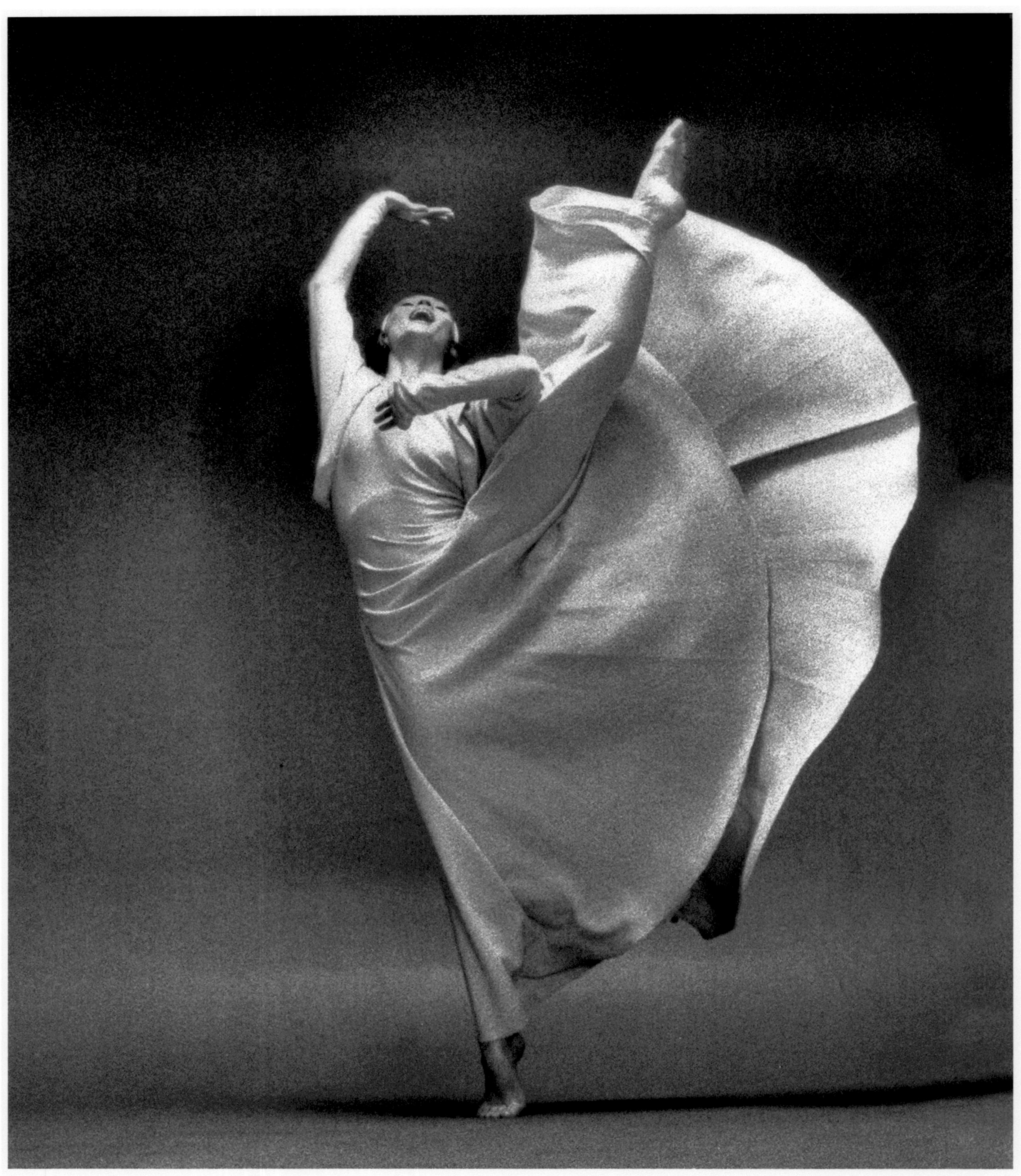

Janet Eilber dancing in *Frontier*. Photograph by Max Waldman.

INTRODUCTION

JANET EILBER

It may surprise people to know that Martha Graham was a great believer in stillness. Though she was recognized as the genius inventor of an entirely new way of moving, Graham was a devotee of stopping time. The many tableaus and moments of arrested motion in her choreography testify to this. She taught us that when the body is stationary, the inner life can provide intense psychological movement—the growing fury, crushing grief, deepening desire, dawning recognition, or any number of emotional revelations that can stop us in our tracks. And in those moments, Martha wanted us to vibrate with intention that could be felt in the balcony of the theater while never moving a muscle.

I was thrilled to have NYC Dance Project, the brilliant artistic duo of Deborah Ory and Ken Browar, willing to take on the challenge of capturing the historic span of the Martha Graham Dance Company heritage—in stillness. Their assignment was to illuminate a legacy of motion—one hundred years of relentless creative activity, unique personalities, and theatrical presentations—all through the power of the suspended image.

These pages contain the dancers of the Martha Graham Dance Company in its tenth decade—dancers who never met Martha Graham. Yet these photos not only reverberate with Martha's insistence on activated stillness but also evoke generations of her most essential collaborators—her dancers. She called them "athletes of God."

Consider that, as today's dancers don the costumes that were designed for others many years earlier, as they perform the now-classic movements that were invented for other bodies, they literally follow the footsteps of their predecessors.

I was part of the Graham generation of the 1970s—the current midpoint of our history. I danced in the celebration of our fiftieth season. (Imagine my surprise at arriving at our hundredth.) From this vantage point, I was fortunate to know many of the extraordinary dancers who came before me and, by now, all of those who have followed. Artists, mentors, teachers, keepers of the Graham flame, these foundational dancers from years past are beautifully evoked in Deborah and Ken's photos (though today's dancers are most visible). You will find the names of original cast members later in these pages. This book is an homage to all who have gone before and a testament to the timelessness of our legacy.

The ferocious dedication and investment of those earlier generations—our Graham ancestors—have propelled our history. As today's dancers invigorate the Graham dances with their own sensibilities, artistry, and place in time, they become part of the continuum. When they press into the air, fling themselves impossibly off-balance, or simply define the space with the intensity of their gaze, they are alive with all that has gone before. They are the current—but temporary—custodians of an ephemeral body of work that has reached its one hundredth year by the grace of Martha Graham's athletes of God.

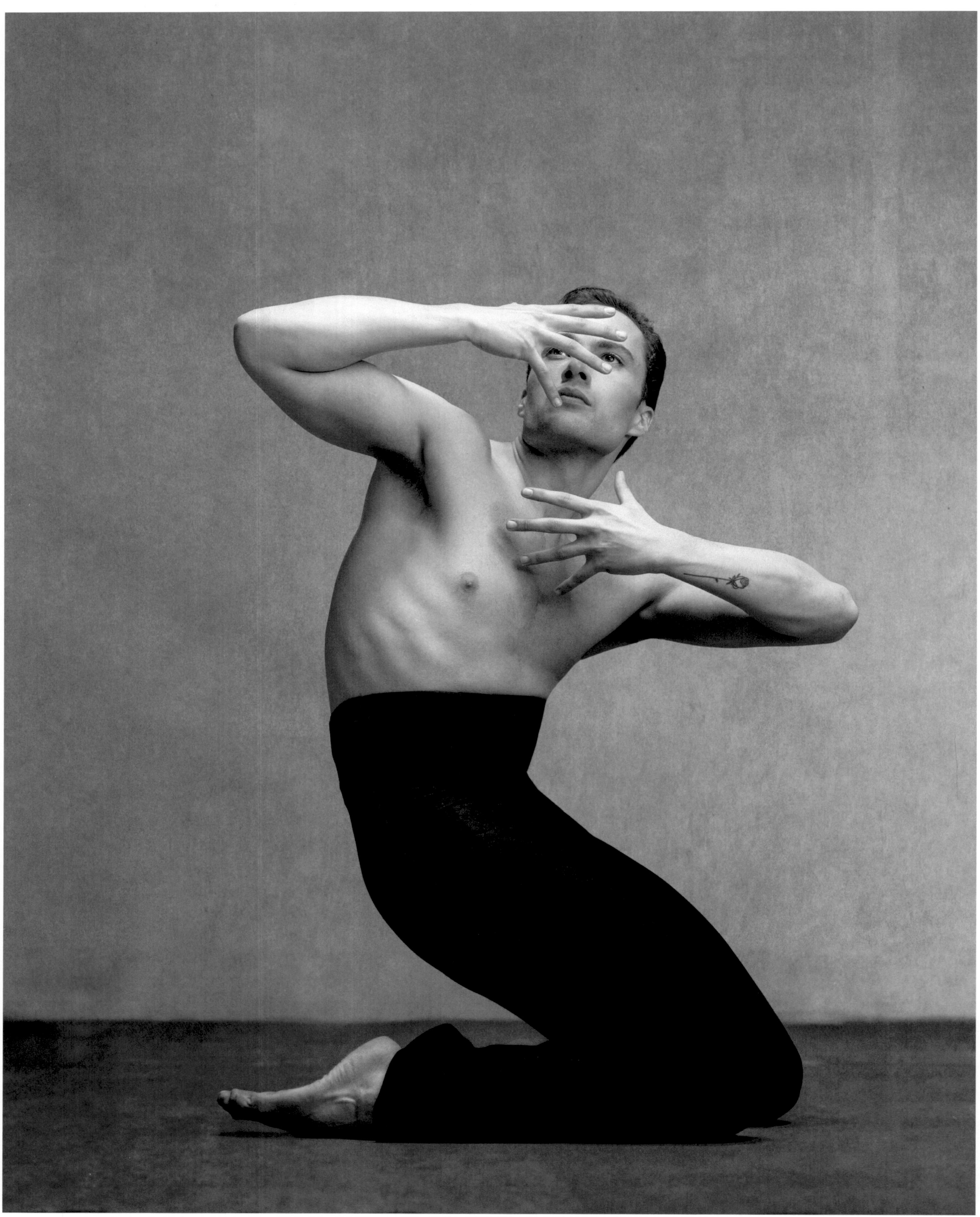

Alessio Crognale-Roberts dancing in *Embattled Garden*.

Dance is the hidden language of the soul.

—MARTHA GRAHAM

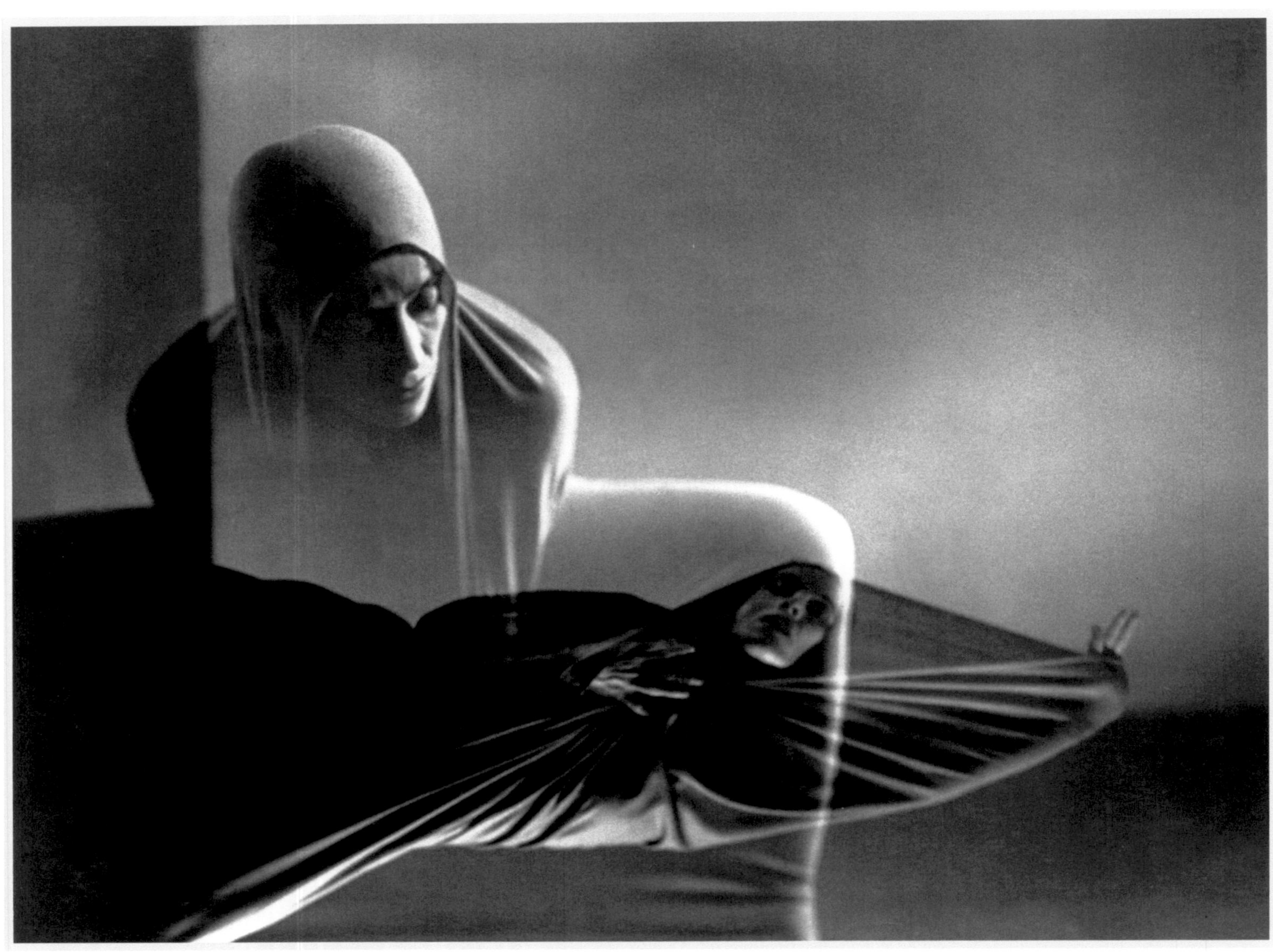

Martha Graham. Photograph by Barbara Morgan.

LAMENTATION, 1930

An ode to the vicissitude and dignity of mourning.

Martha Graham's most iconic solo is a metaphor in motion for grief itself. Graham's mourner sits alone on a bench encased in a tube of purple stretch jersey that doubles as shawl and burial shroud. She pulls the fabric taut around her contorted form, carving ever-shifting shapes into the darkness. The movement communicates a visceral and emotional experience, or the sensation of skin moving over bone. The gestures of pleading and the agony of loss are amplified into pure sculpture.

One might imagine that Graham needed to at first externalize the oppositional pull of fabric to better understand the body's capacity to express extreme states of inner emotion. As Graham continued her movement explorations with her early company of women throughout the 1930s, she evolved a unique movement vocabulary of contraction and release, of extreme, sustained tension through both angular and curvilinear shapes.

COSTUME DESIGN
Martha Graham

COMPOSER
Zoltán Kodály

Lamentation

DANCER
Natasha Diamond-Walker

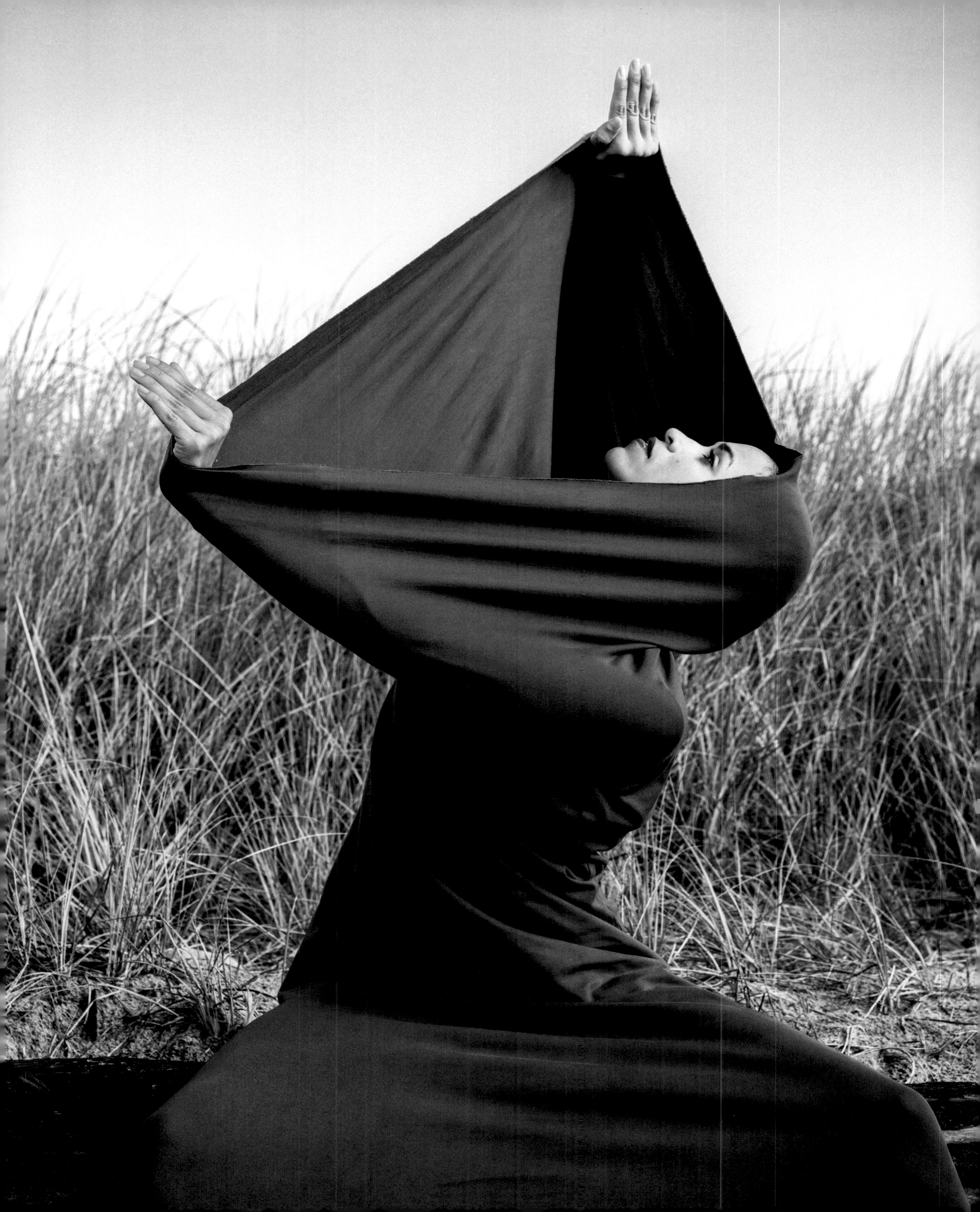

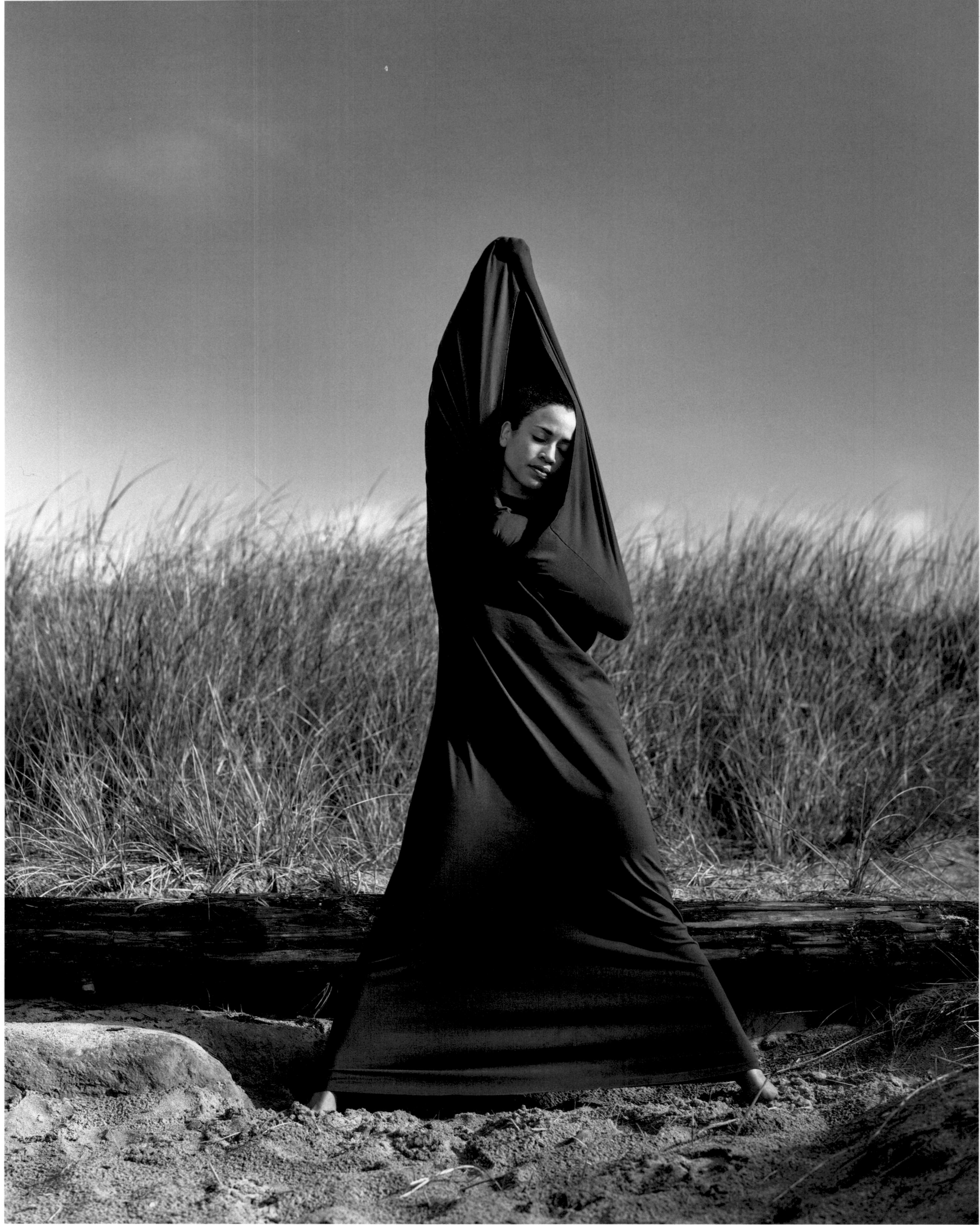

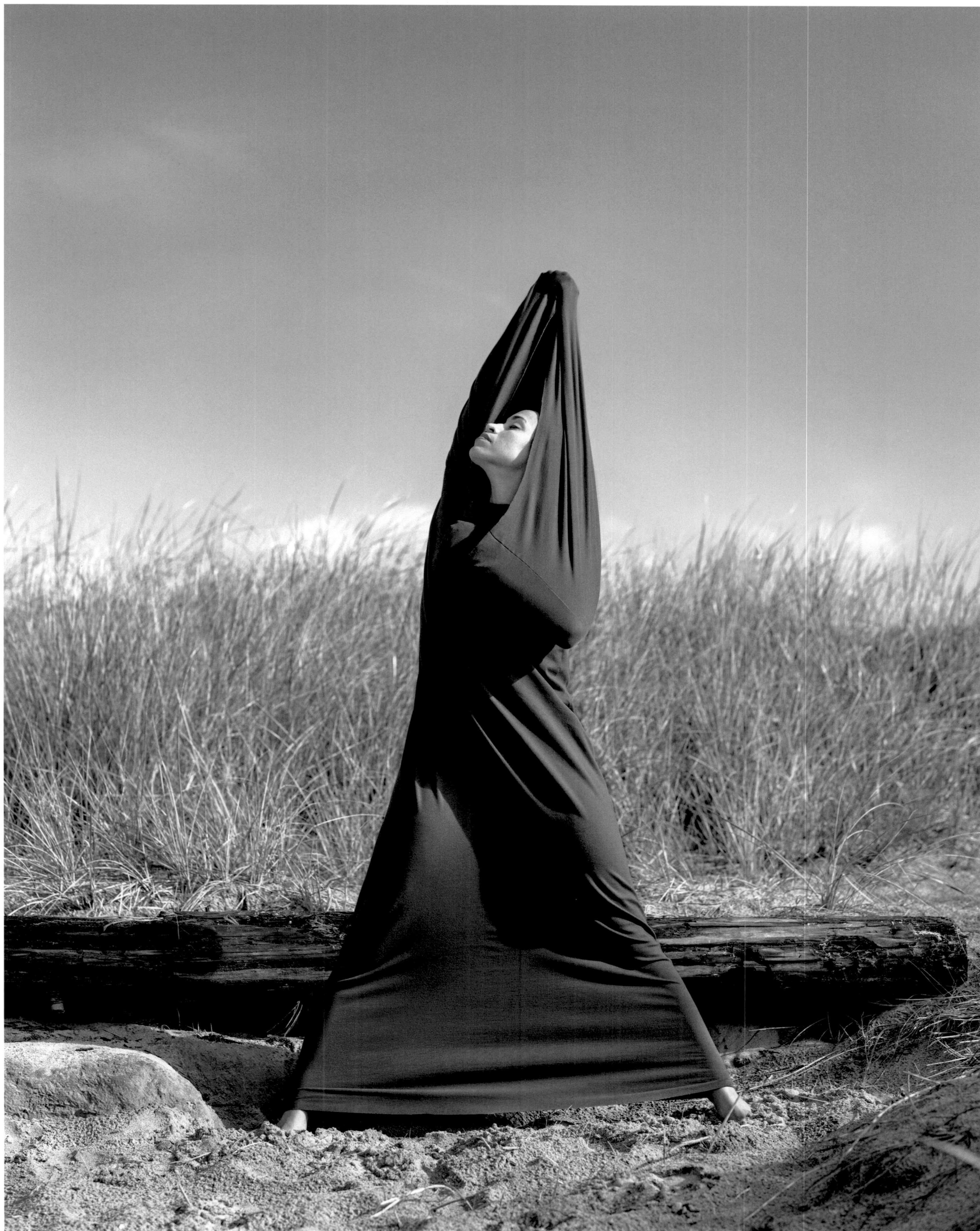

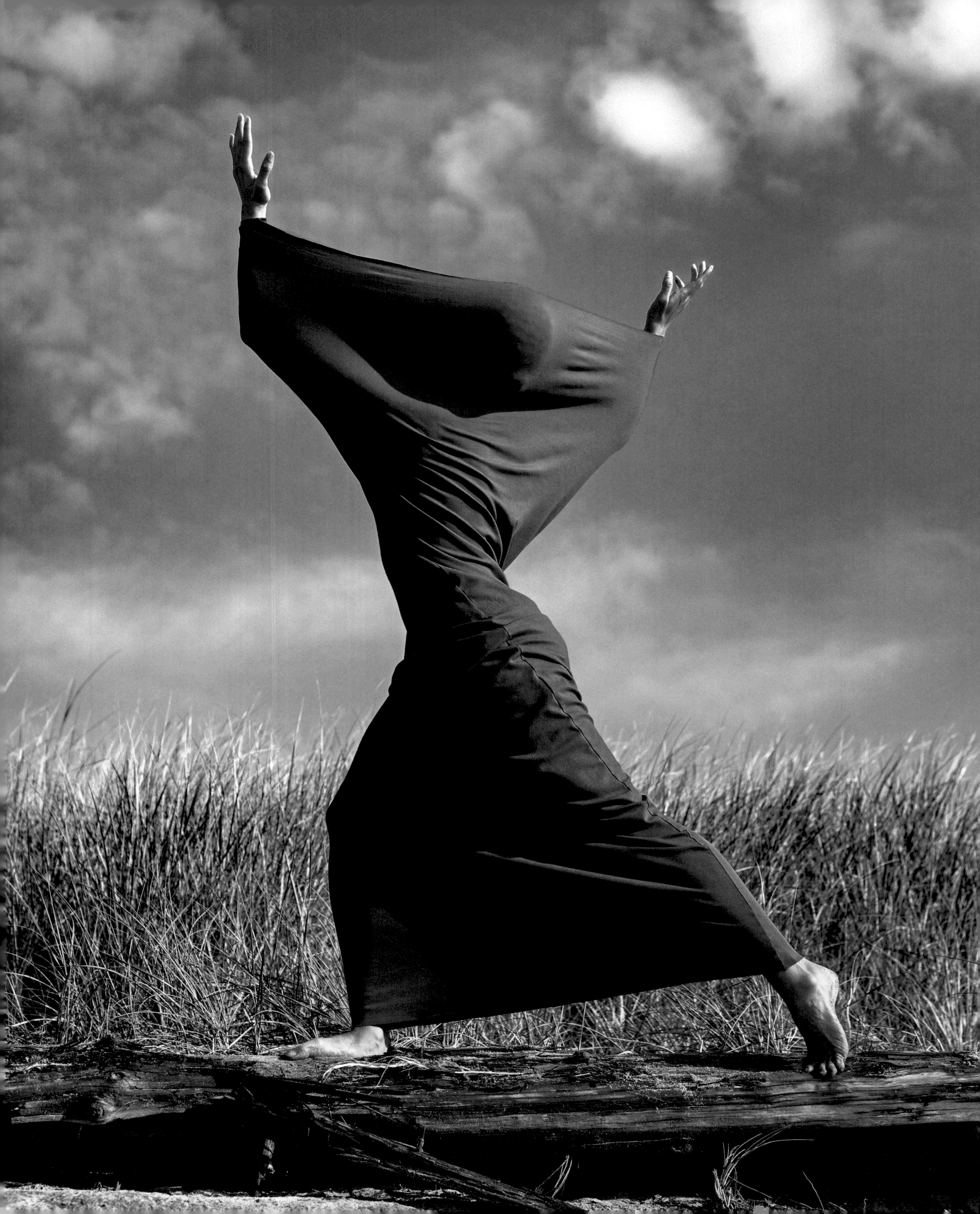

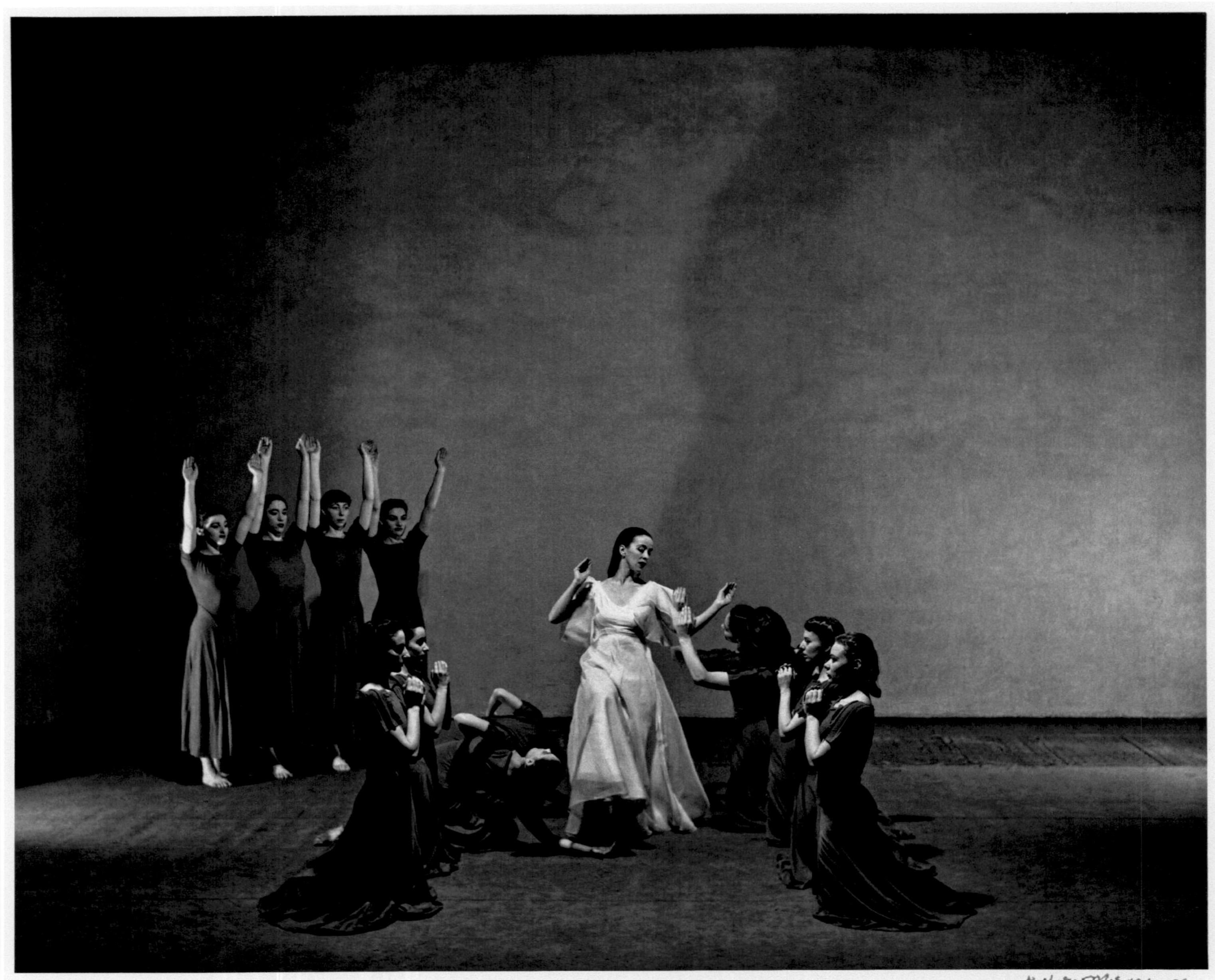

Martha Graham and Company. Photograph by Barbara Morgan.

PRIMITIVE MYSTERIES, 1931

A demonstration of the human desire for transformative ritual.

Graham's 1931 masterwork *Primitive Mysteries* draws its influence from both Catholic ritual and Indigenous ceremonial dances of the American Southwest. Each of three sections is bookended with a solemn, silent processional of dancers entering and exiting the stage. A single figure in a white organdy gown, inspired by the night-blooming Cereus flower, assumes the role of Mary, the matriarch, or the Virgin. She is surrounded in each dance by her acolytes dressed in royal blue.

In "Hymn to the Virgin," Mary blesses her followers, who respond with gestures of prayer and reverence. "Crucifixus" evokes images of the crucified Christ as the women assume poses of grief and mourning. For the joyous closing section, "Hosannah," the women's steps become light and buoyant. Mary rises from her pietà-like position to spread her arms wide, emanating rebirth and an ecstatic dominion. She exits, exalted, with her flock of celebrants.

COSTUME DESIGN
Martha Graham

COMPOSER
Louis Horst

Primitive Mysteries

VIRGIN

So Young An

DANCERS

Laurel Dalley Smith, Devin Loh, Marzia Memoli,
Amanda Moreira, Anne O'Donnell Passero,
Kate Reyes, Anne Souder

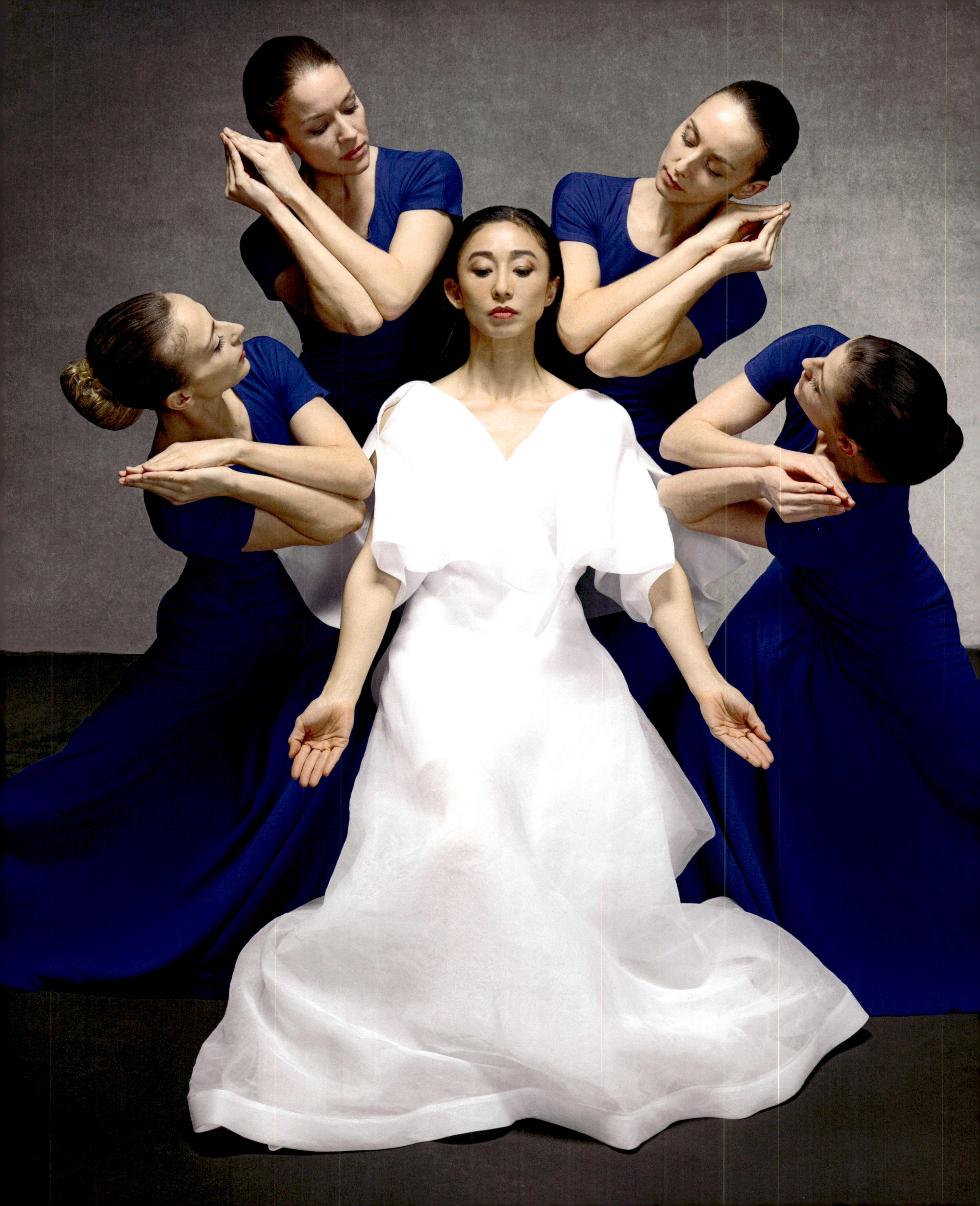

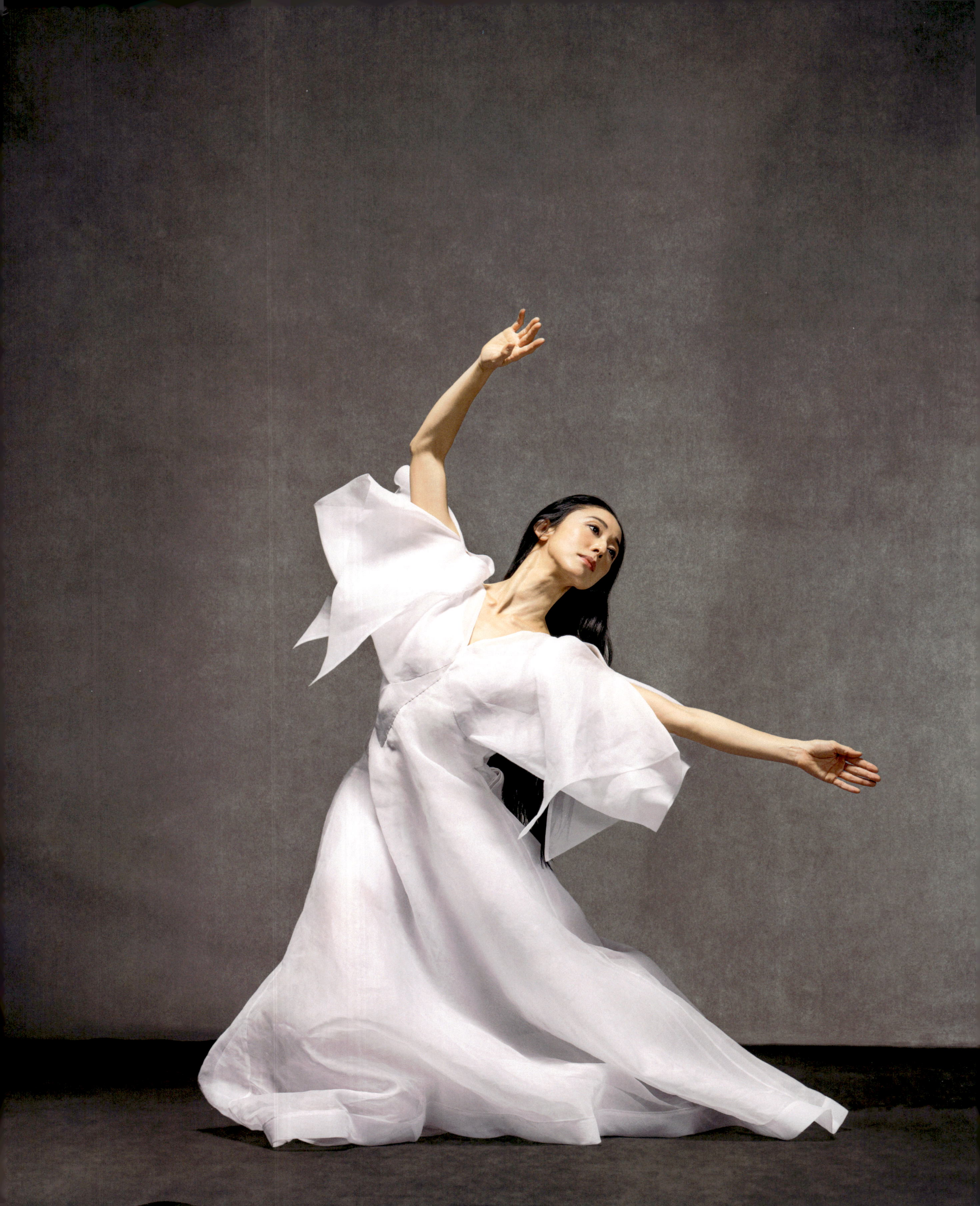

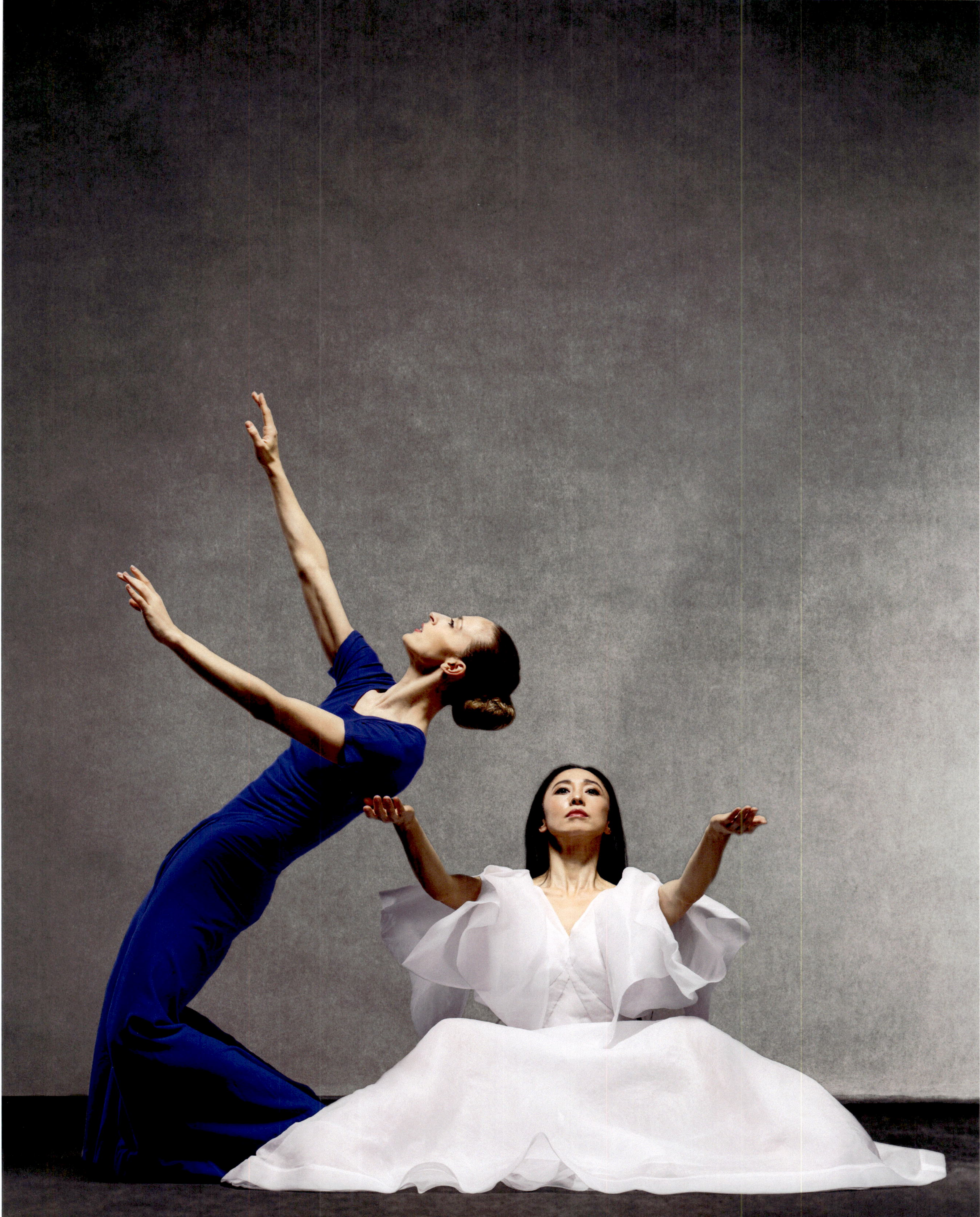

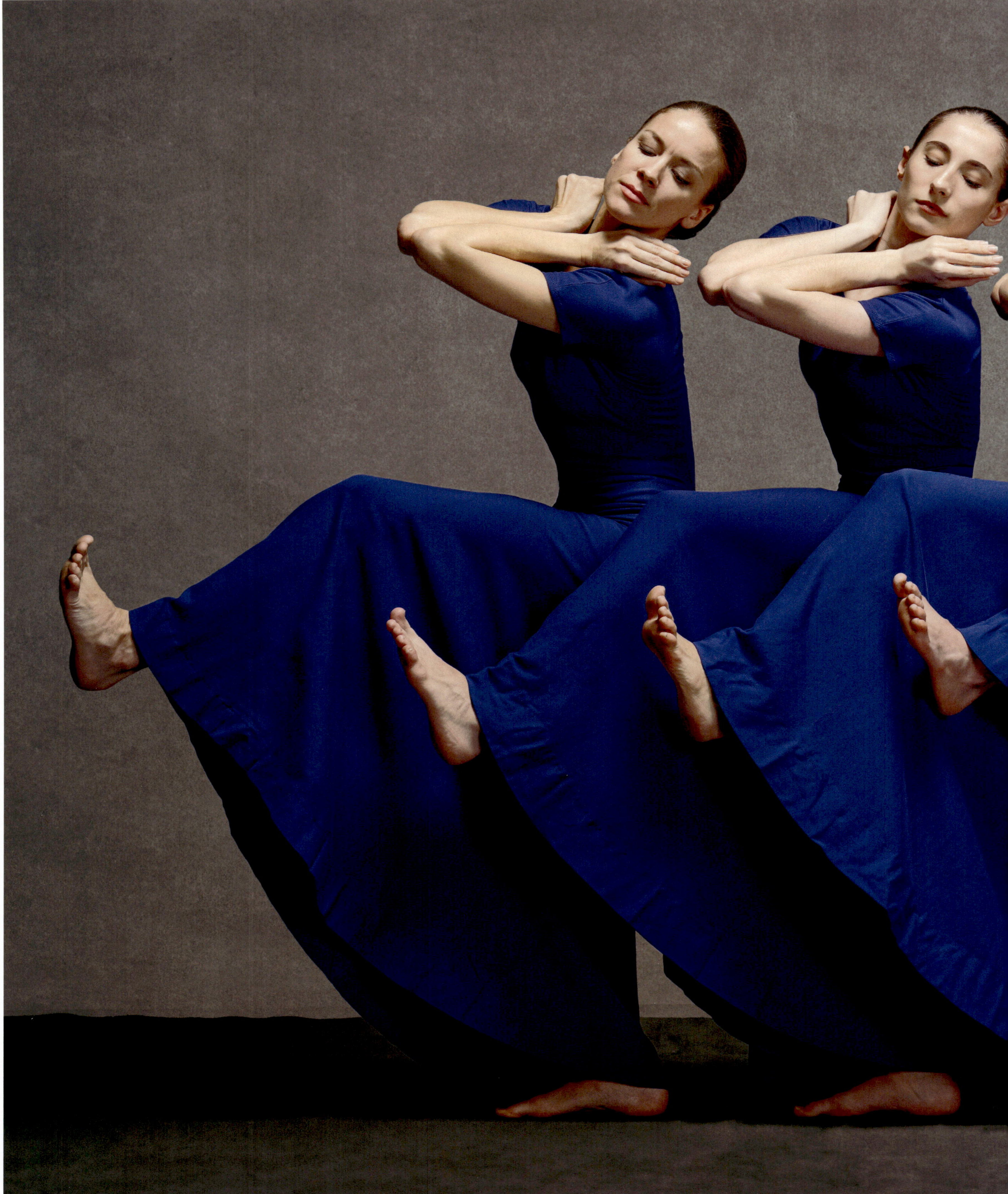

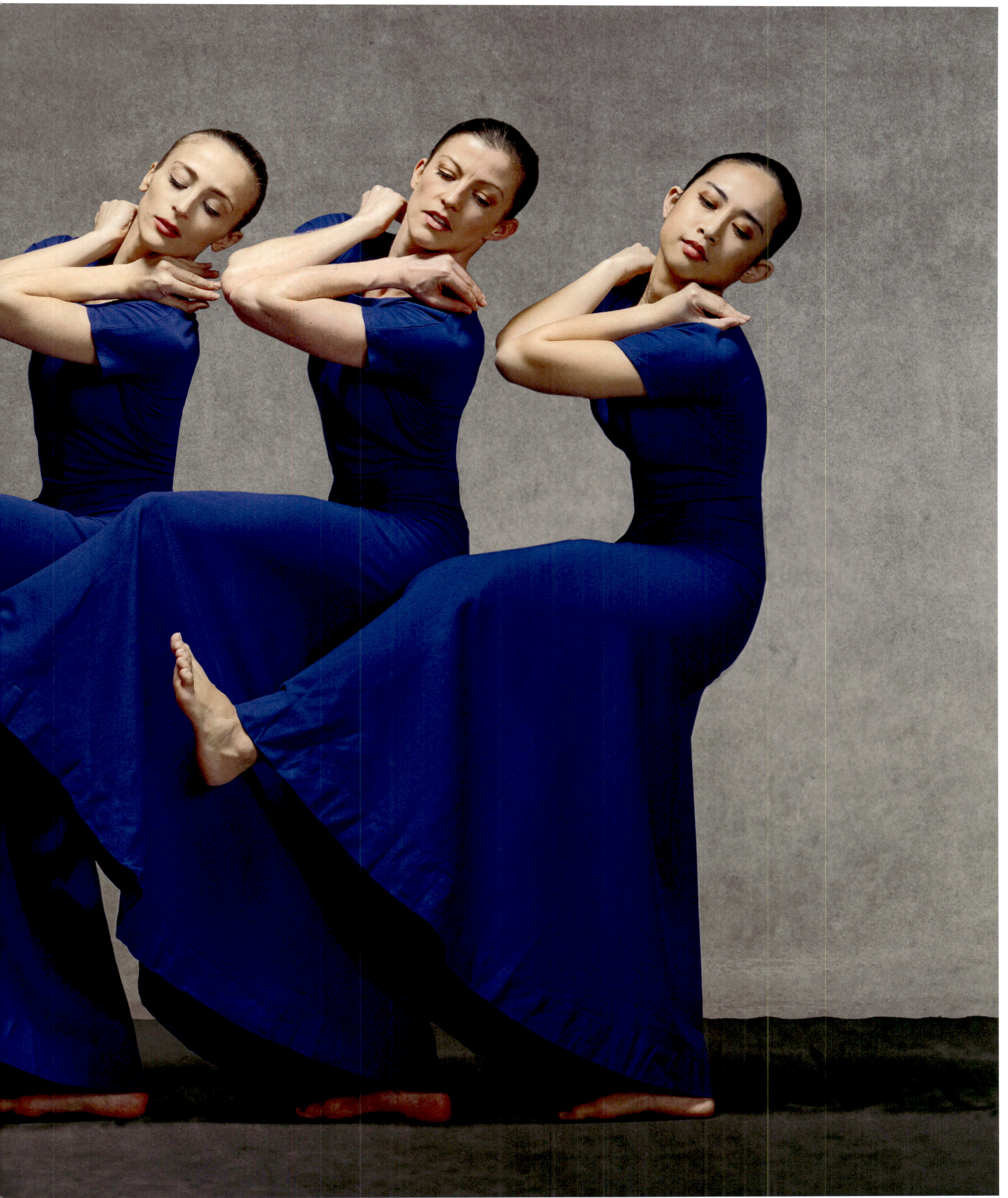

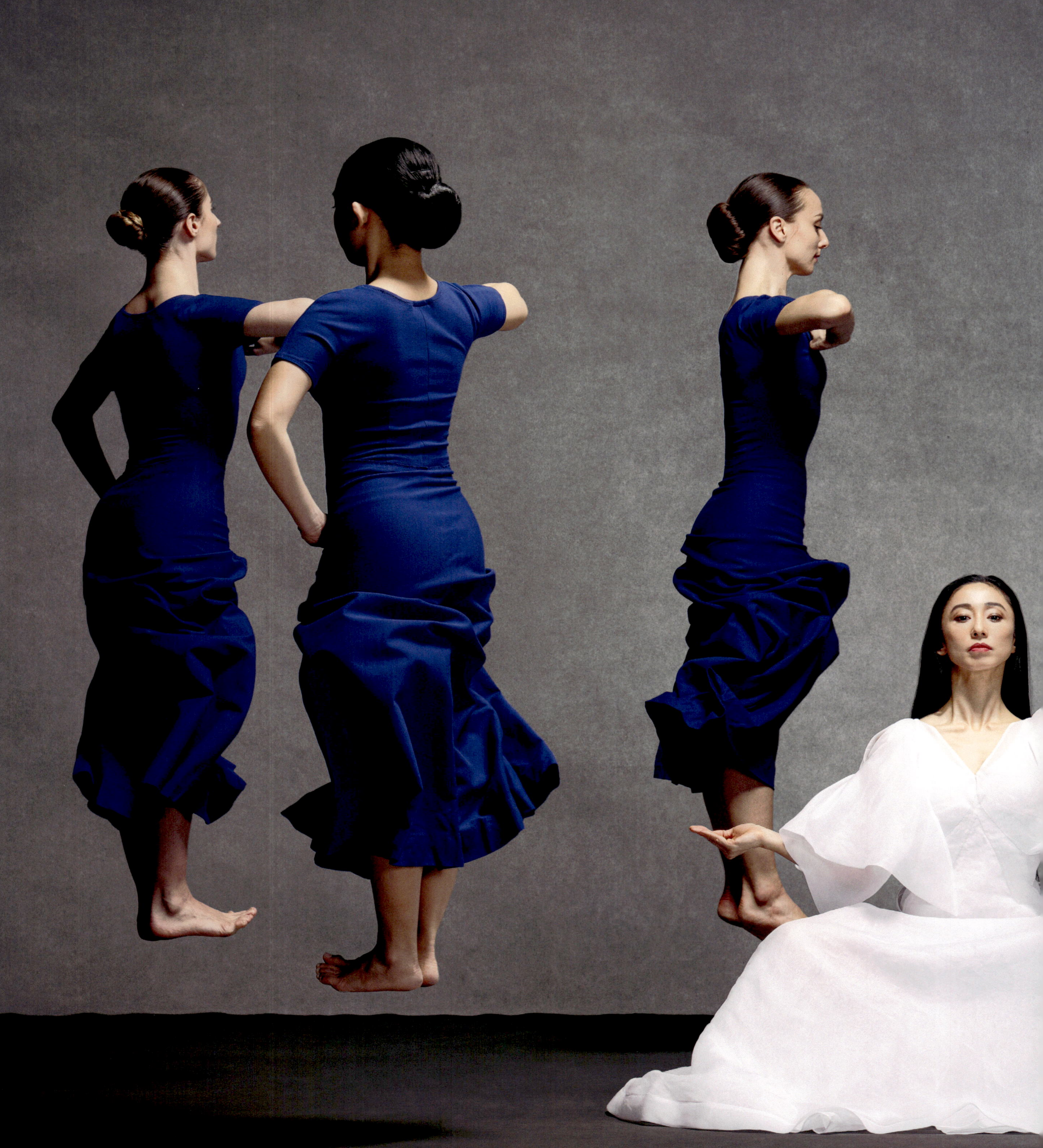

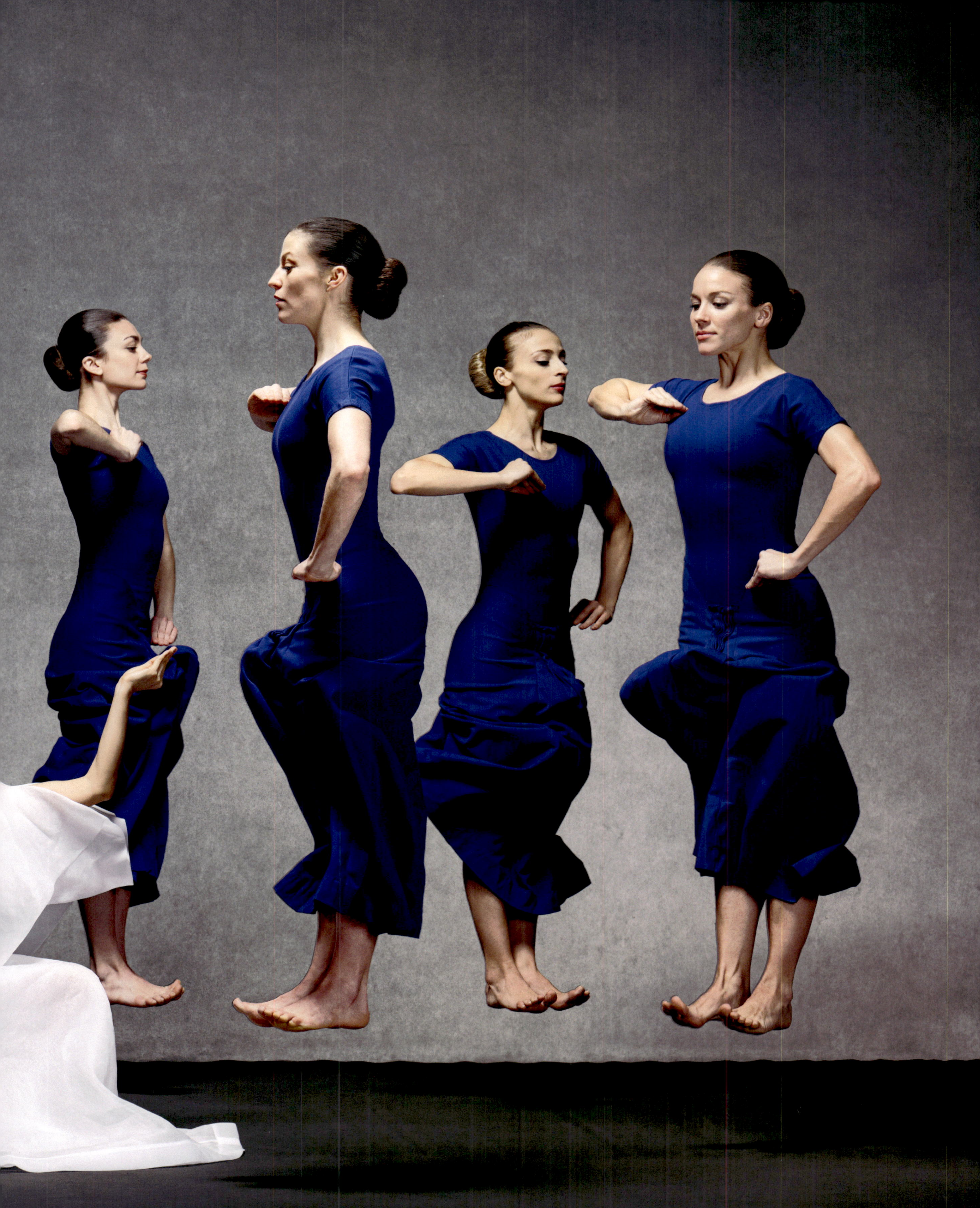

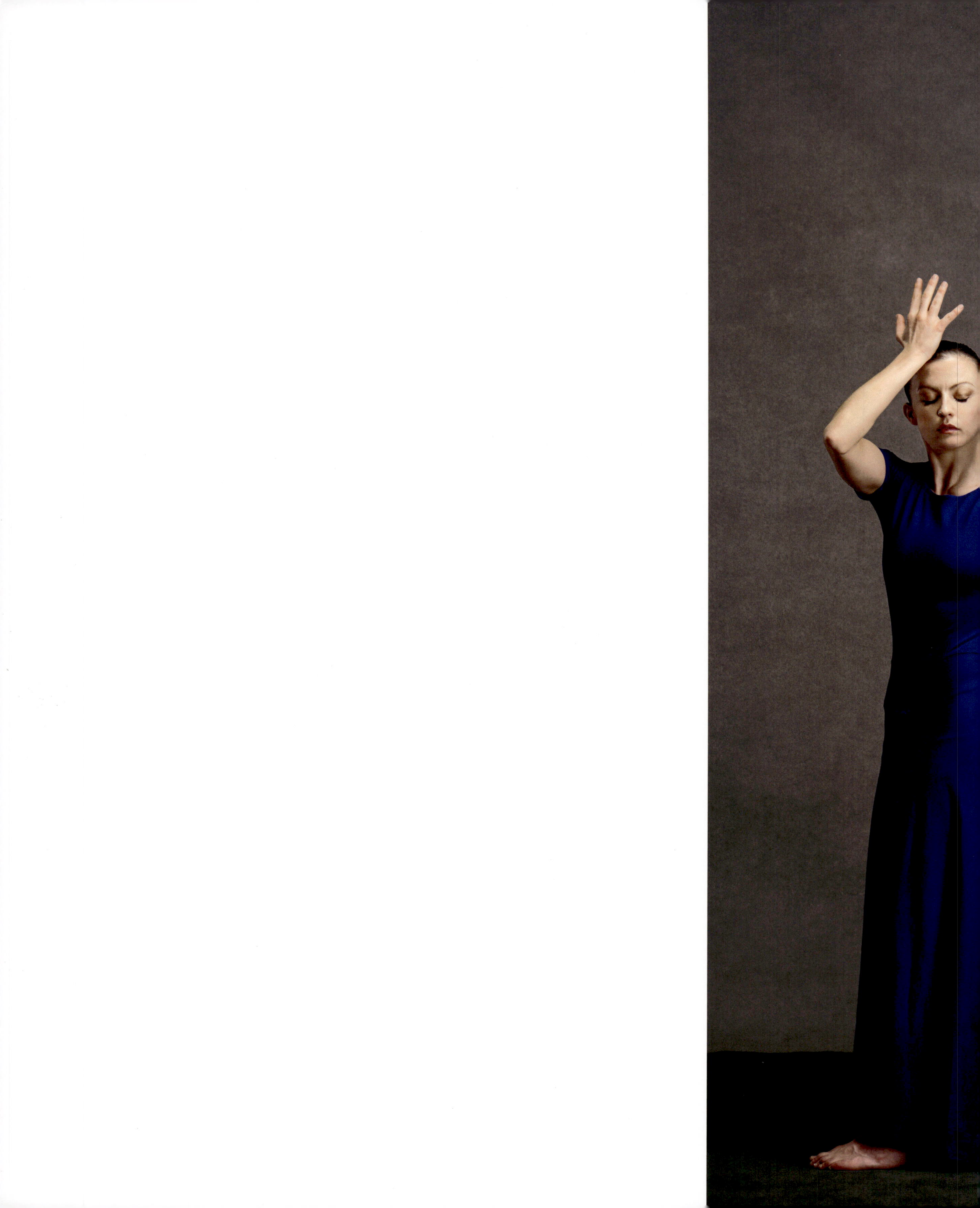

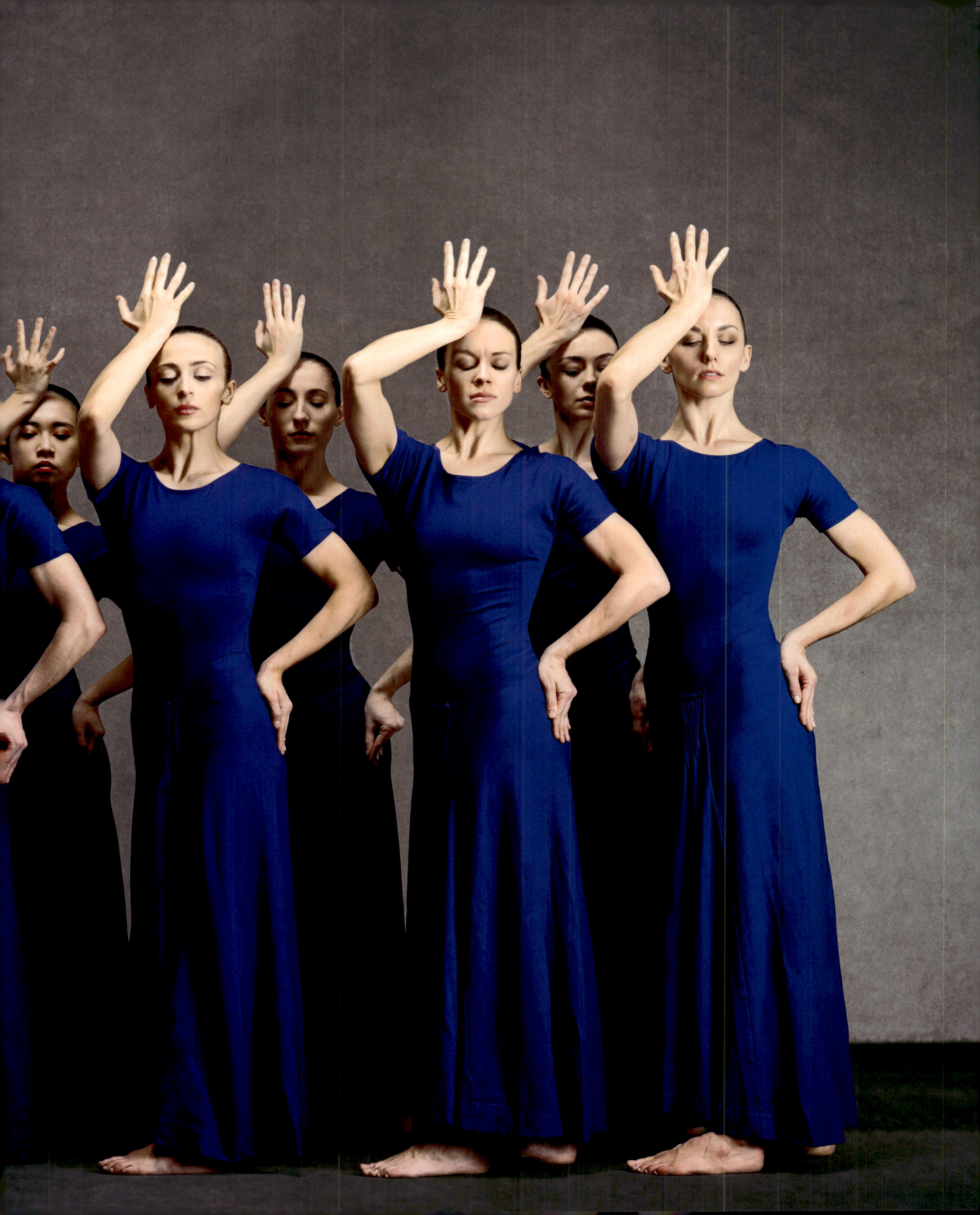

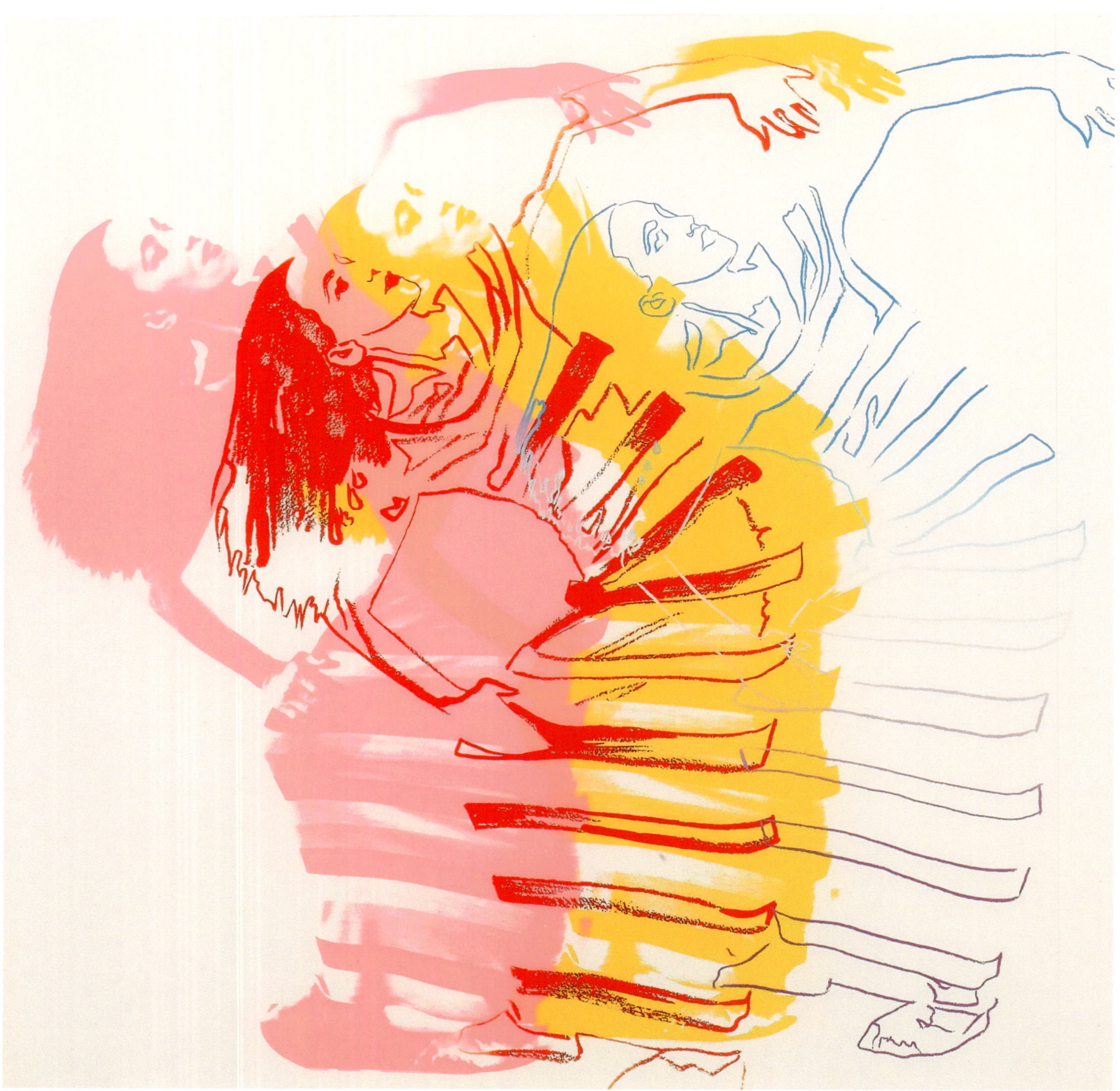

Illustration by Andy Warhol.

SATYRIC FESTIVAL SONG, 1932

A playful, sly trickster mocks her own seriousness.

Satyric Festival Song is a rare example of Graham's witty, comedic flair. It features a solo dancer who is part vaudeville performer and part trickster, inspired by the clowns of American Indian Pueblo culture who mock sacred rituals.

As the piece begins, a bright light reveals a female figure in a long, formfitting, green-and-yellow-striped dress. She springs repeatedly into the air, flinging her loose hair in all directions and punctuating the motion with a series of gestural exclamations.

After this exuberant opening, our trickster engages the audience in a series of brief sketches that parody both herself and theatrical conventions. Peekaboo gestures and quick foot patterns across the stage create a coy and lighthearted mood. The dance ends with a false exit and return to springlike jumps where it all began.

Lost for decades, this solo was reimagined by Diane Gray and Janet Eilber in 1994 using photos of Graham by Barbara Morgan.

COSTUME DESIGN

Martha Graham

COMPOSERS

Imre Weisshaus, Fernando Palacios

Satyric Festival Song

DANCER
Marzia Memoli

COSTUME RE-CREATION
Russell Vogler

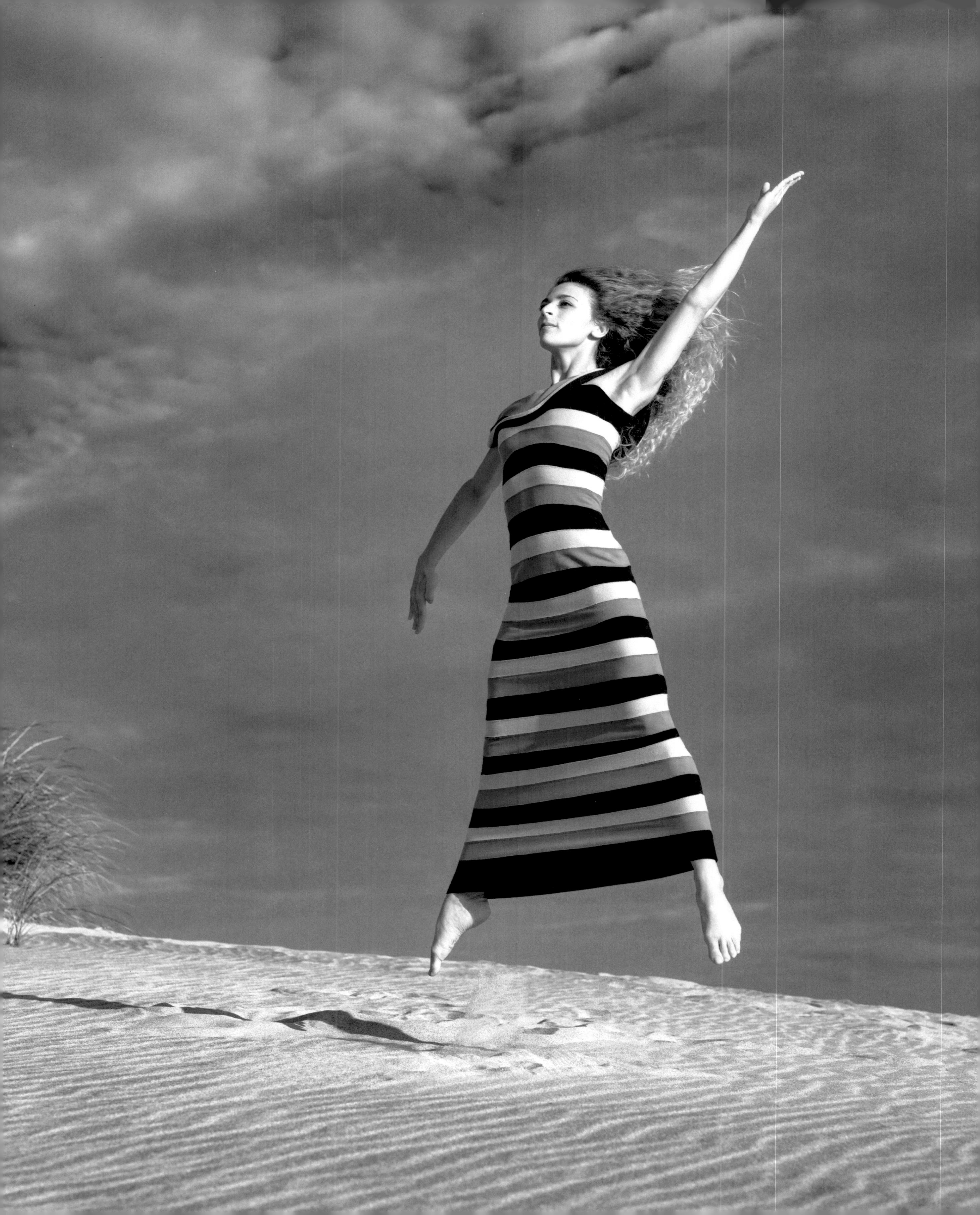

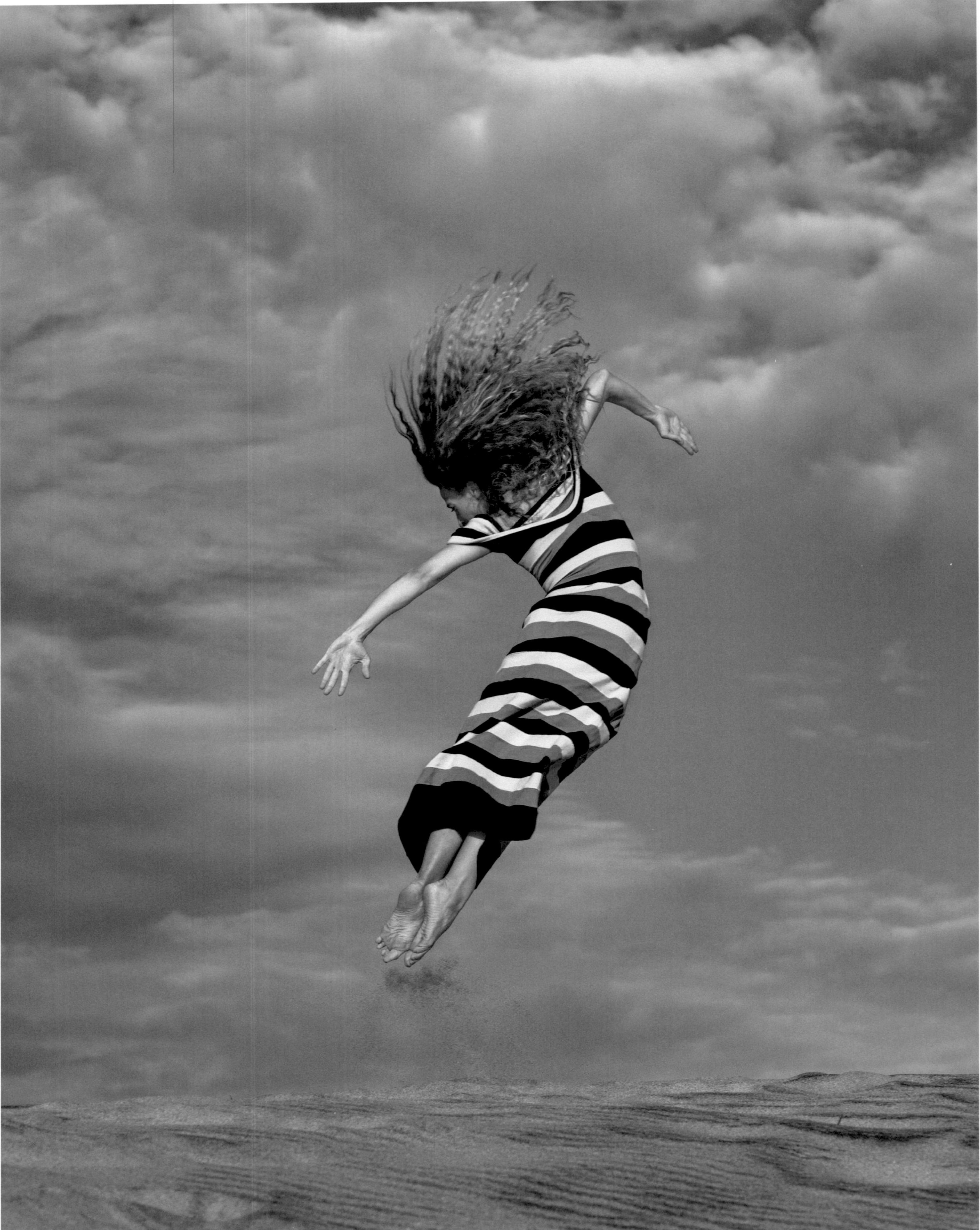

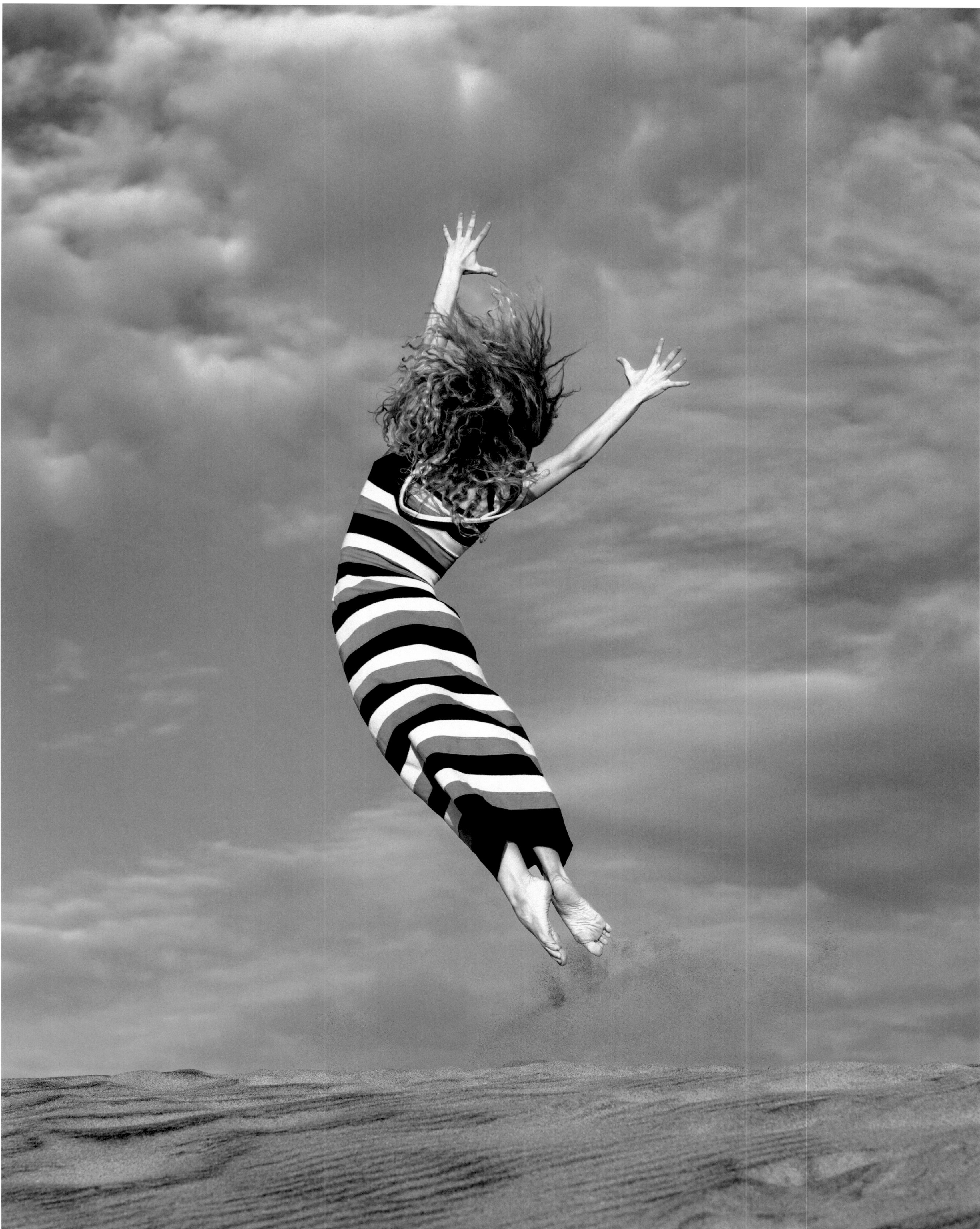

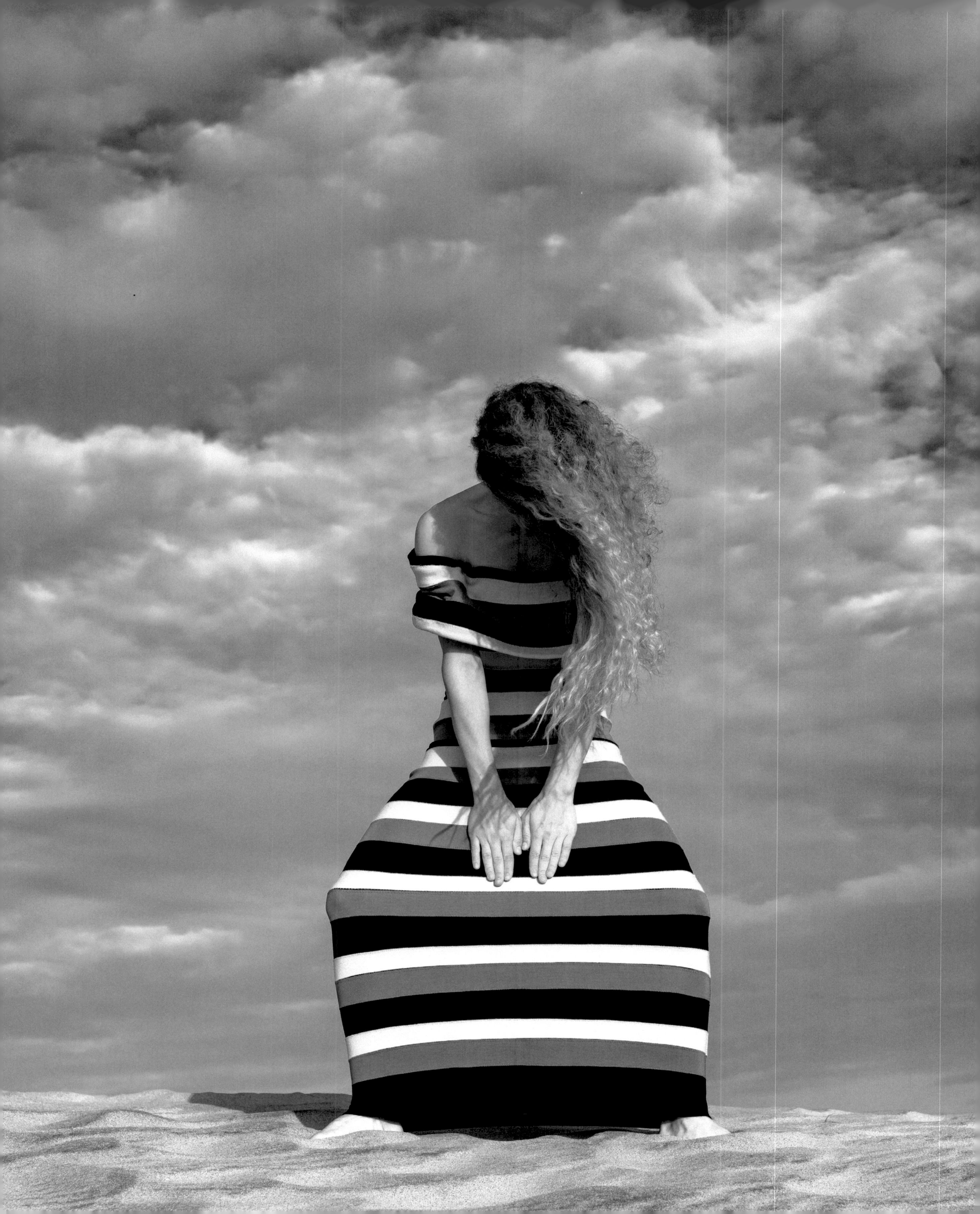

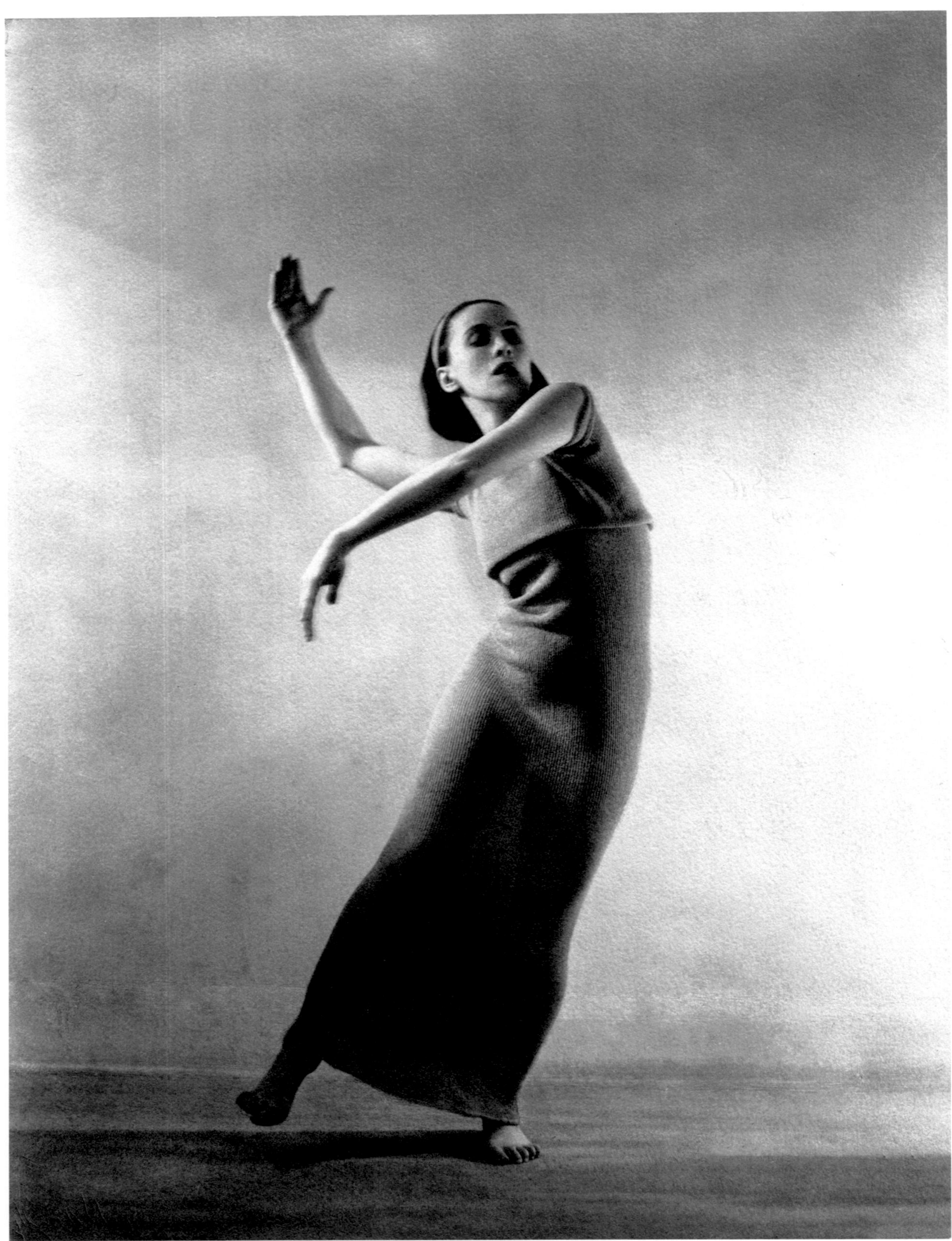

Martha Graham. Photograph by Soichi Sunami.

EKSTASIS, 1933

An exploration of the human body as a sculpture brought to life.

Ekstasis embodies the purely sculptural possibilities of the female form moving within and against a sheath of stretch fabric. Spiraling, thrusting the hip outward, and shape-shifting gyroscopically from the pelvis and center of gravity, the dancer creates images that are archaic, erotic, and totemic. In Graham's own words from her autobiography, *Blood Memory*, "I wear a long tube of material to indicate the tragedy that obsesses the body, the ability to stretch inside your own skin, to witness and test the perimeters and boundaries of grief."

Ekstasis is a duet between the performer and the viewer. The dancer guides the eye to follow the contours she creates from the impulses of her hips and shoulders while allowing the viewer's gaze to actively survey the morphing and evocative shapes vividly revealed in the precisely angled stage lighting.

Ekstasis disappeared from the Company's repertory and was returned to the stage in 2016, when Virginie Mécène used photos and other archival materials to reimagine the choreography.

COSTUME DESIGN
Martha Graham

COMPOSERS
Lehman Engel, Ramon Humet

Ekstasis

DANCERS
Anne Souder and
Natasha Diamond-Walker

COSTUME RE-CREATION
Karen Young

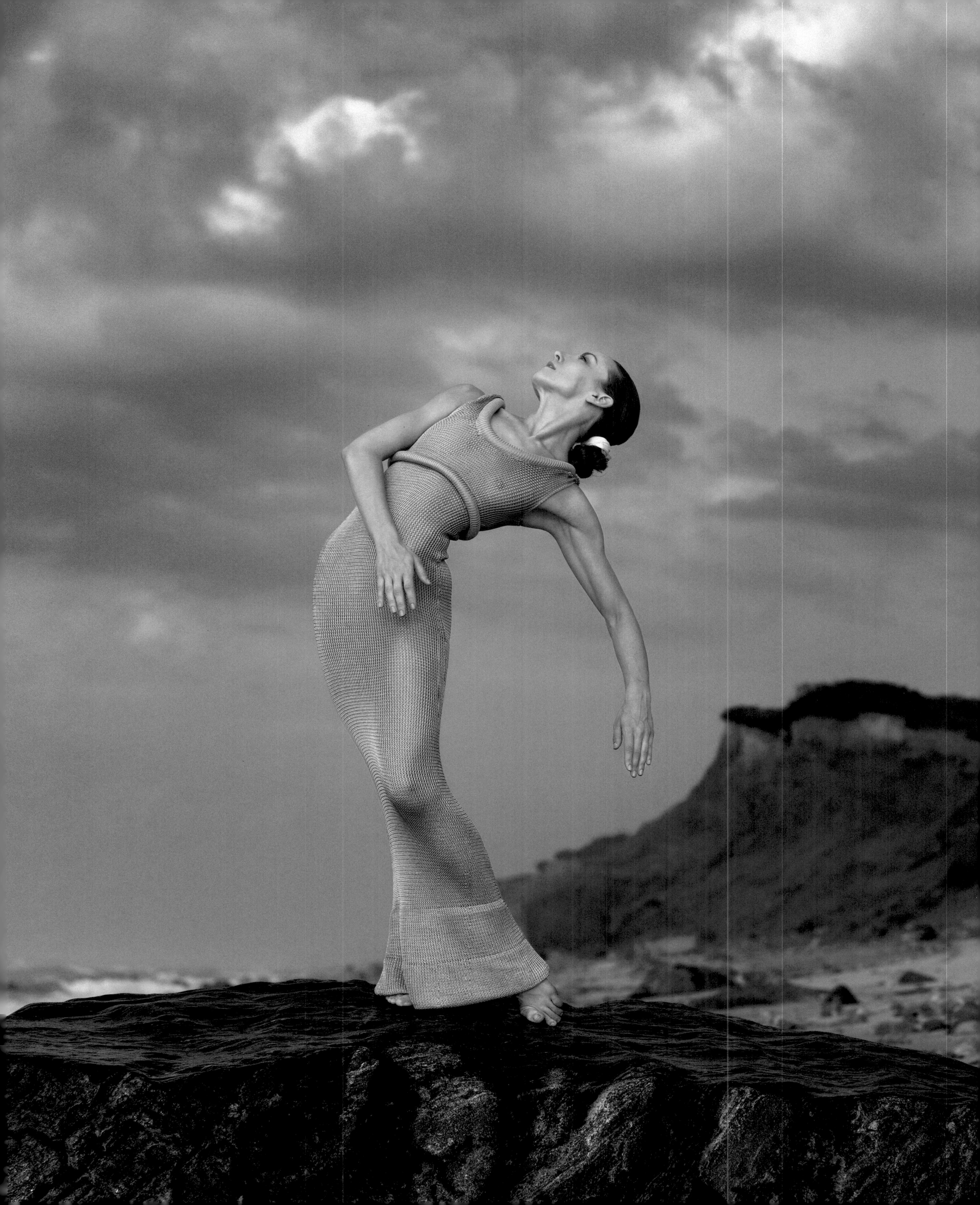

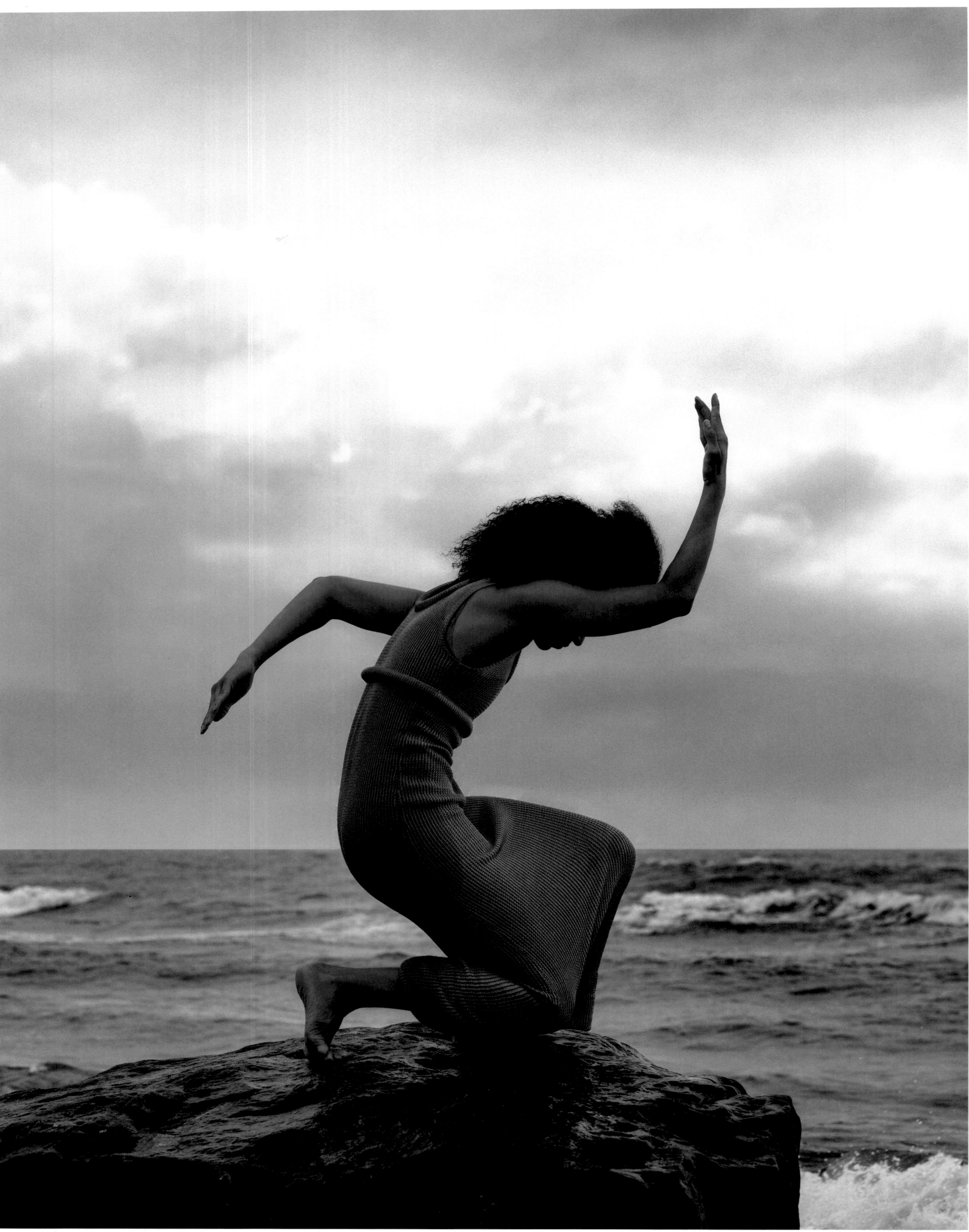

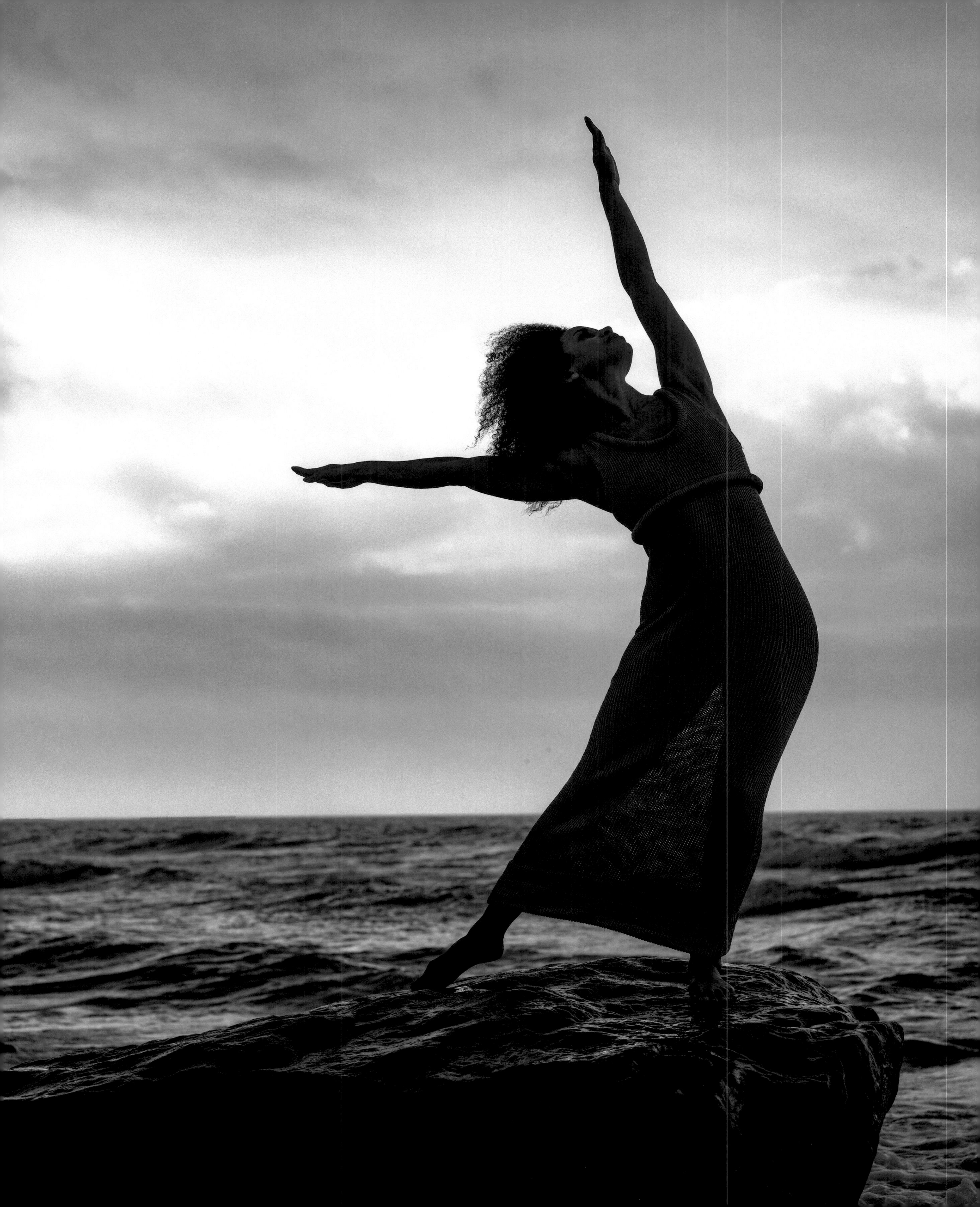

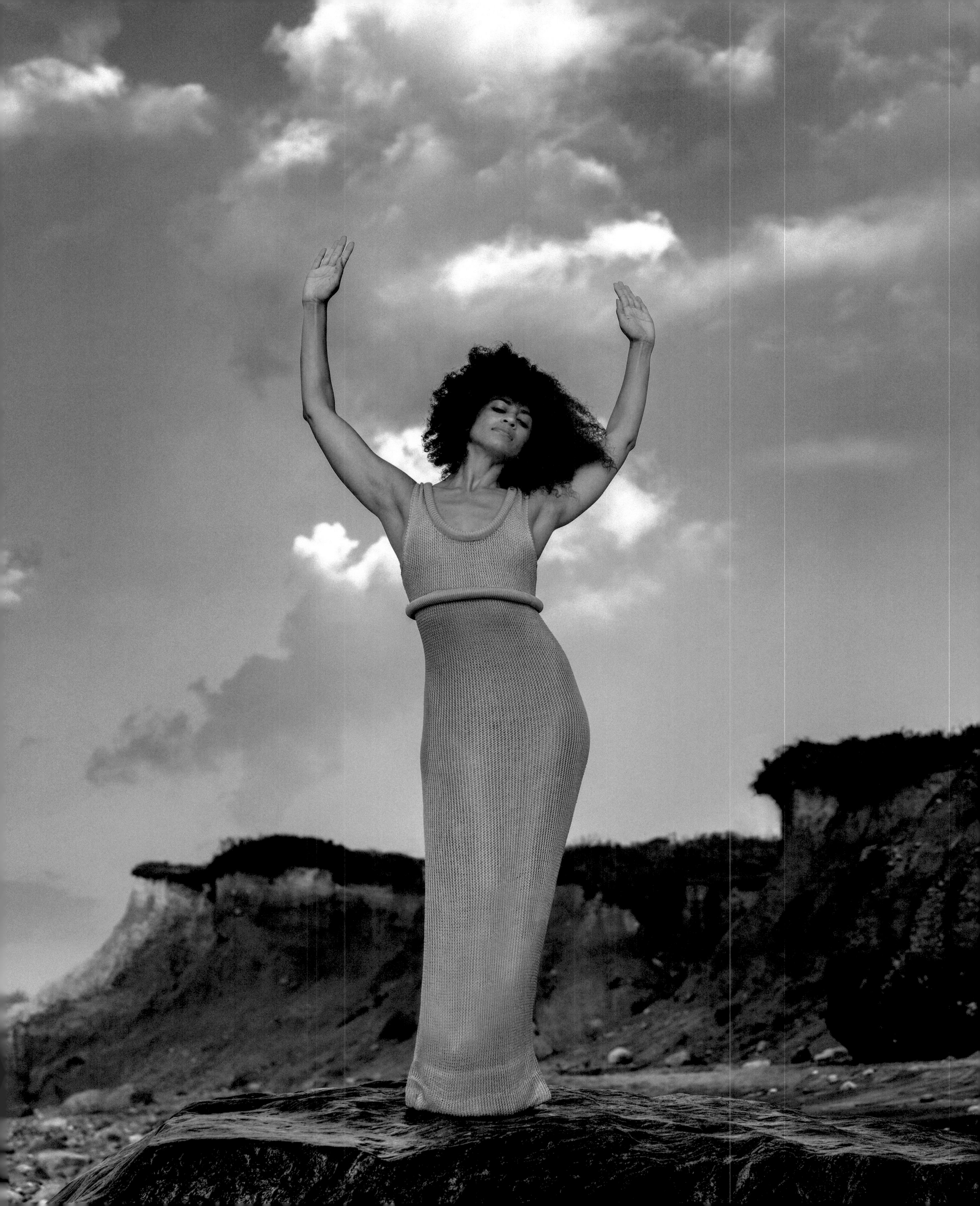

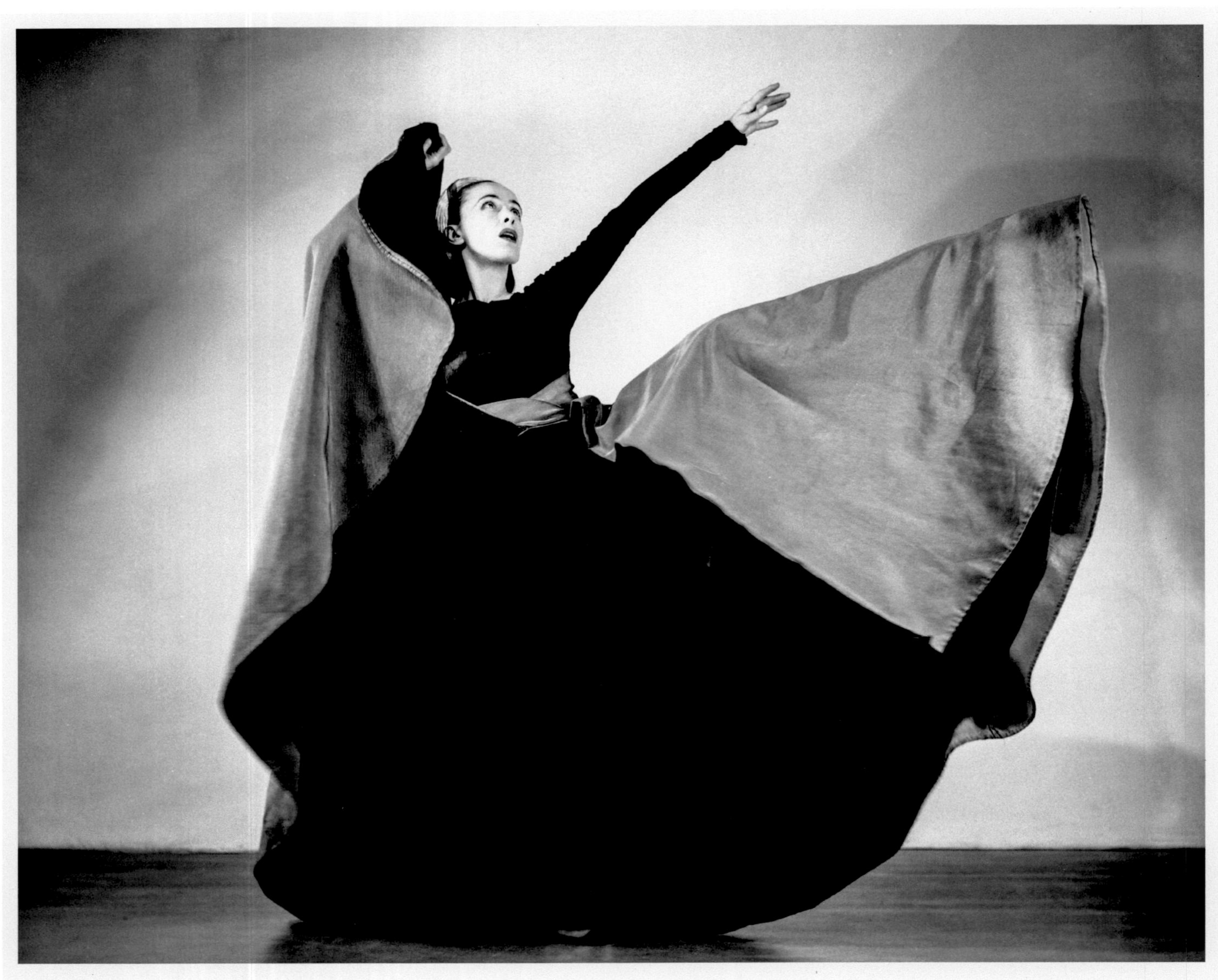

Martha Graham. Photograph by Barbara Morgan.

IMPERIAL GESTURE, 1935

A portrait of demagoguery that foreshadowed the rise of dictators.

In 1935, with fascism on the rise in Europe, Graham rejected an invitation by Nazi officials in Germany to perform at the 1936 Summer Olympics in Berlin and created this solo. At the time it was described in a review by the *Dance Observer* as "the essence of the megalomania that conquers continents." *Imperial Gesture* disappeared from the Graham repertoire not long after its premiere, only to be revived decades later in 2013 by former Company member Kim Jones, who used photographs by Barbara Morgan of Graham in the original for inspiration.

The reimagined solo holds the fierce tension characteristic of Graham's choreography. Emphatic arm gestures, finger snaps, and pounding footwork embody the fervor of entitlement and imperialism.

COSTUME DESIGN
Martha Graham

COMPOSERS
Lehman Engel, Patrick Daugherty

Imperial Gesture

DANCER
Xin Ying

COSTUME RE-CREATION
Karen Young

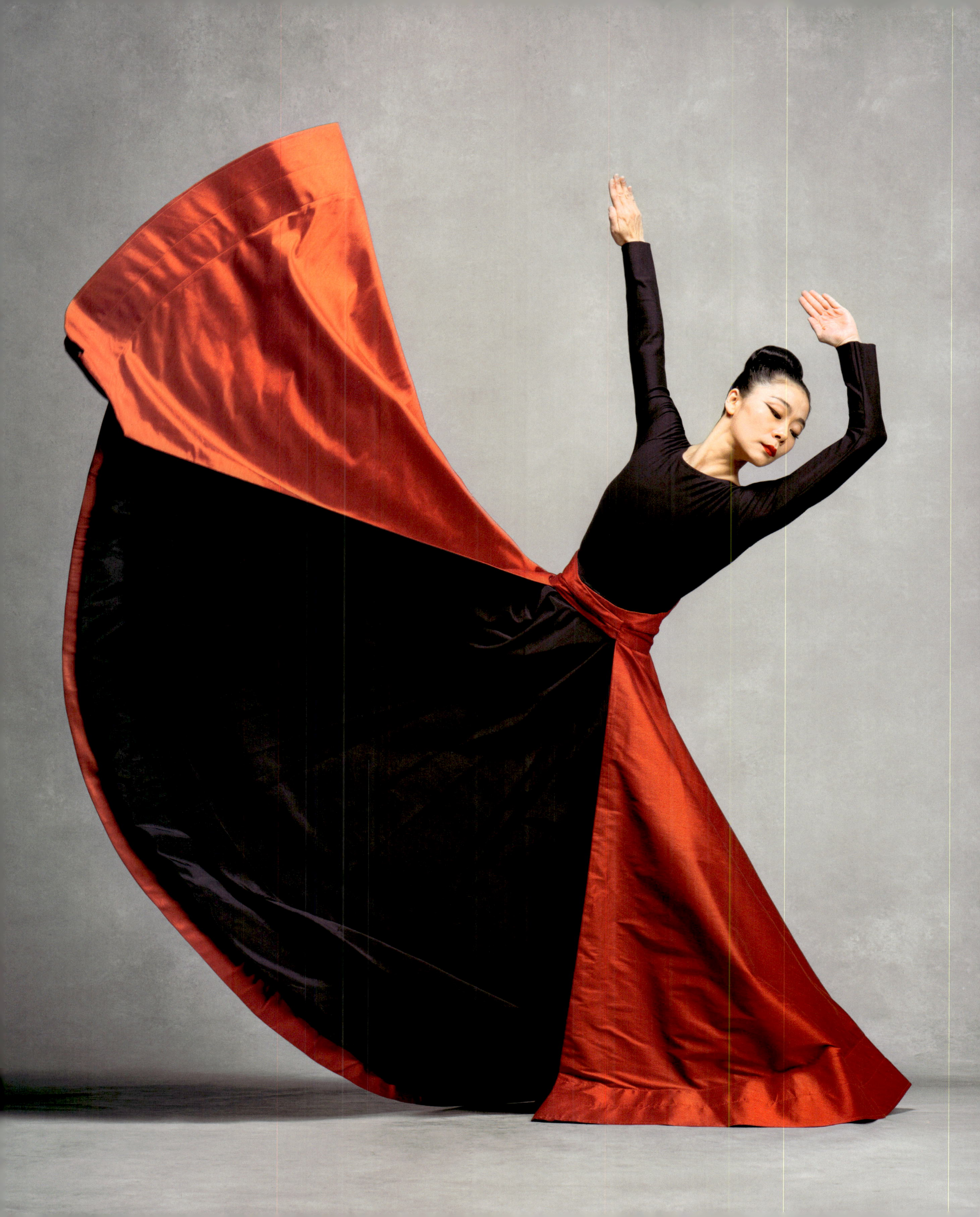

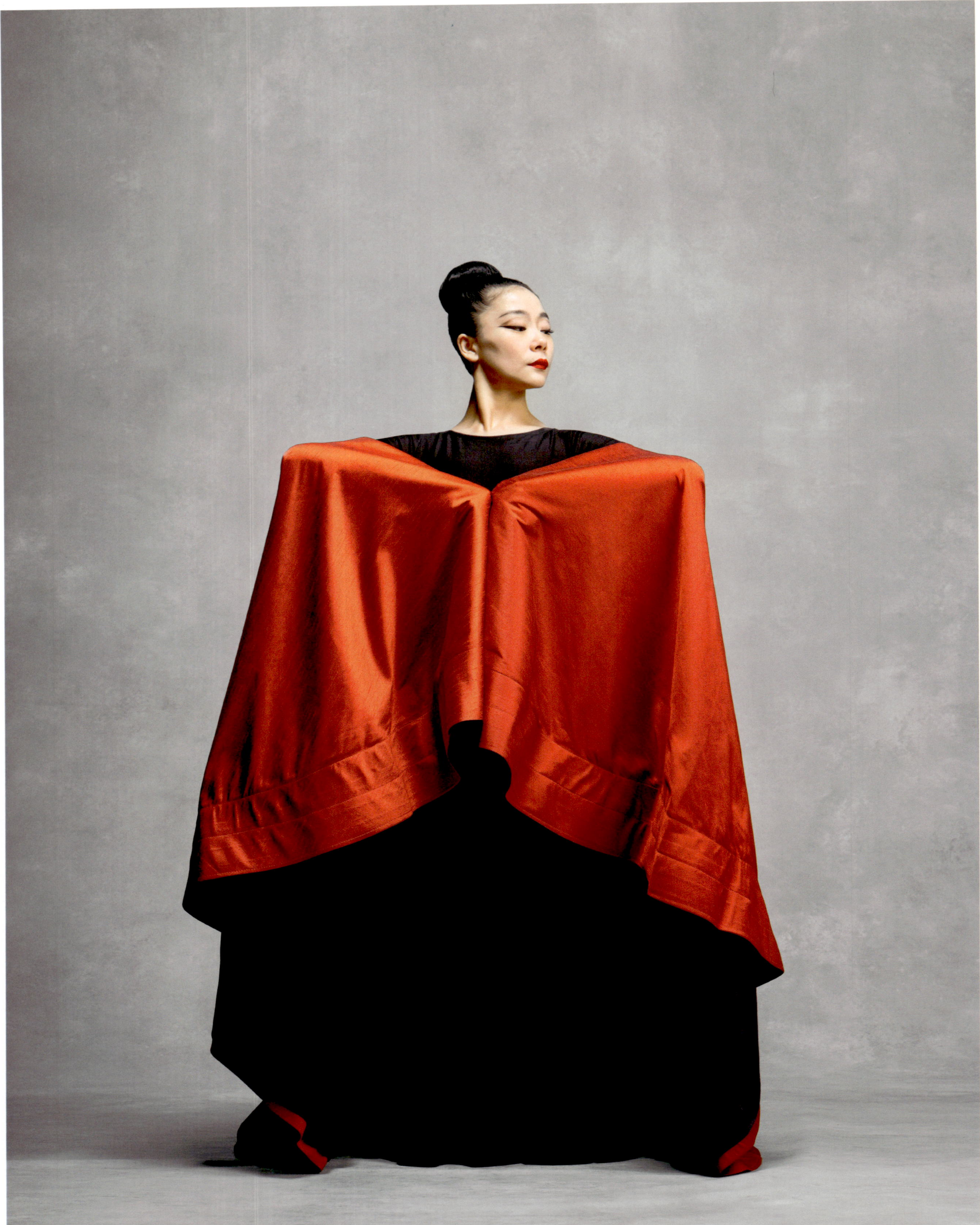

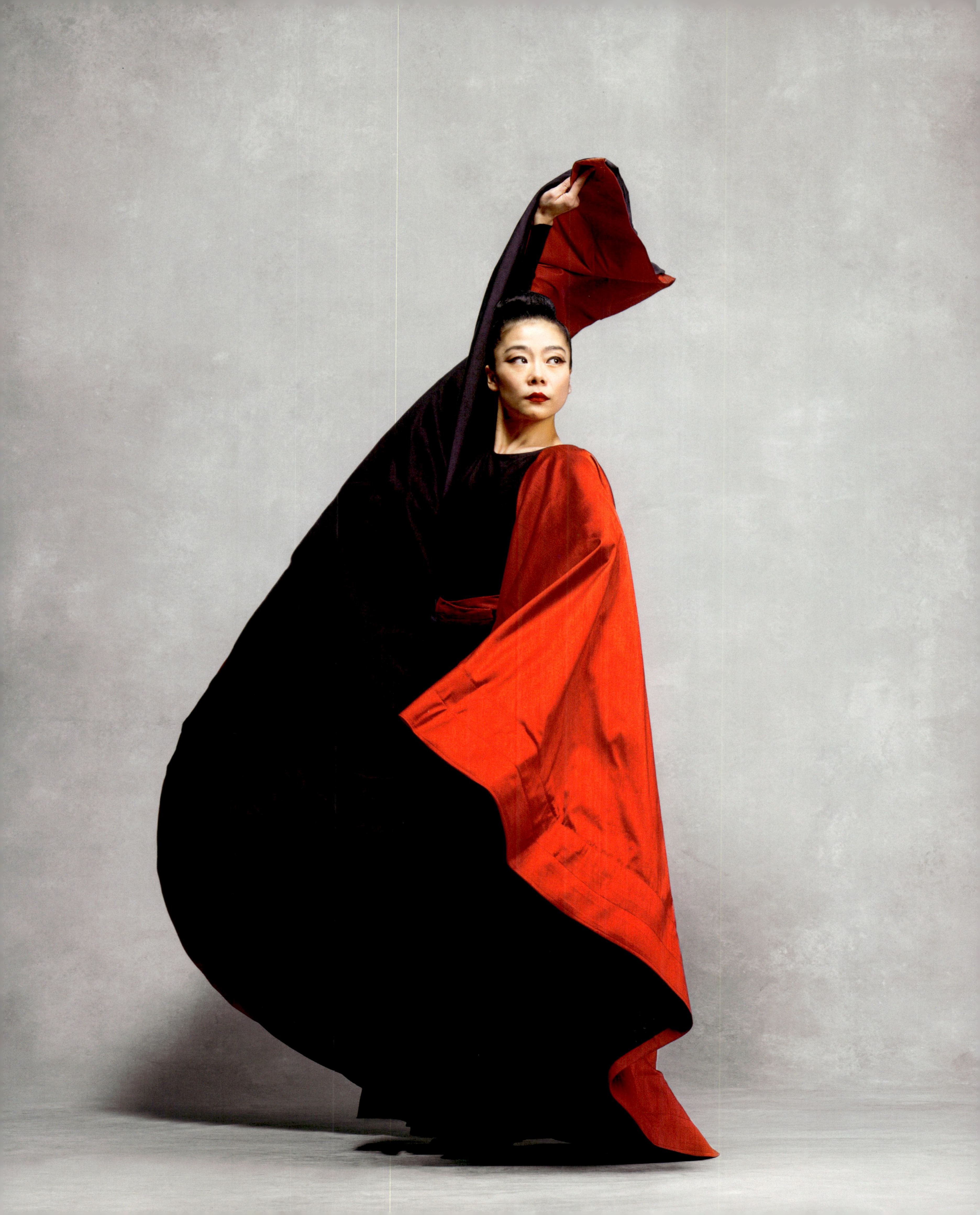

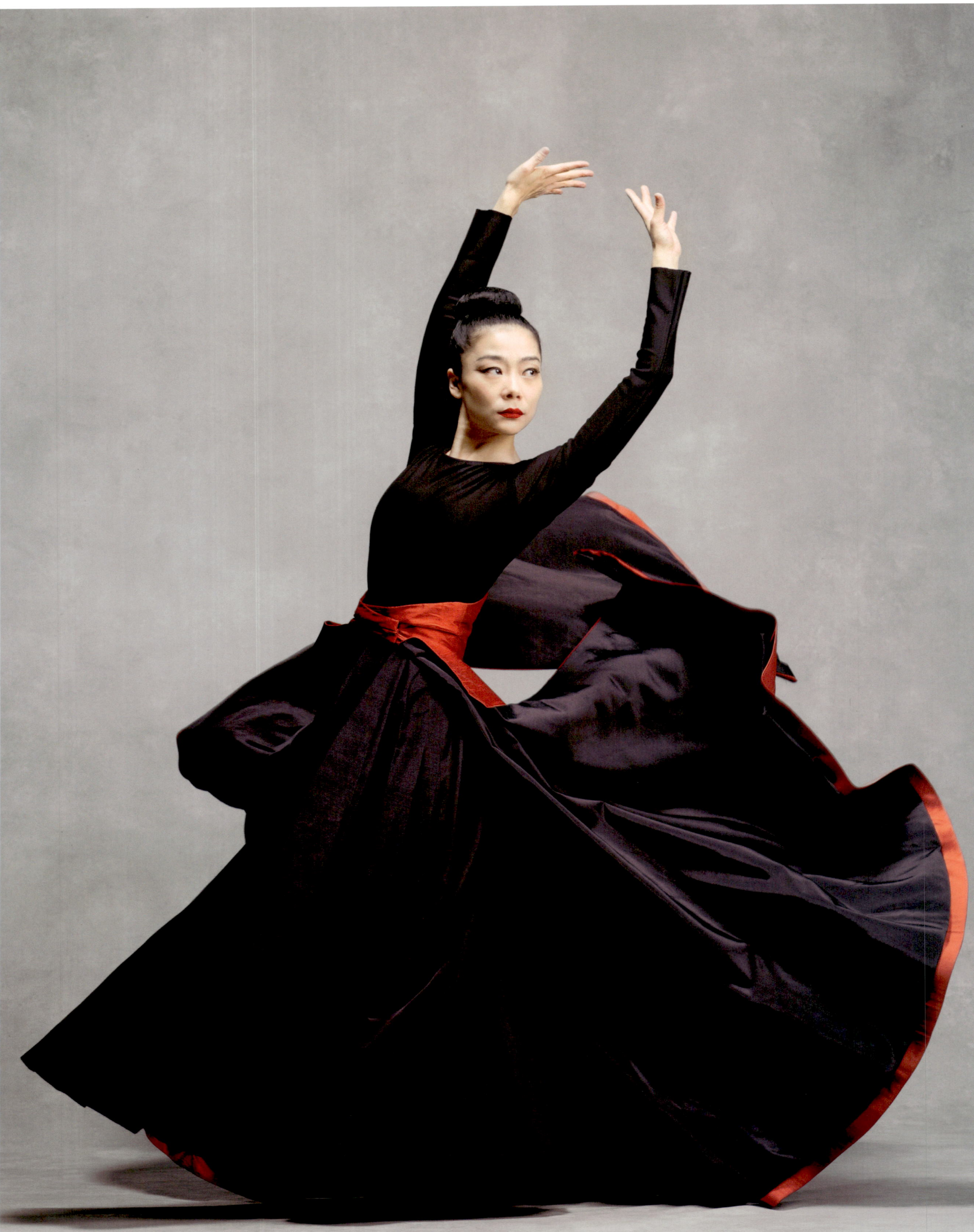

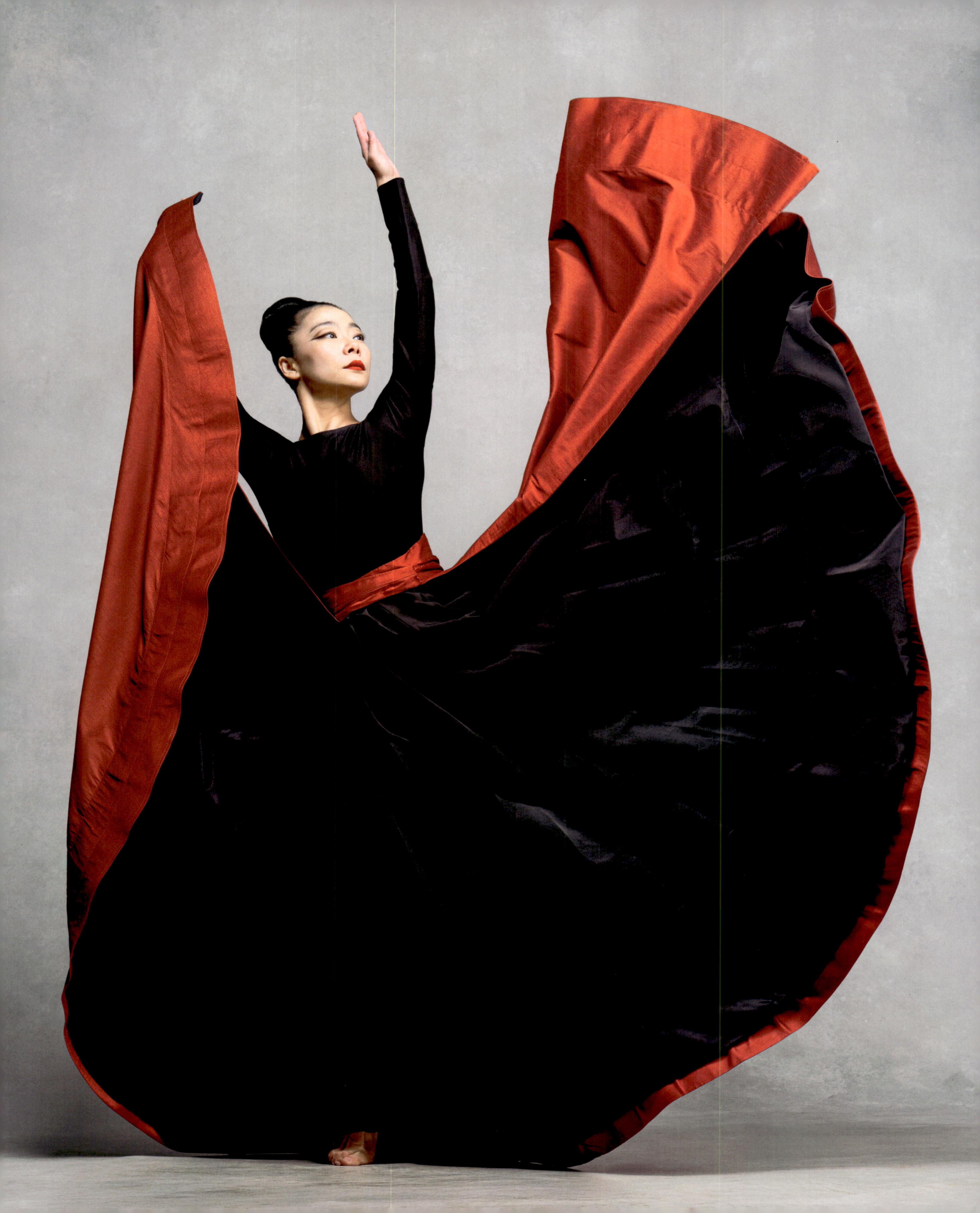

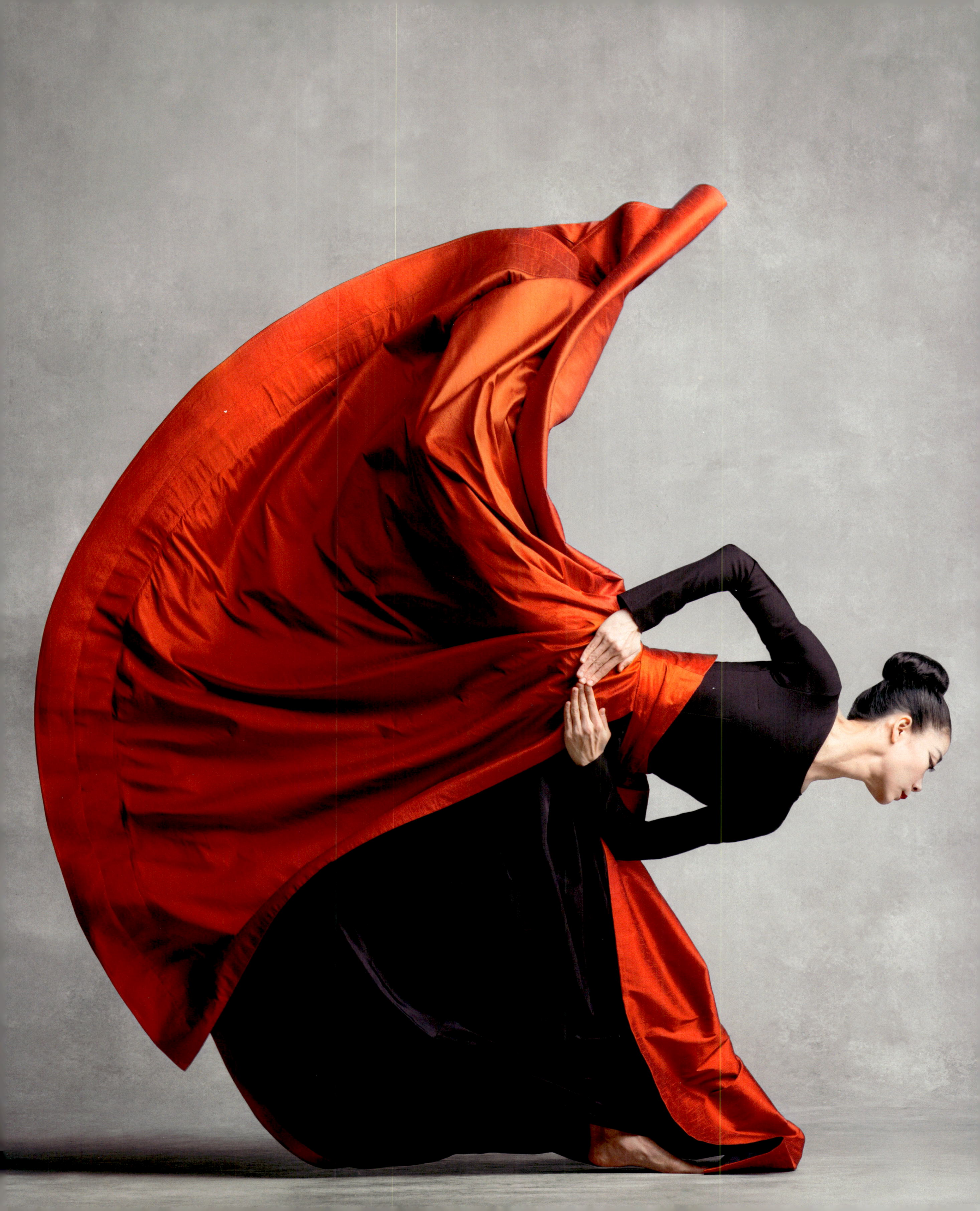

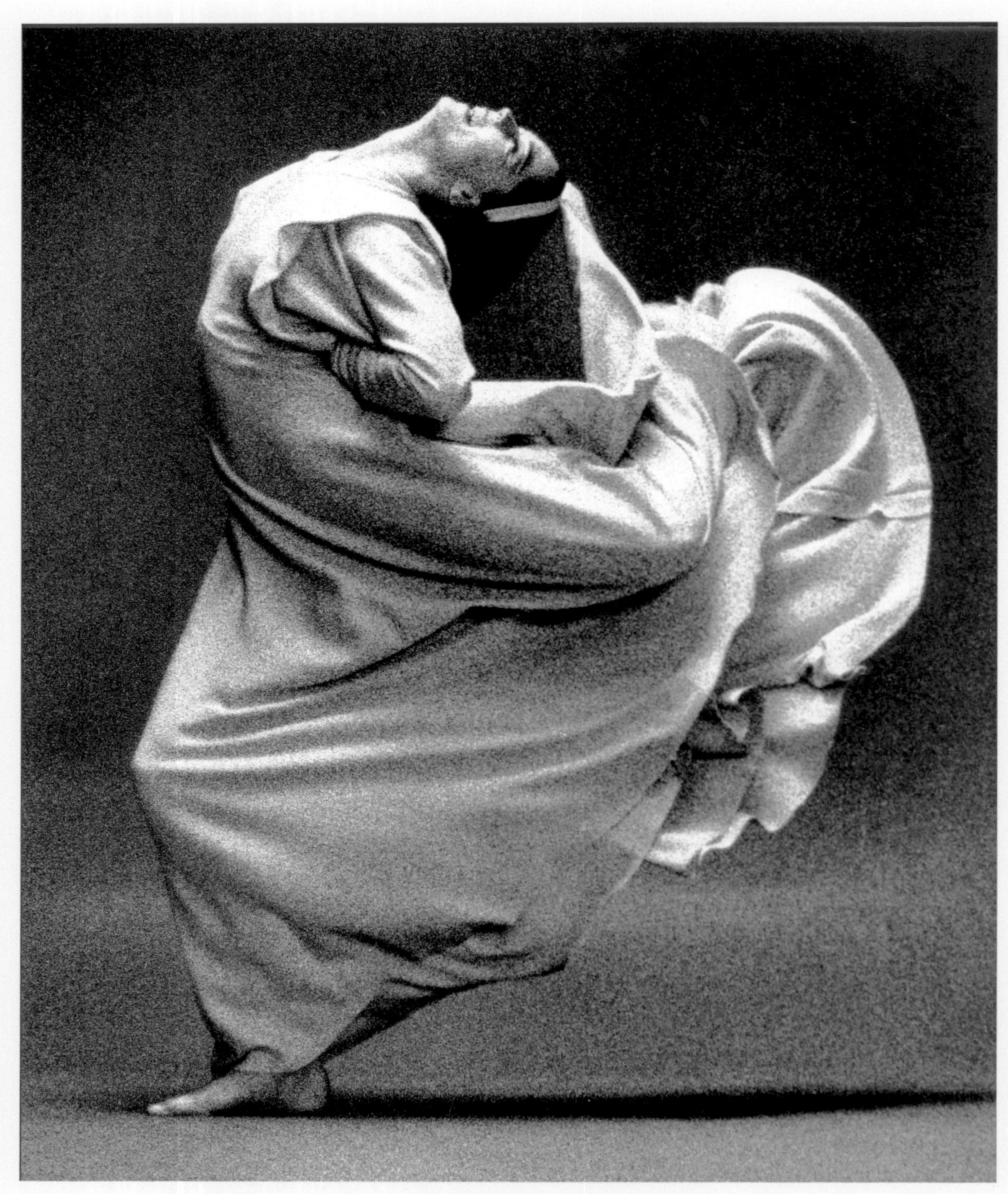

Janet Eilber. Photograph by Max Waldman.

FRONTIER, 1935

A solo dancer evoking the uniquely American quest for vast open spaces.

Claiming a vantage point from her perch against Noguchi's two-railed fence, the lone female figure in a long dress greets the morning with a sweeping gesture that defines the distant horizon line. She surveys her domain until propelled forward with a set of spirited hops and high side kicks. She sits legs spread wide on the floor in the shape of a surveyor's measuring tool or compass.

As the musical score shifts into a more solemn, contemplative mode, she glides sideways on tiptoe, then upstage. At one point, she does so with folded arms as if cradling a baby.

Returning to her perch at the fence, she defiantly lowers her fist onto her raised knee. In Graham's words, introducing *Frontier* for a PBS broadcast in 1976, "That girl, who was myself, is seeing a great landscape—untrammeled, and I felt it when I danced . . . flinging myself against the sky."

SET DESIGN
Isamu Noguchi

COSTUME DESIGN
Martha Graham

COMPOSER
Louis Horst

Frontier

DANCER
Leslie Andrea Williams

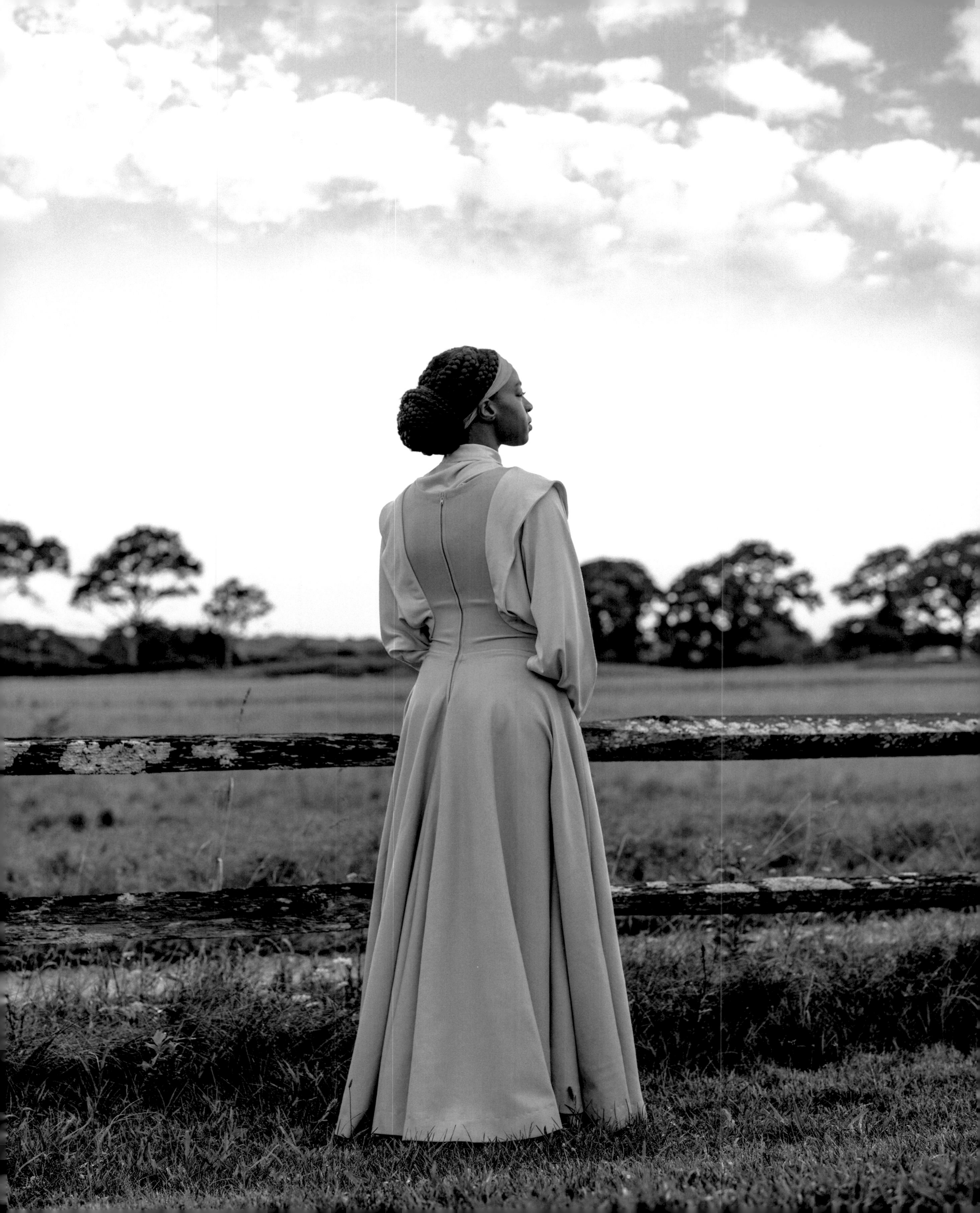

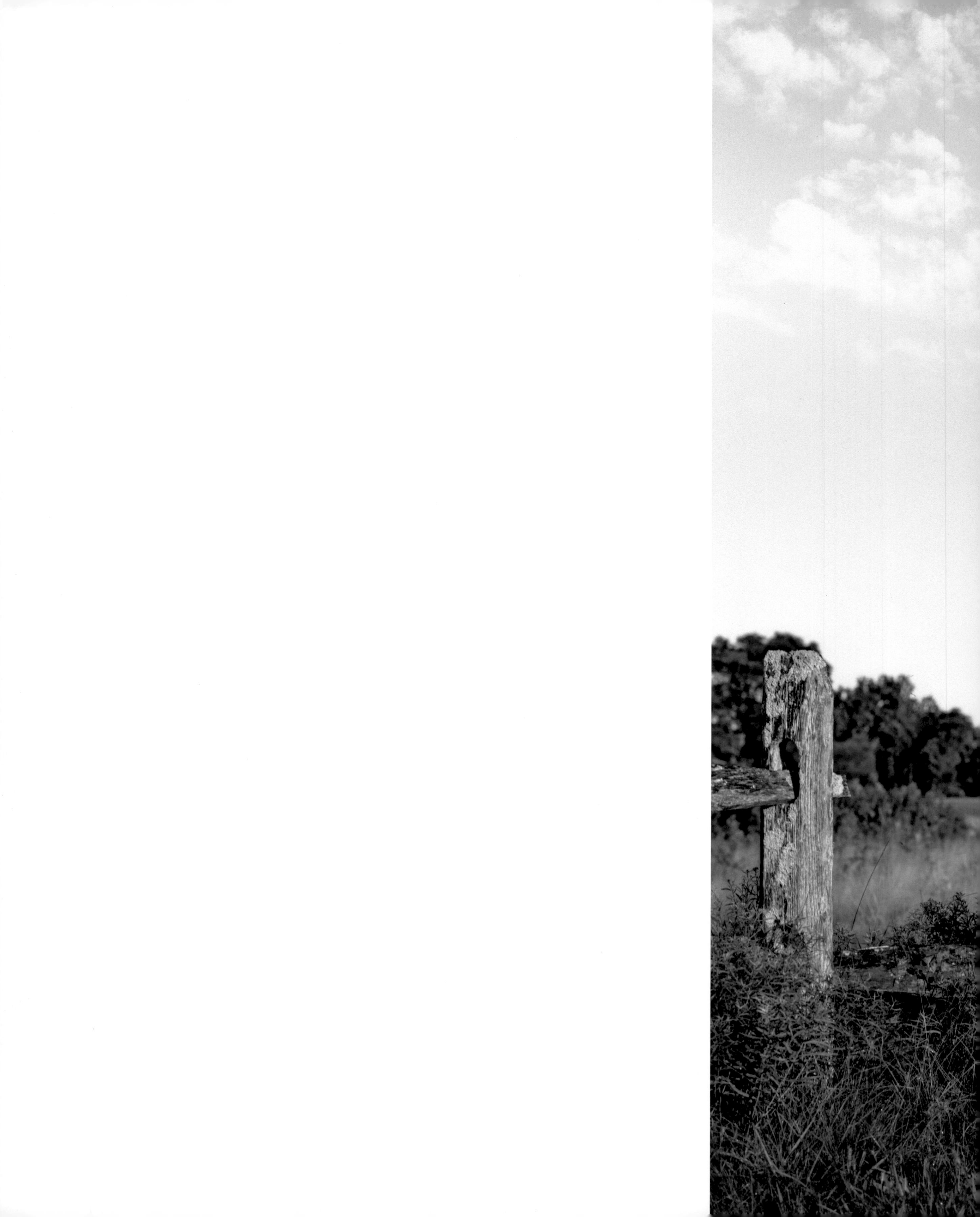

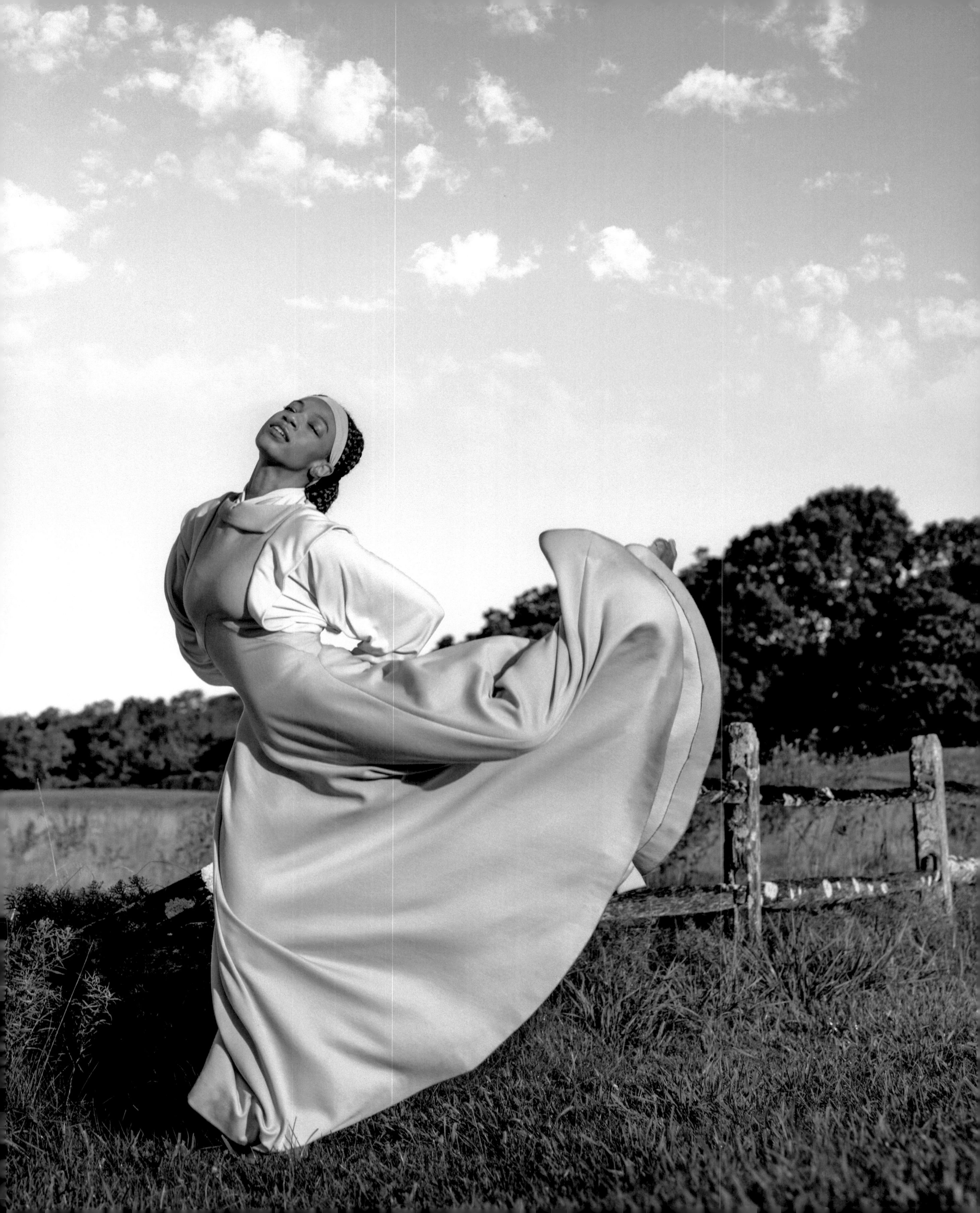

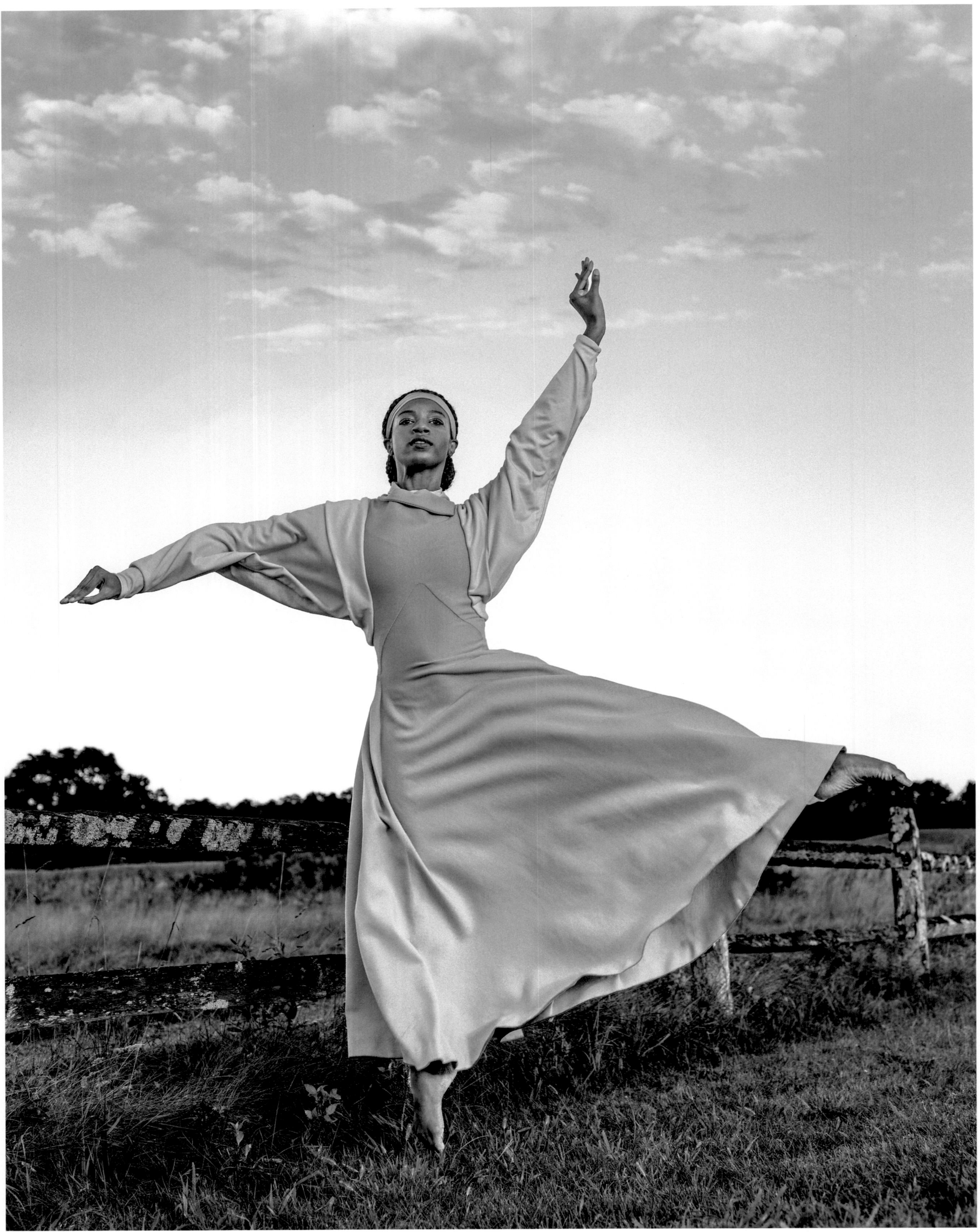

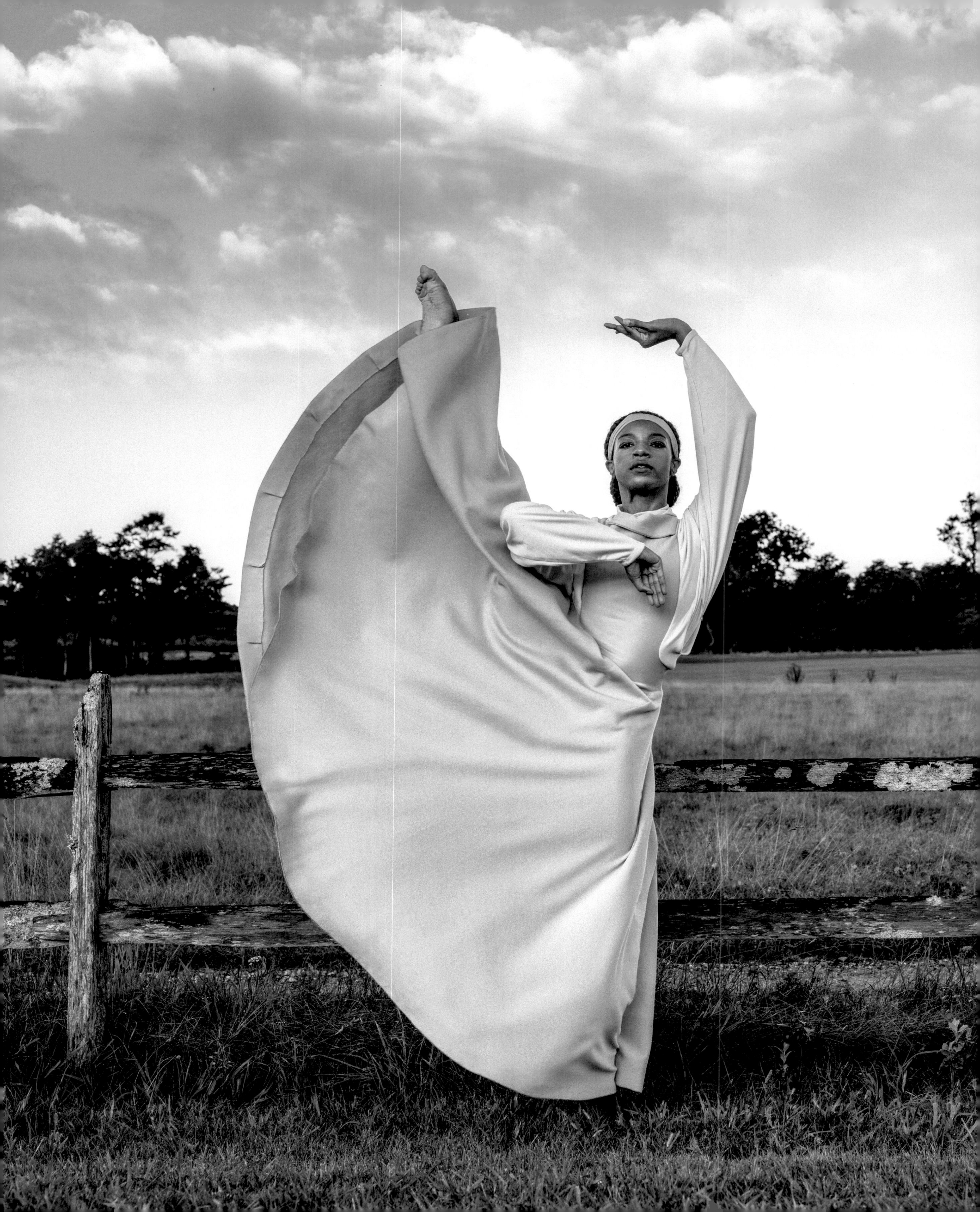

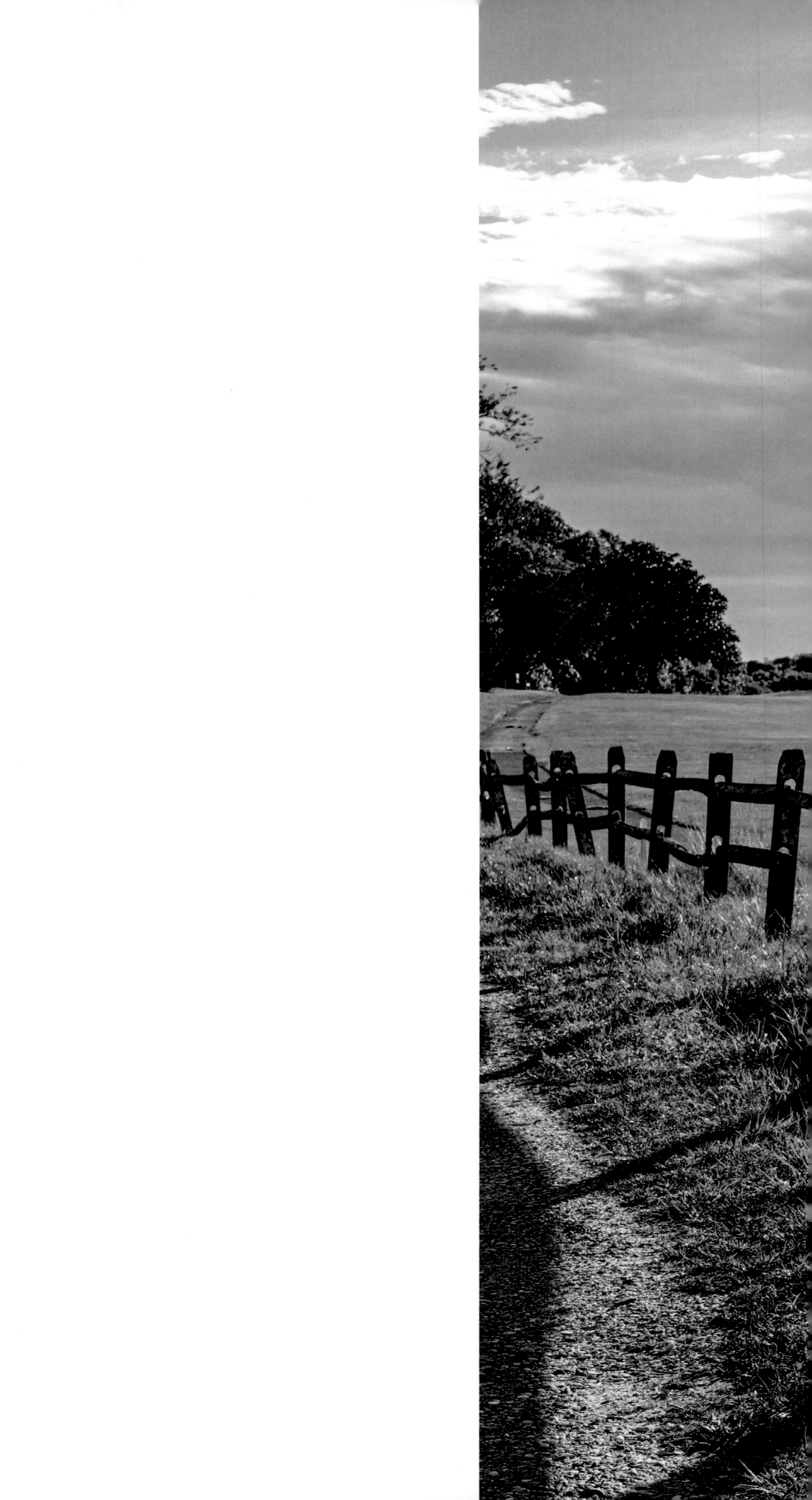

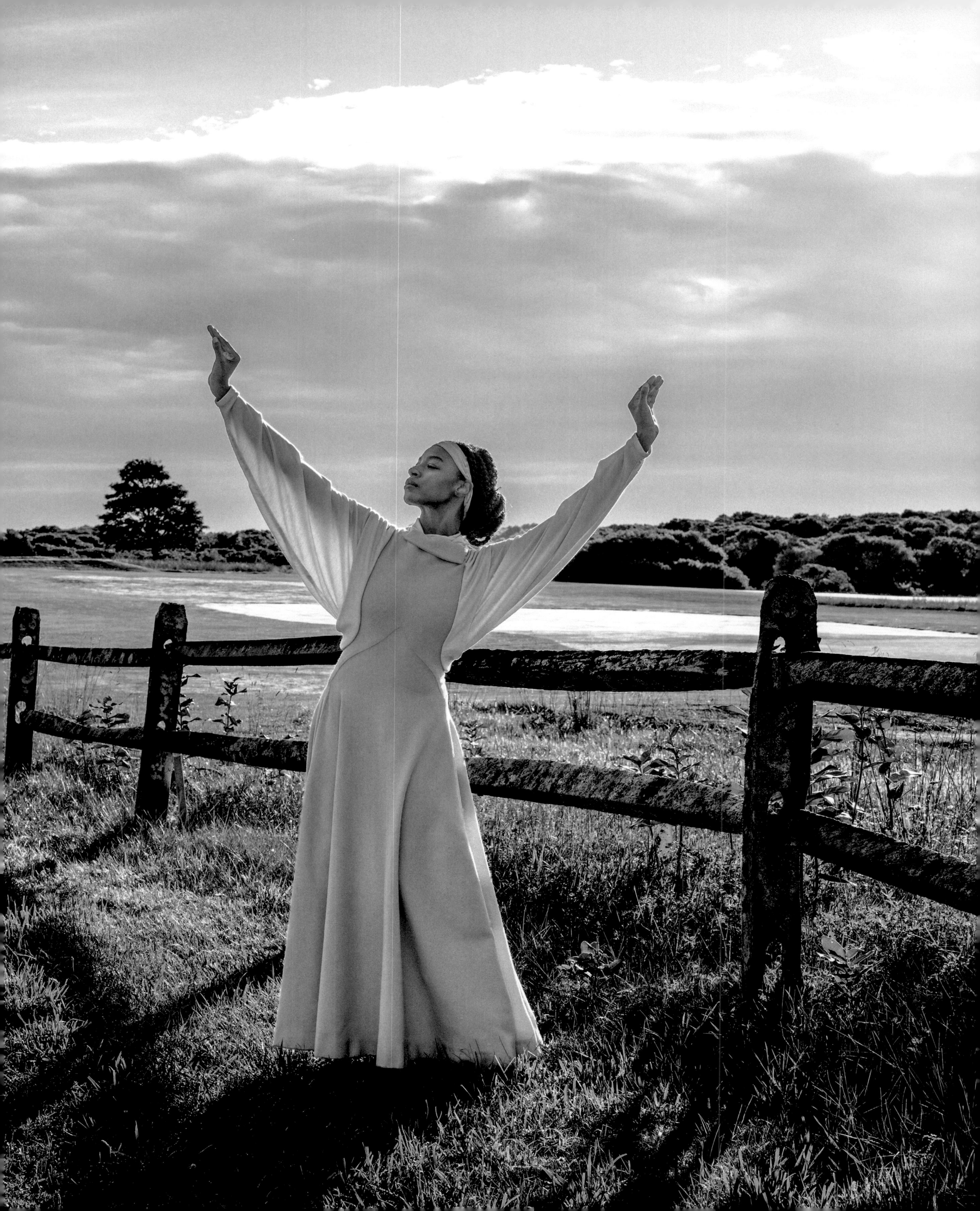

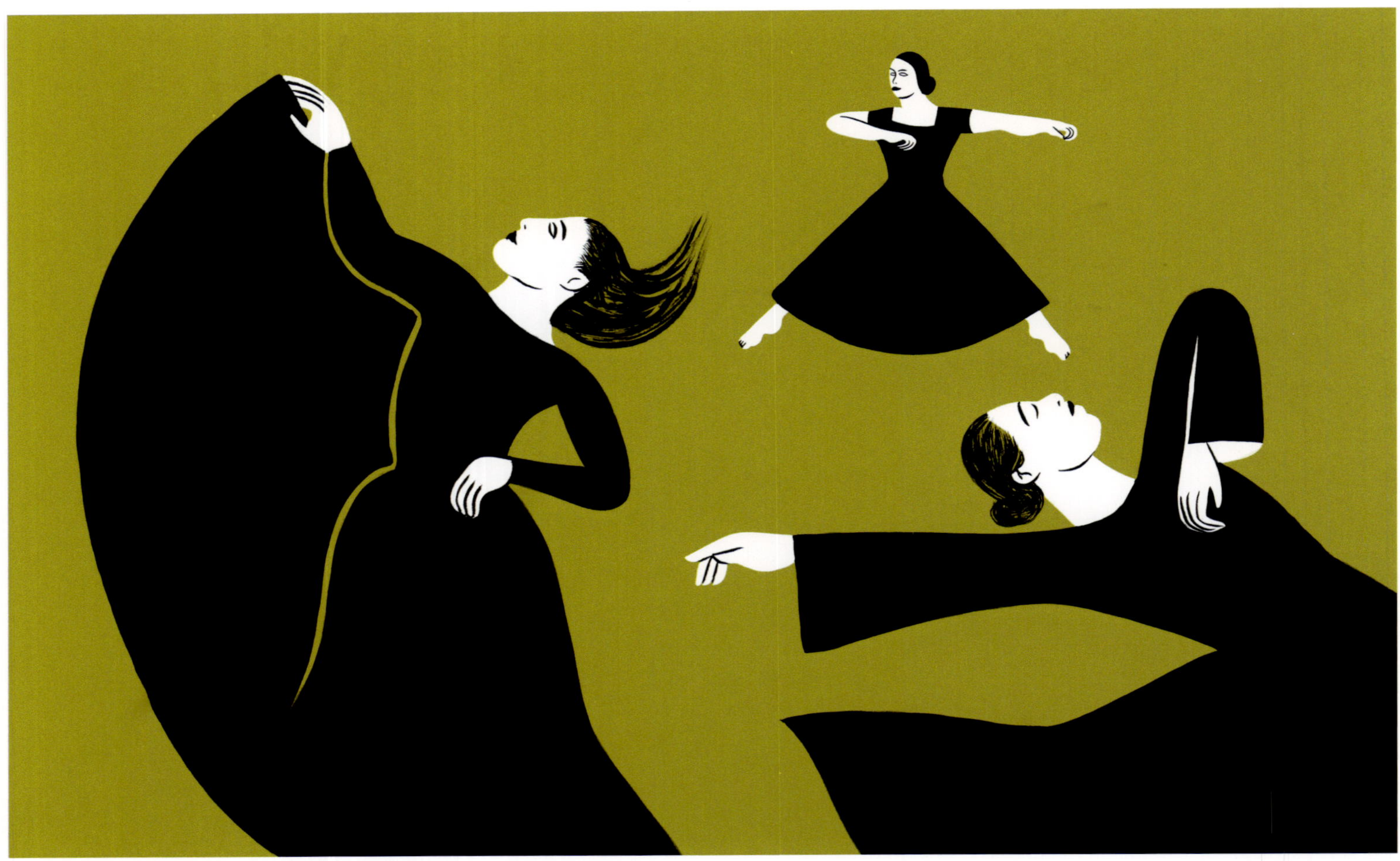

Illustration by Rachel Levit Ruiz.

CHRONICLE, 1936

A searing indictment
of the consequences of war.

Originally a work in five sections, the dance was created in 1936 in reaction to the rise of fascism in Europe. Lost for five decades, three sections were reclaimed using newly discovered film footage and photos. The first, "Spectre-1914," evokes the foreboding prelude to war and features a solo dancer who manipulates her skirt like a banner or flames that threaten to consume her. "Steps in the Street" begins in silence as the dancers make staggered entrances onto the stage, then organize themselves into masses as the propulsive music begins, moving with resistance against some invisible force.

In the final section, "Prelude to Action," the solo figure, now in white, summons the dancers onto the stage. They enter with a newfound purpose, having shed any sign of victimhood, unified and fit for protest or battle.

SET DESIGN
Isamu Noguchi

COSTUME DESIGN
Martha Graham

COMPOSER
Wallingford Riegger

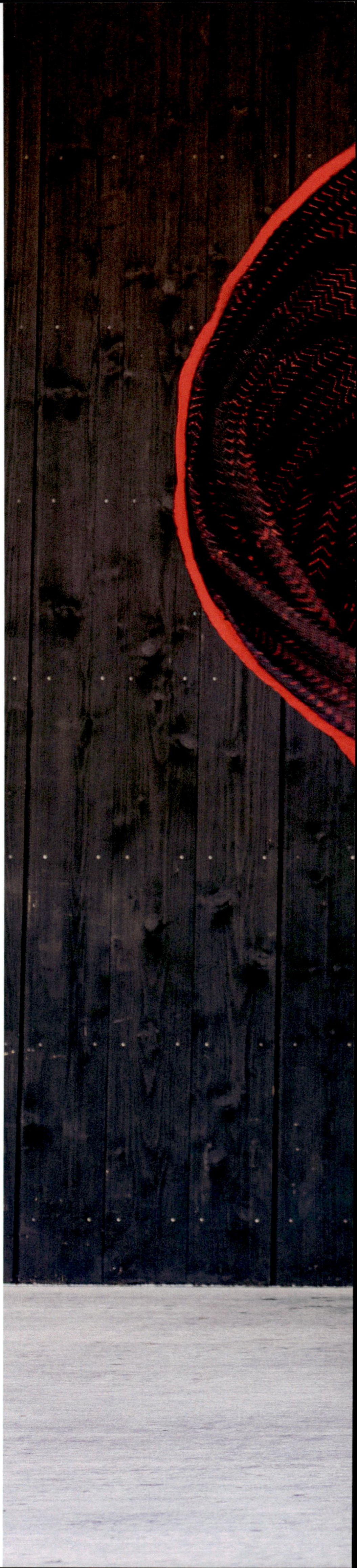

"Spectre" from *Chronicle*

DANCER
Leslie Andrea Williams

COSTUME RE-CREATION
Russell Vogler

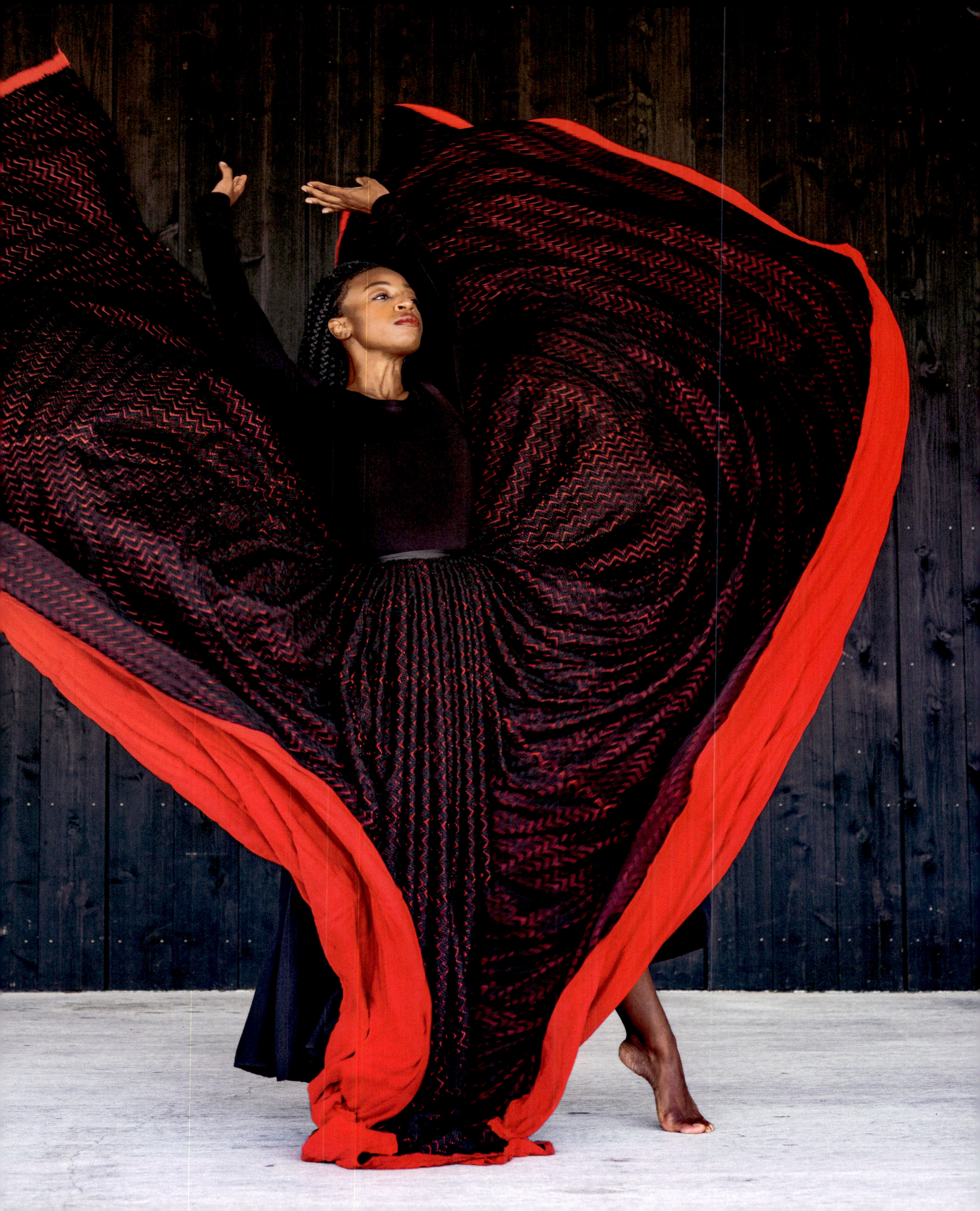

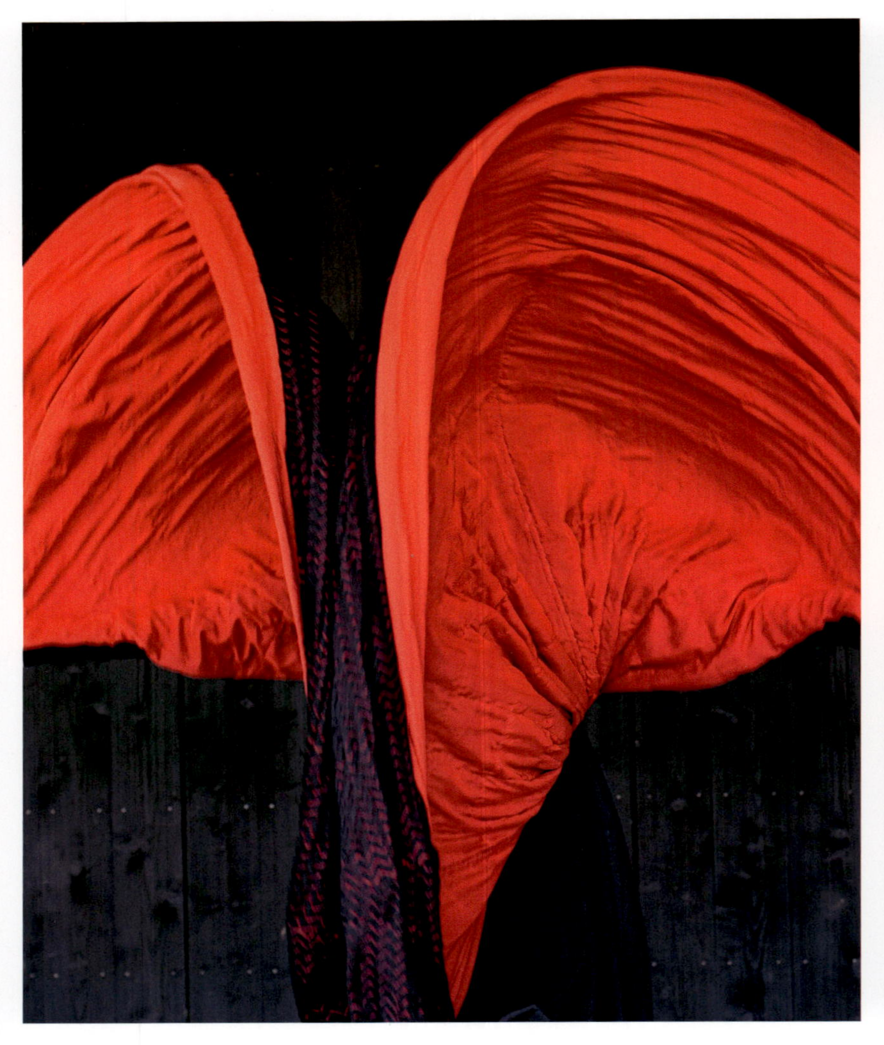

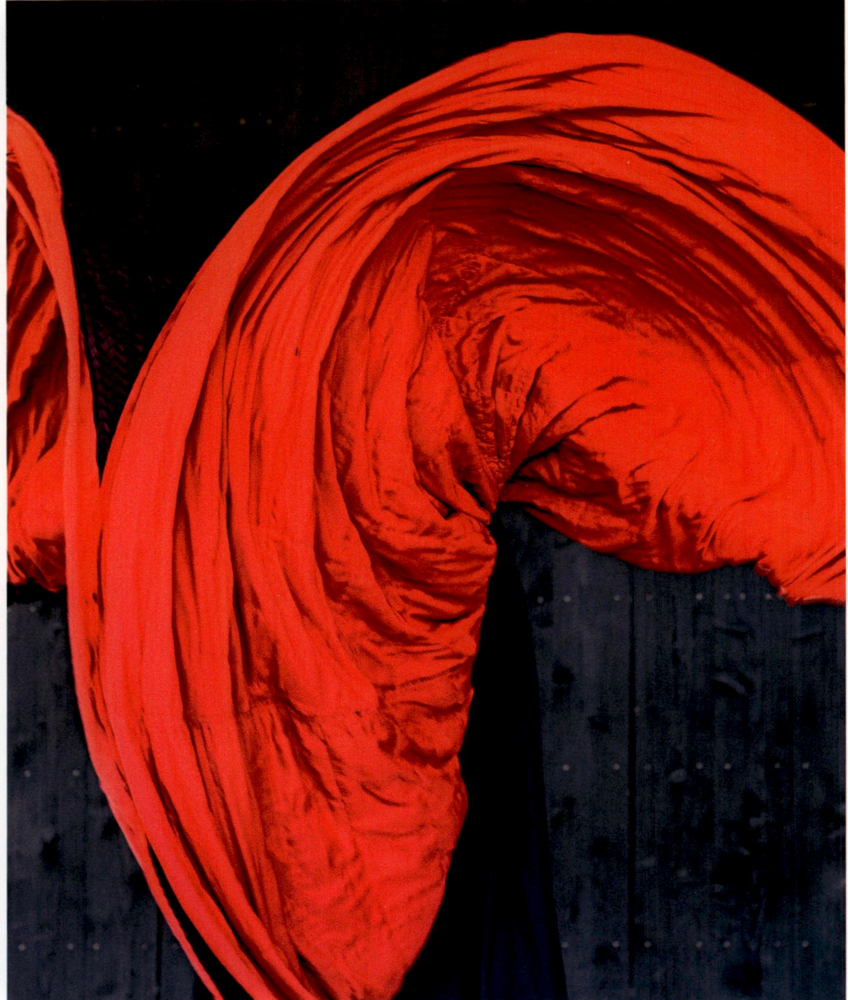

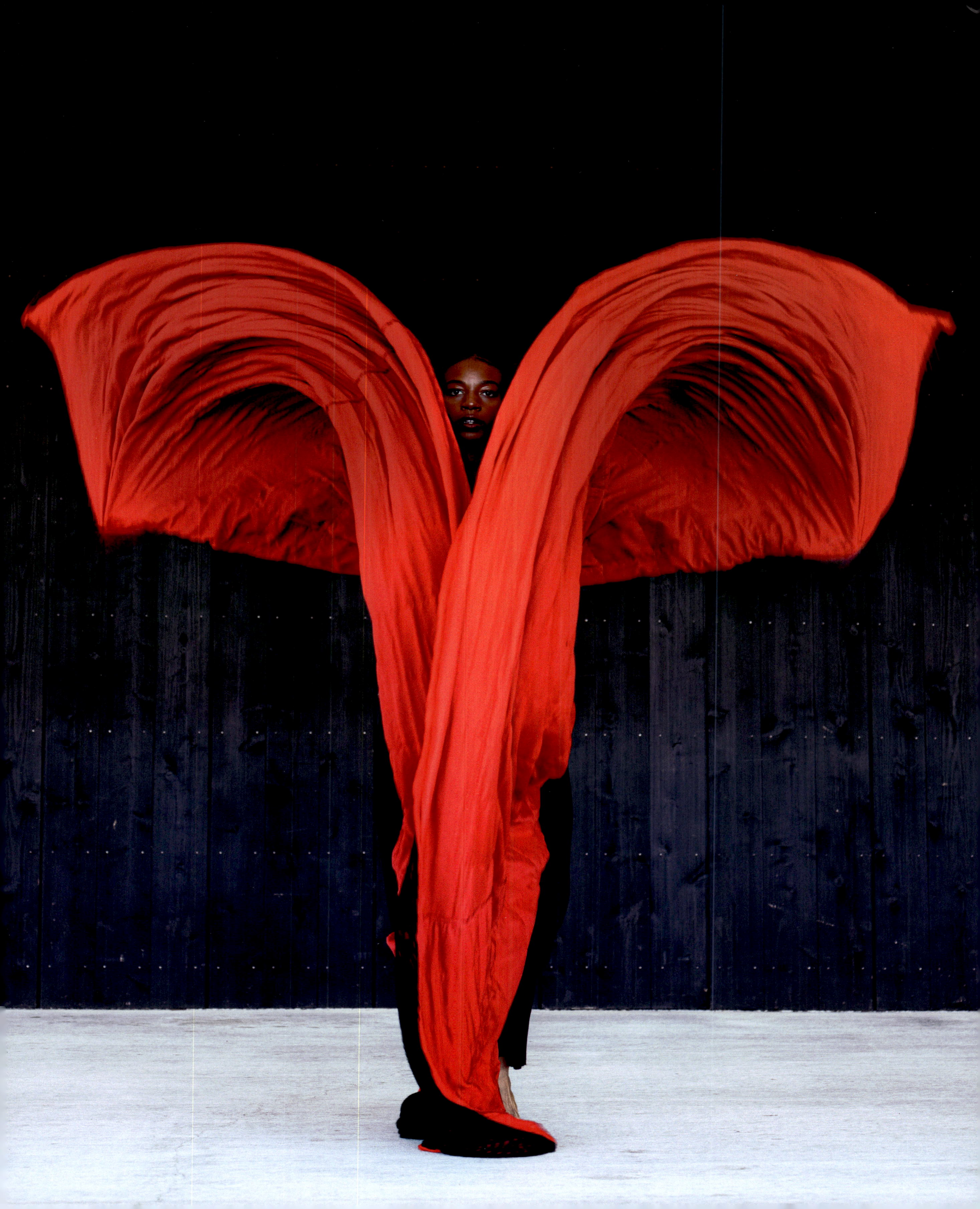

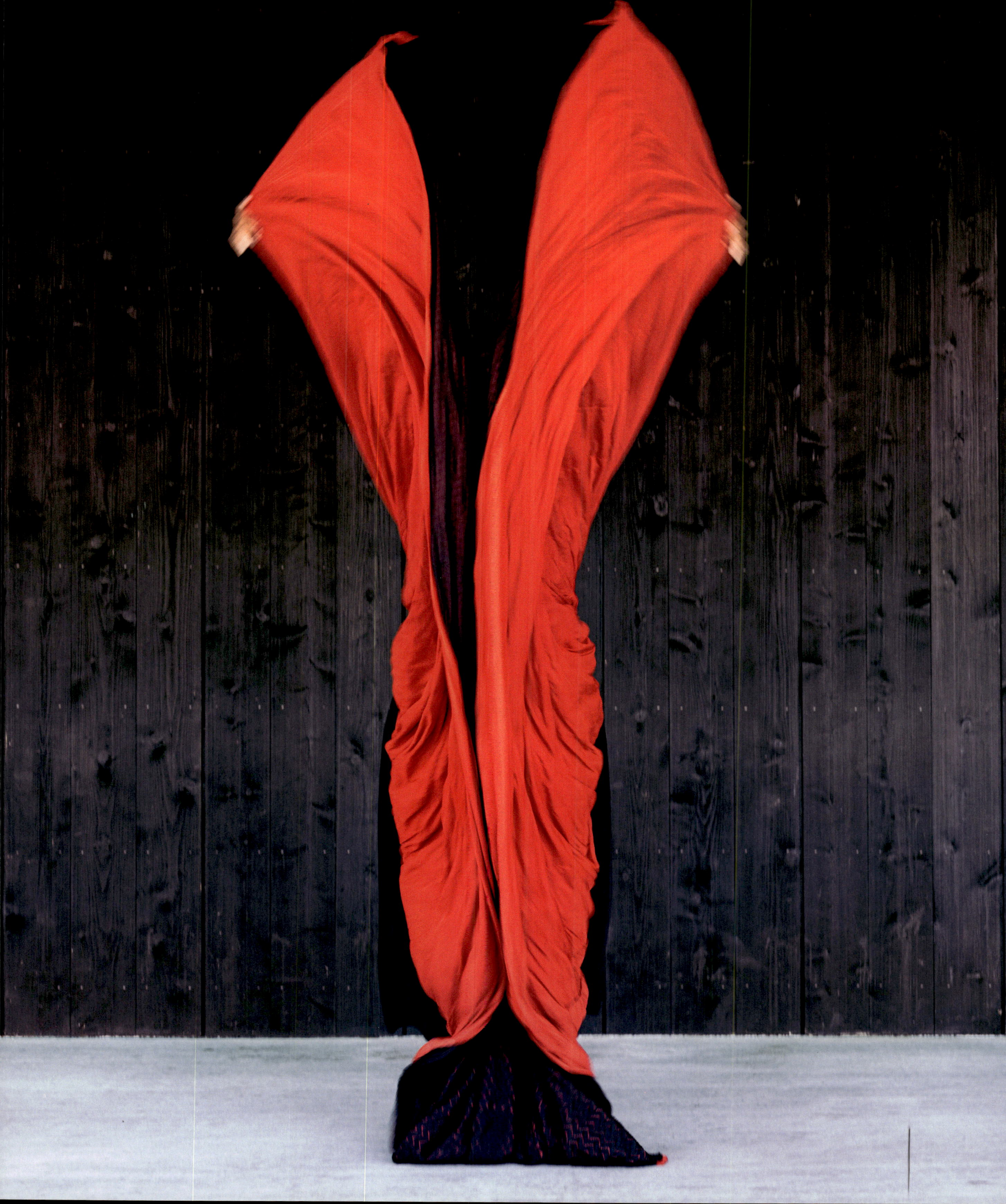

"Prelude to Action"
from *Chronicle*

LEAD DANCER

Leslie Andrea Williams

DANCERS

Laurel Dalley Smith, Devin Loh, Marzia Memoli,
Amanda Moreira, Anne O'Donnell Passero,
Kate Reyes, Anne Souder

SET DESIGN

Isamu Noguchi

COSTUME RE-CREATION

Russell Vogler

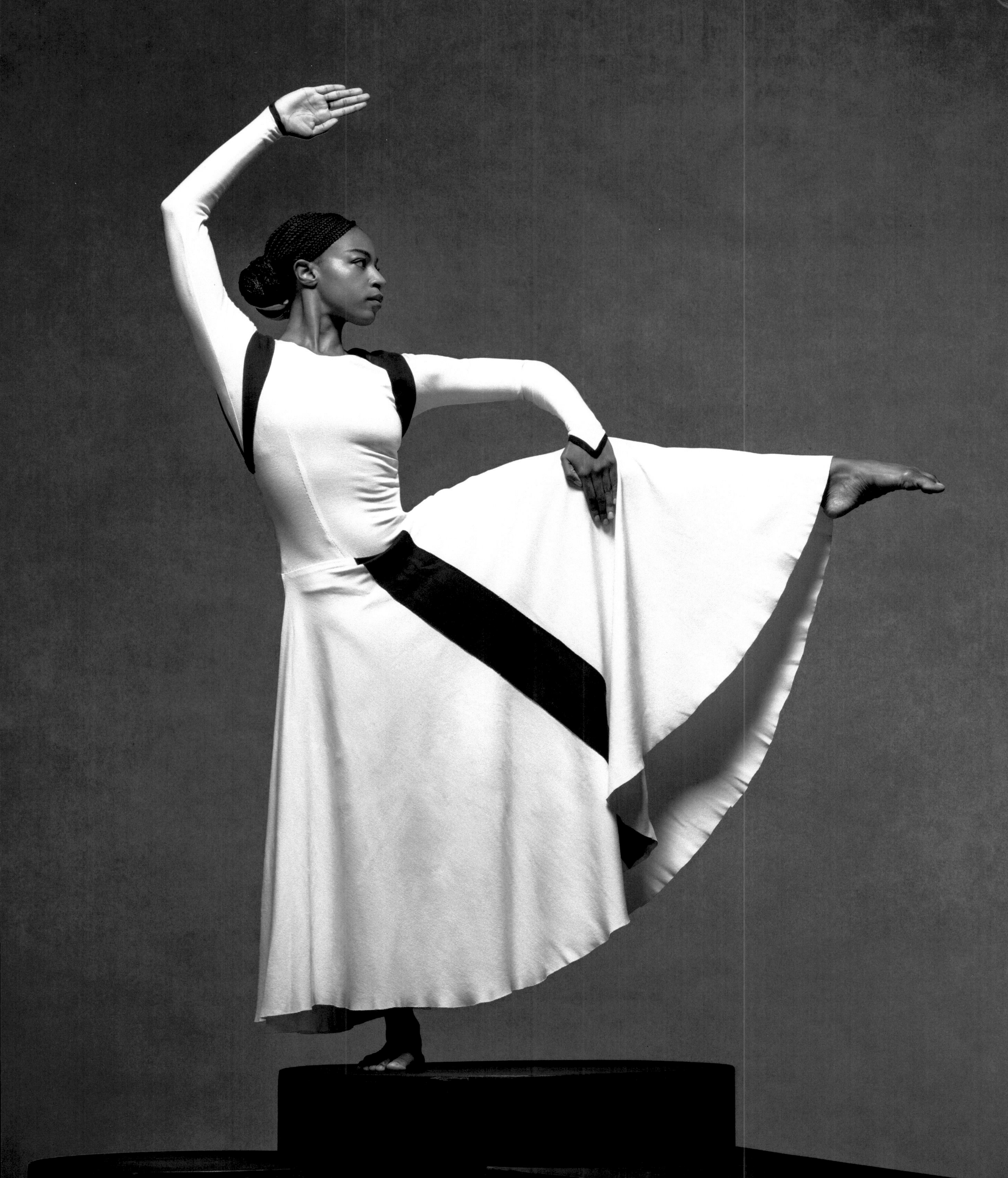

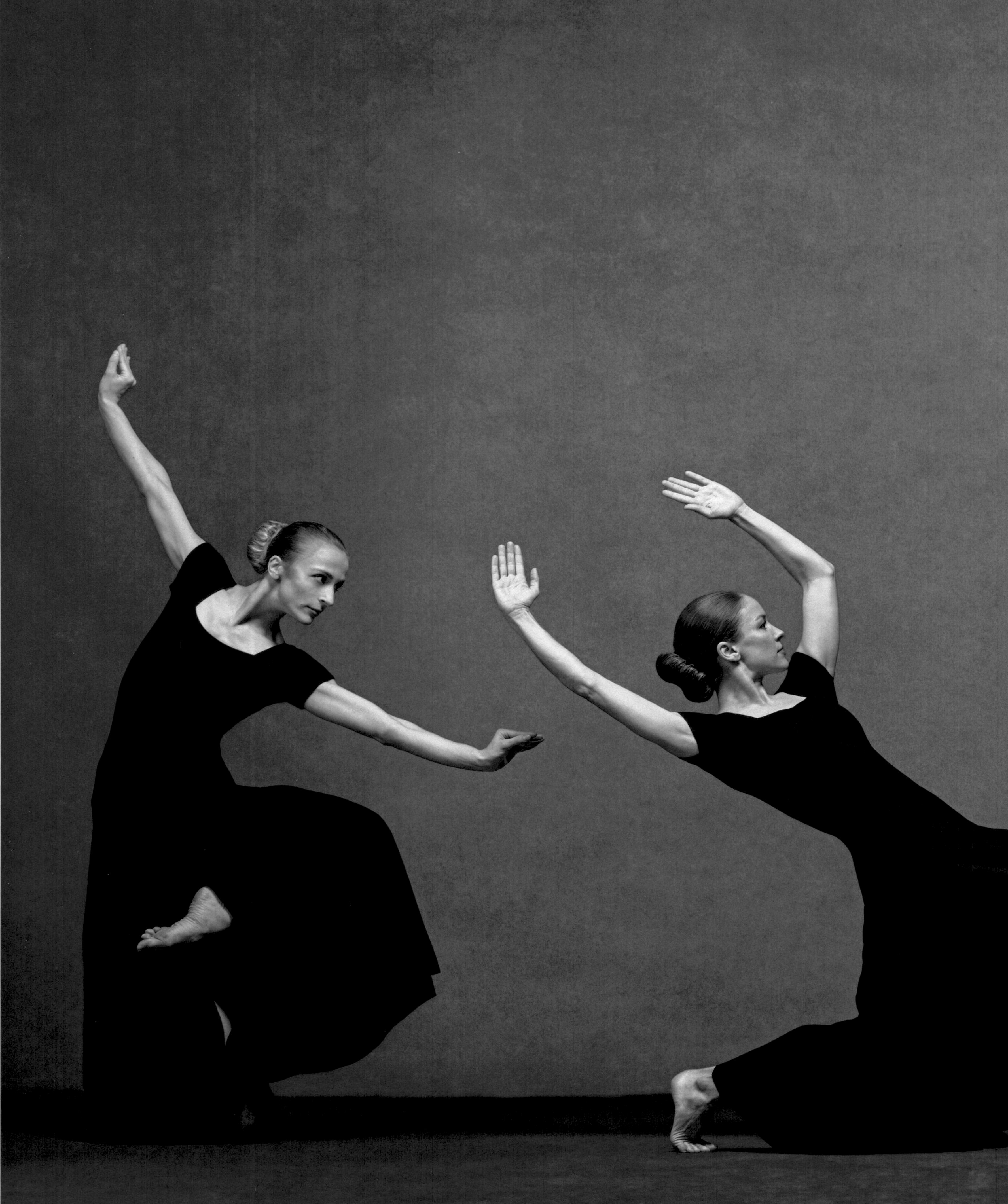

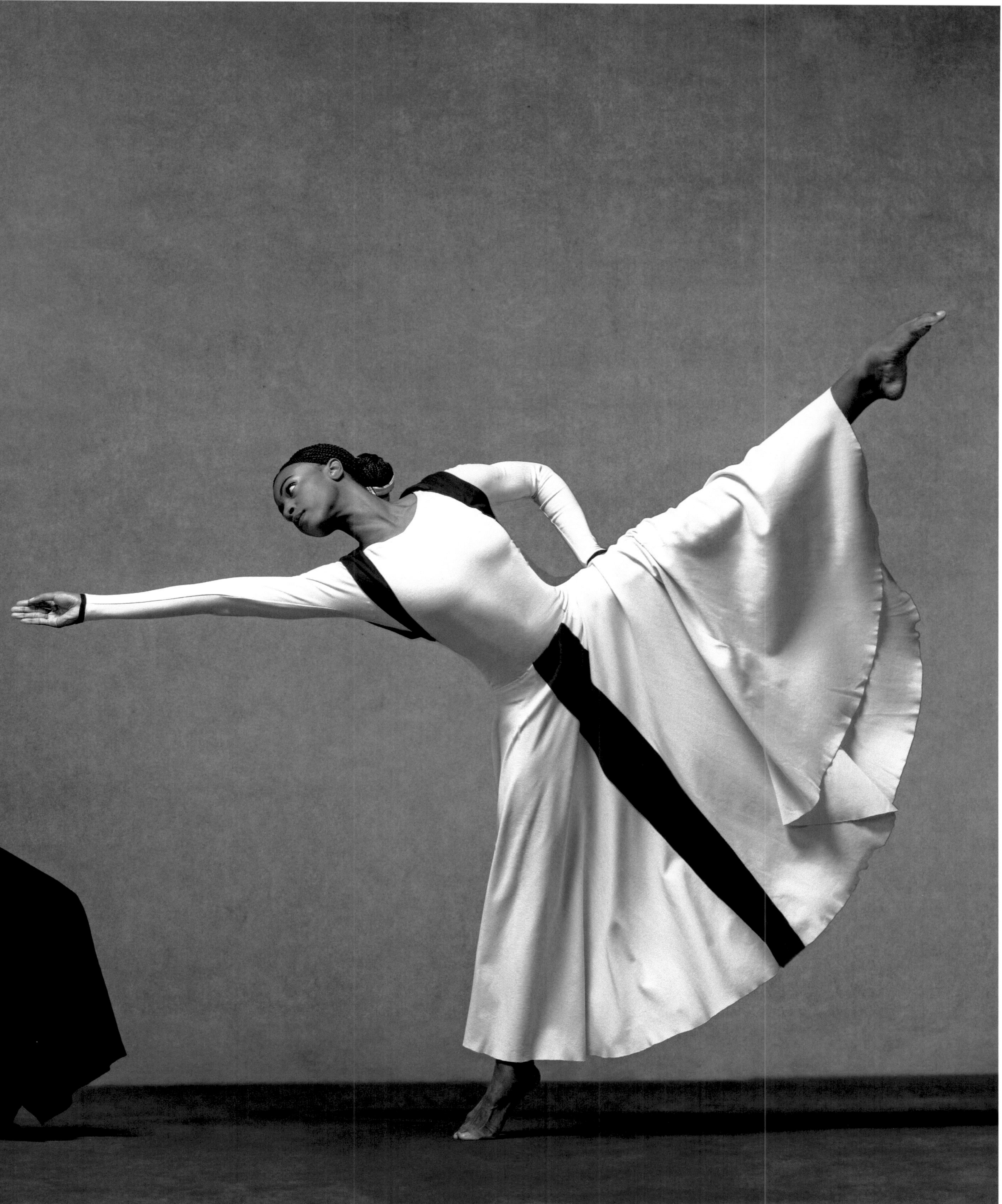

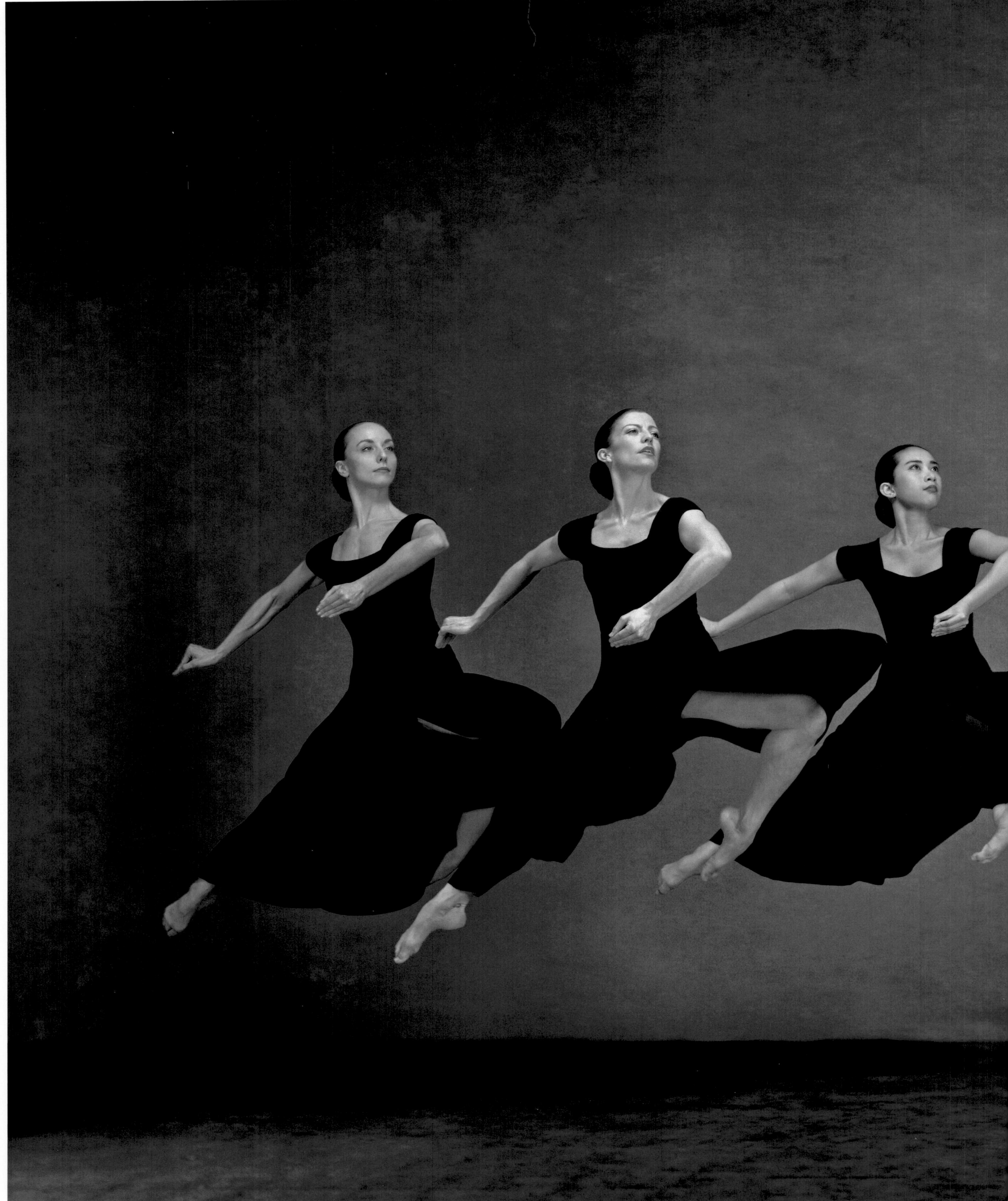

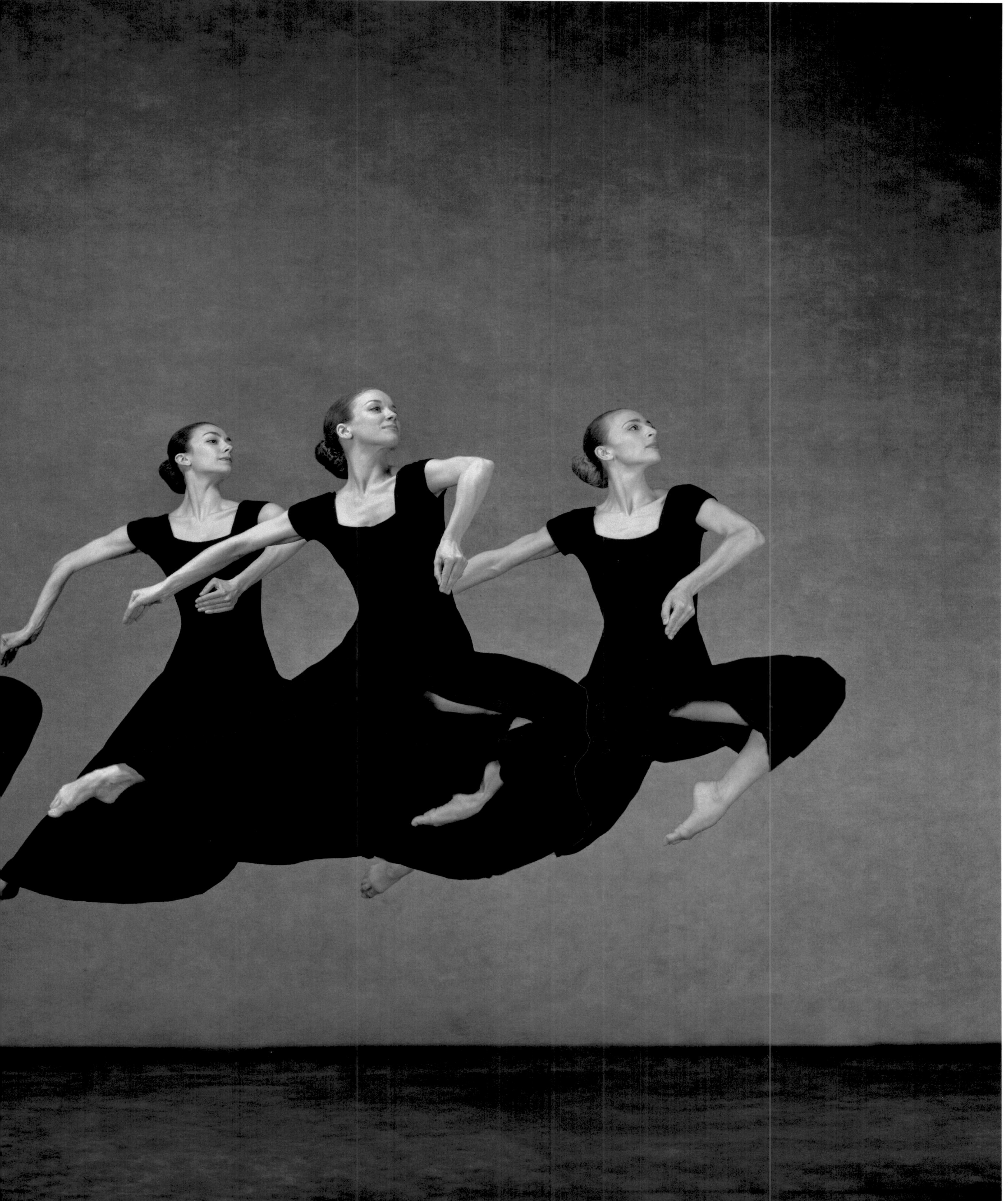

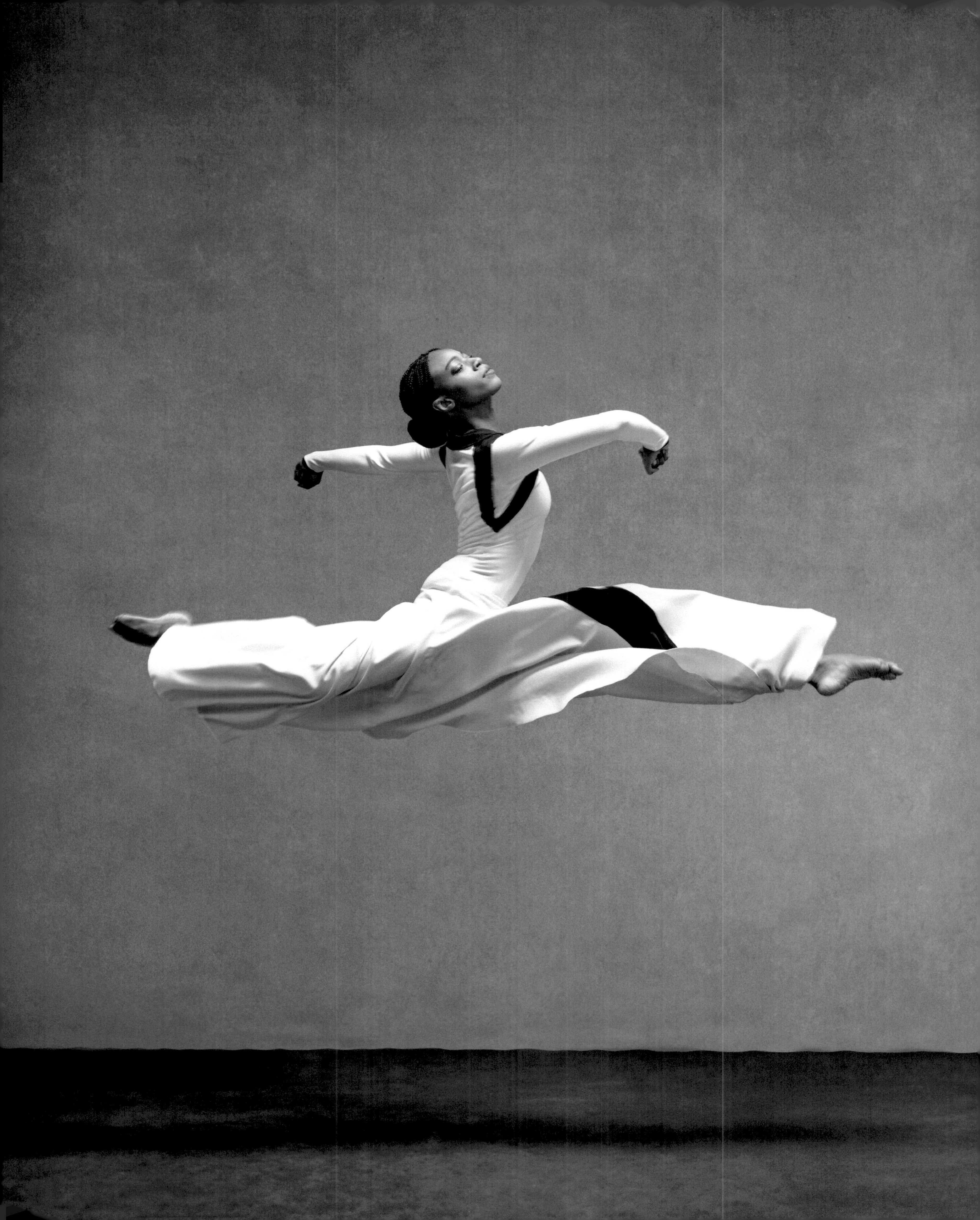

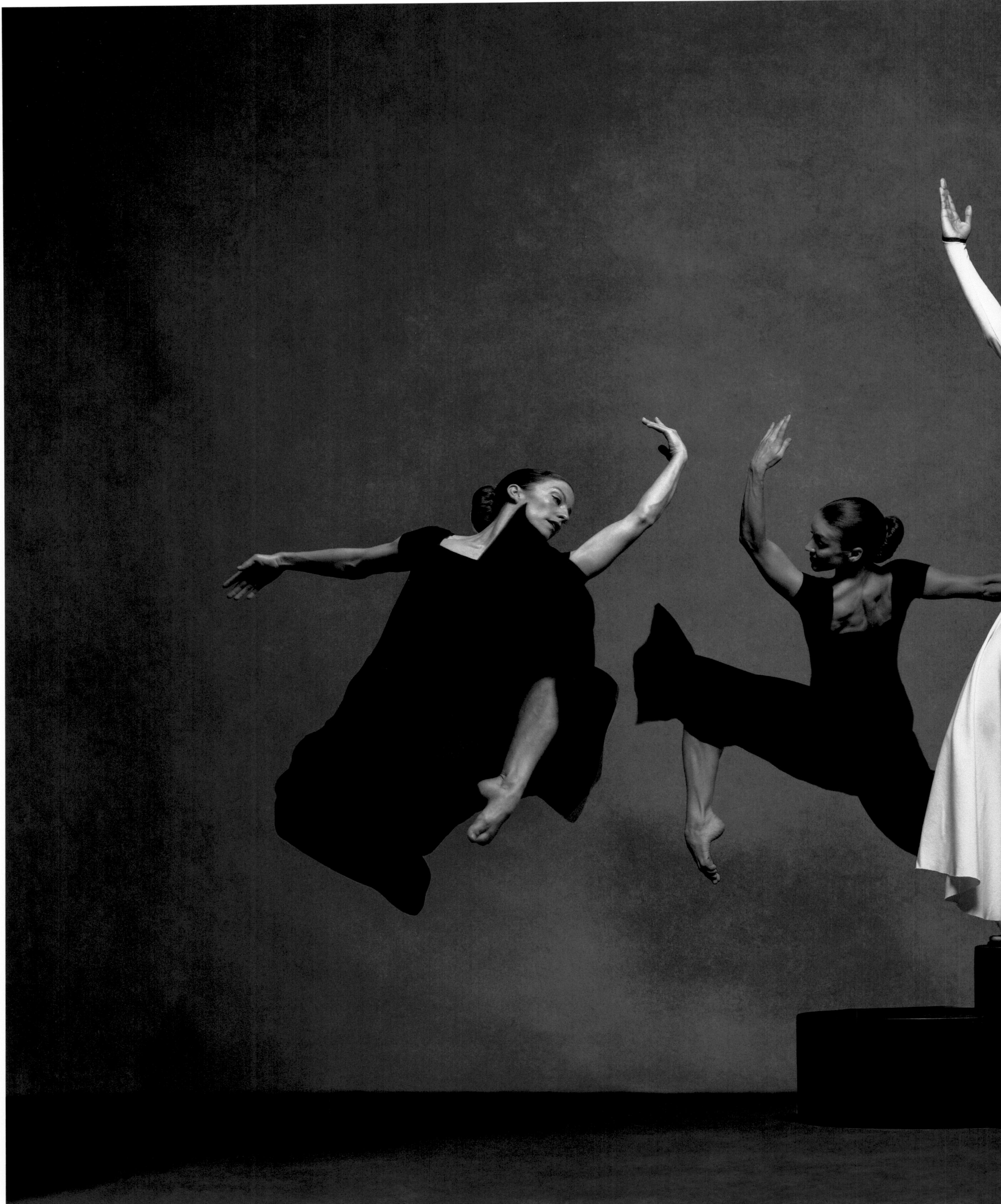

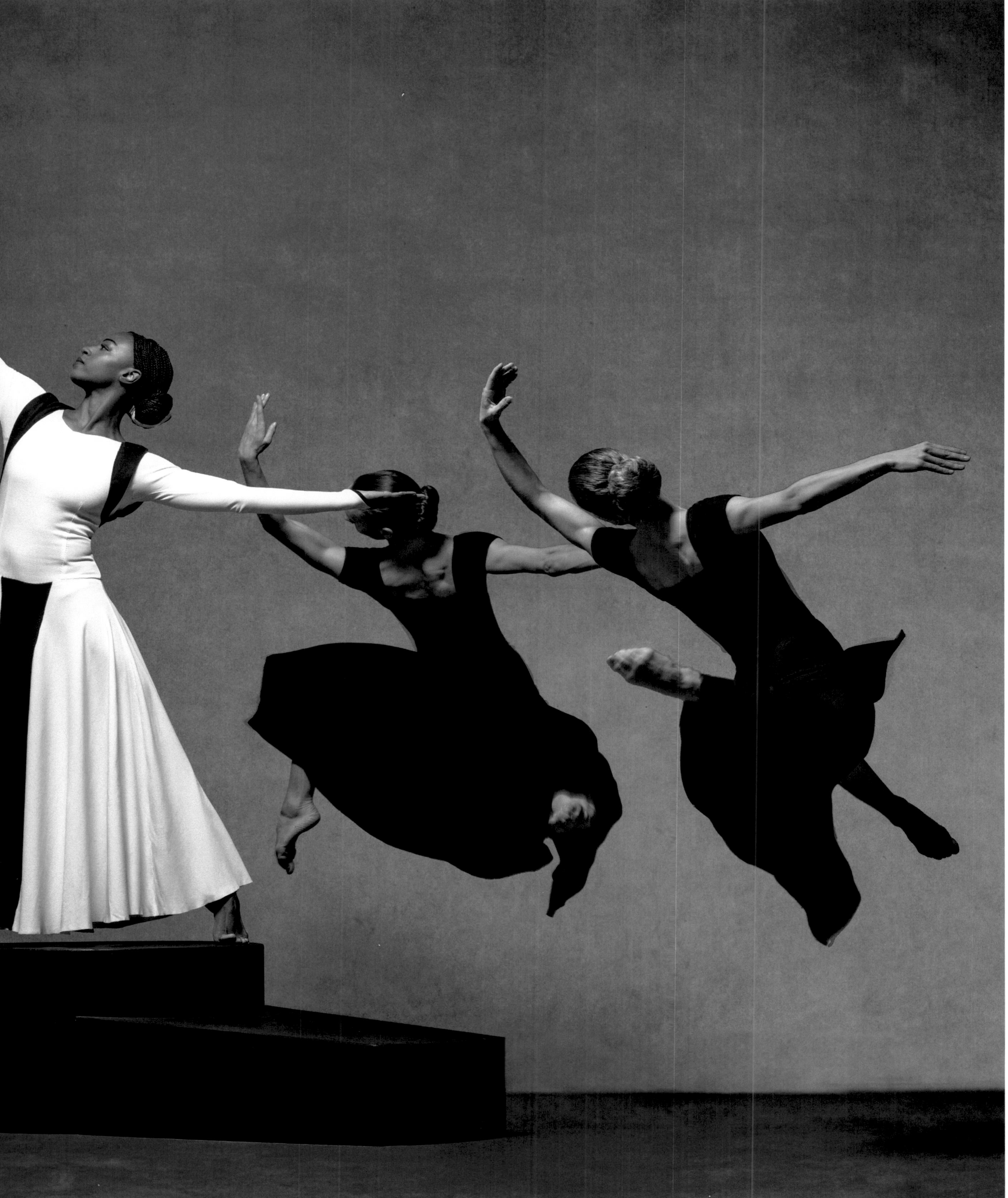

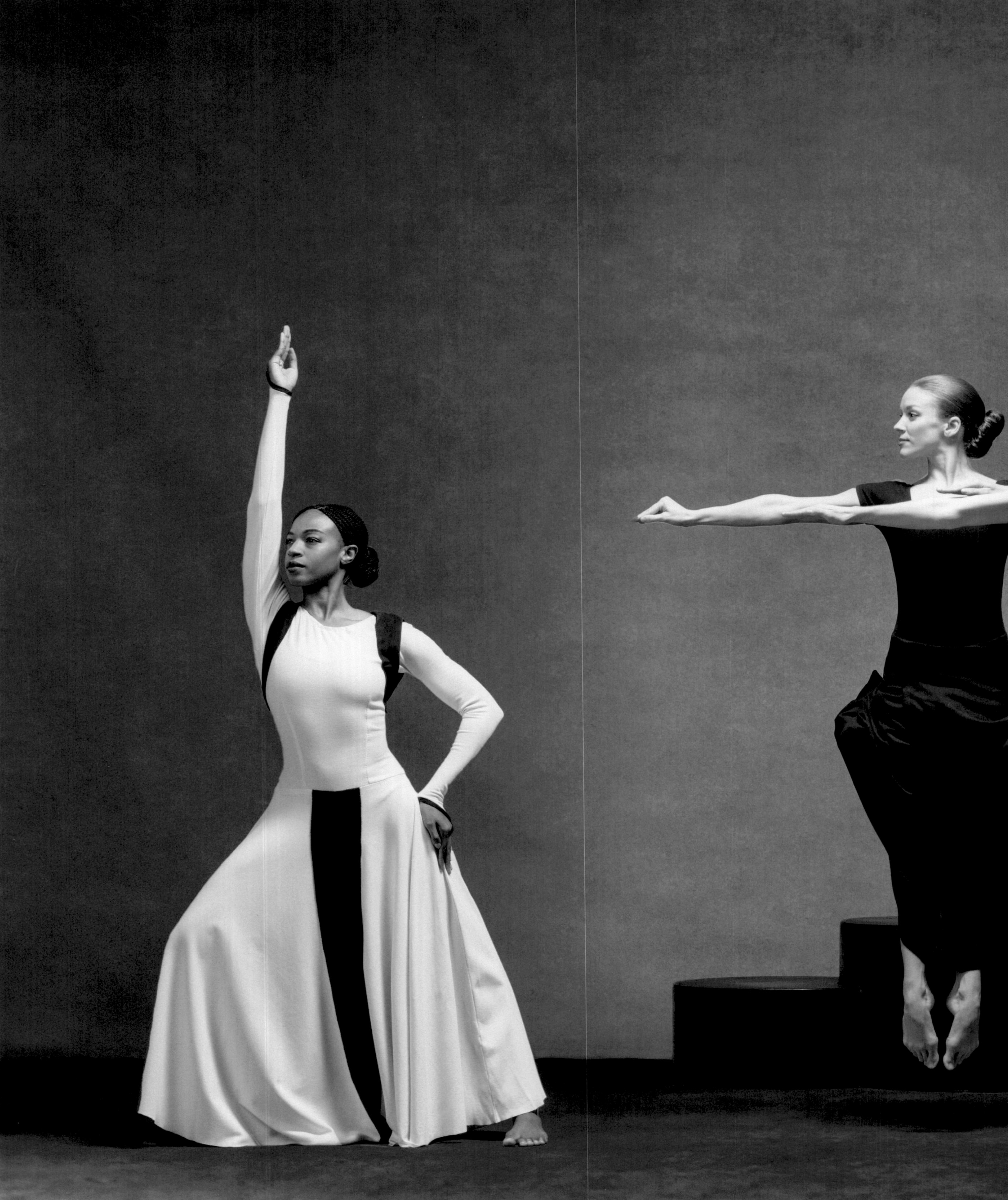

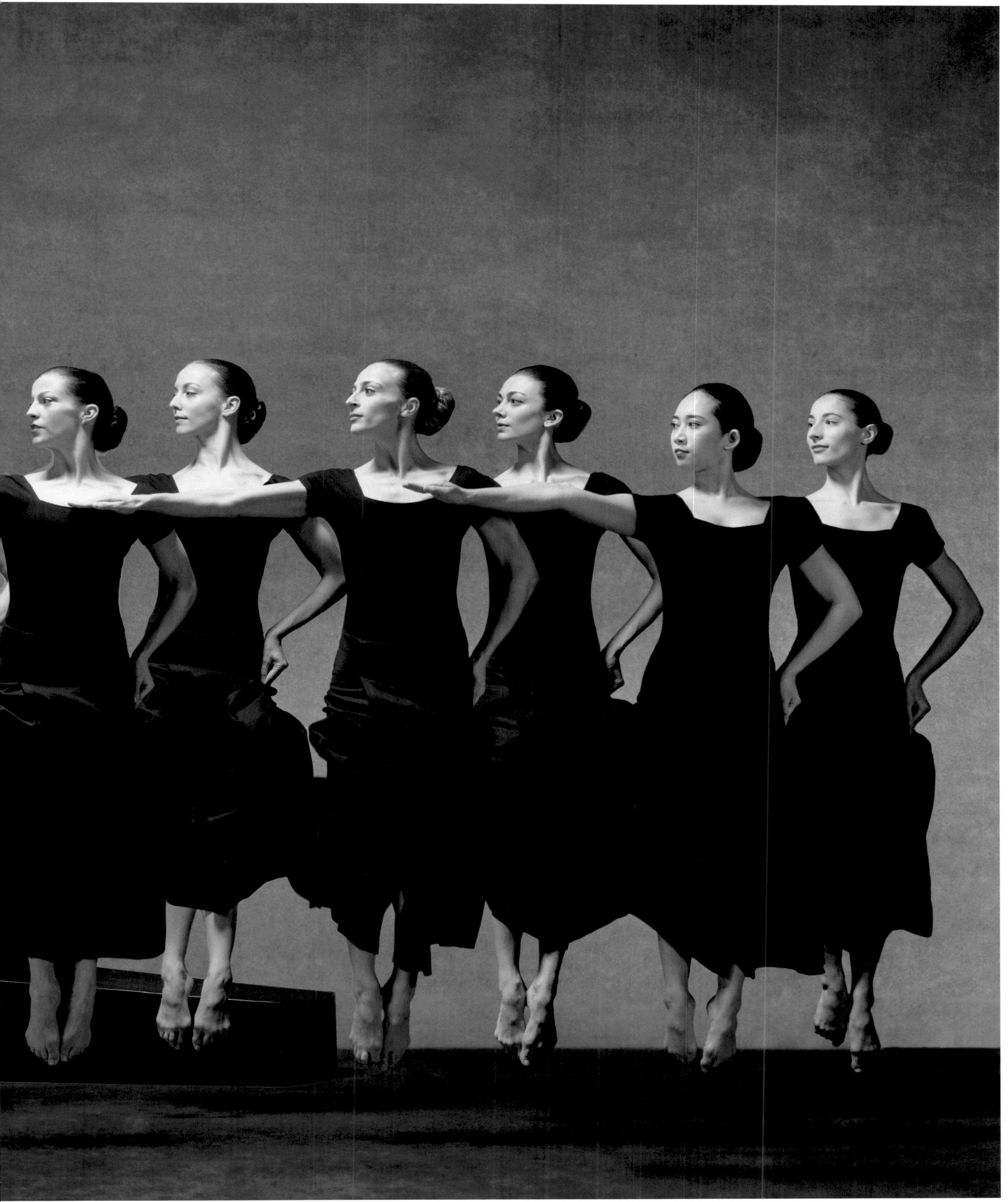

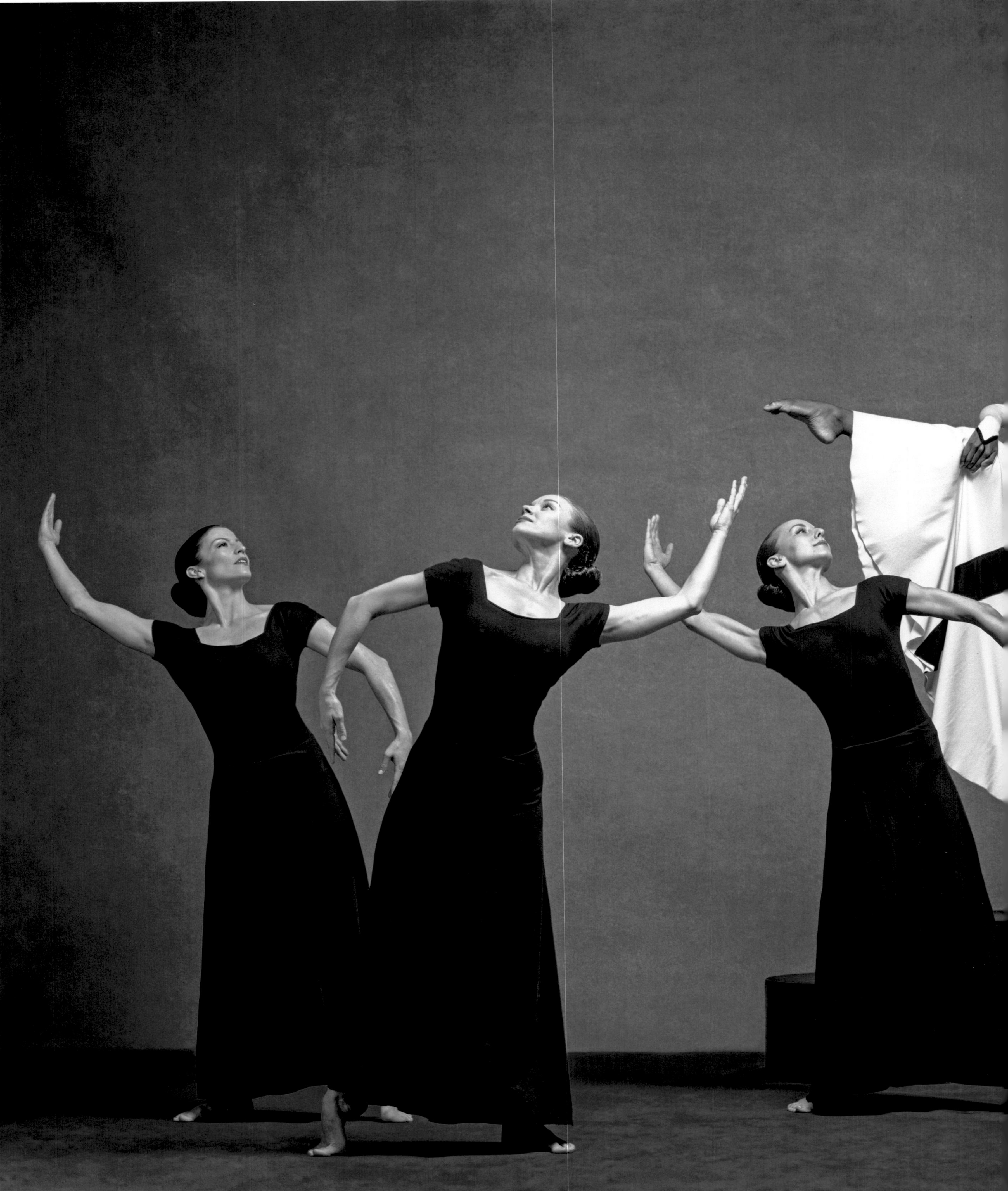

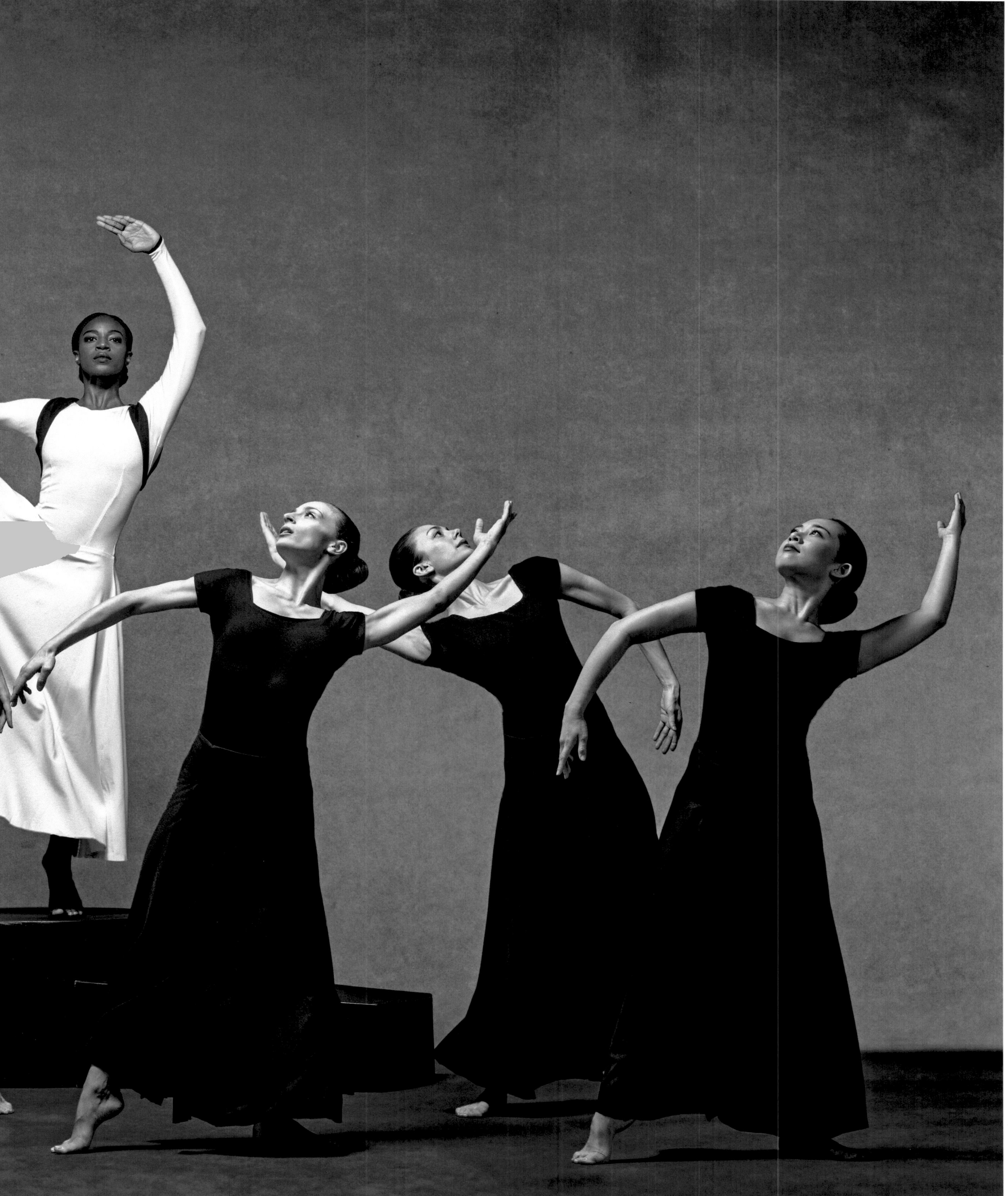

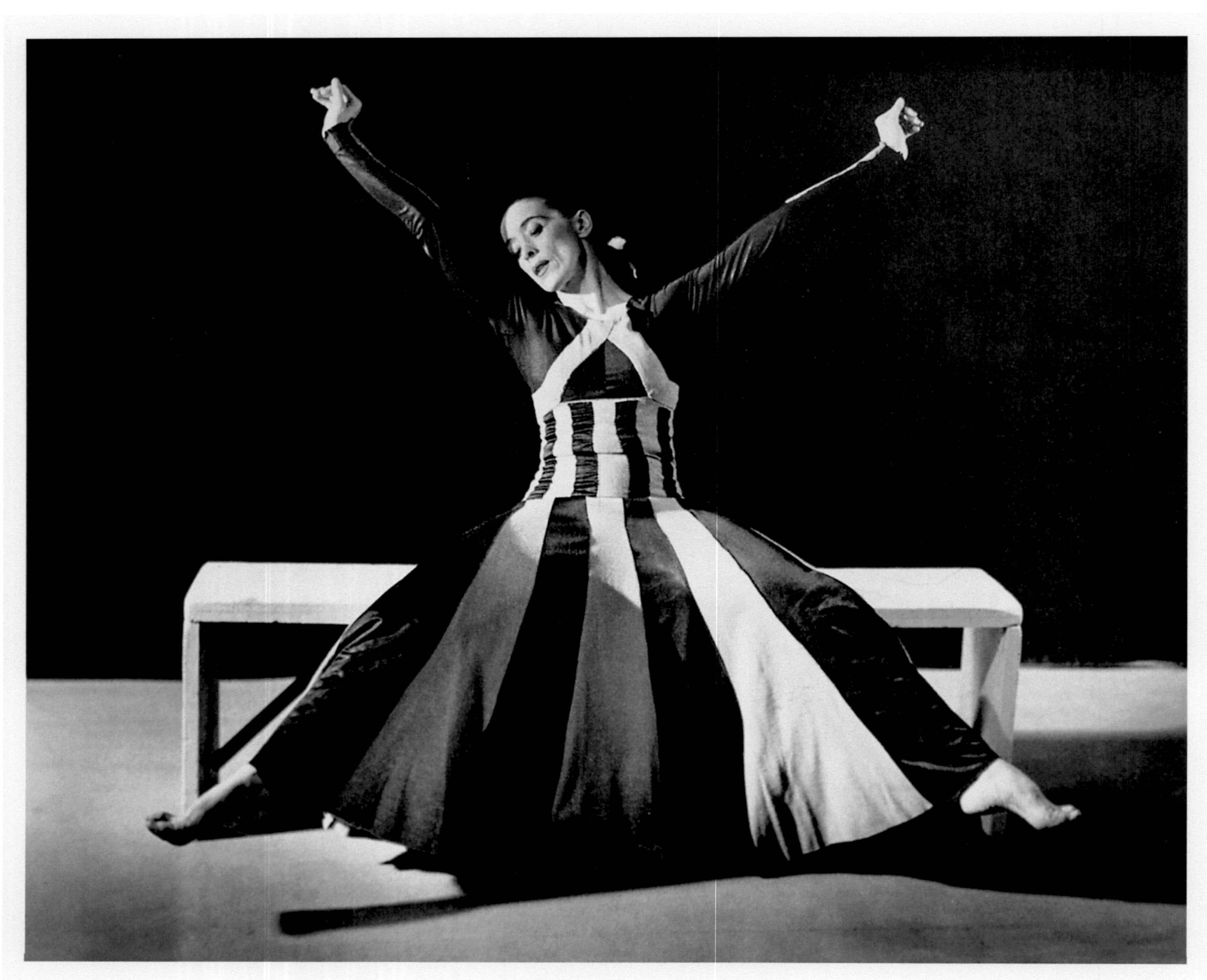

Martha Graham. Photograph by Barbara Morgan.

DEEP SONG, 1937

A cri de coeur against the inhumanity and cruelty of the Spanish Civil War.

Deep Song opens with a lone female figure perched on a simple low white bench that doubles as a coffin and mourner's pew. The vertical lines of her black-and-white-striped dress warp into bold, graphic distortions as her body carves out deep contractions and produces an angular jutting of hips that gesture agony and pleading. Her movements are characterized by crawls across the floor, stuttering side steps, and moments of defiance that quickly dissolve into crumpled forms. She crawls beneath the low bench and lies as if buried alive, then frees herself to walk defiantly toward audience, only to finally collapse on the bench, sobbing in slow motion as the lights fade.

This solo was lost for decades until Graham reconstructed it with company member Terese Capucilli in 1988, using photographs by Barbara Morgan.

SET DESIGN
Martha Graham

COSTUME DESIGN
Martha Graham

COMPOSER
Henry Cowell

Deep Song

DANCER

Anne Souder

COSTUME RE-CREATION

Russell Vogler

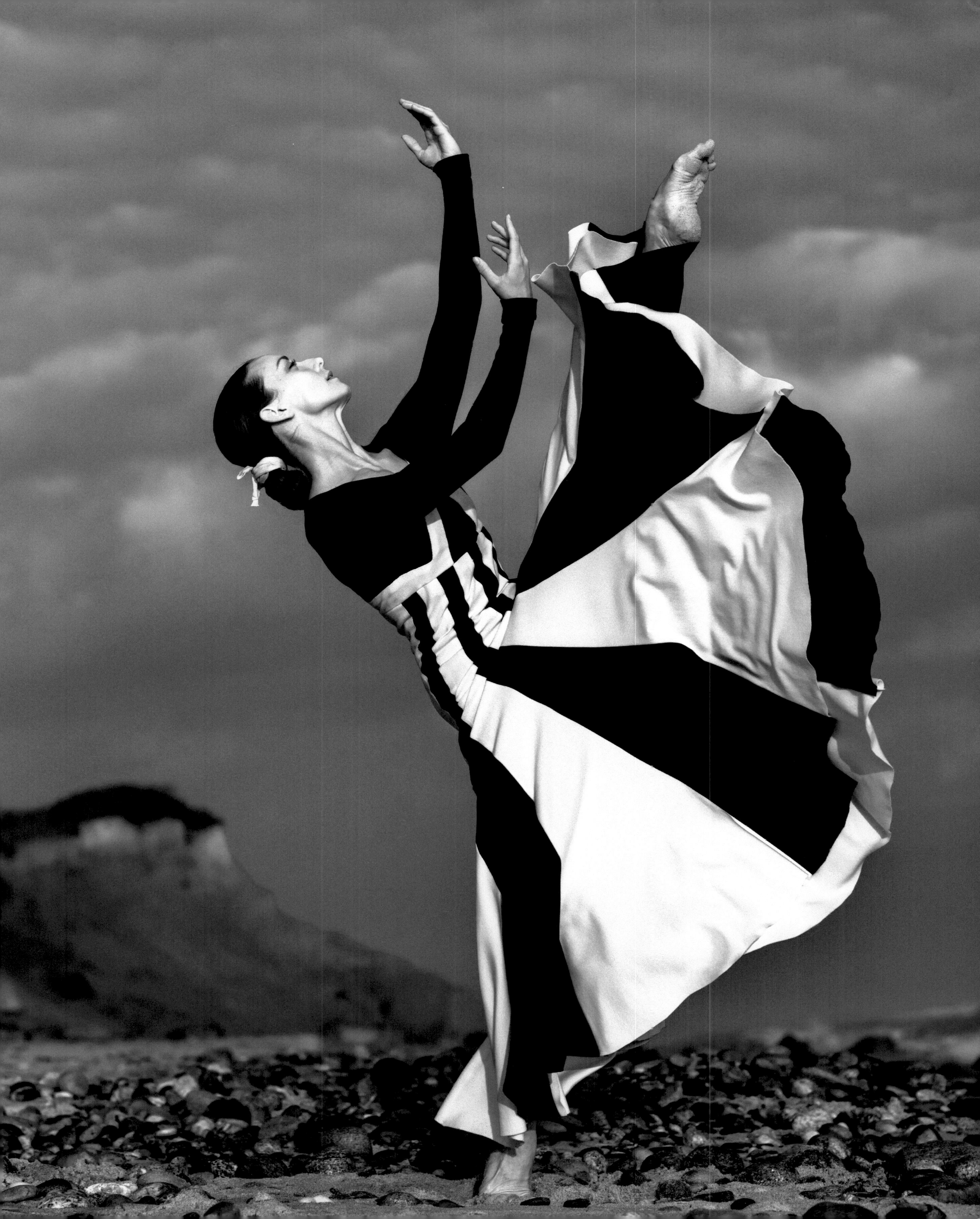

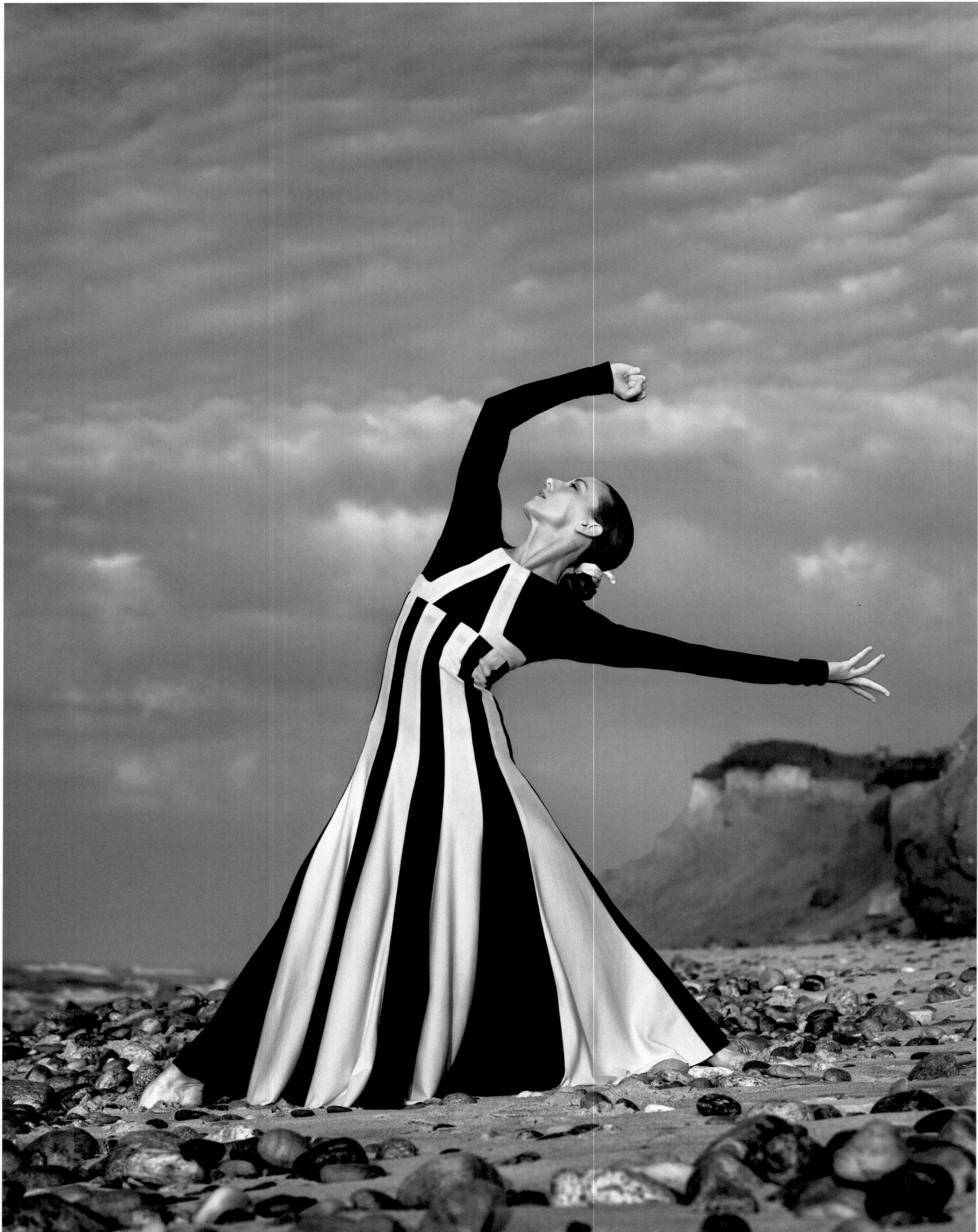

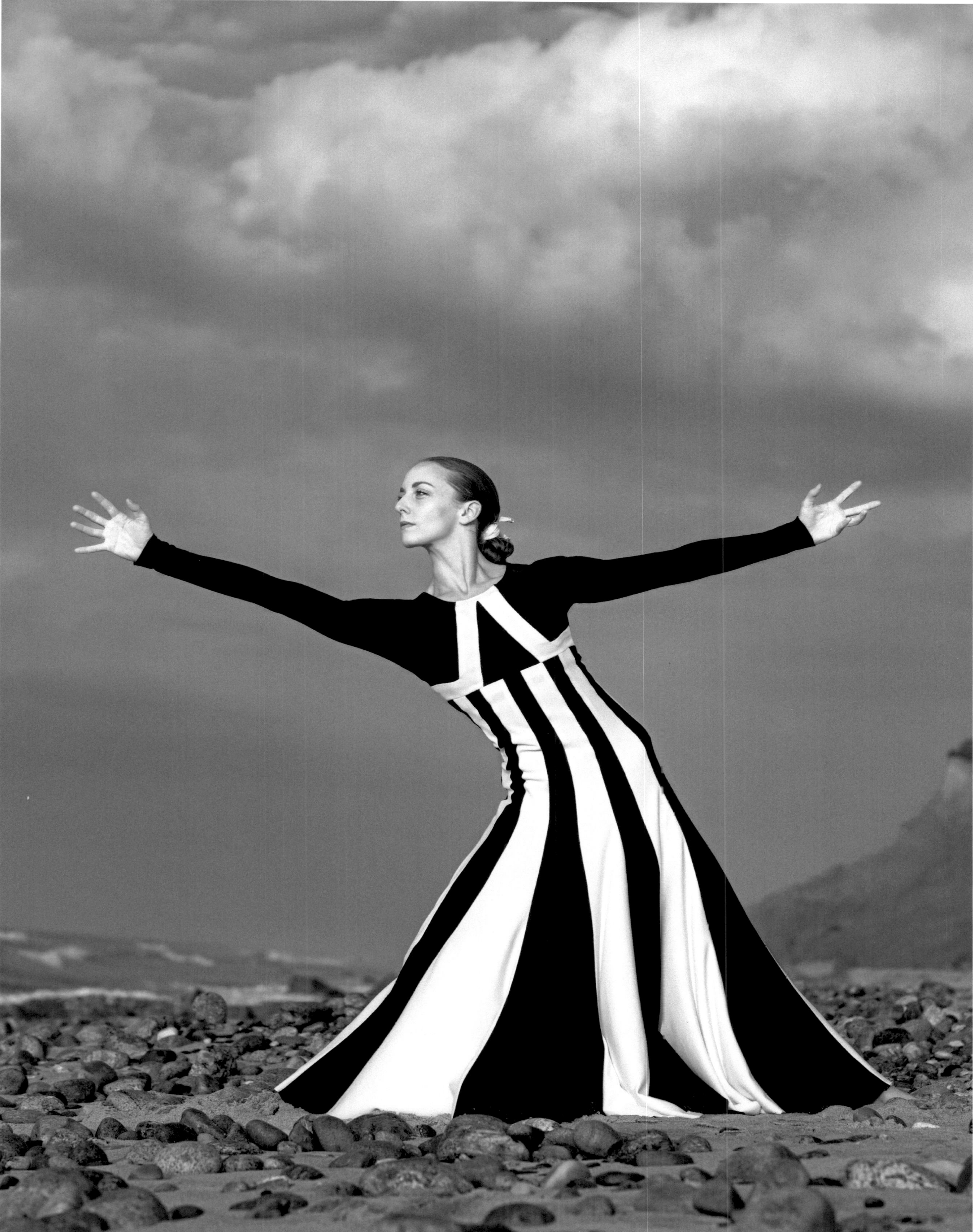

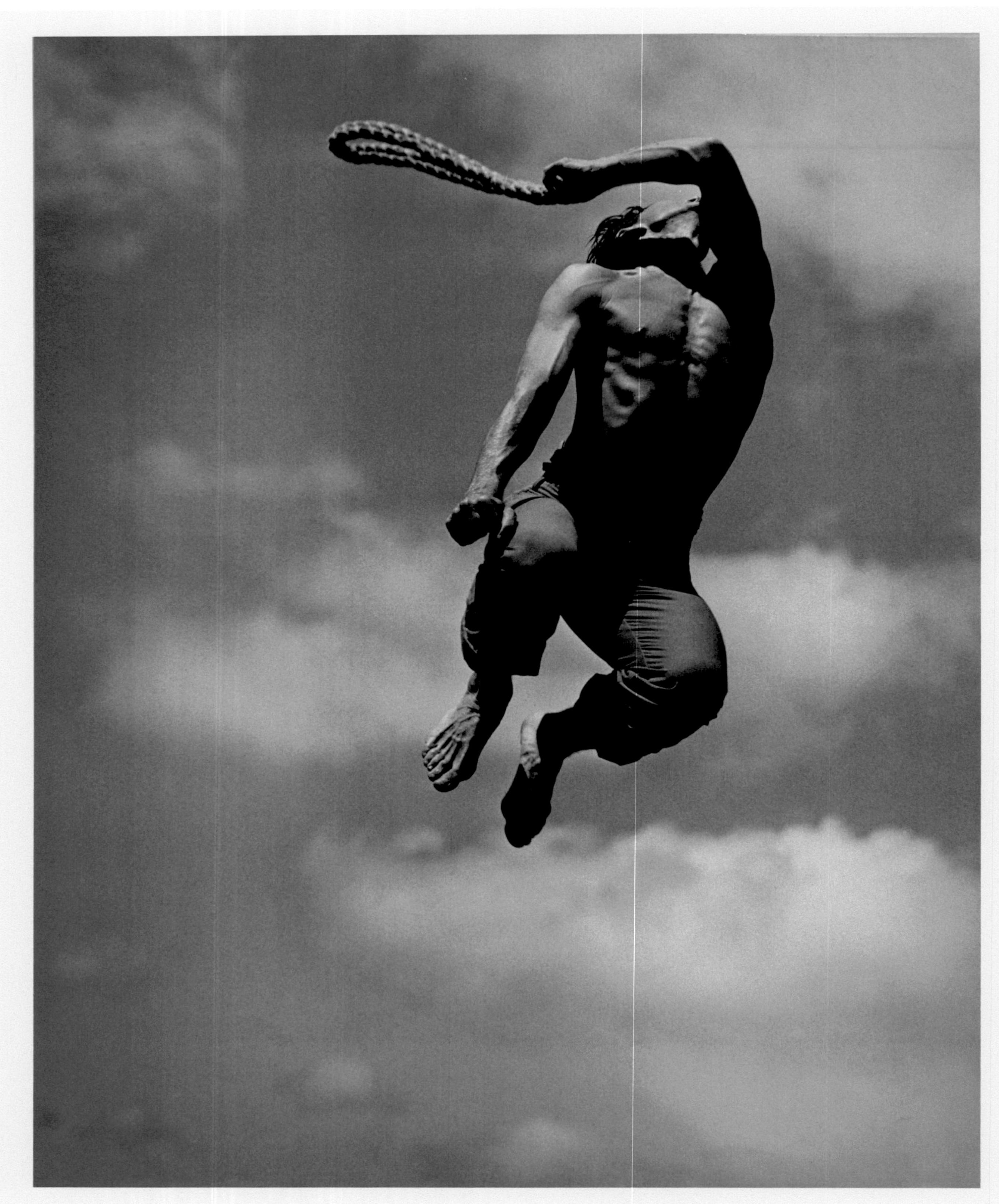

Erick Hawkins. Photograph by Barbara Morgan.

EL PENITENTE, 1940

A series of biblical tableaux performed by a trio of traveling players.

This stylized medieval miracle play features the Mary figure transformed from Virgin to Magdalene to Mater Dolorosa, a self-punishing Penitent, and a benign but chastising Christ figure. The dance proceeds through ten vignettes that present episodes of flagellation, revelation, temptation, contrition, crucifixion, and redemption, each connected by a simple walking processional.

The Penitent whips himself with a knotted rope. The black-robed Christ figure in an imposing mask topped with a crown of thorns angles a wooden cross to become the spar for a sail. Mary seduces the Penitent with an apple, and the Penitent later steps into a collapsible wooden death cart. Mary wipes the tears of the cross-bearing Christ as on the Via Dolorosa, and the three players end in a festive folk dance, hopping and skittering like carved puppets on strings.

SET DESIGN
Arch Lauterer/Isamu Noguchi

COSTUME DESIGN
Edythe Gilfond

COMPOSER
Louis Horst

El Penitente

PENITENT
Lloyd Knight

CHRIST FIGURE
Alessio Crognale-Roberts

MARY AS VIRGIN, MAGDALEN, MOTHER
Marzia Memoli

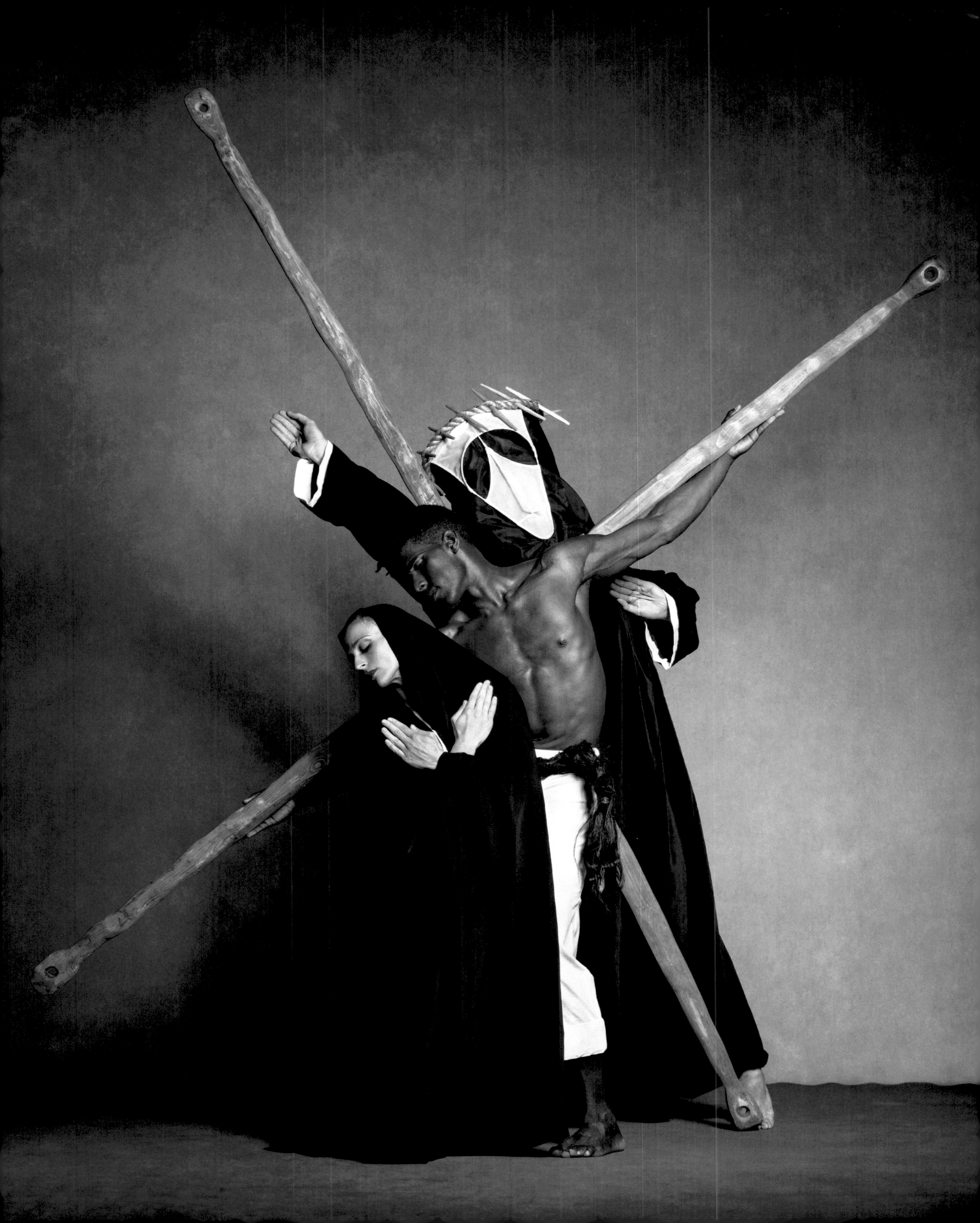

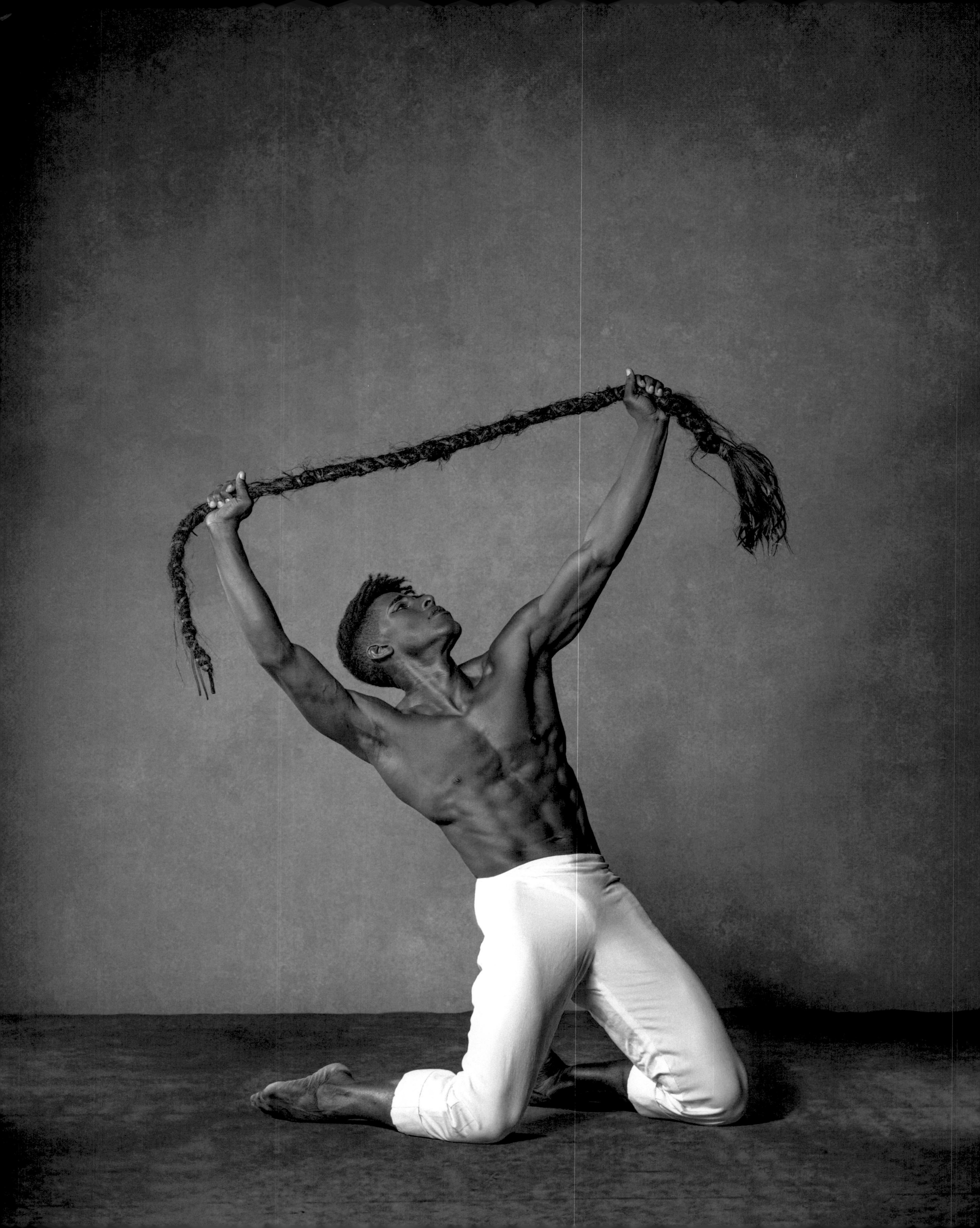

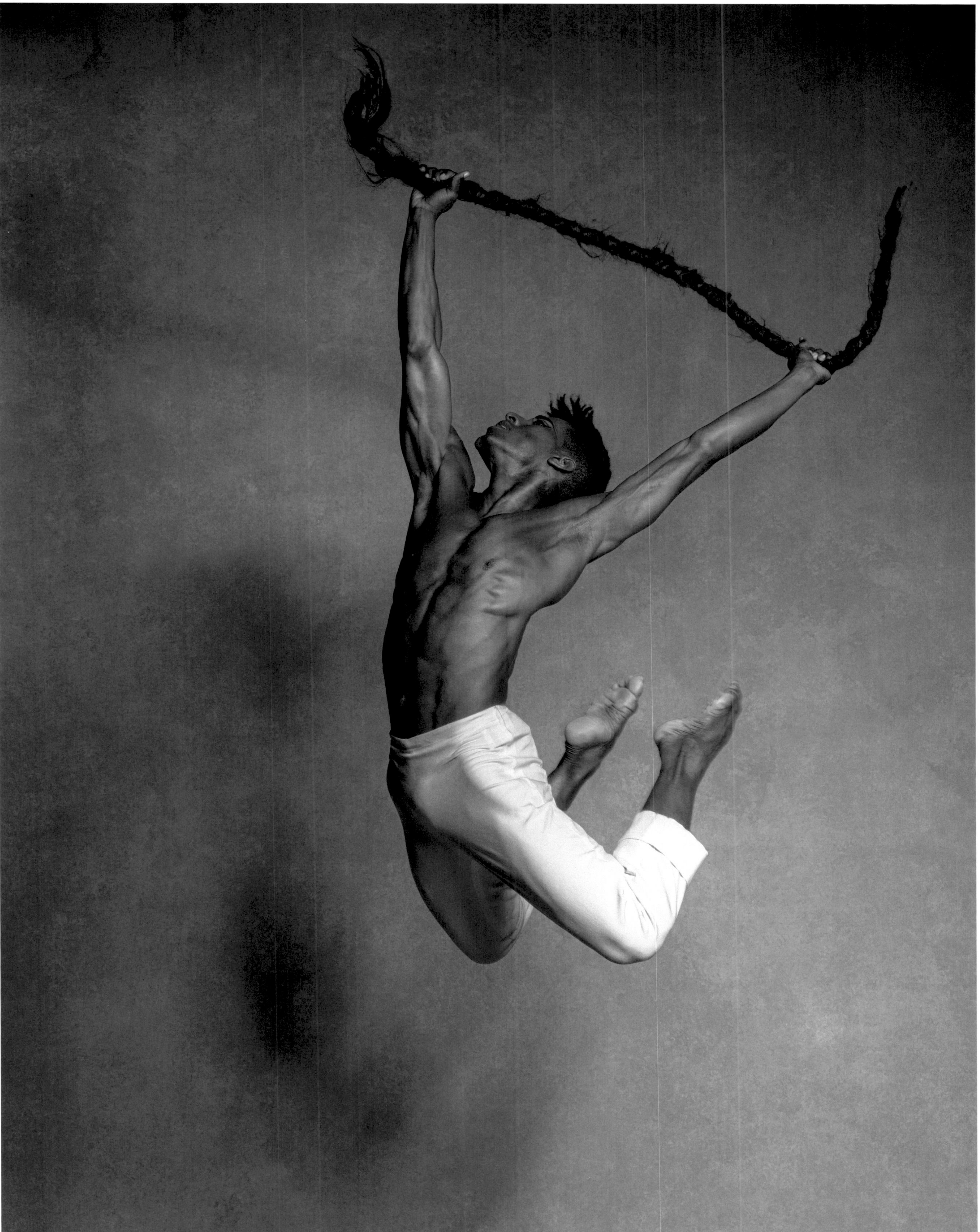

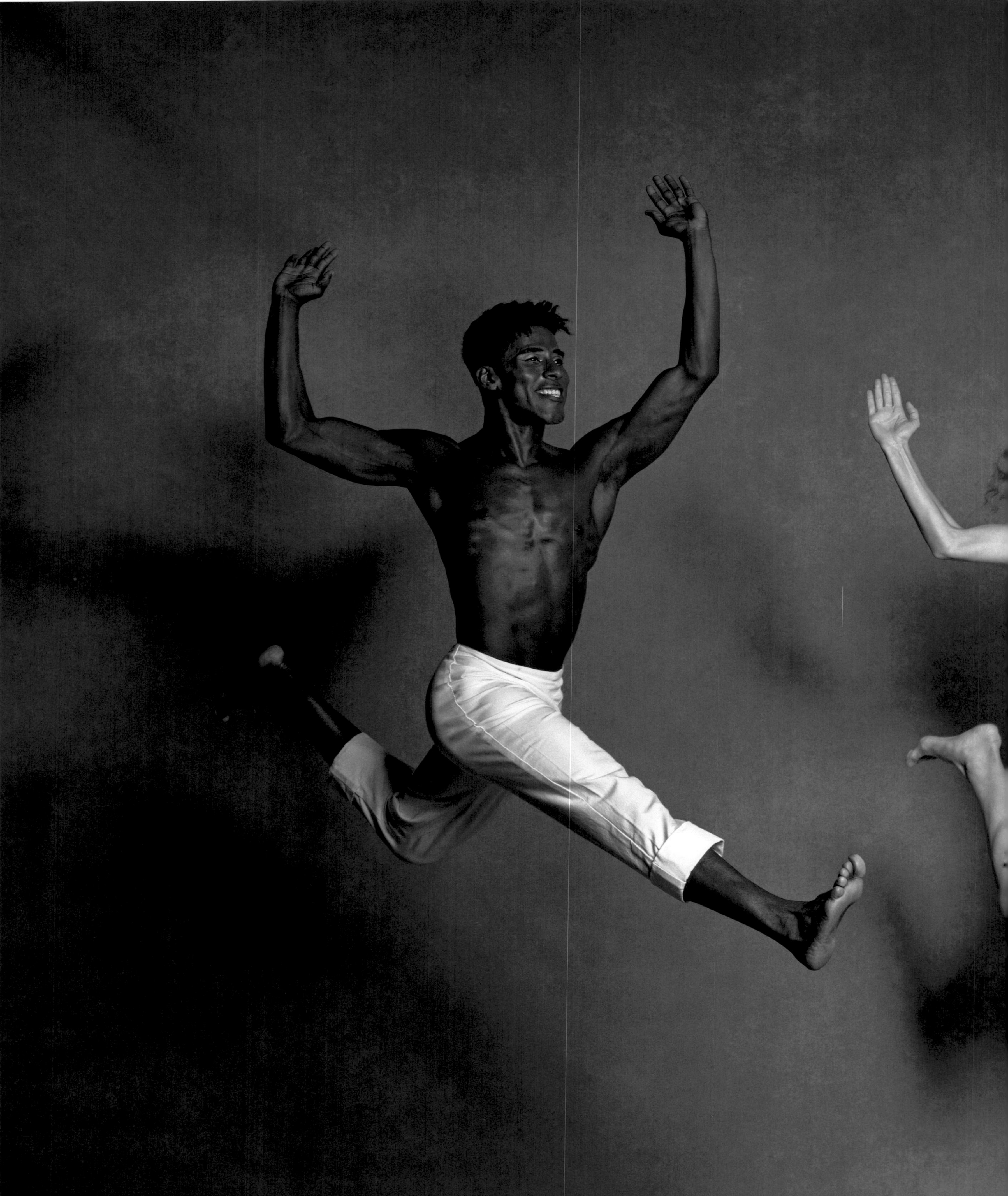

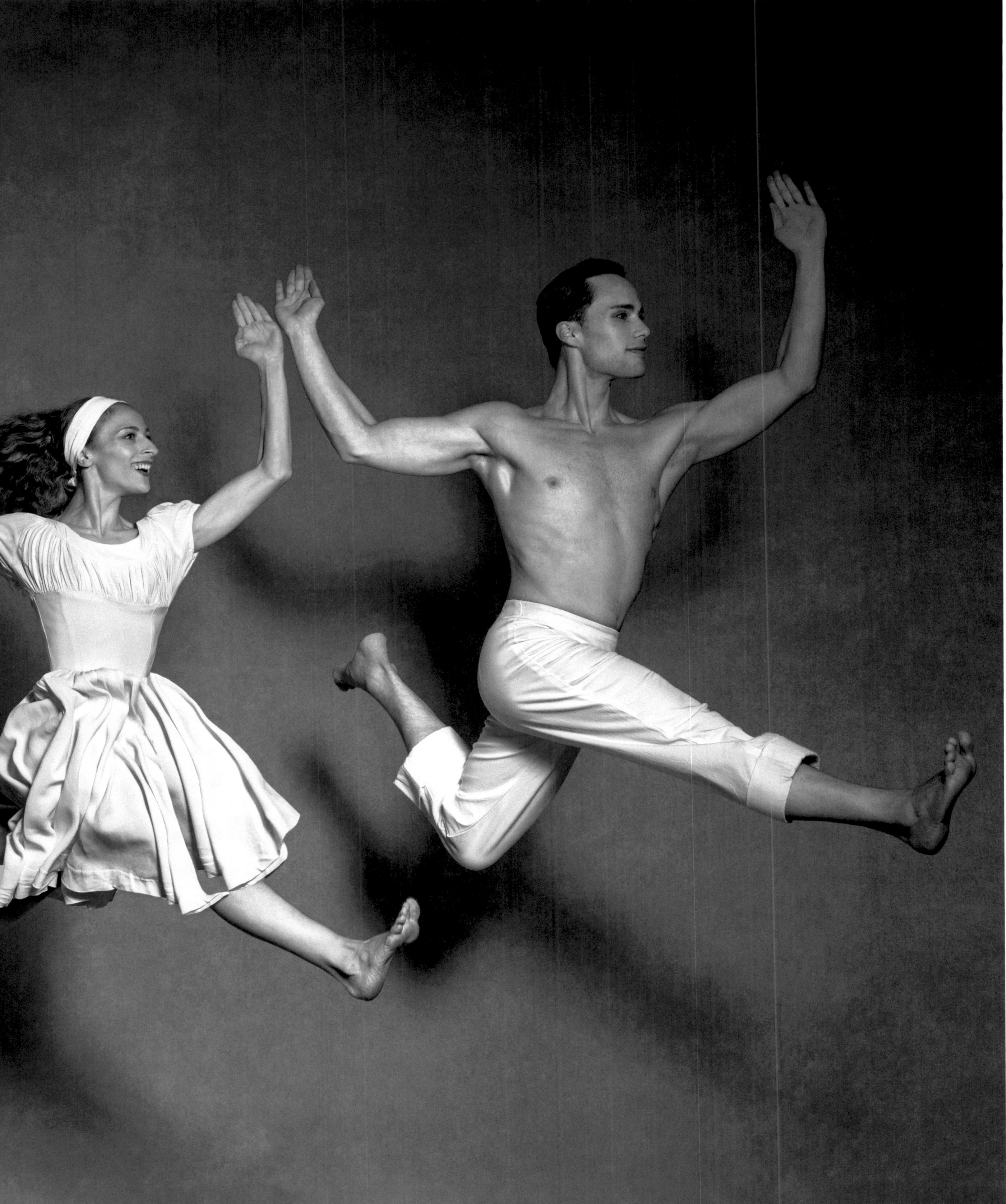

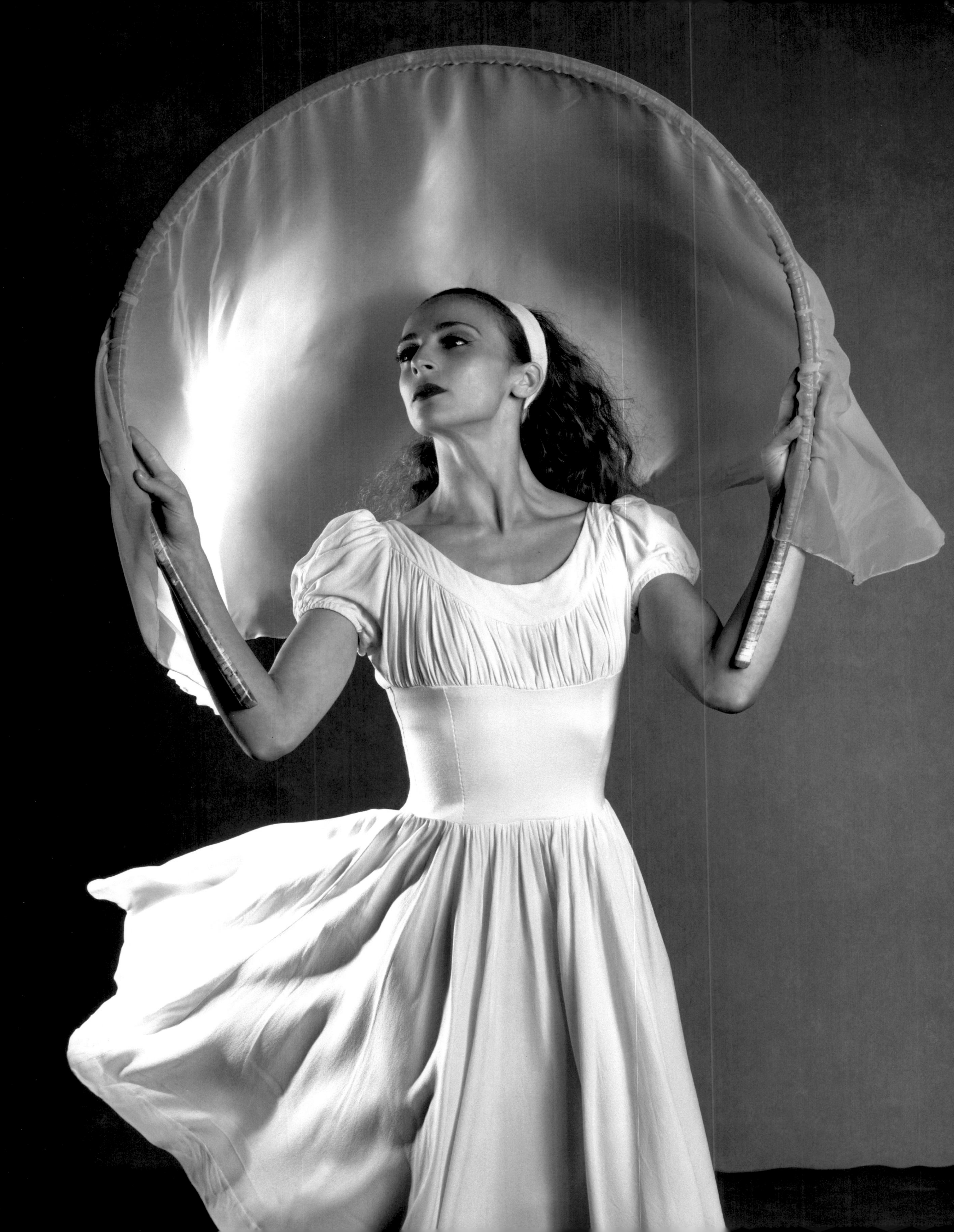

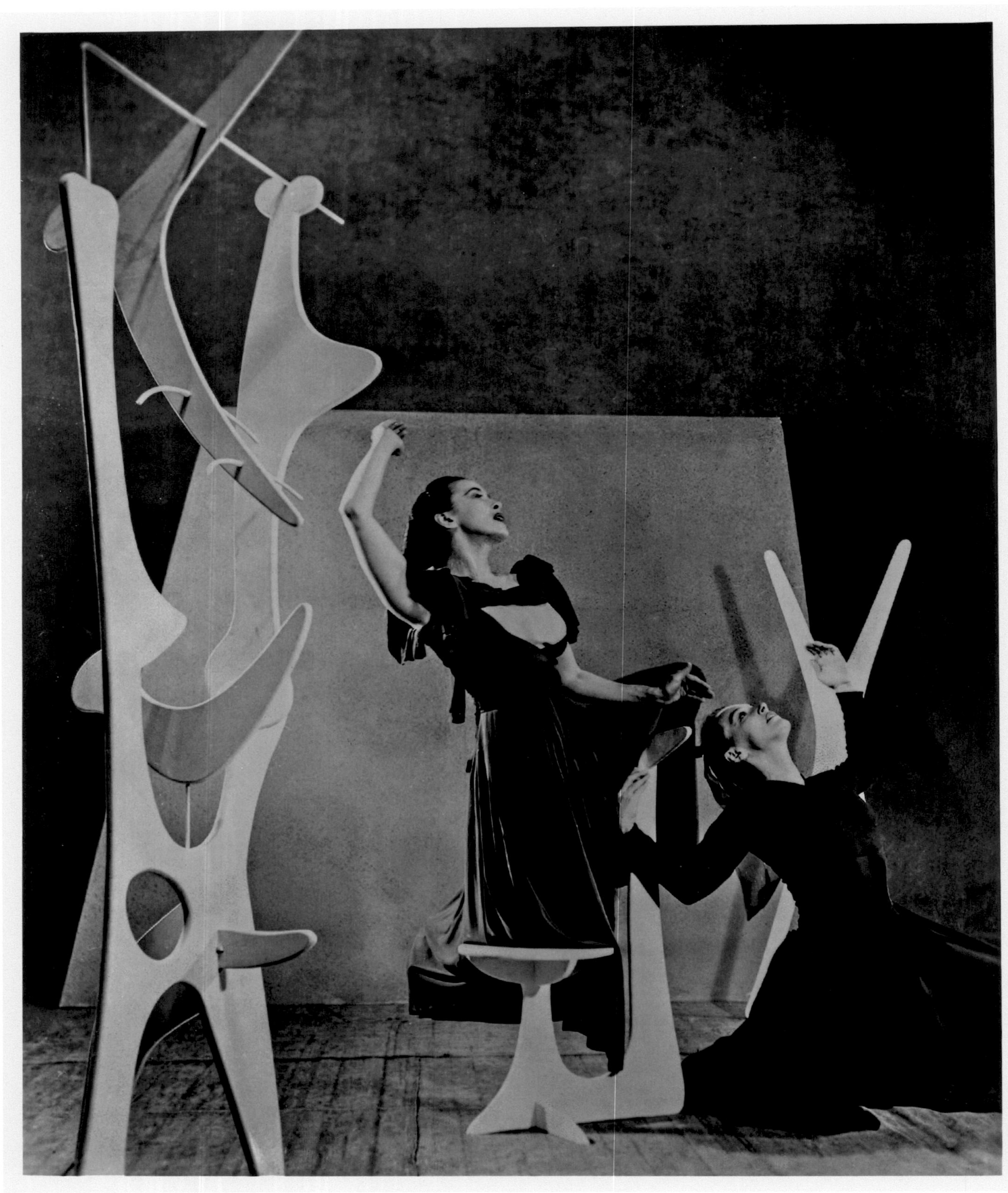

Martha Graham and May O'Donnell. Photograph by Arnold Eagle.

HÉRODIADE, 1944

An artist willfully asserts her creative voice against her own mortality.

Drawn from a symbolist poem of the same name by French poet Stéphane Mallarmé, Graham's *Hérodiade* provides no easy answers and follows no obvious narrative line, but instead offers a moving portrait of the woman-as-artist waging an inner battle between fate and the will to choose her identity. Danced as a duet between the protagonist and her female attendant, the woman confronts her reflection in a "mirror" by Noguchi suggesting bleached bones, while her attendant tries to persuade her to give up her struggle. With each extended utterance or argument, the protagonist accumulates the strength and determination to reject her attendant's pleas. Left alone on stage, she bows one last time to her own reflection, wraps herself in a large black cloth, and turns away from the audience, her body obliterated with only her head visible above, as she chooses the unknown.

SET DESIGN
Isamu Noguchi

COSTUME DESIGN
Martha Graham

COMPOSER
Paul Hindemith

Hérodiade

A WOMAN
Xin Ying

HER ATTENDANT
Anne Souder

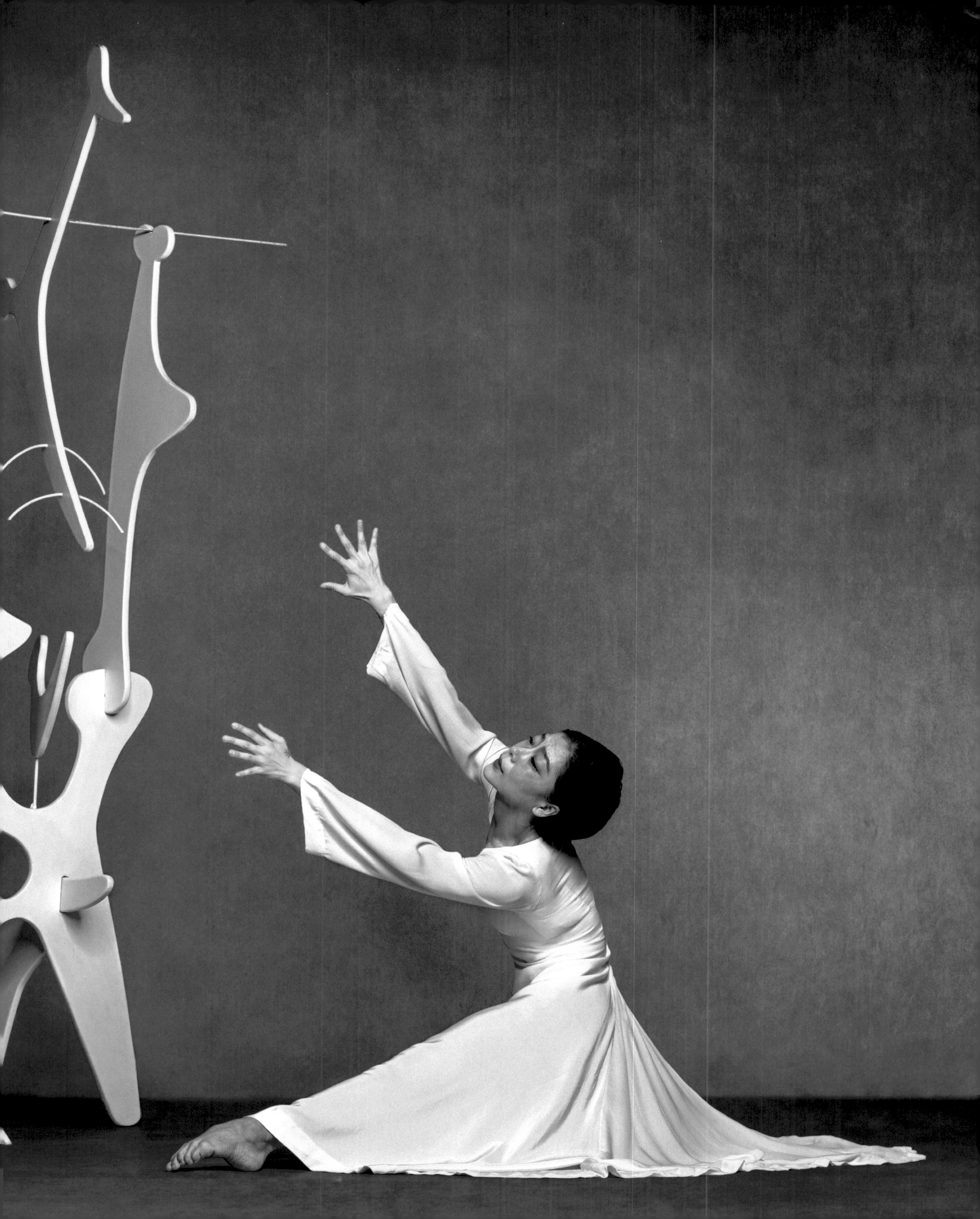

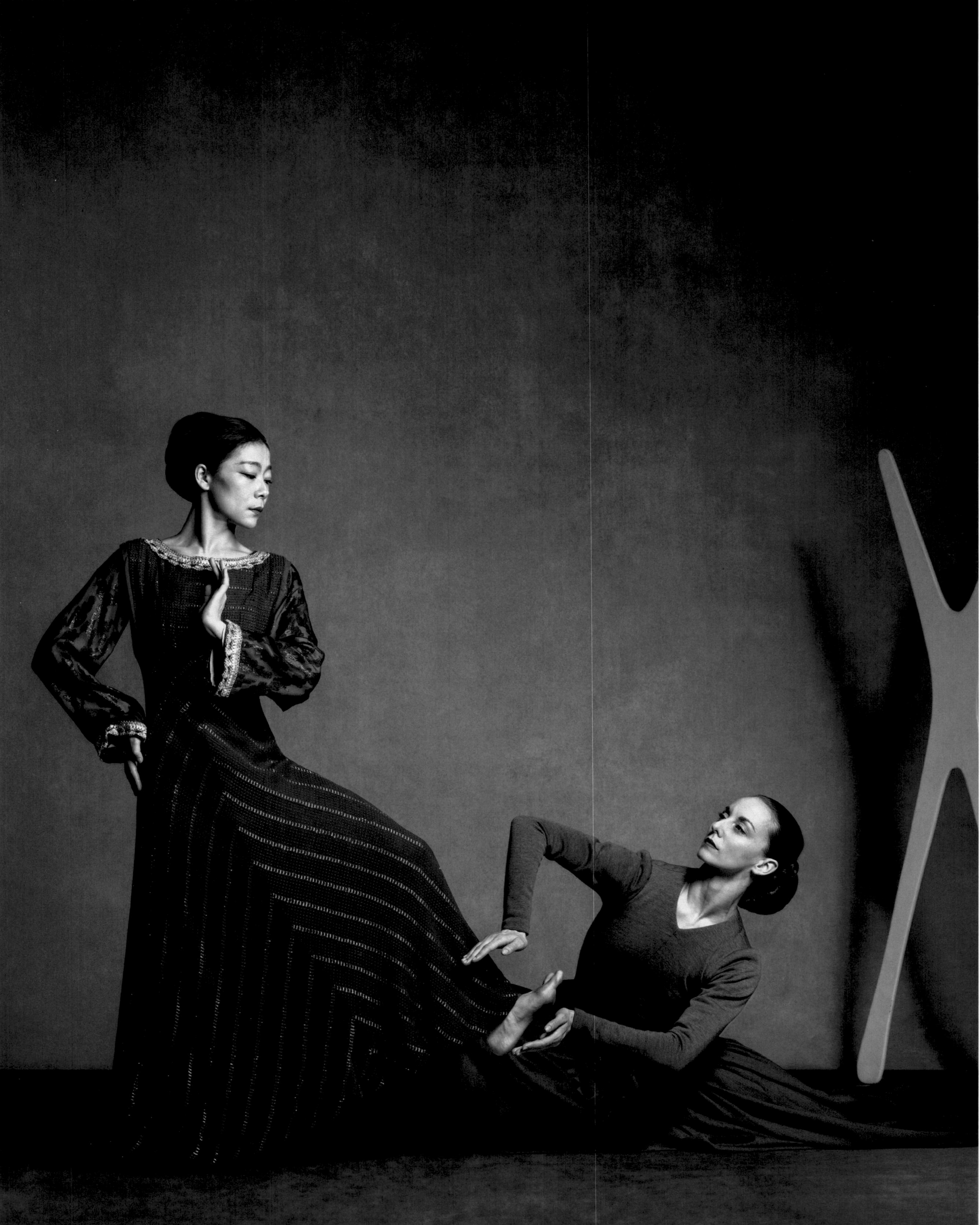

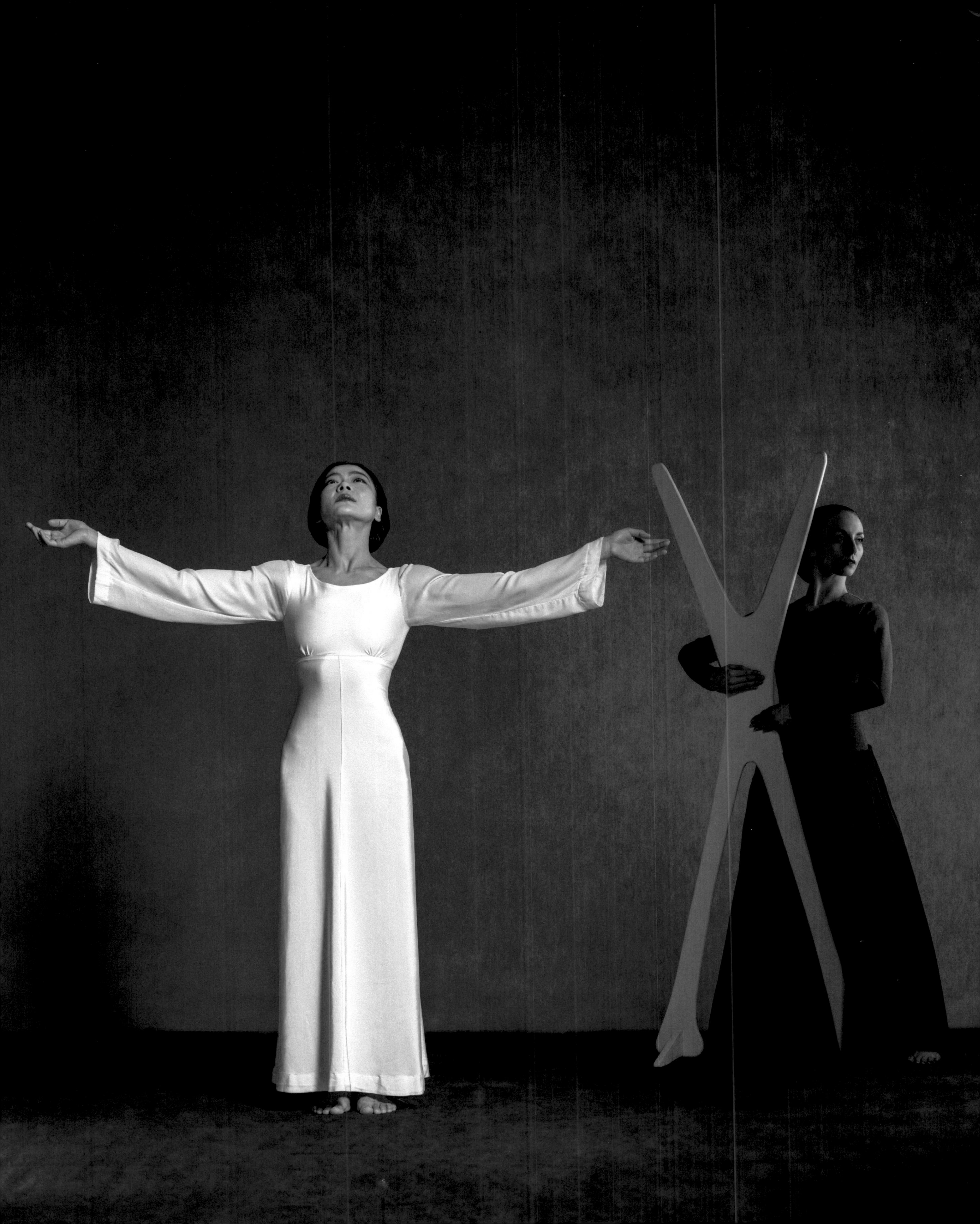

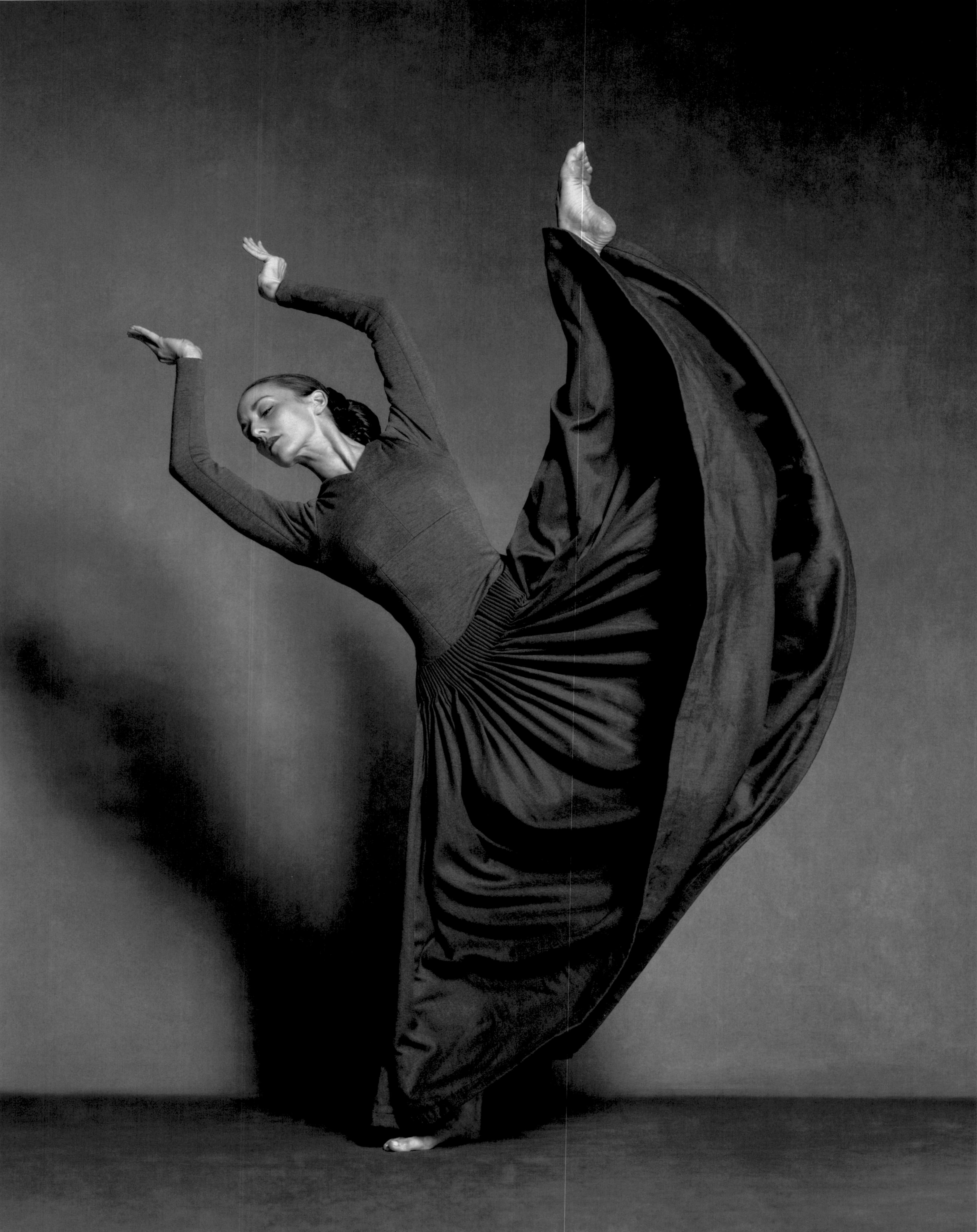

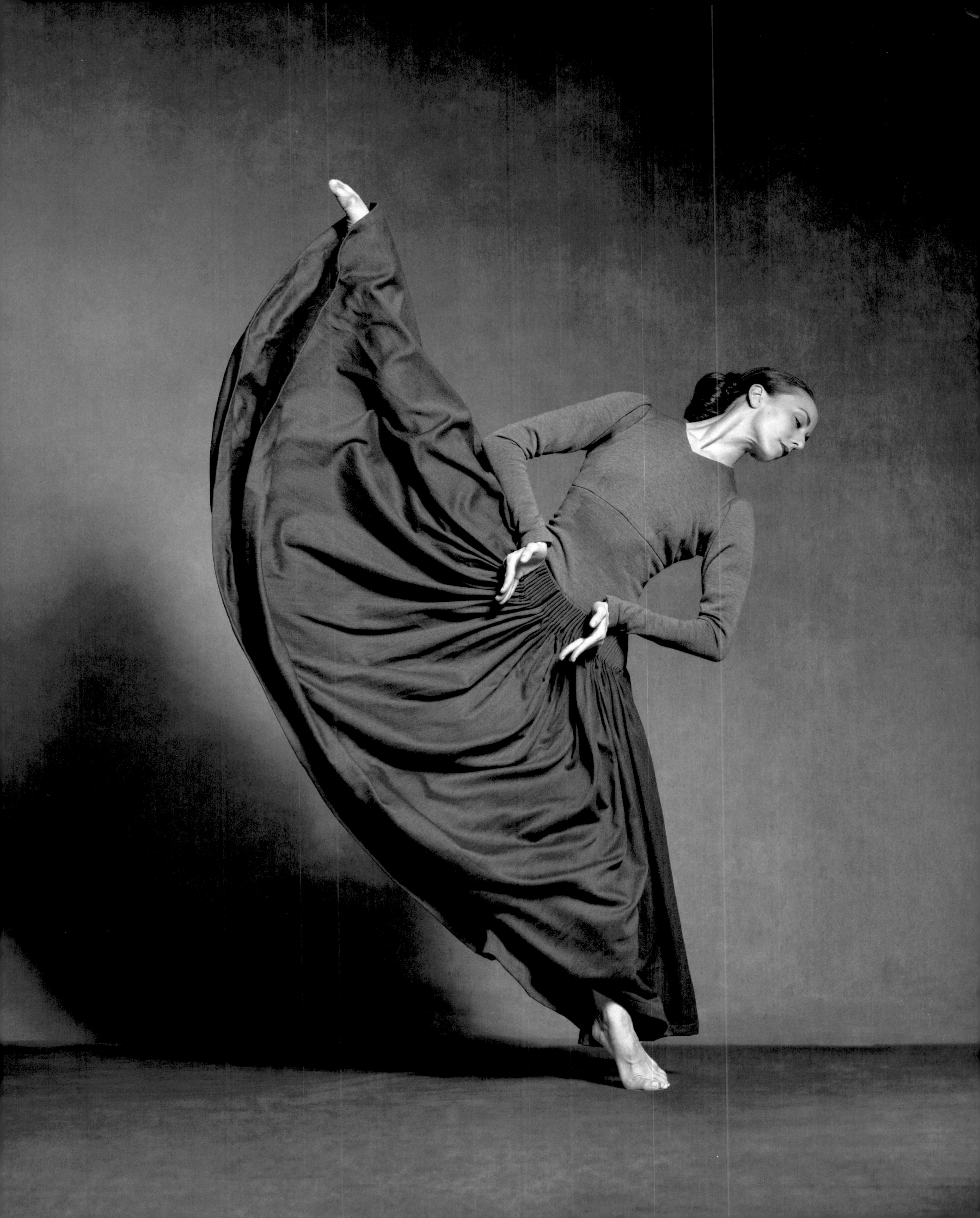

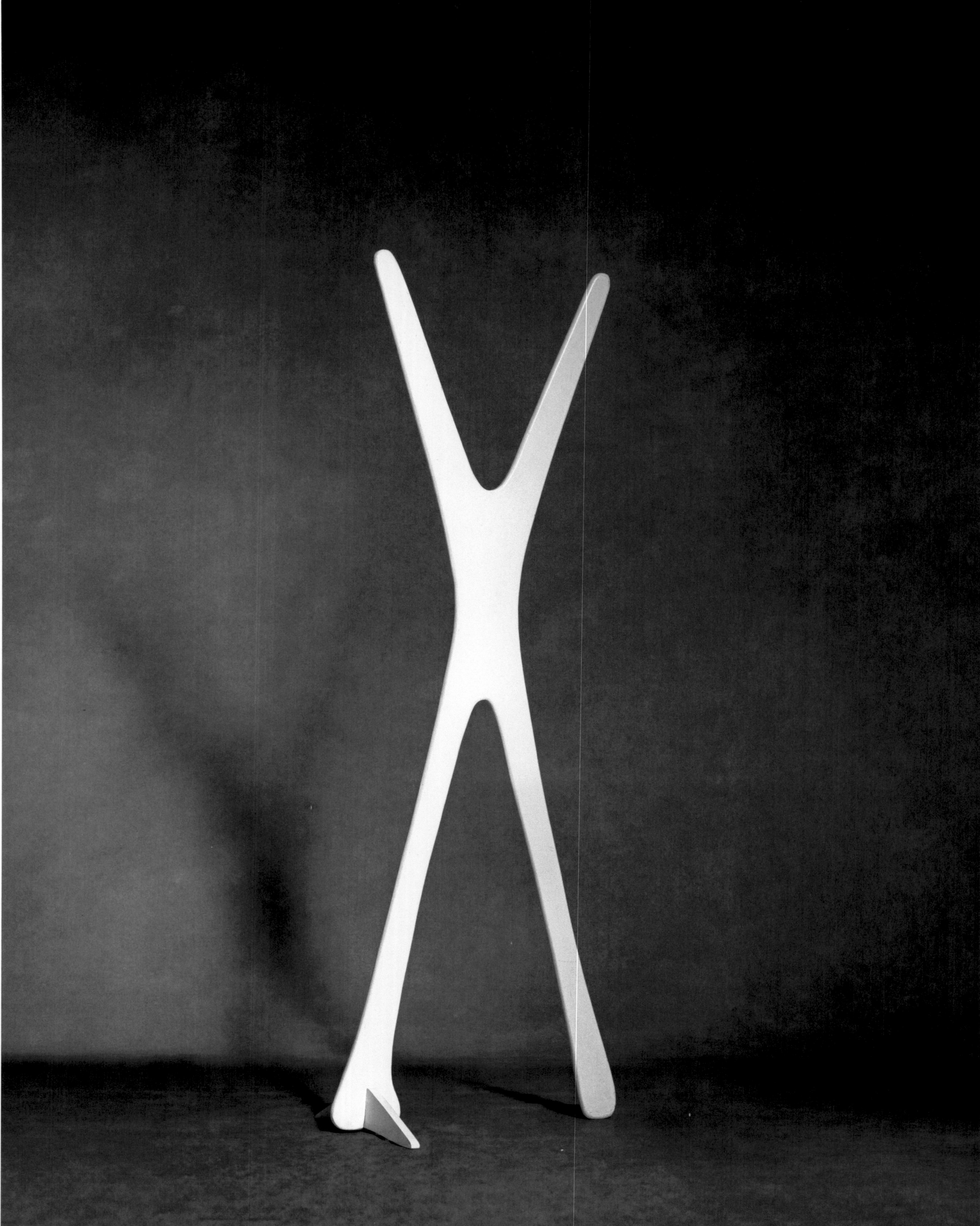

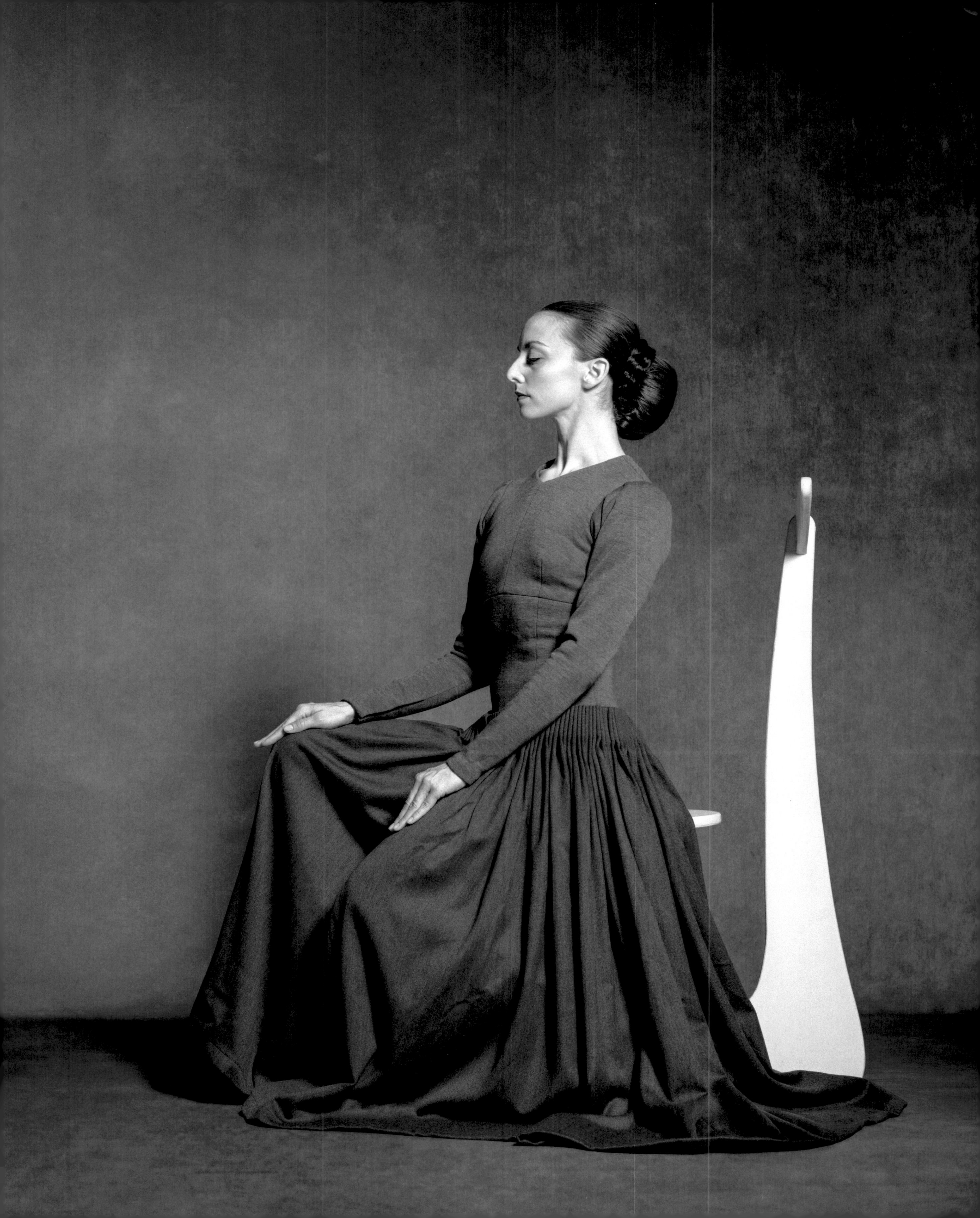

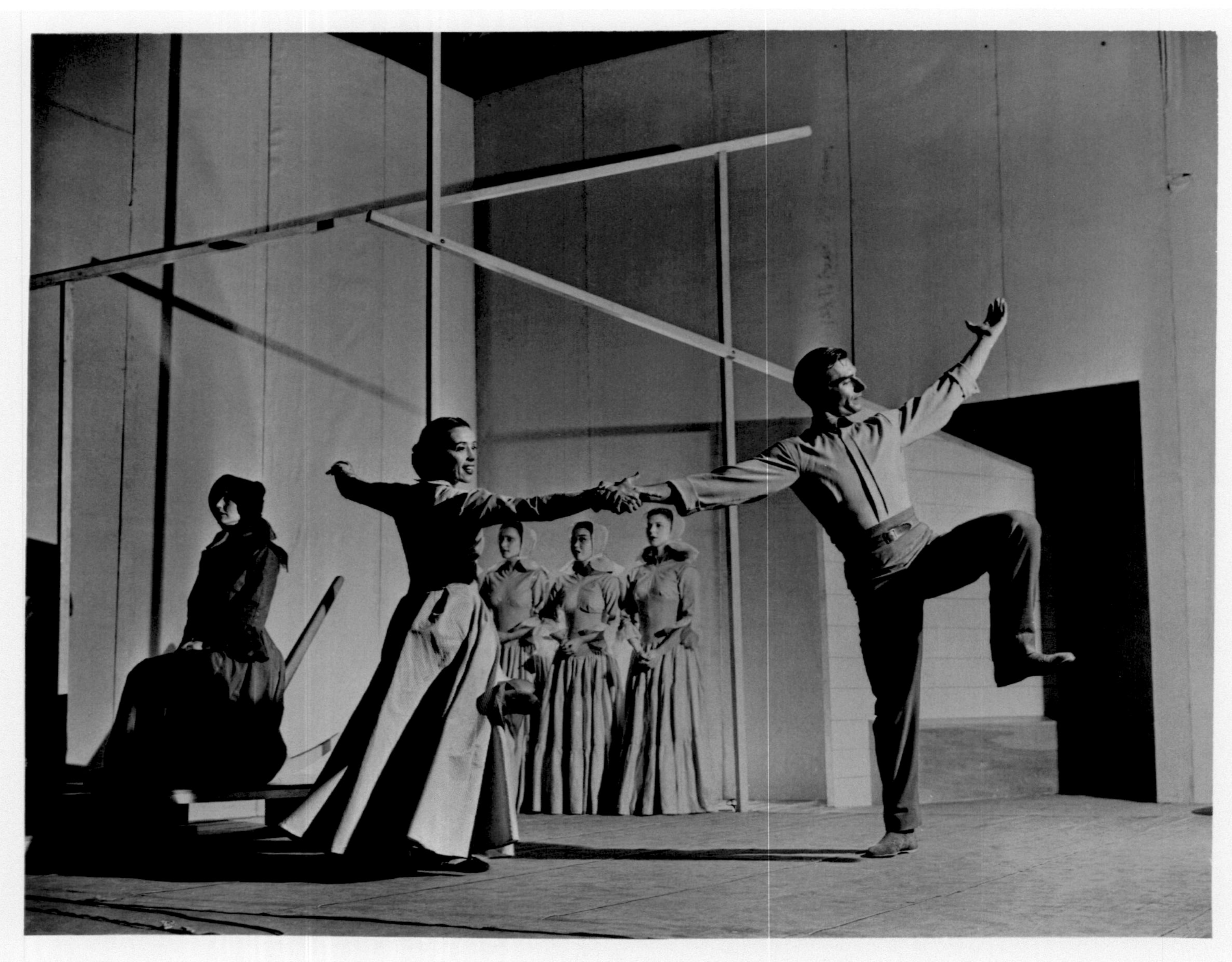

Martha Graham and Erick Hawkins (leads), May O'Donnell (seated), Marjorie Mazia, Yuriko, and Nina Fonaroff. Photograph by Arnold Eagle.

APPALACHIAN SPRING, 1944

An ode to the American pioneering spirit of the Appalachian wilderness.

With the Shaker hymn "'Tis a gift to be simple . . ." at its heart, Aaron Copland's beloved musical score, composed specifically for Graham, evokes the vast spaces surrounding a new homestead somewhere in the American wilderness.

The curtain opens on Isamu Noguchi's minimalist set to reveal a quiet, sun-dappled morning, soon to be enlivened by the celebration of a young couple and their entourage on their wedding day. Although the tone is uncharacteristically cheerful and romantic for Graham, a darker side of the tableau soon reveals itself in the bride's moments of doubt, the husbandman's concern in providing for his future family, and the fervent itinerant preacher's fire-and-brimstone sermon. An ethos of spirited determination emanates from the 1944 work, created during World War II. Even the US Department of State took notice and, following the end of the war, sent Graham's company around the world to perform *Appalachian Spring* as cultural ambassadors.

What audiences witnessed was an unprecedented artistic collaboration at the highest level between three iconic American artists, in which movement, music, and design combine to portray the essential soul of the American way.

SET DESIGN
Isamu Noguchi

COSTUME DESIGN
Martha Graham

COMPOSER
Aaron Copland

Appalachian Spring

BRIDE

Laurel Dalley Smith

HUSBANDMAN

Richard Villaverde

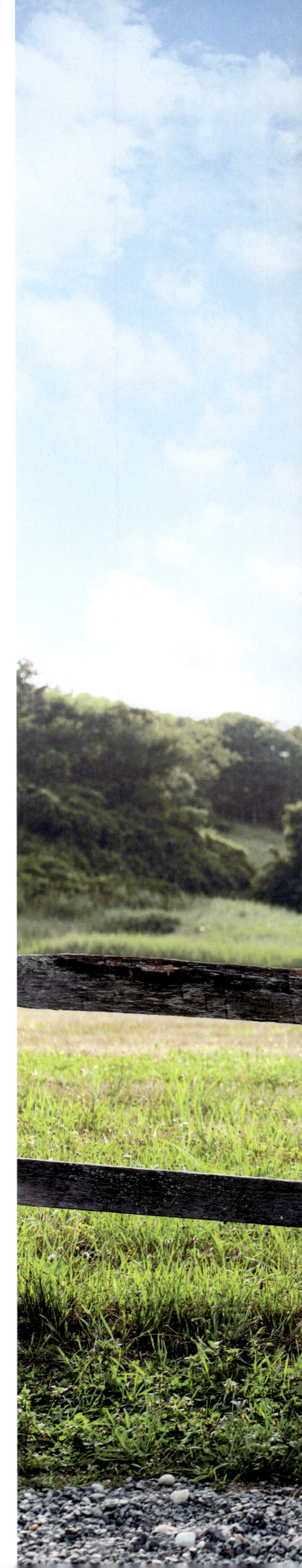

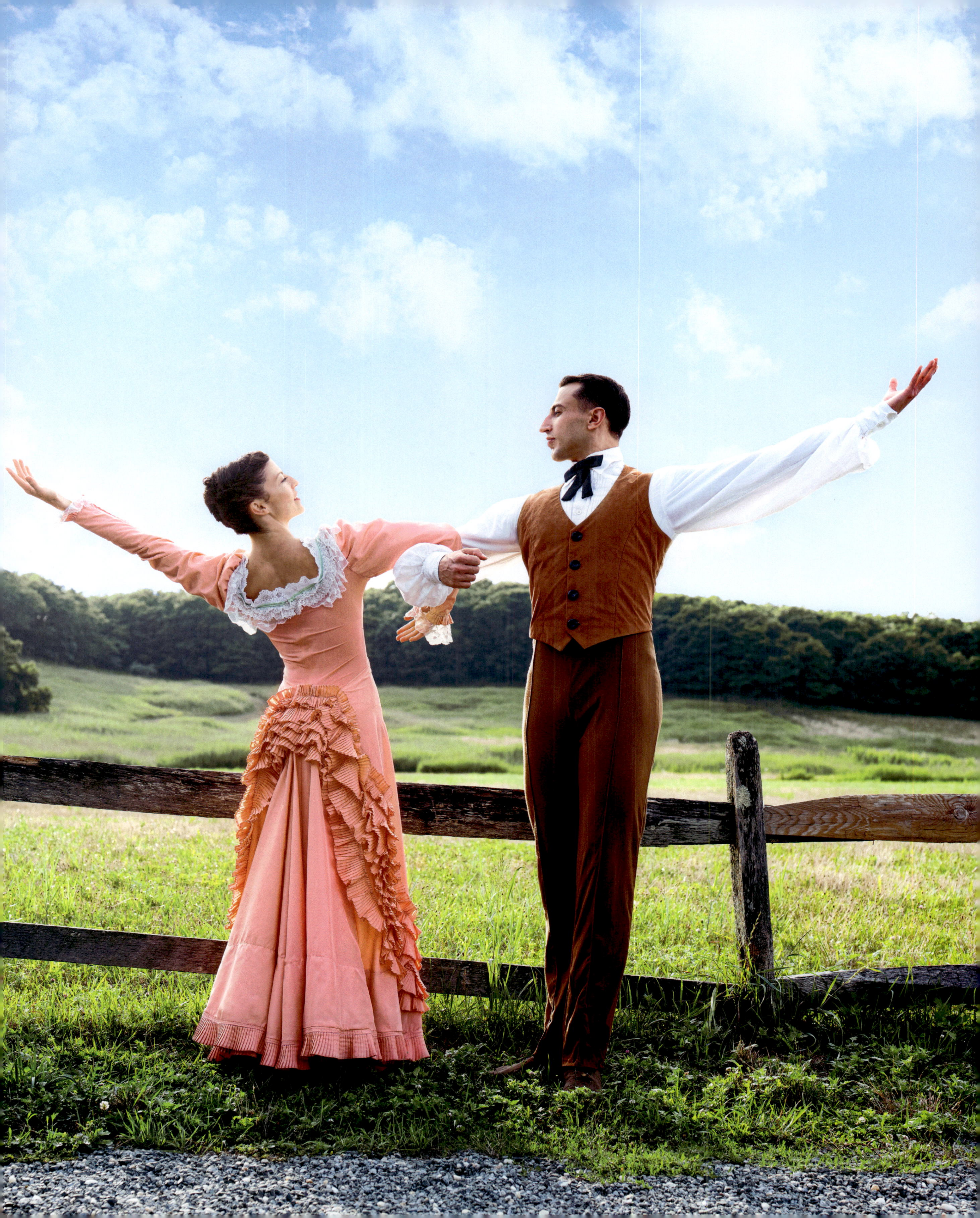

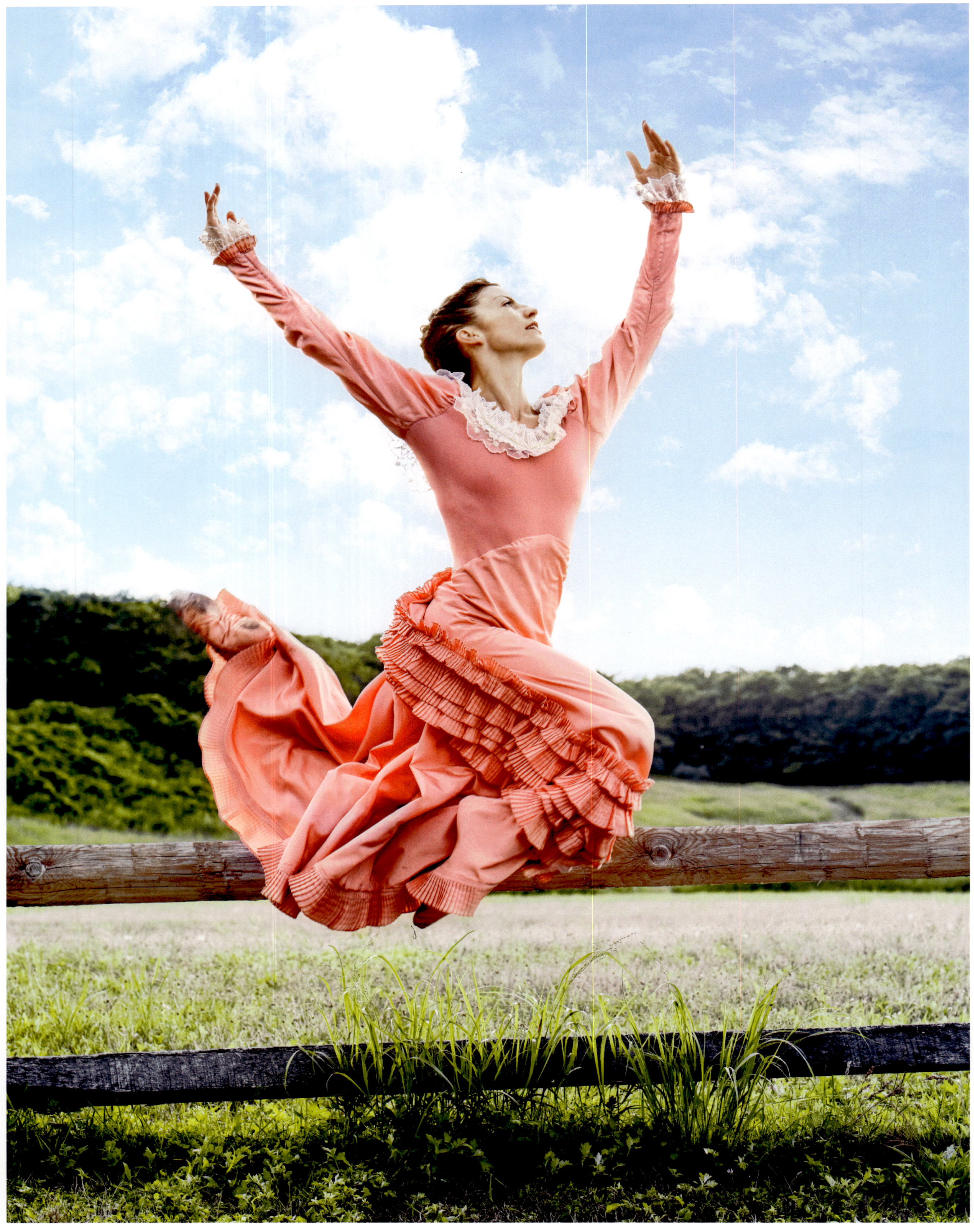

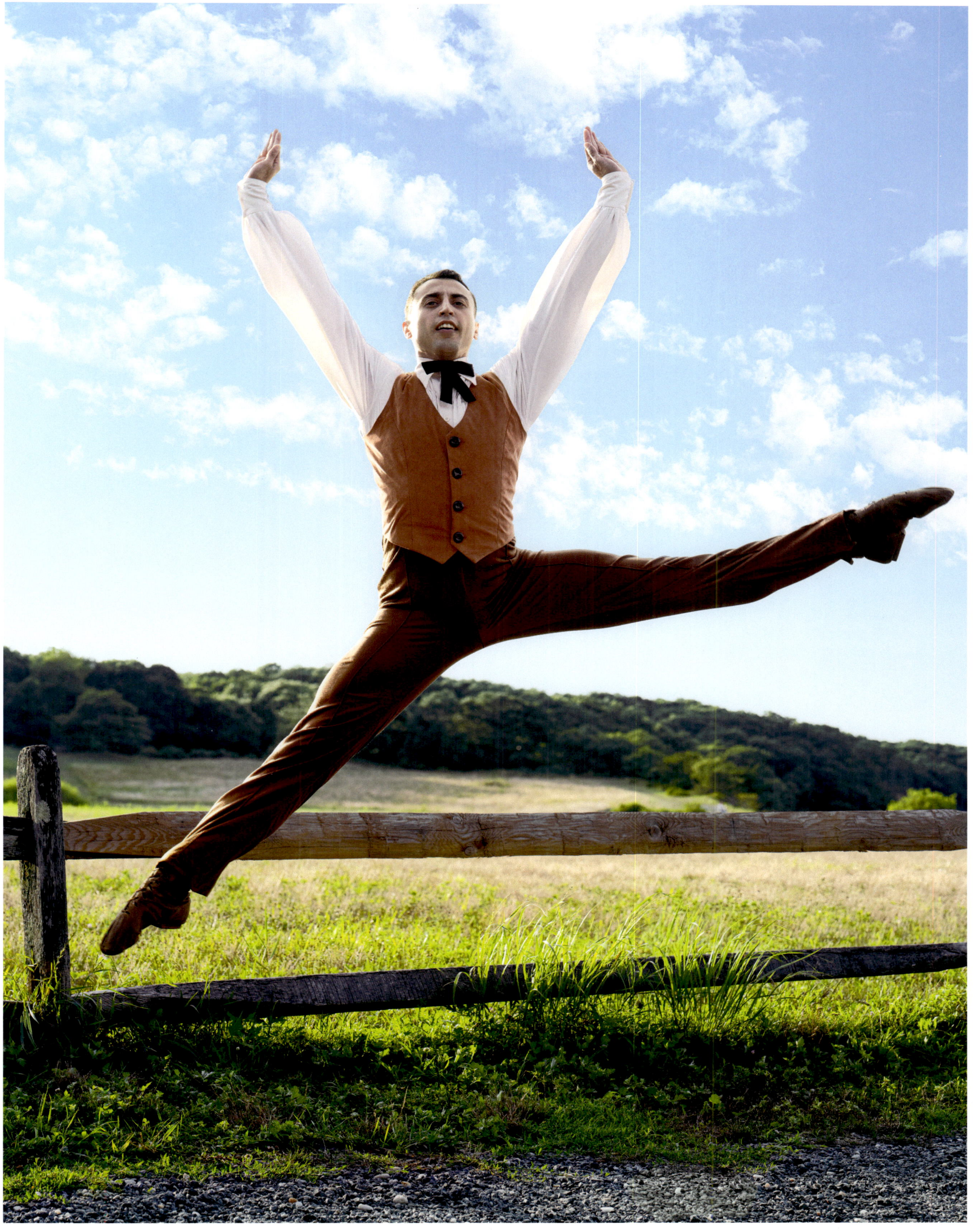

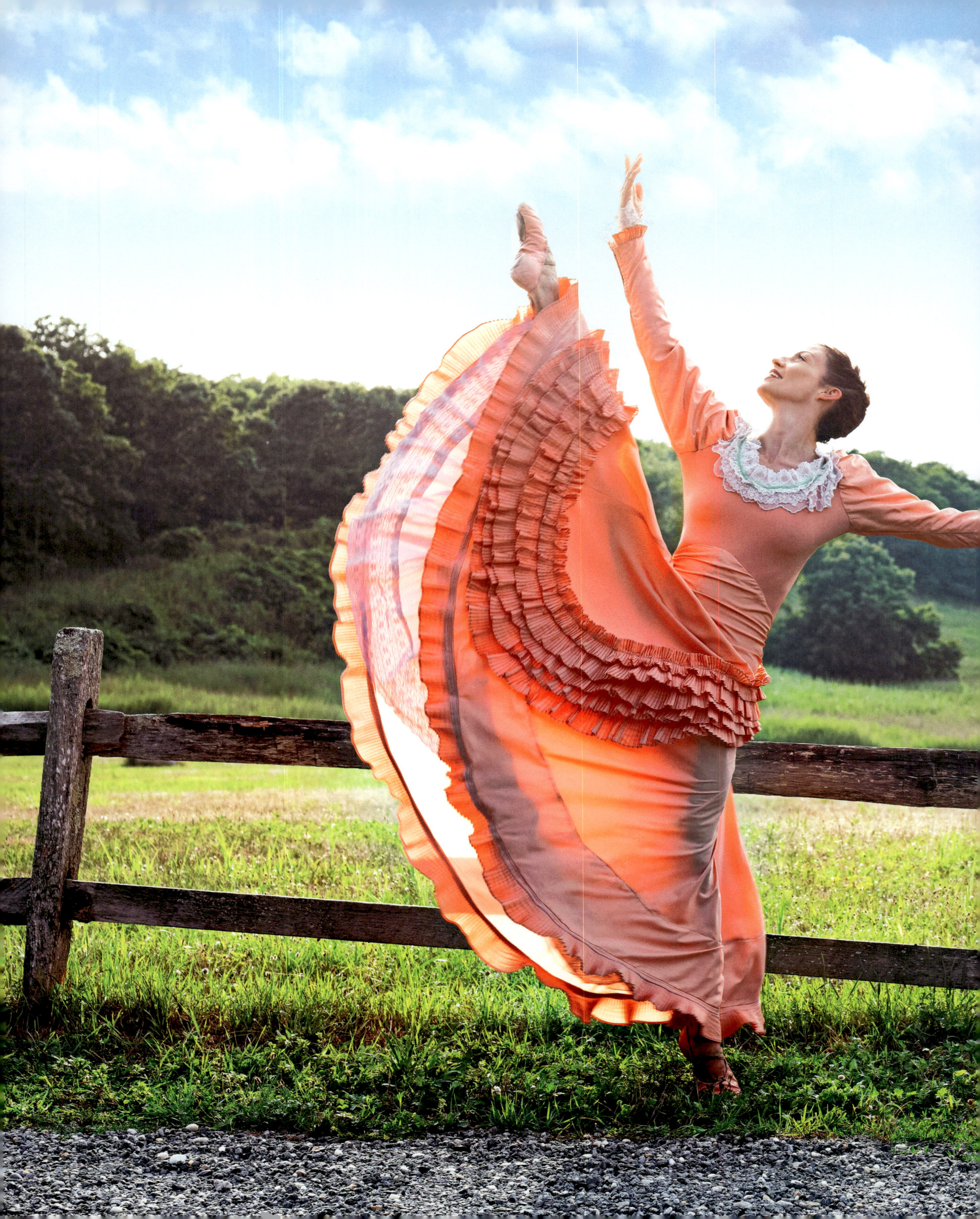

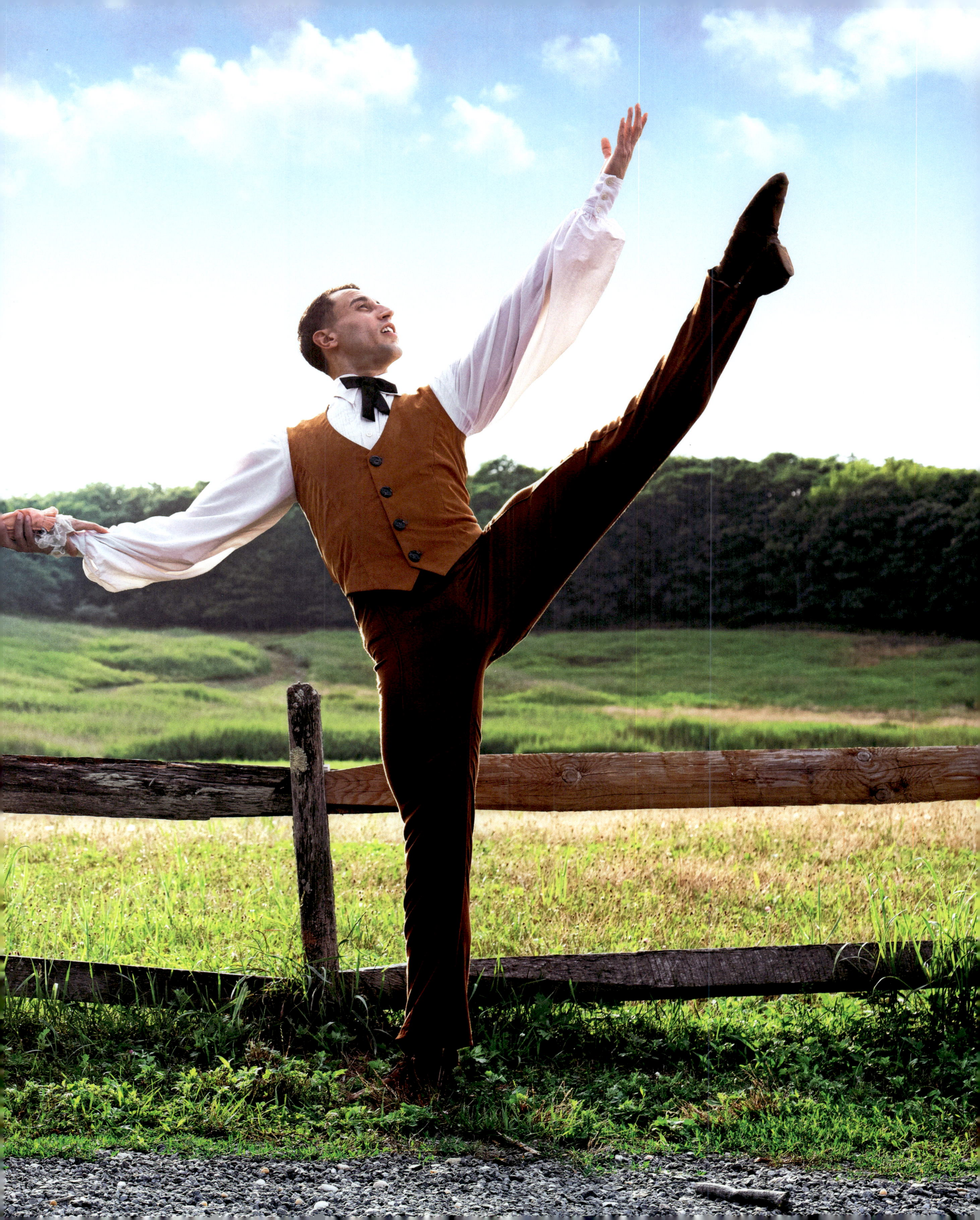

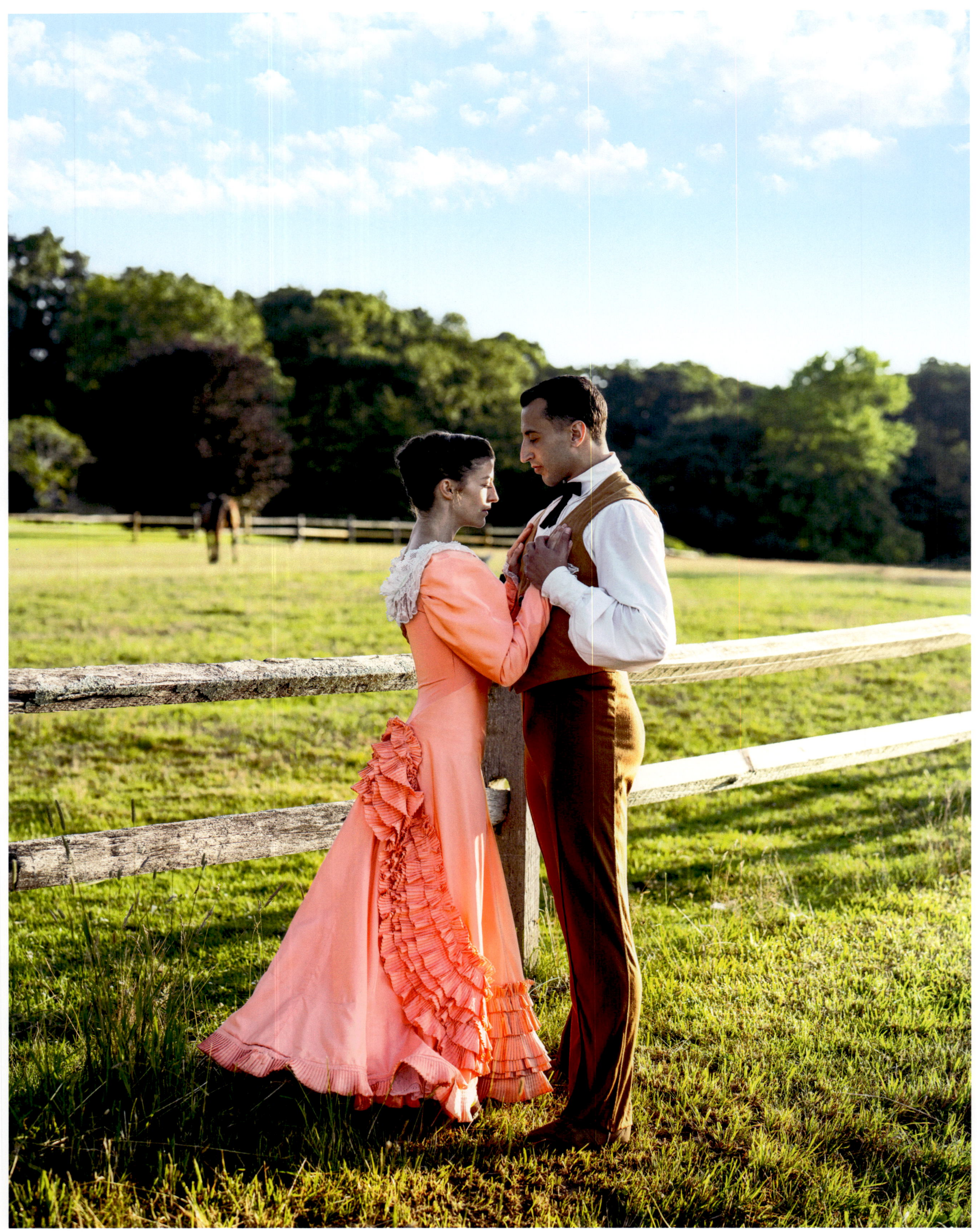

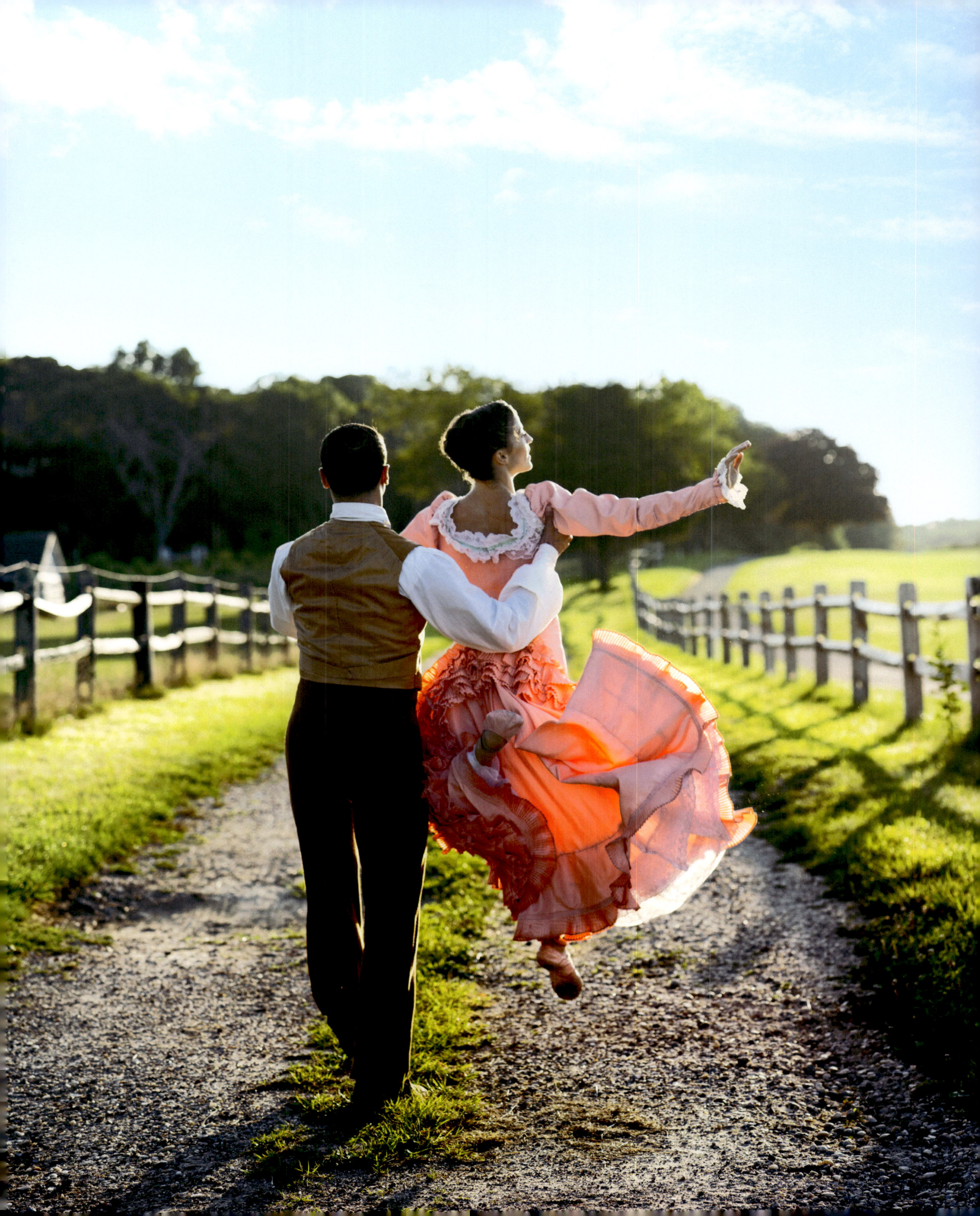

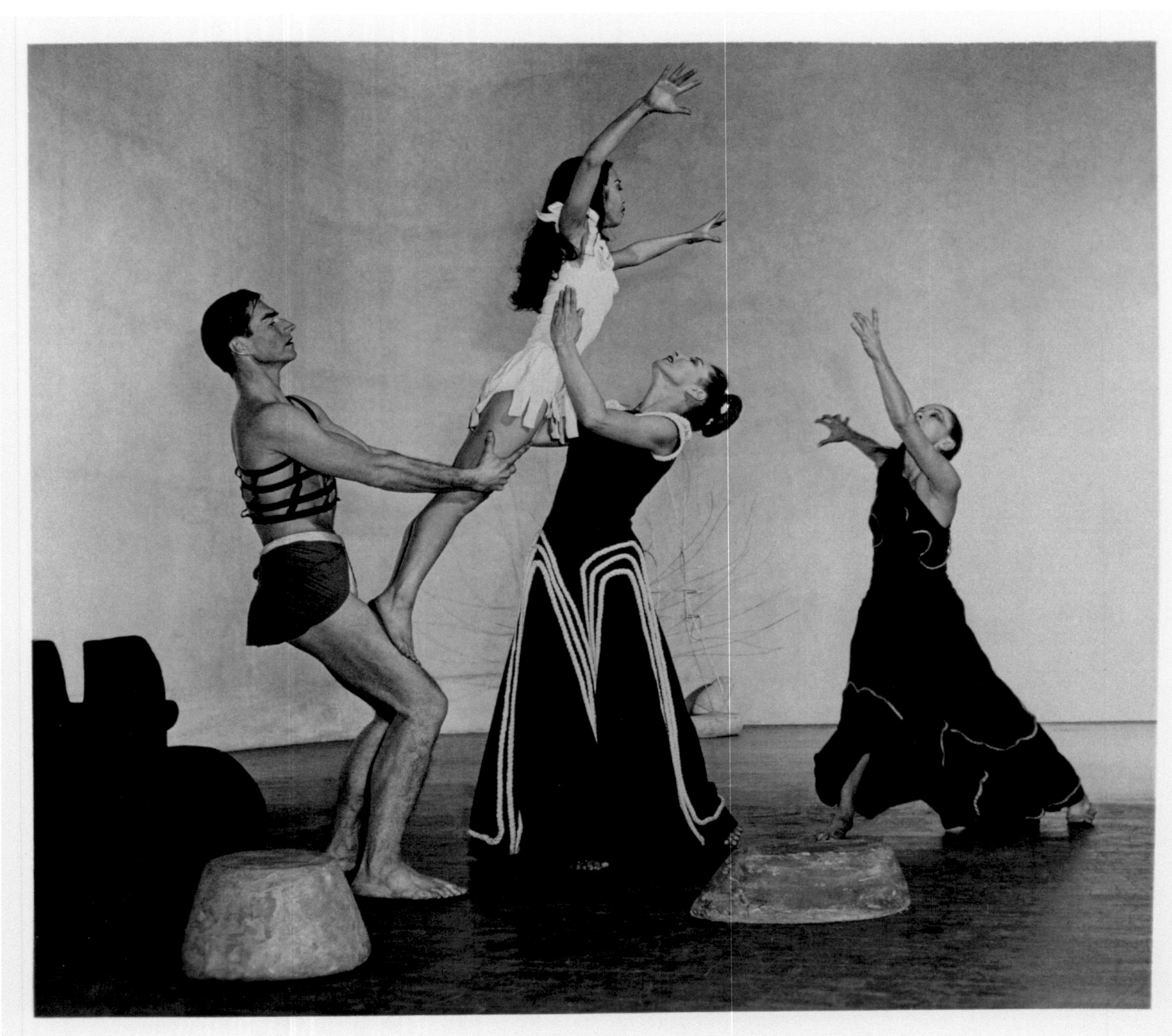

Erick Hawkins, Yuriko, May O'Donnell, and Martha Graham. Photograph by Philippe Halsman.

CAVE OF THE HEART, 1946

A modernist Greek tragedy portraying the destructive powers of love.

In Graham's *Cave of the Heart*, the sorceress Medea exacts revenge on her disloyal partner, Jason, while the Chorus, represented by a single dancer, forecasts the doomed fates of Jason and his betrothed, the Princess of Corinth. Consumed by jealousy, Medea plots to mortally wound the young princess. Pretending to offer a gift, she places a poisoned crown on the young bride's brow and watches as she is overwhelmed by its destructive power. The sorceress then explodes with a maniacal dance of vengeance in which she consumes her own entrails before she escapes the crime scene. She returns shrouded in a purple burial cloth, hauling the dead body of the princess behind her to present to an agonized Jason. Victorious, Medea seizes the flaming brass cage and mounts her throne, evoking the chariot of her father, the sun god Helios.

SET DESIGN
Isamu Noguchi

COSTUME DESIGN
Martha Graham

COMPOSER
Samuel Barber

Cave of the Heart

MEDEA
Xin Ying

JASON
Lorenzo Pagano

THE PRINCESS
Marzia Memoli

THE CHORUS
Natasha Diamond-Walker

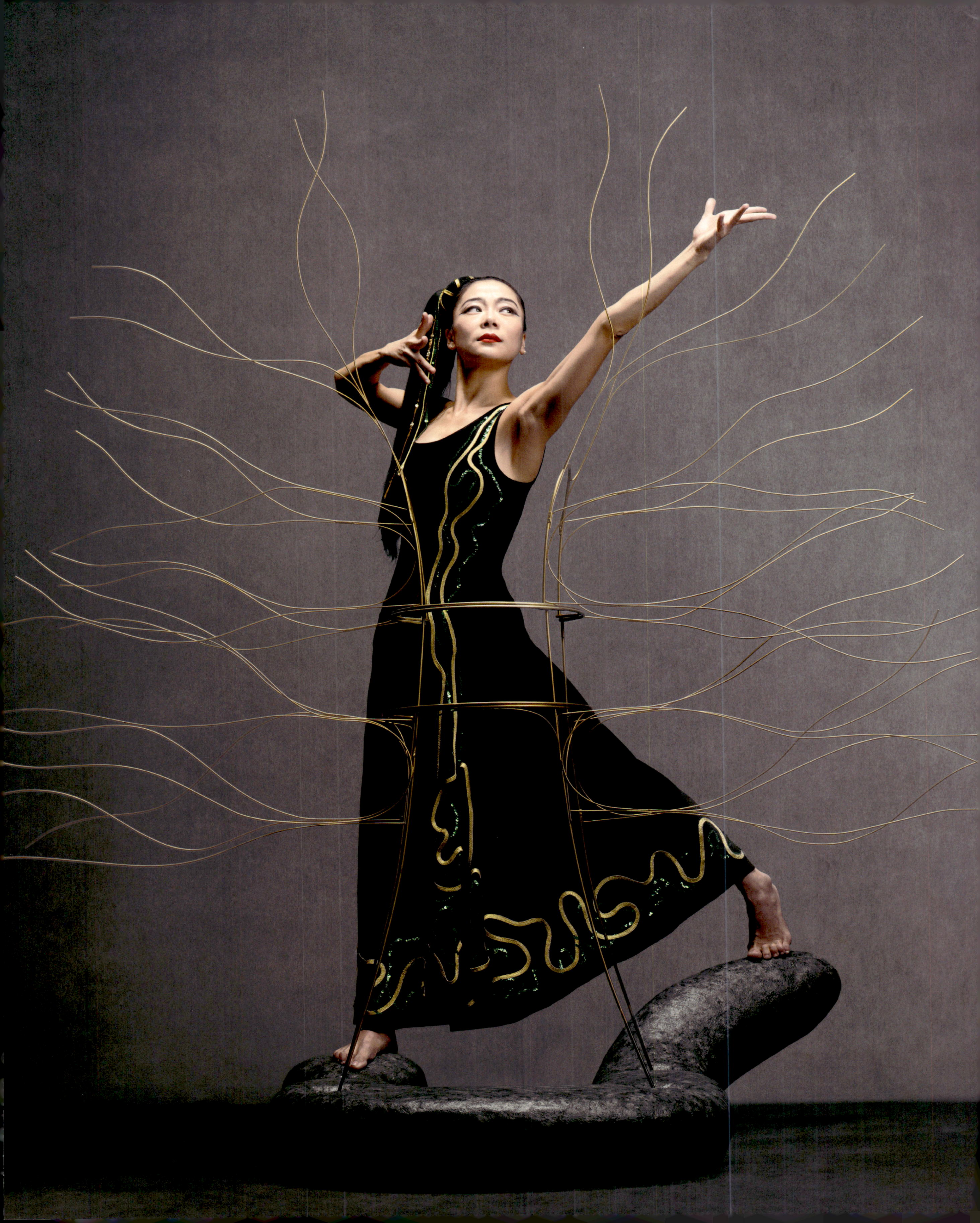

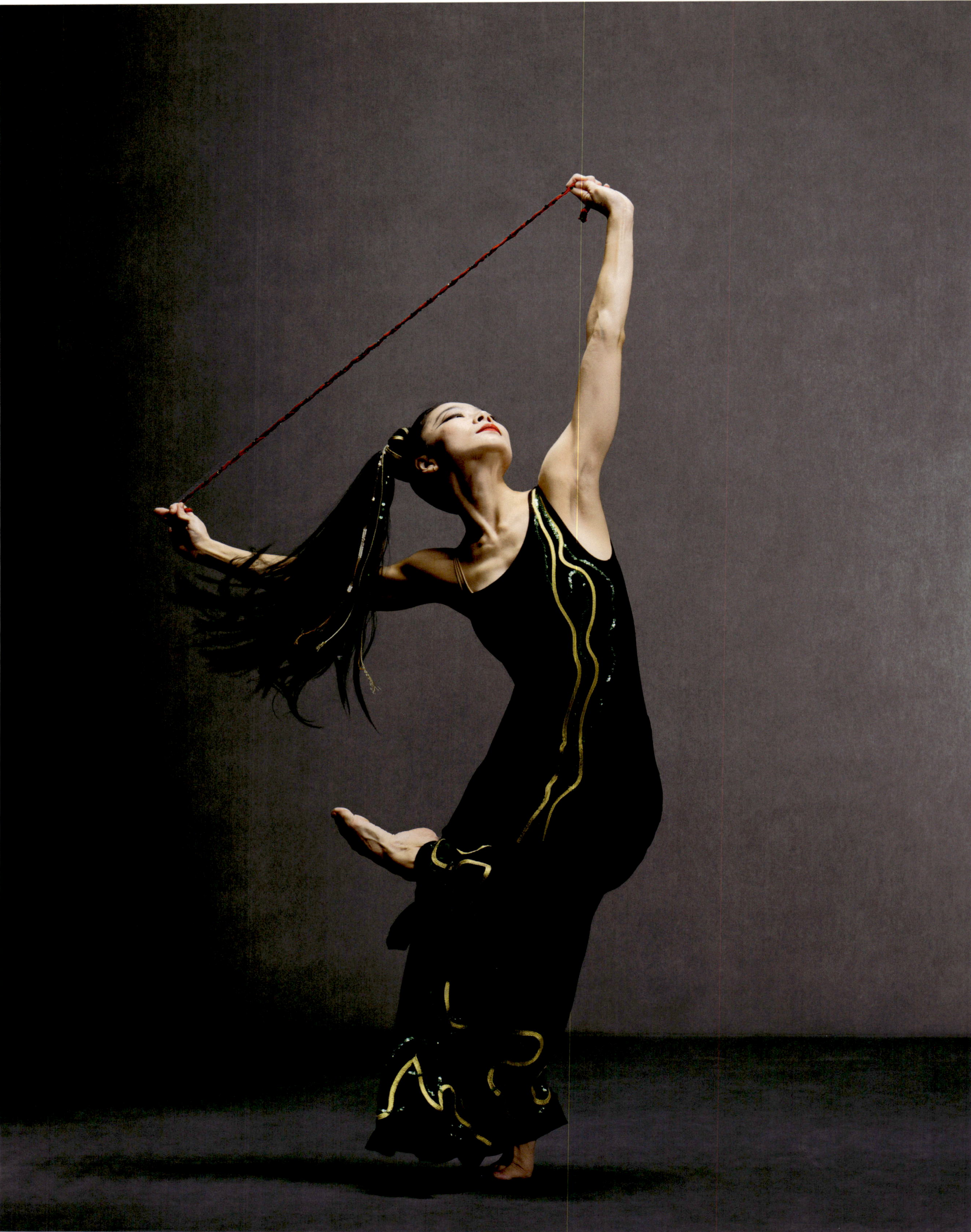

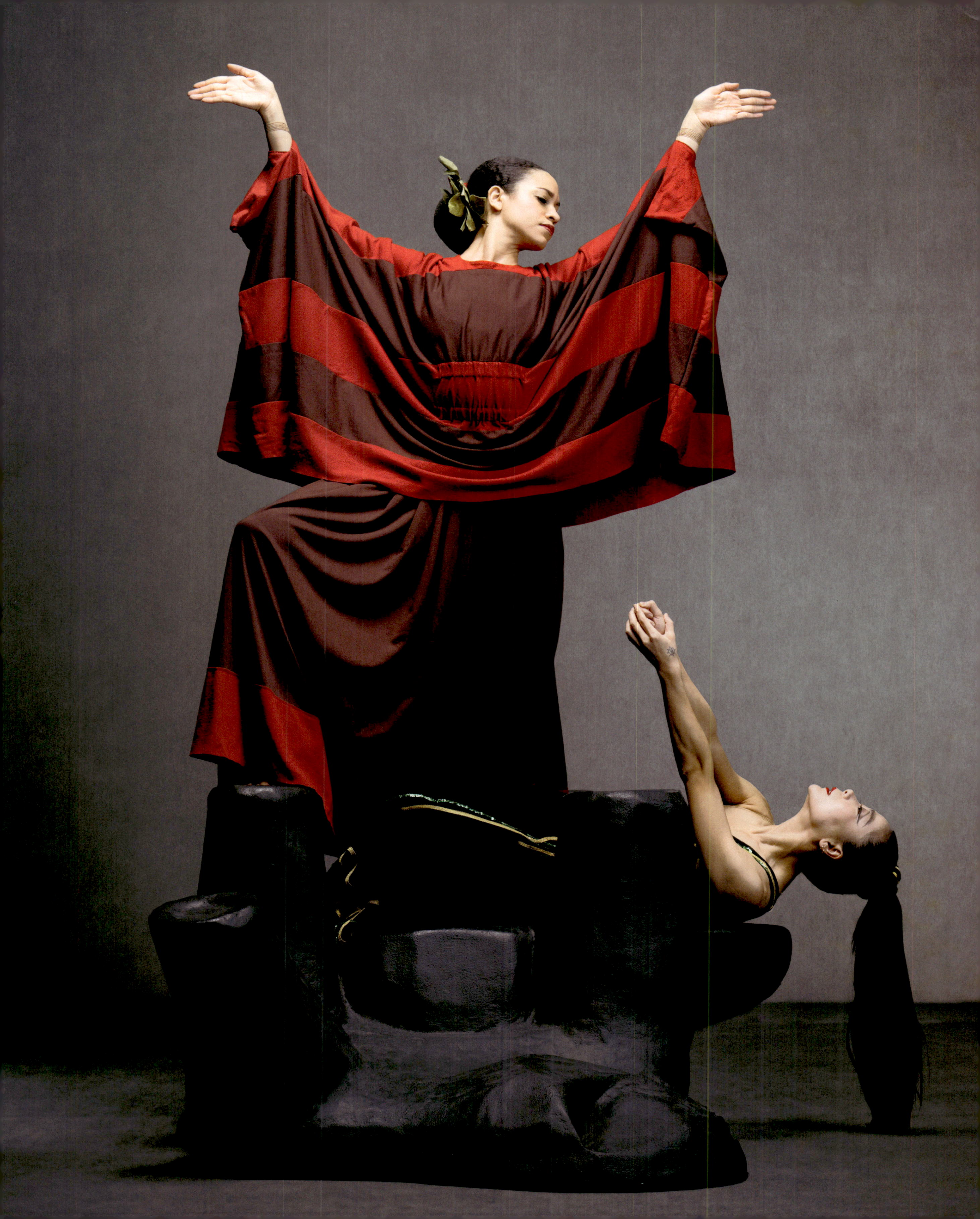

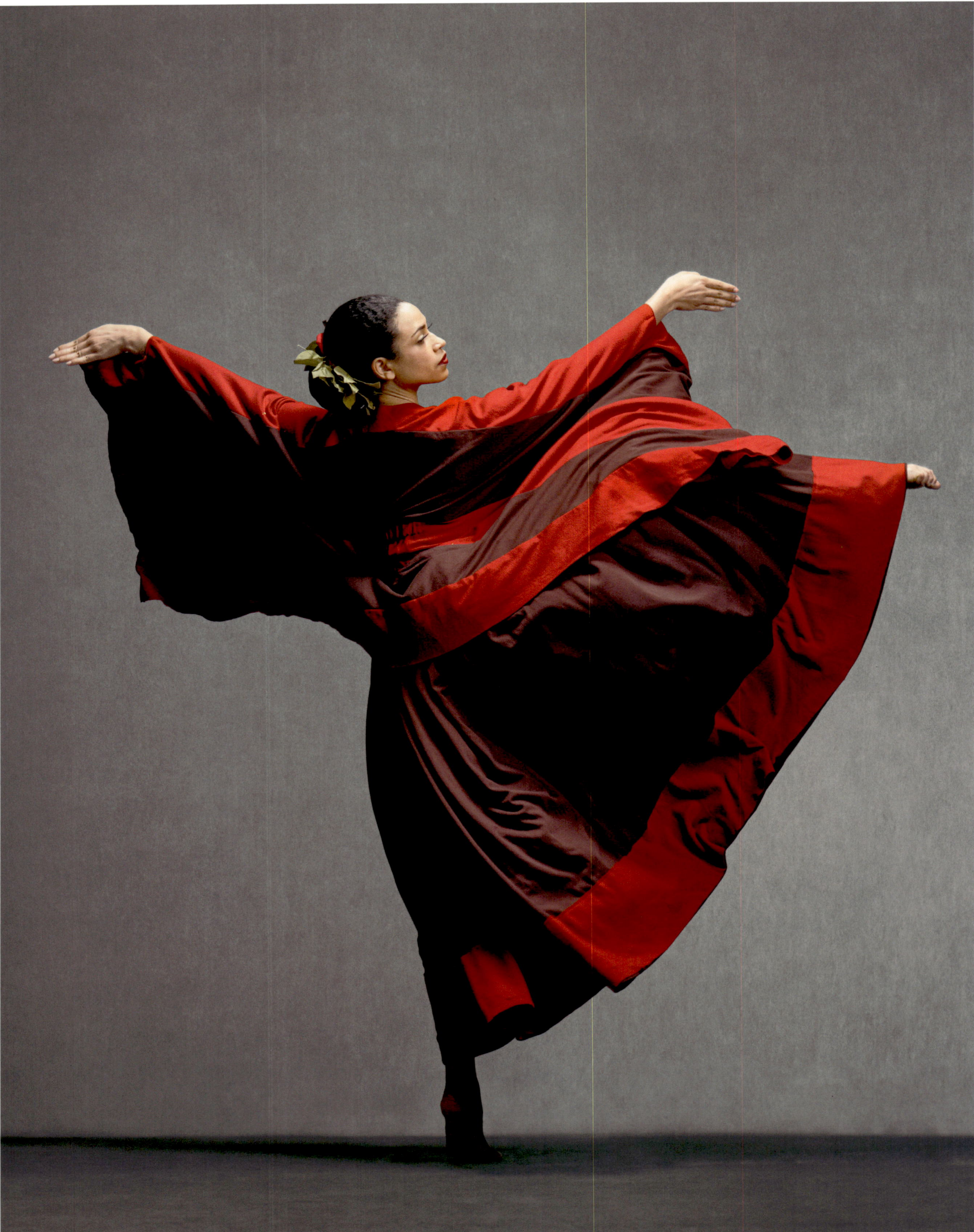

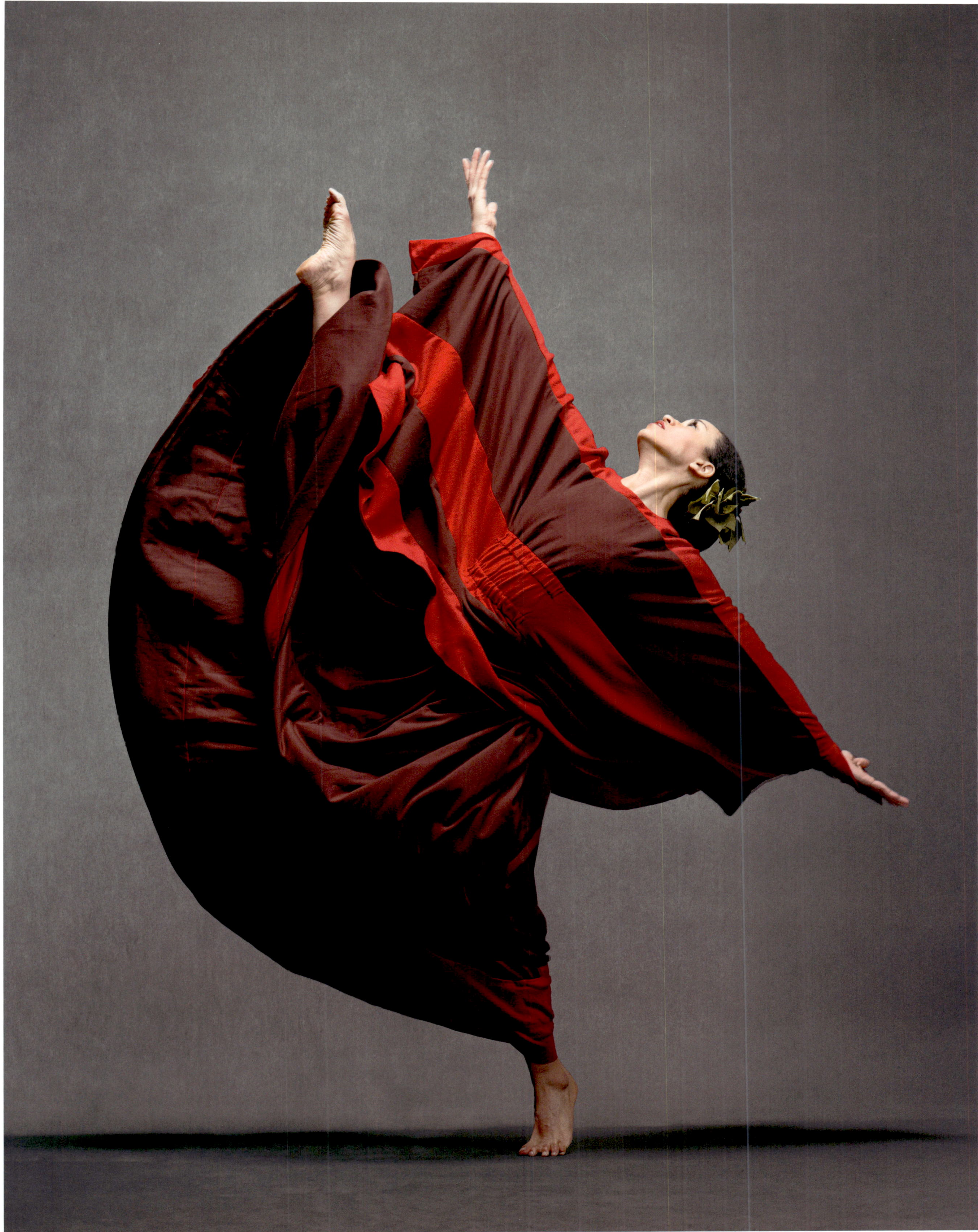

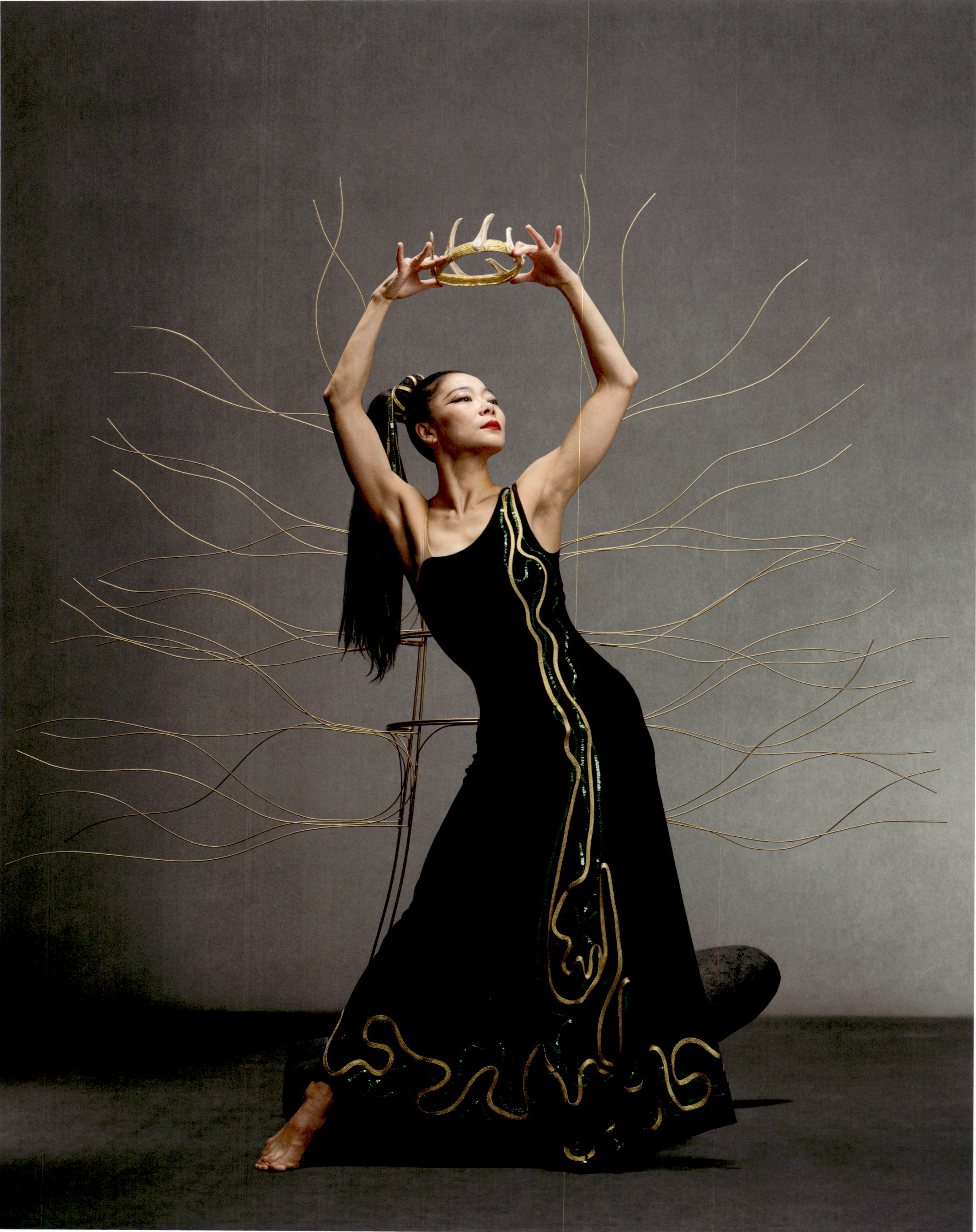

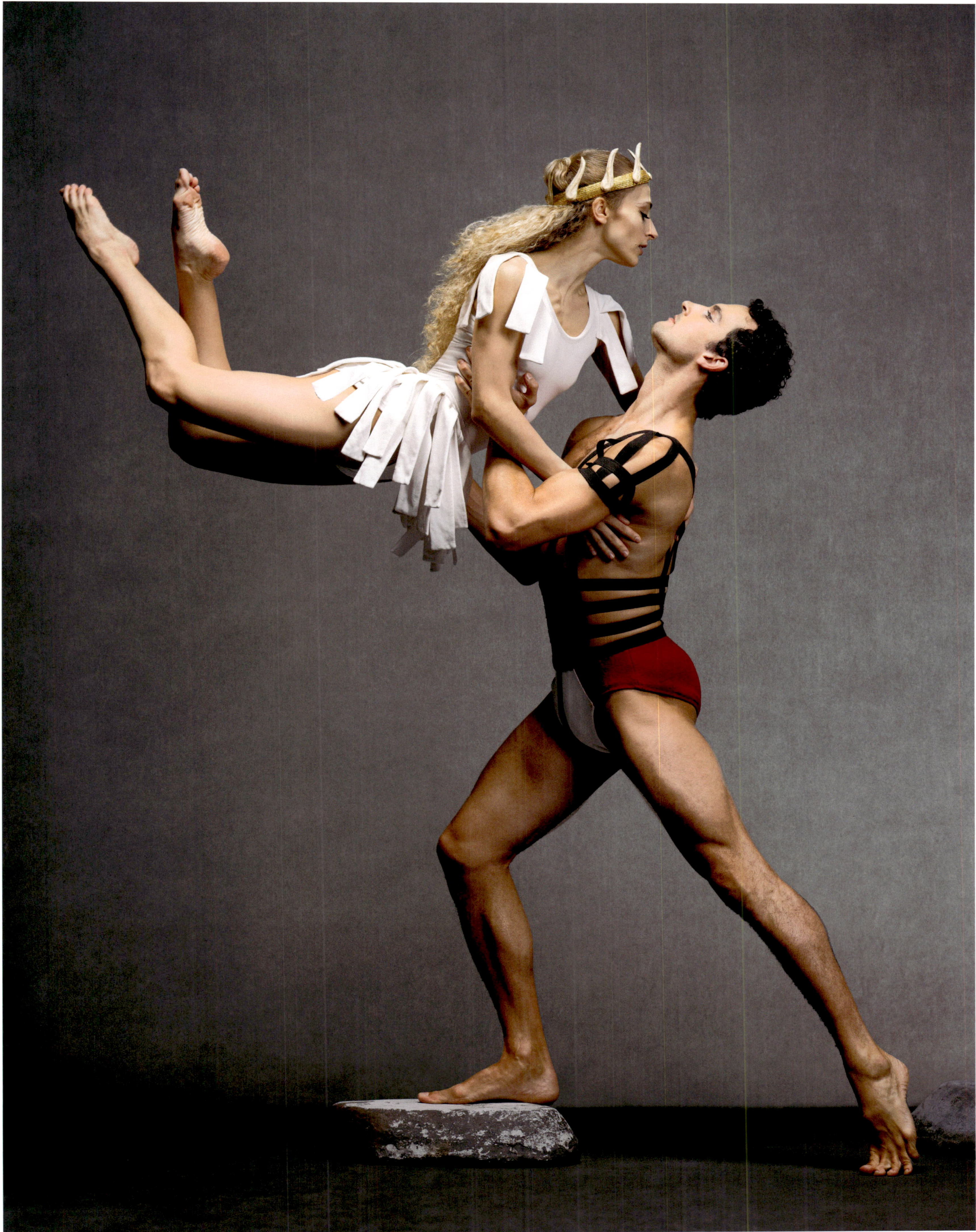

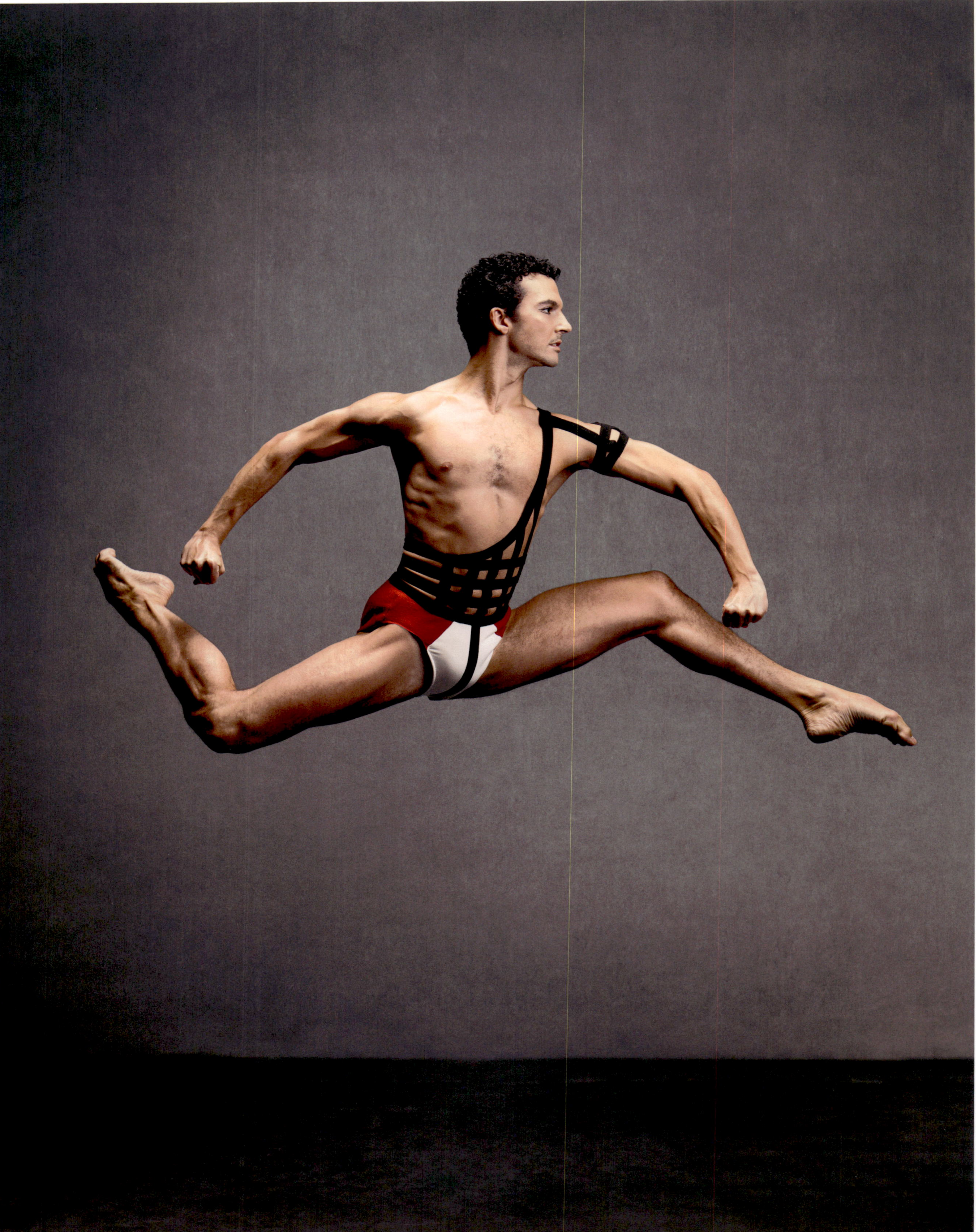

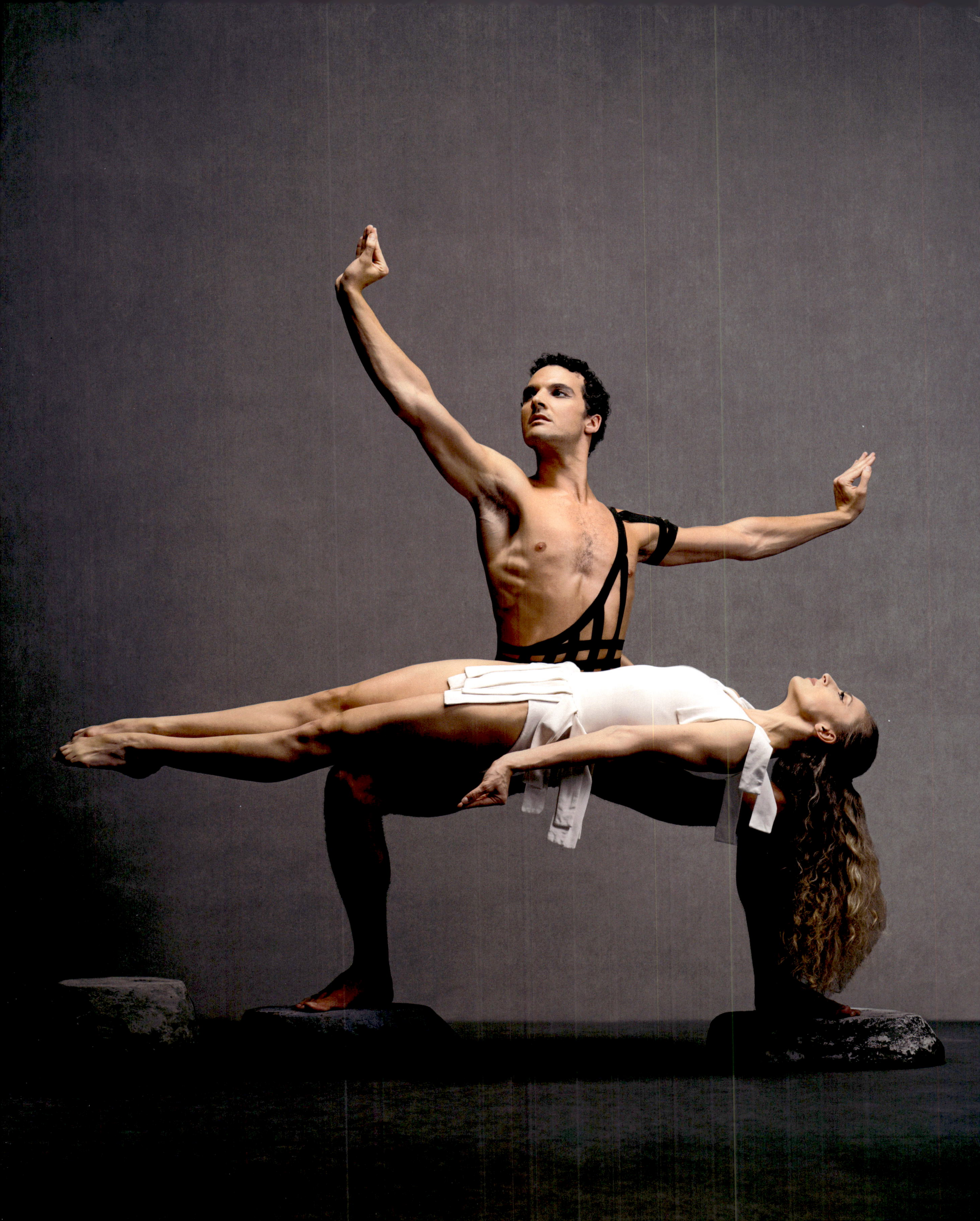

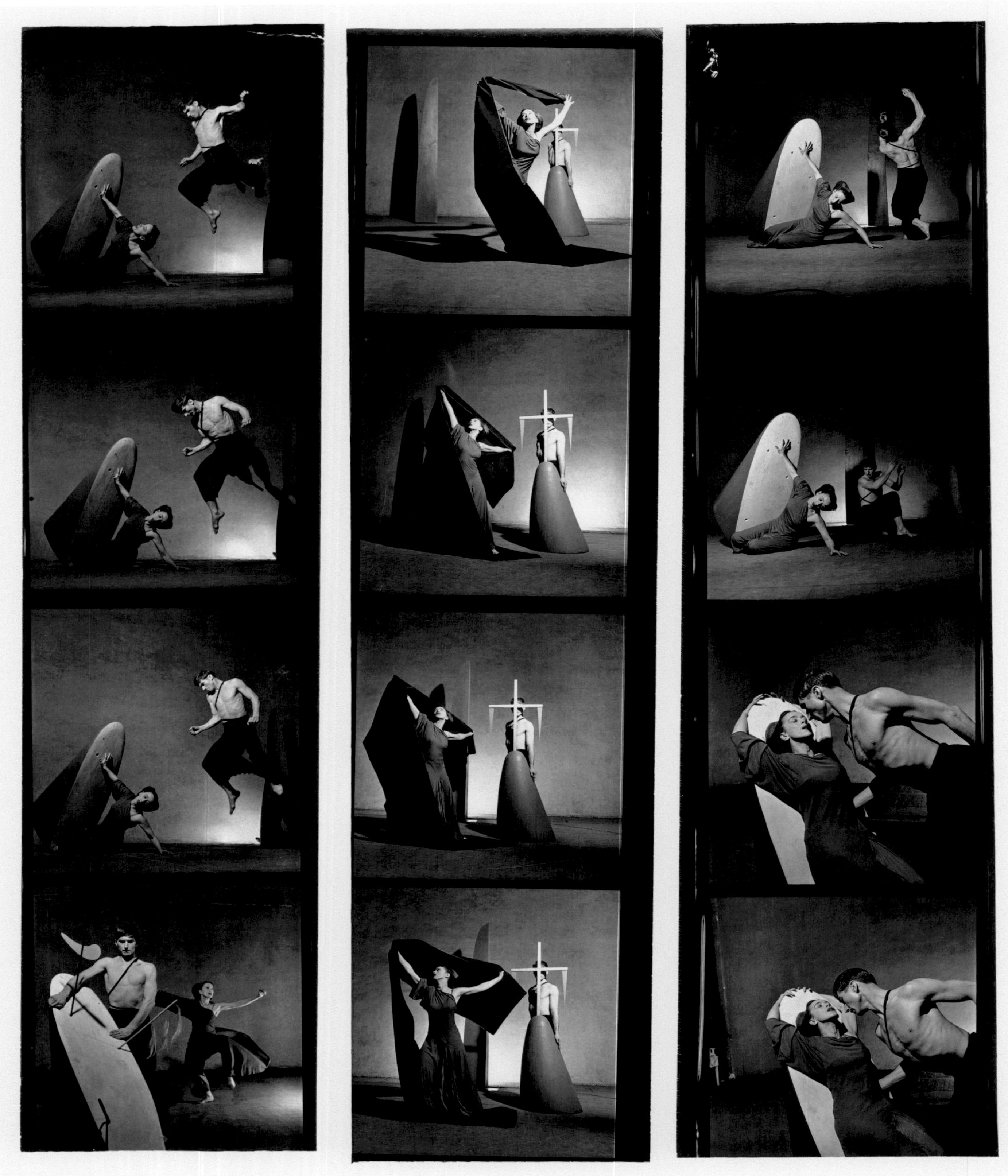

Martha Graham and Erick Hawkins. Photographs by Philippe Halsman.

DARK MEADOW, 1946

A heroine navigates her unconscious to mine the source of her sexual and spiritual energies.

Isamu Noguchi's set for *Dark Meadow* suggests a Jungian inner landscape in which a female protagonist, She Who Seeks, reckons with primal archetypes on a journey of self-discovery. Her male counterpart, He Who Summons, accompanies her through ritual dances performed by a chorus of four couples, They Who Dance, and a matriarch or fertility goddess, She of the Earth.

Dark Meadow unfolds as dancers etch paths that seem to unearth a lost civilization and long-forgotten ritual. She Who Seeks wrestles with a long black cloth that she transforms from shroud to pathway to tunnel into the underworld to protective shawl. She of the Earth consecrates the ground traversed by the dancers and assists in various rites of passage depicted by the dancers. The dance ends with the promise of light and growth in the dark meadow of a woman's soul.

SET DESIGN
Isamu Noguchi

COSTUME DESIGN
Edythe Gilfond

COMPOSER
Carlos Chavez

Dark Meadow

DANCERS

So Young An, James Anthony,
Alessio Crognale-Roberts,
Jacob Larsen, Marzia Memoli

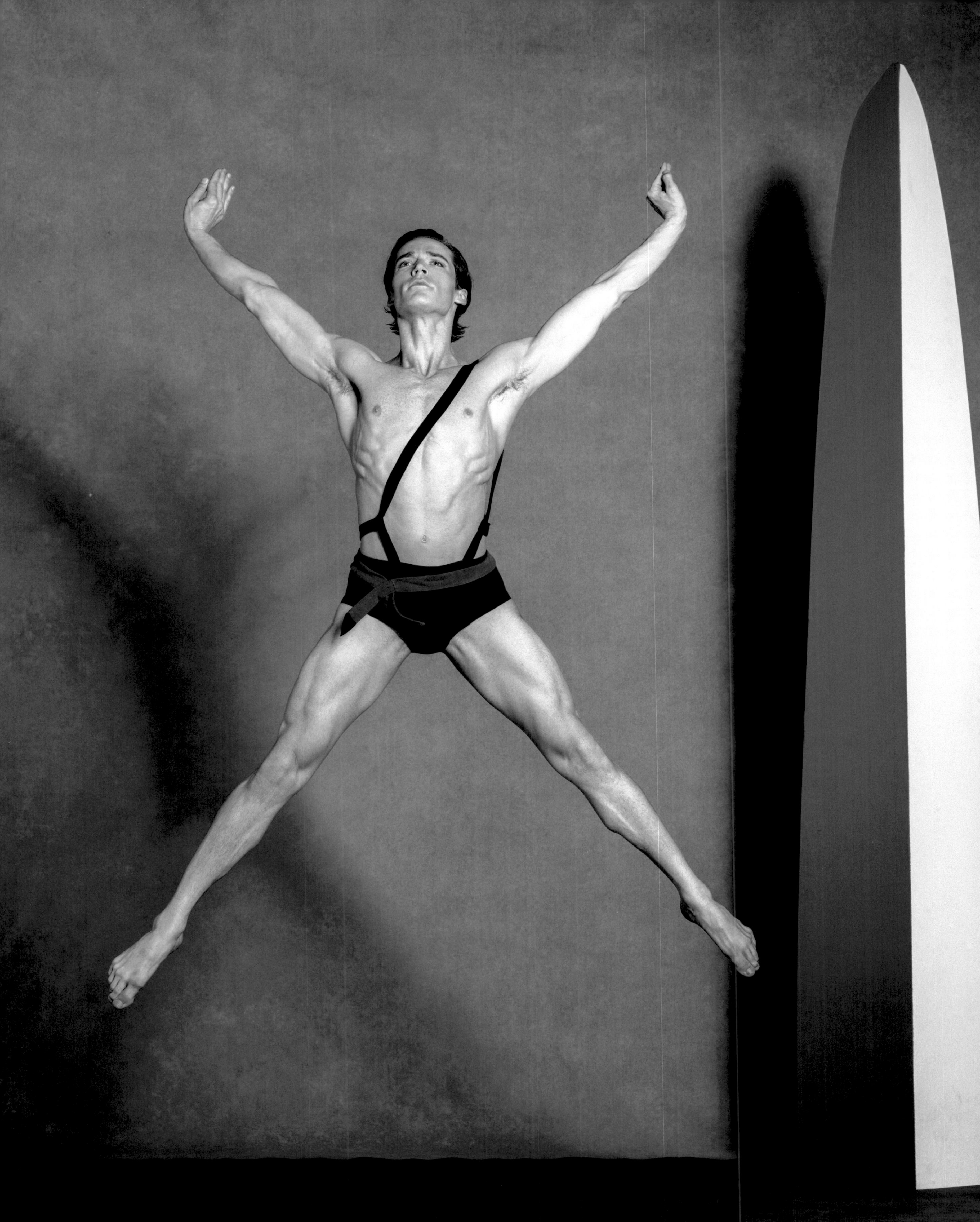

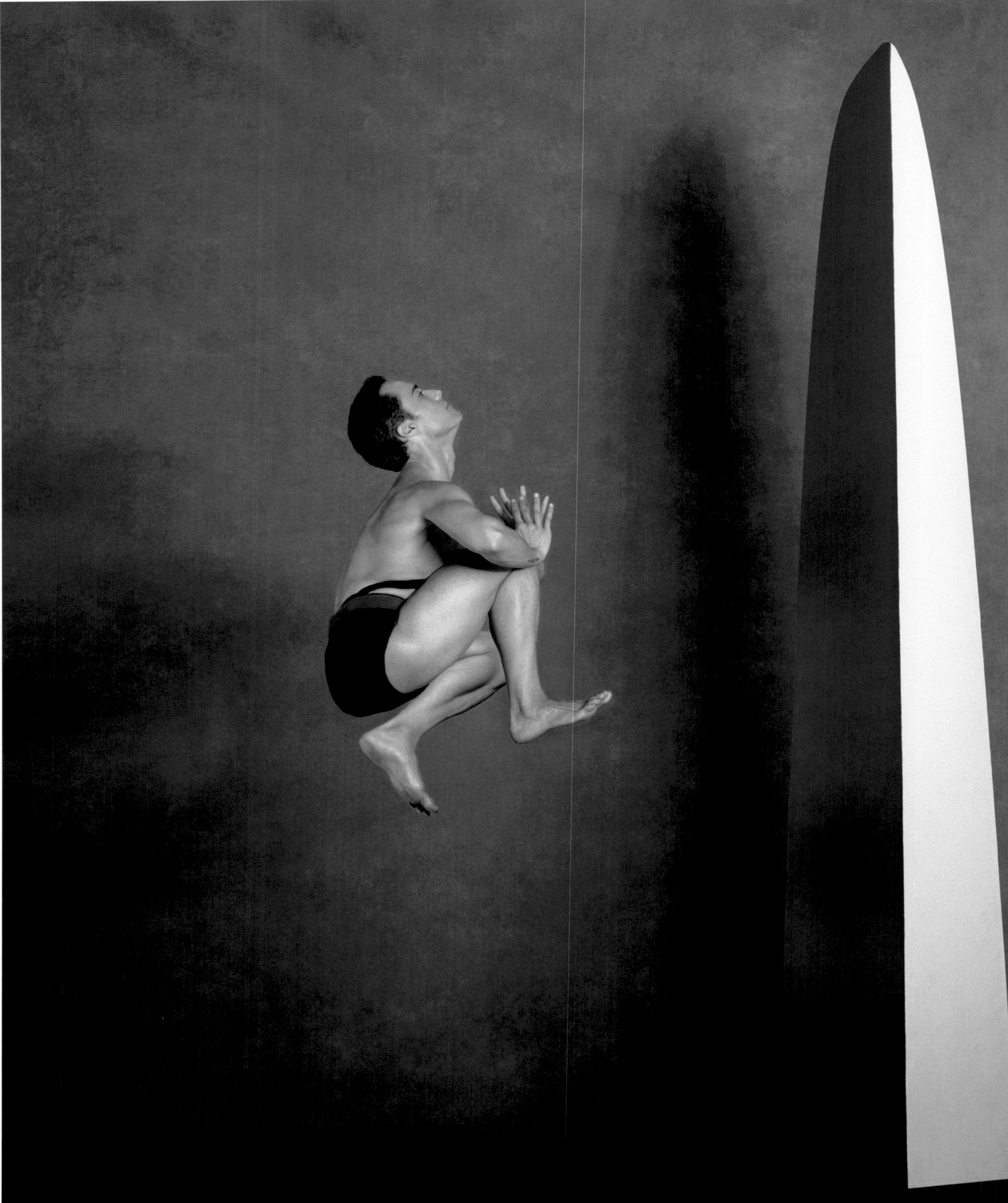

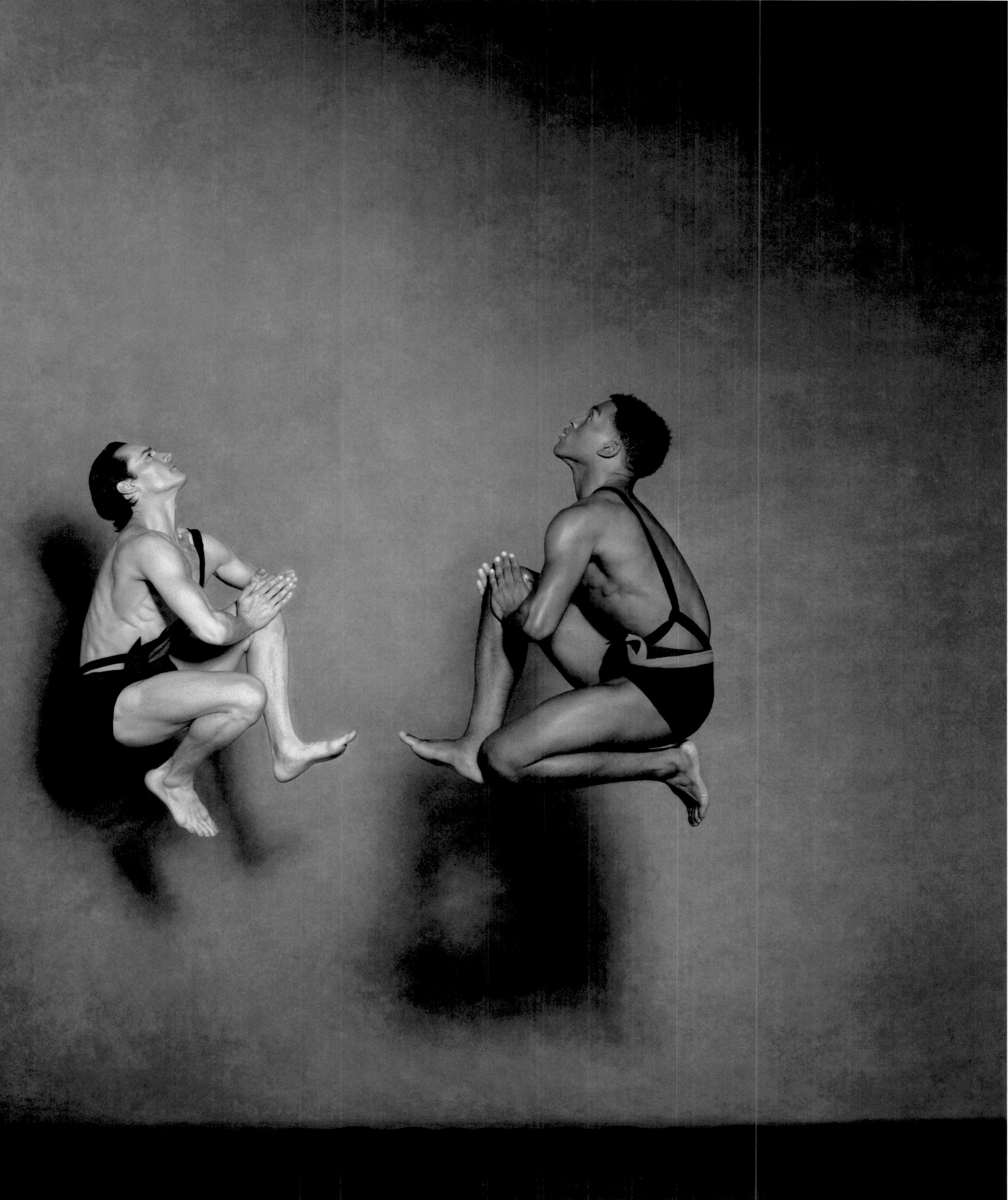

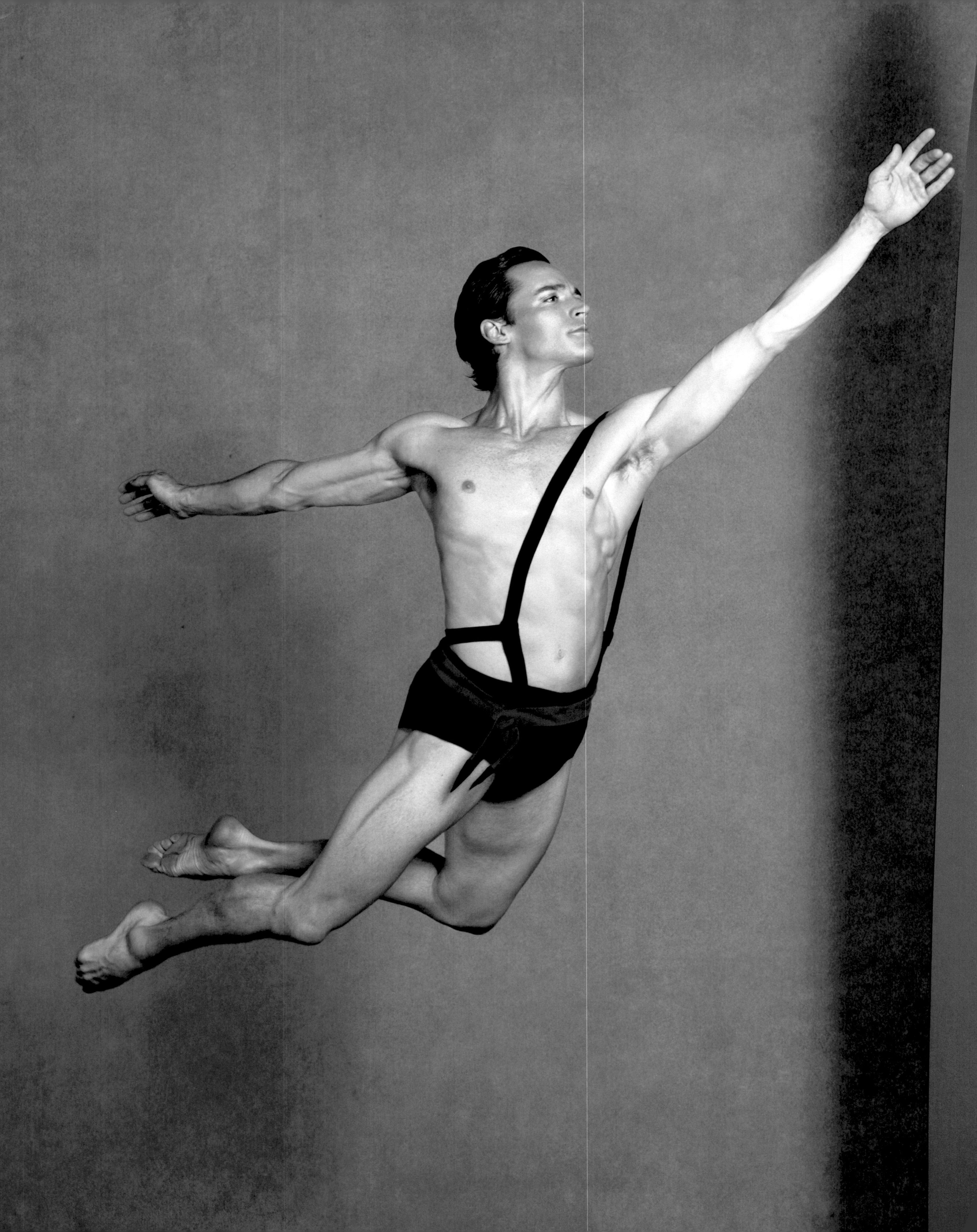

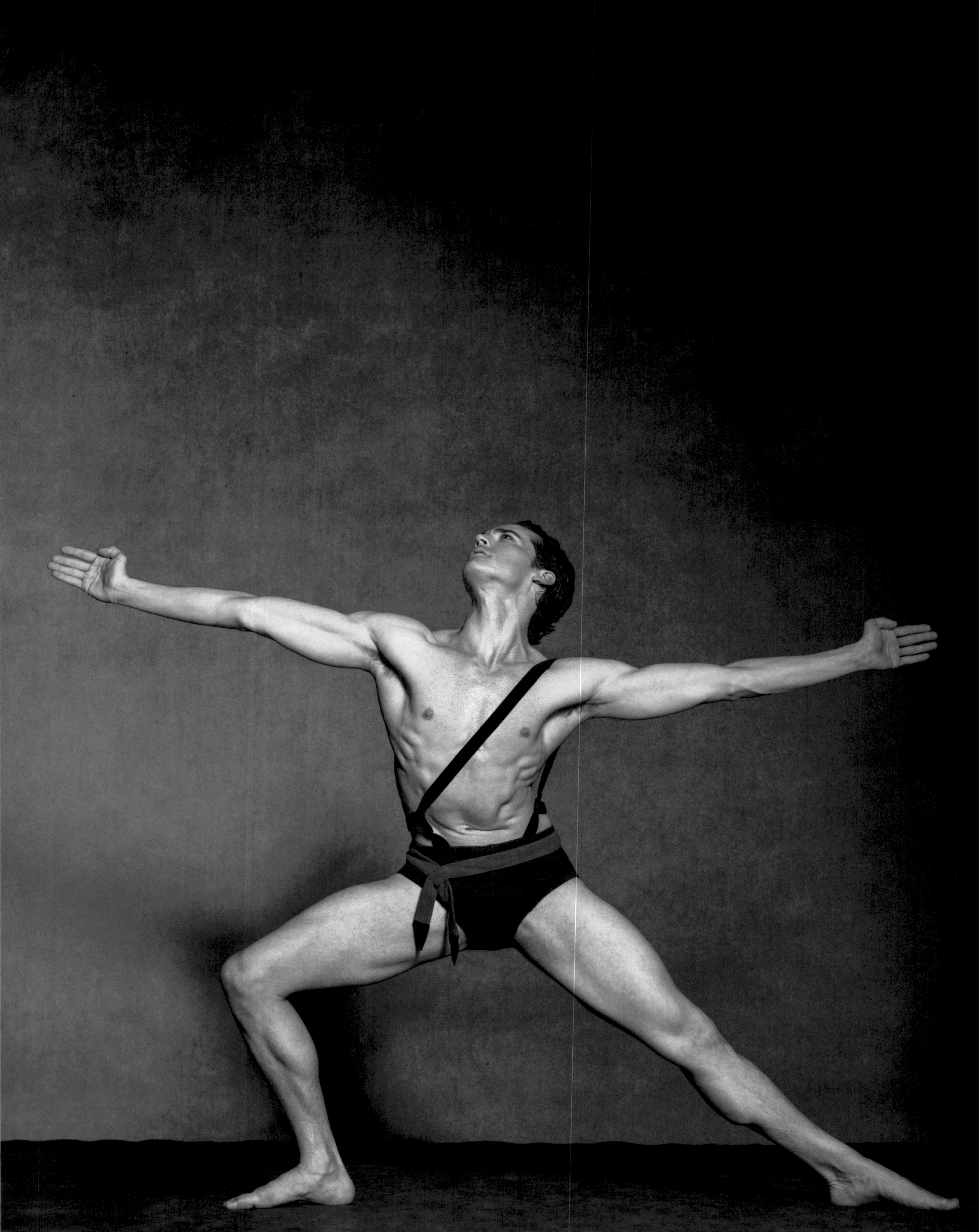

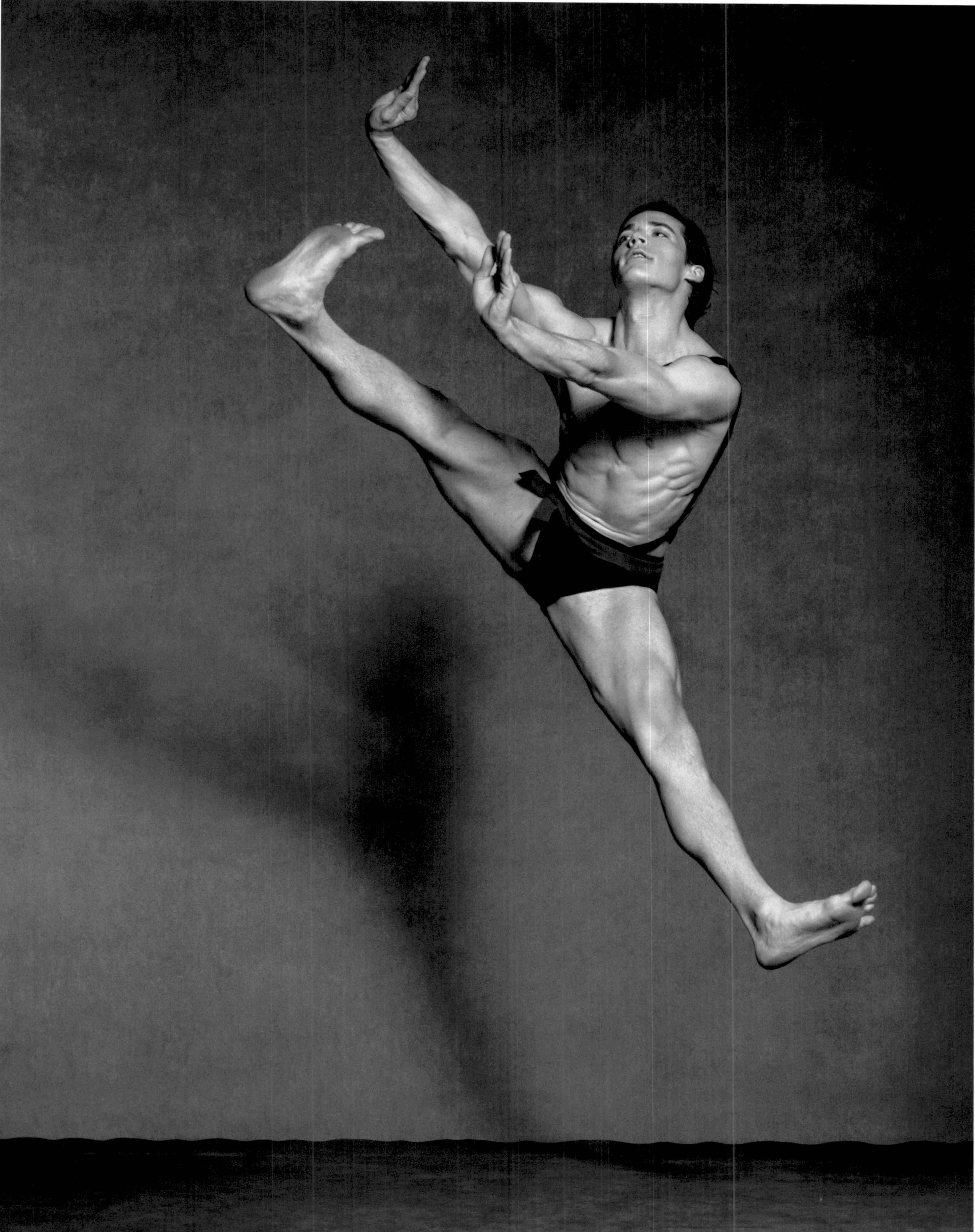

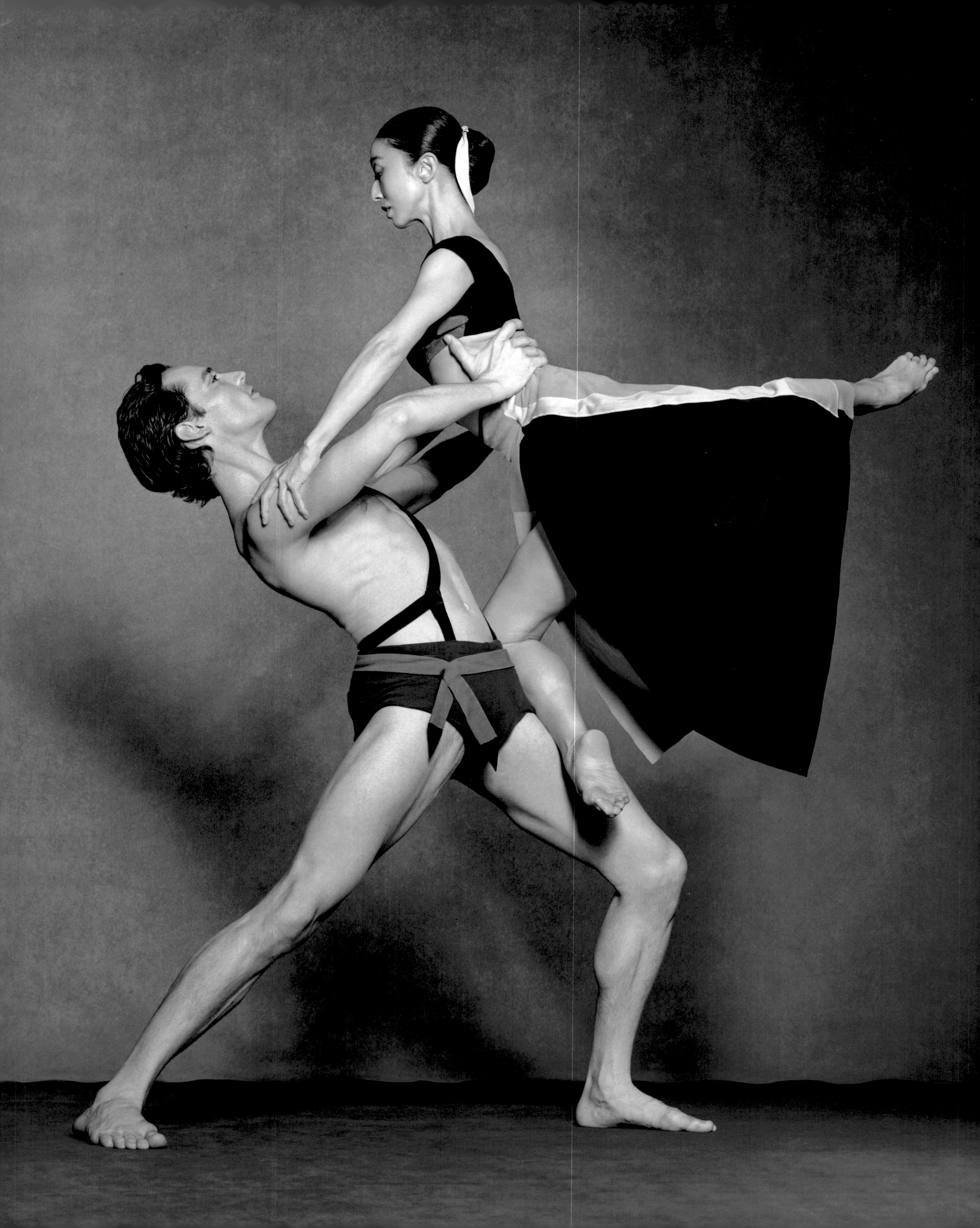

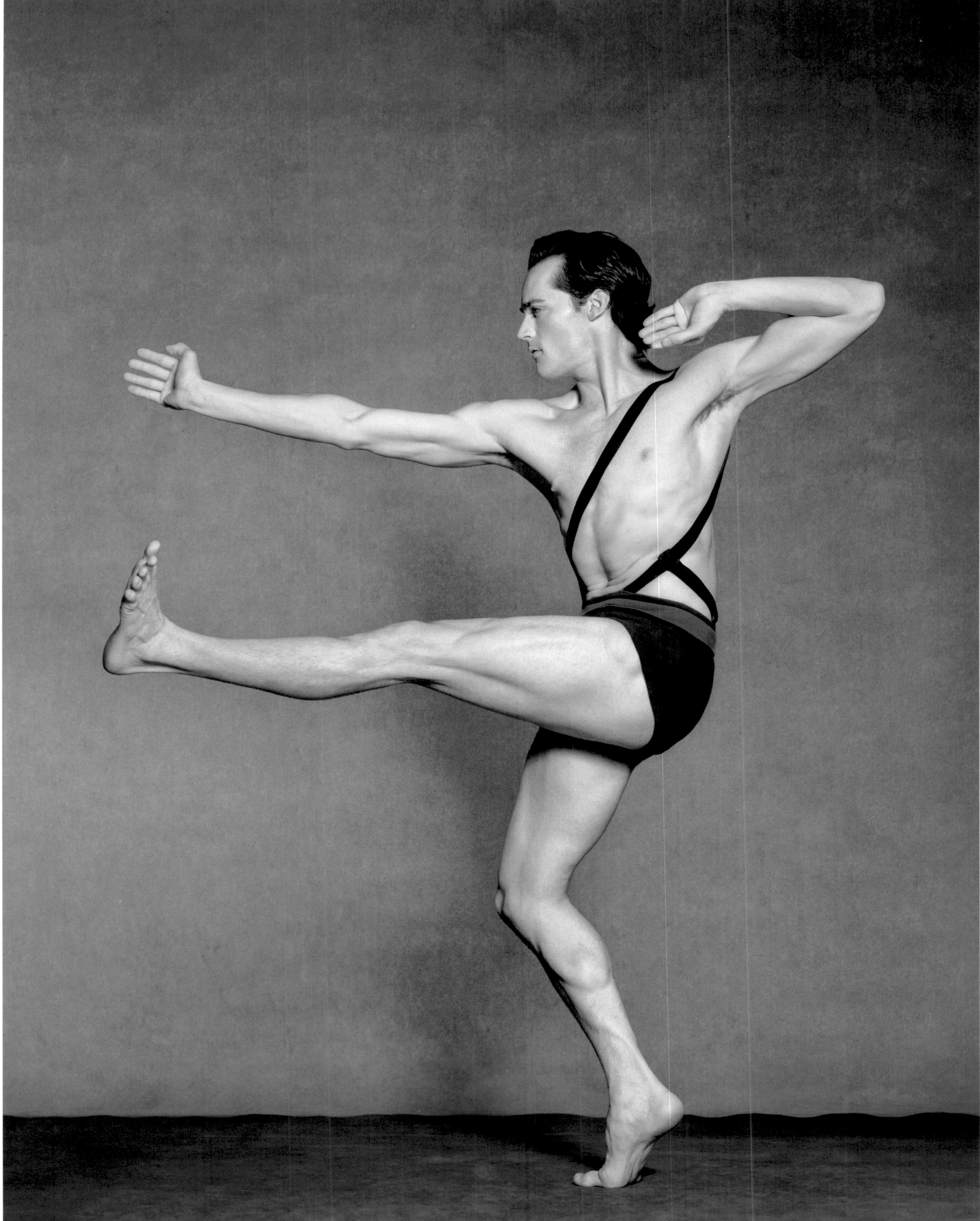

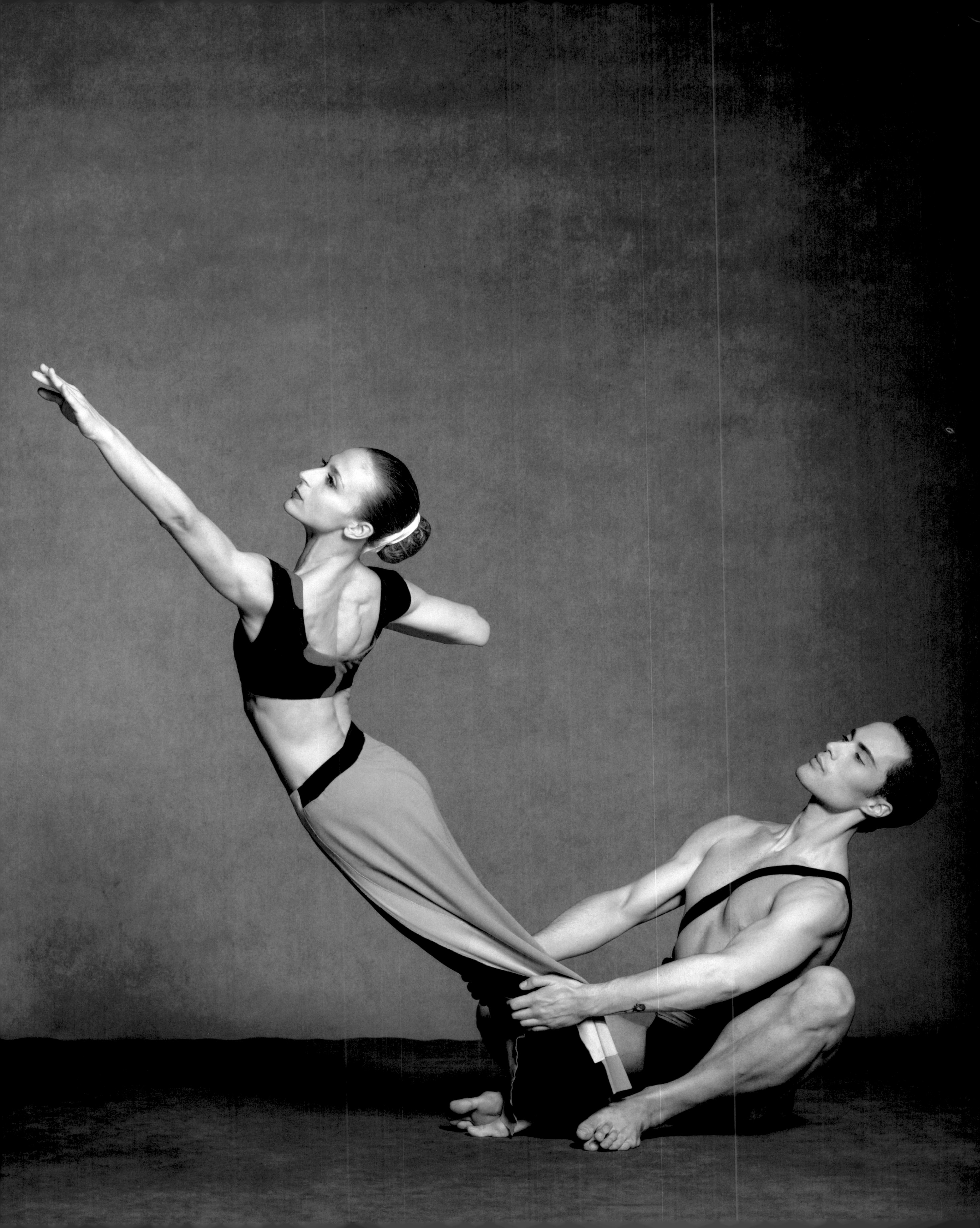

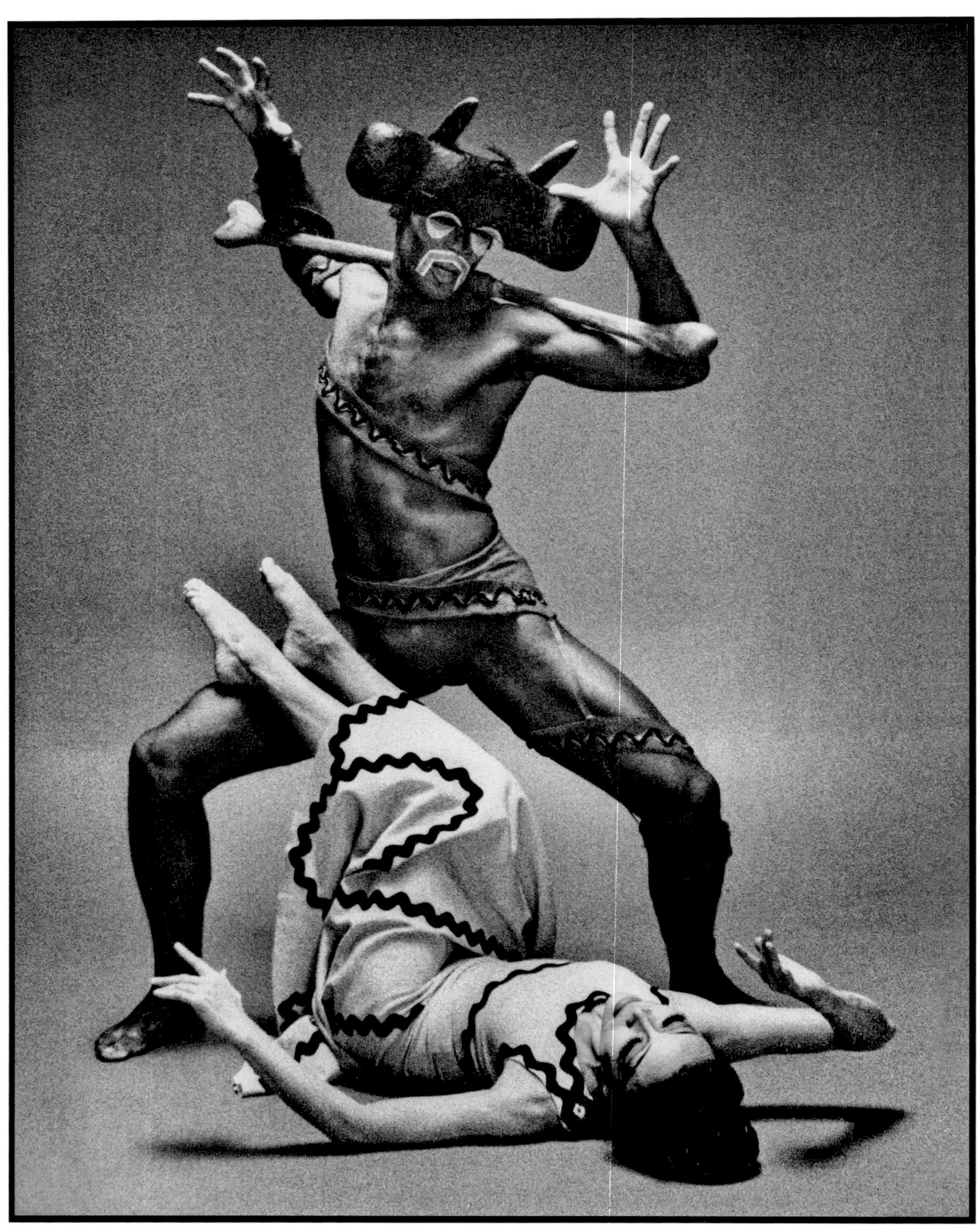

Yuriko Kimura and Daniel Maloney. Photograph by Max Waldman.

ERRAND INTO THE MAZE, 1947

A woman's journey into the psyche to confront her innermost fears.

The maze into which the lone female dancer enters is one of her own unresolved fear, which is embodied by the character of the Minotaur or Creature of Fear, a creature half man, half monster, who lies in wait at the end of a coiling thread the dancer lays to mark her path.

Long before there was feminism, Graham blazed a trail as a woman unafraid of autonomy and her voice as an artist. Her female protagonists, often cast as secondary players in their original context, reflect this willful mission. Graham's heroine Ariadne, a stand-in for Theseus of the Greek myth, appears alone under a sliver of a moon, pacing in the shadows, her muscles taut and twitching with fearful anticipation. Three confrontations with the Creature of Fear bring her closer to freedom until she finally vanquishes him, climbing his thighs and riding him until he crumples at her feet. She steps through a V-shaped portal, designed by Isamu Noguchi, and into the light. The propulsive score by Gian Carlo Menotti creates a pointillist landscape that exquisitely mirrors our heroine's journey into the self.

SET DESIGN
Isamu Noguchi

COSTUME DESIGN
Martha Graham

COMPOSER
Gian Carlo Menotti

Errand into the Maze

DANCERS

Lloyd Knight and Xin Ying

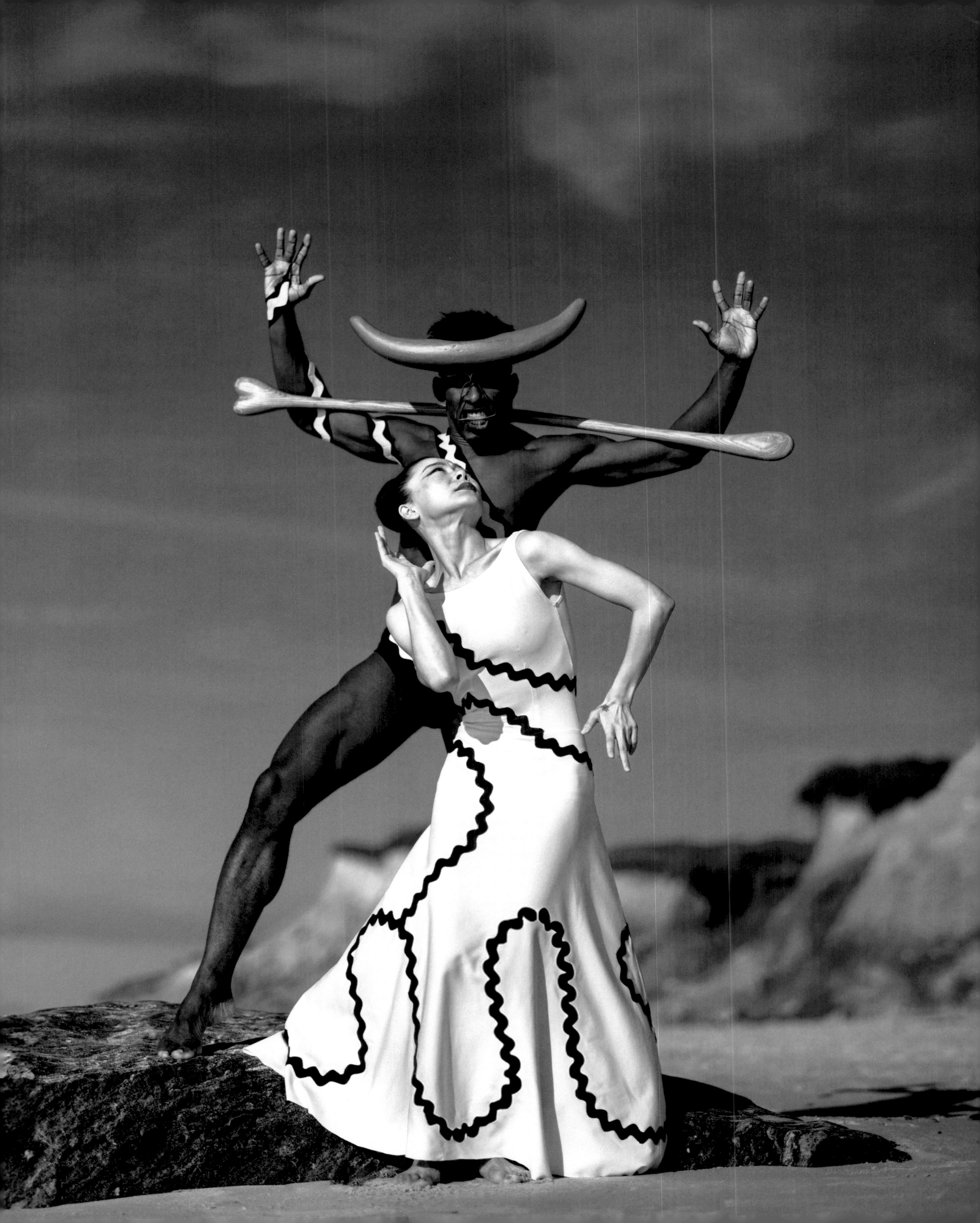

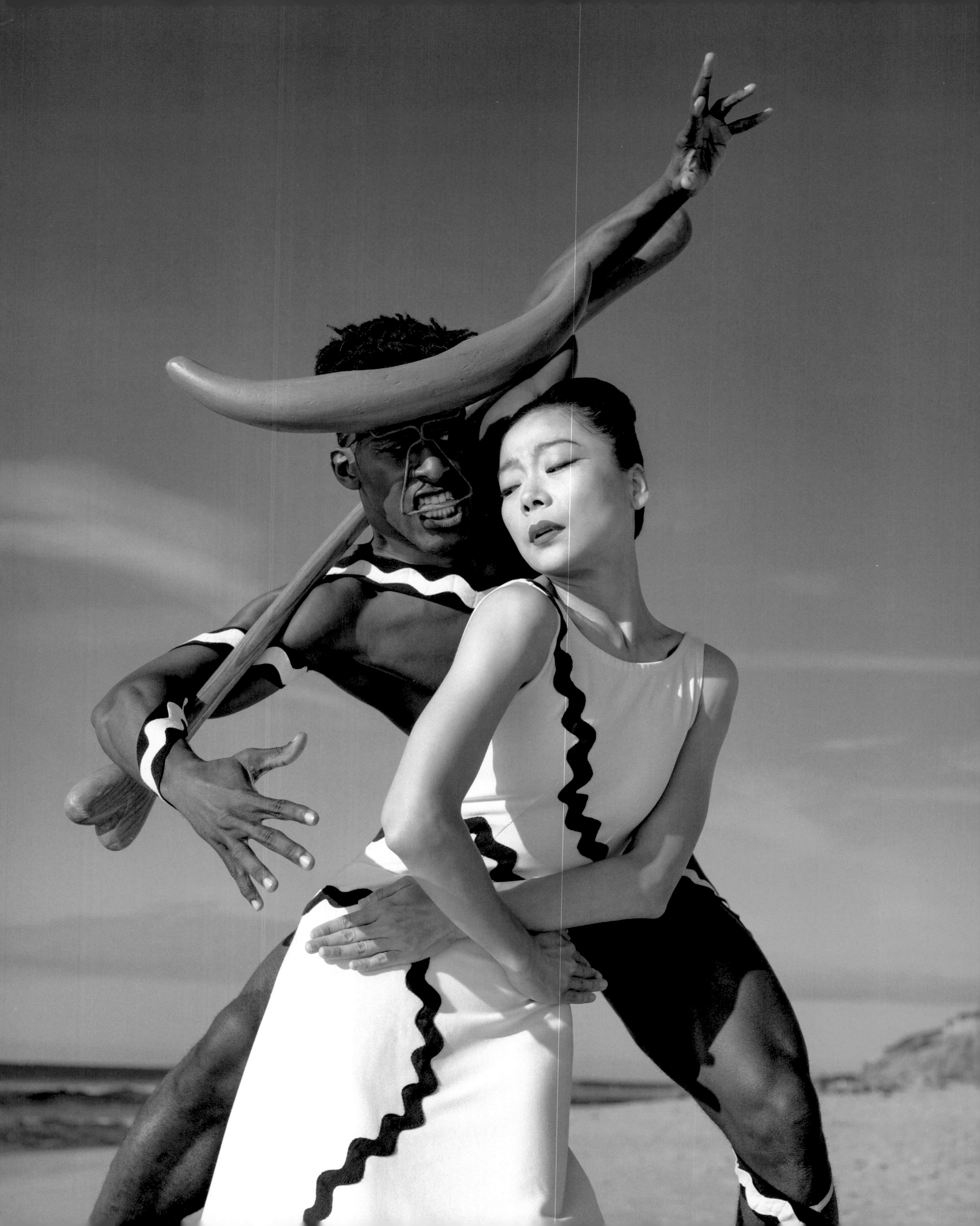

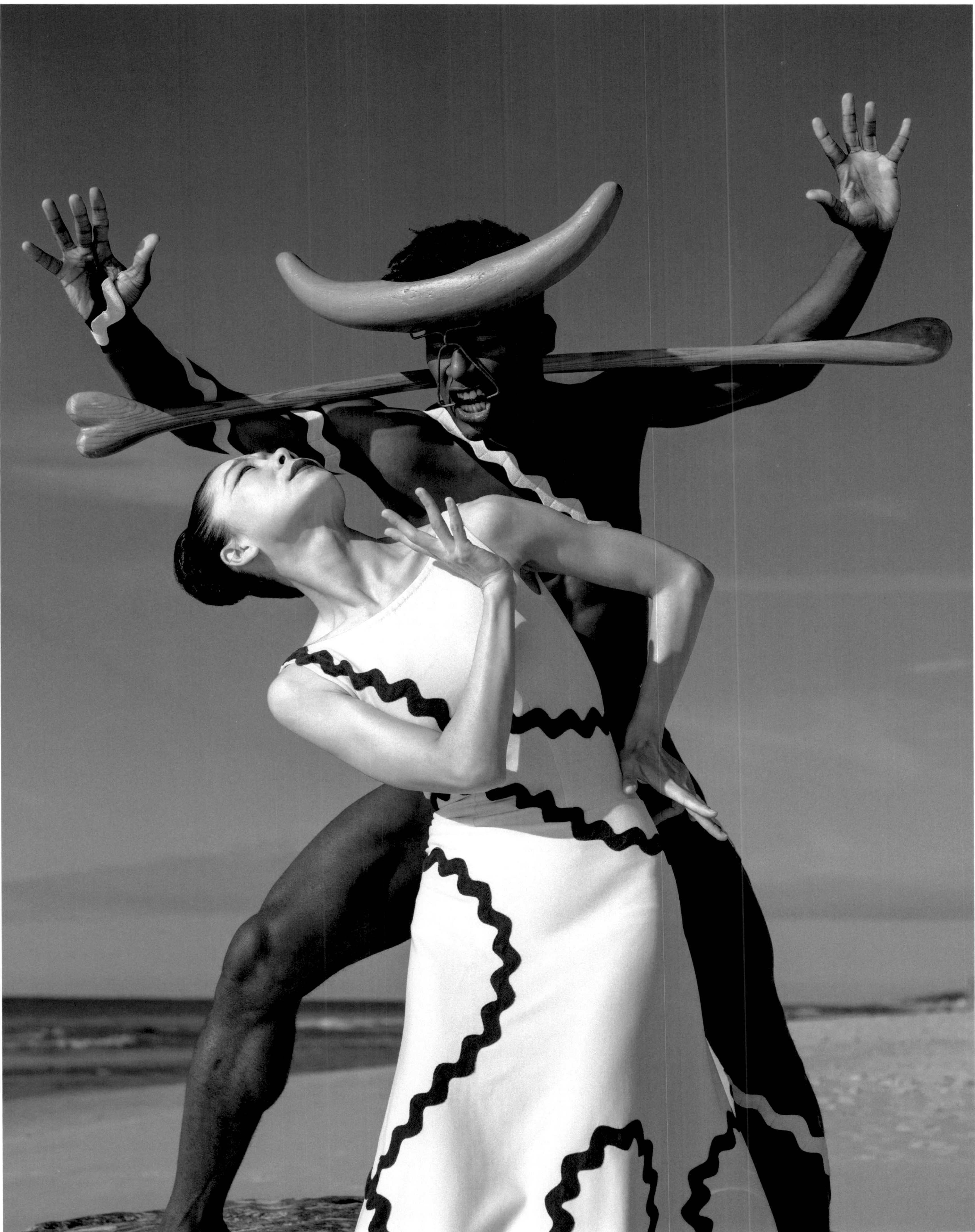

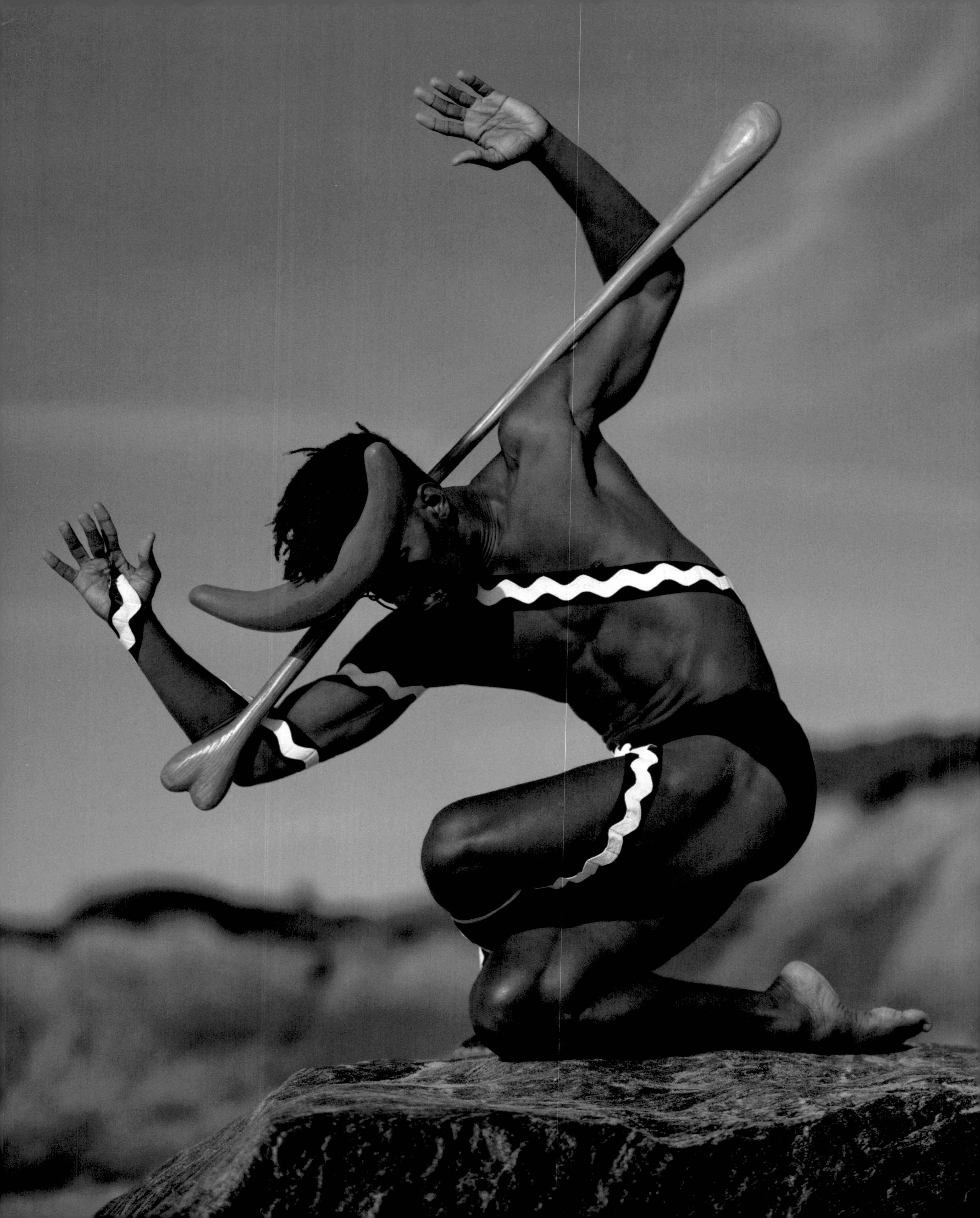

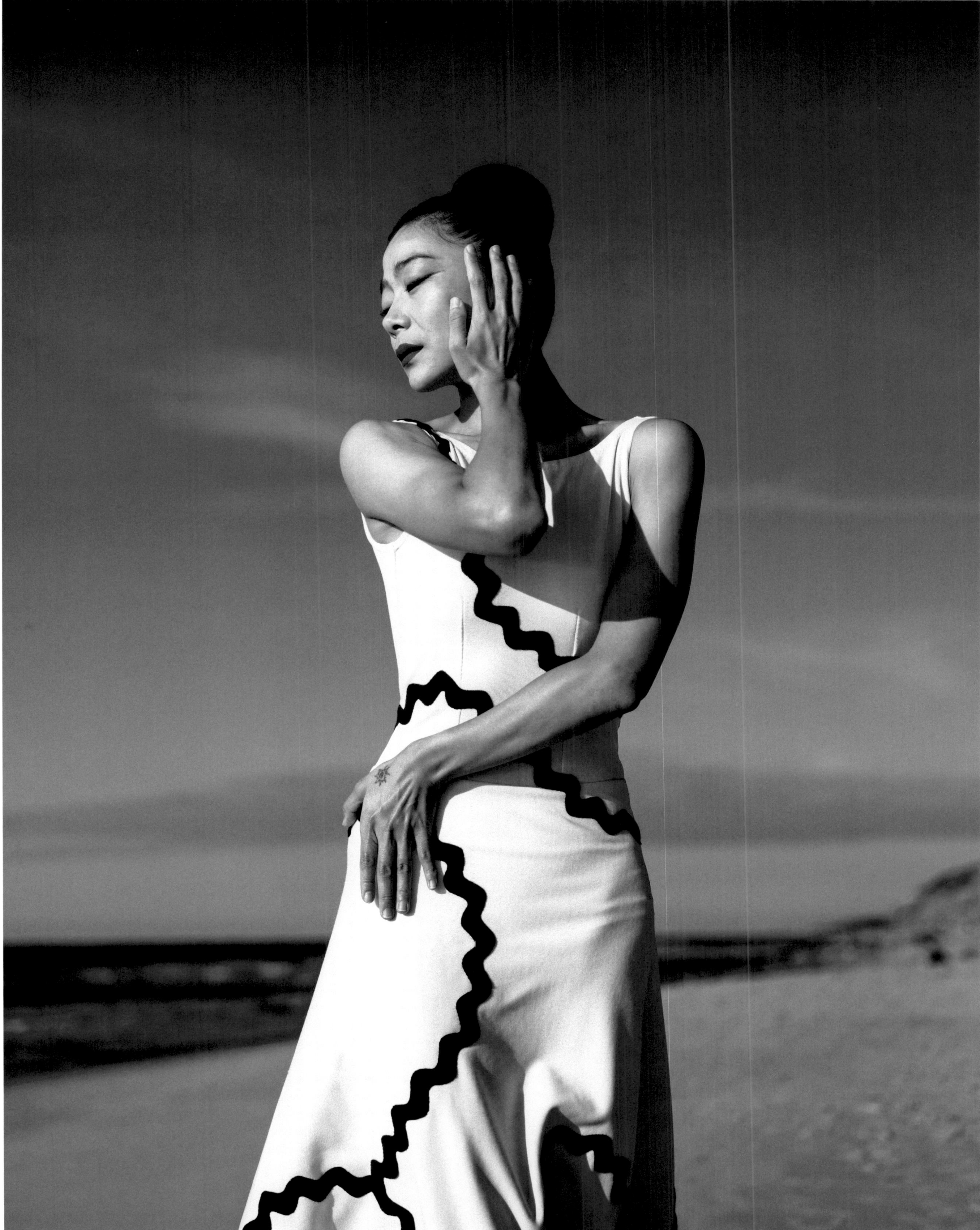

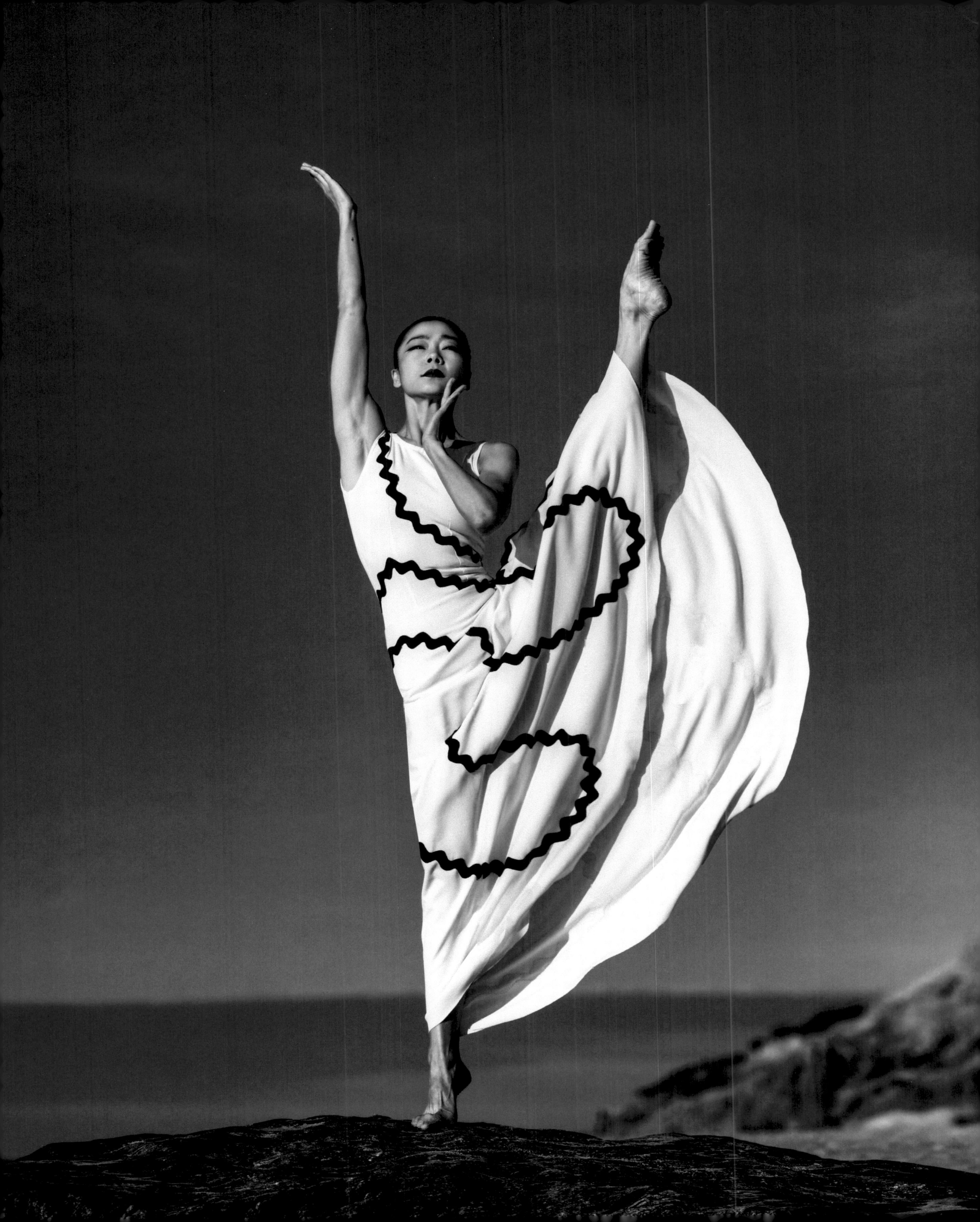

DANCE OBSERVER

VOLUME TWENTY-TWO, NUMBER SIX JUNE-JULY, 1955

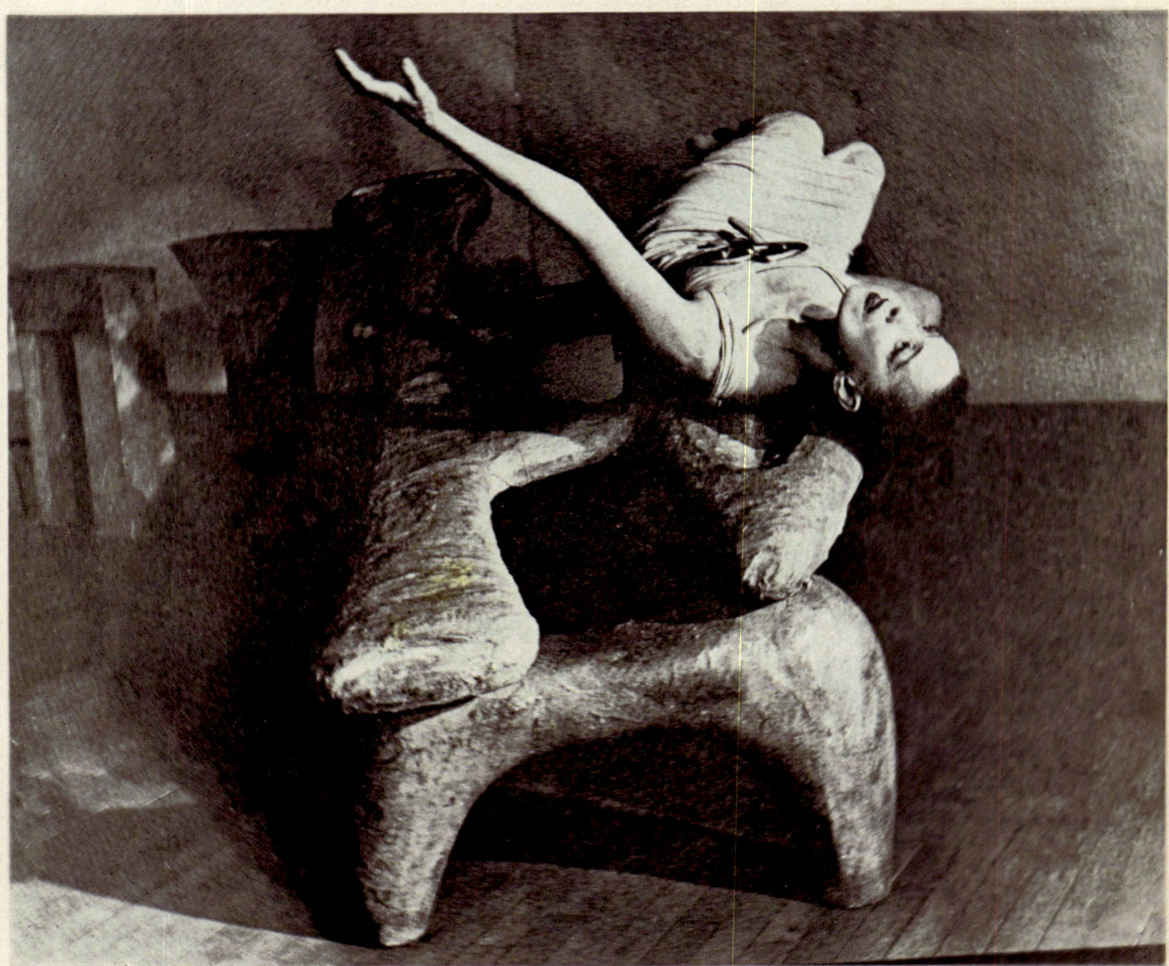

(Philippe Halsman)

MARTHA GRAHAM
in "Night Journey"

25c

Photograph by Philippe Halsman.

NIGHT JOURNEY, 1947

An ingenious reimagining of
a canonical Greek tragedy.

In Graham's extraordinary transformation of Sophocles's tragic play *Oedipus Rex*, she foregrounds the death of her protagonist, Jocasta, and maps her story in flashback.

As the curtain opens, we see Jocasta, having recognized the truth, preparing to hang herself. As she remembers the path that has brought her to this moment, Tiresias, the blind seer, enters accompanied by a chorus of seven women, the Daughters of the Night, who comment on the action with foreboding movement.

Flush with the glory of having answered the Sphinx's riddle, Oedipus enters to win Jocasta's hand in marriage, unaware that he is her son. A highly stylized courtship ritual is followed by the entrance of the chorus who unleash an extraordinary dance of doom. Tiresias then reveals the truth about the unnatural union and Oedipus blinds himself with Jocasta's brooch, leaving Jocasta alone to confront her own fate and complete her fatal task.

SET DESIGN
Isamu Noguchi

COSTUME DESIGN
Martha Graham

COMPOSER
William Schuman

Night Journey

JOCASTA
PeiJu Chien-Pott

OEDIPUS
Lloyd Knight

DAUGHTERS OF THE NIGHT
So Young An, Laurel Dalley Smith,
Charlotte Landreau, Anne O'Donnell Passero,
Anne Souder, Leslie Andrea Williams

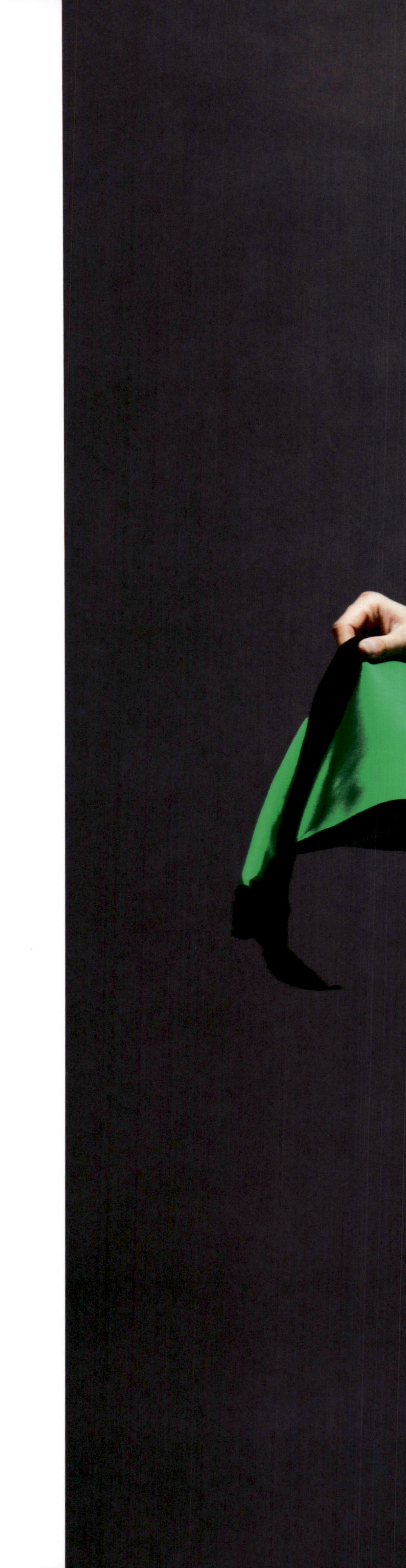

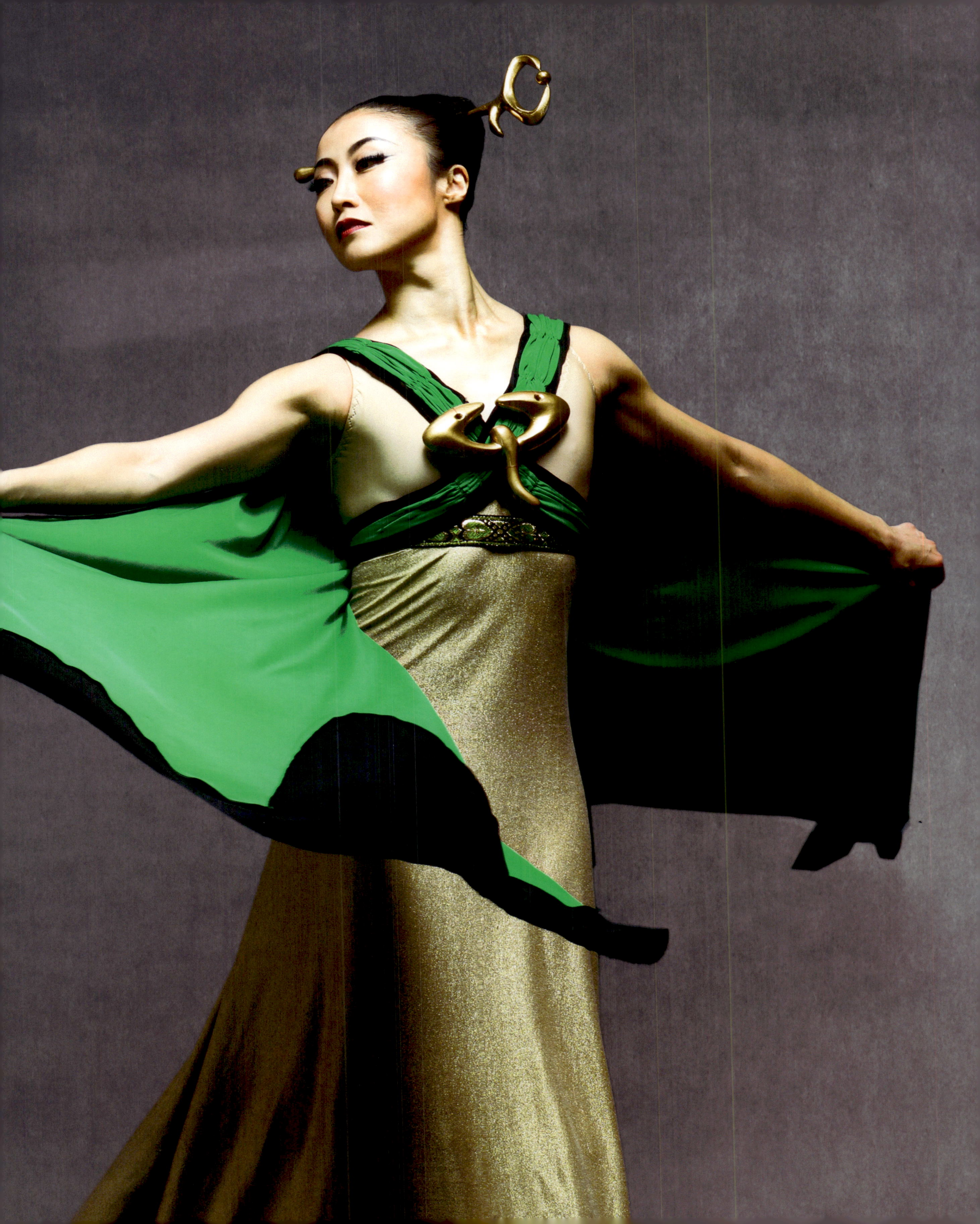

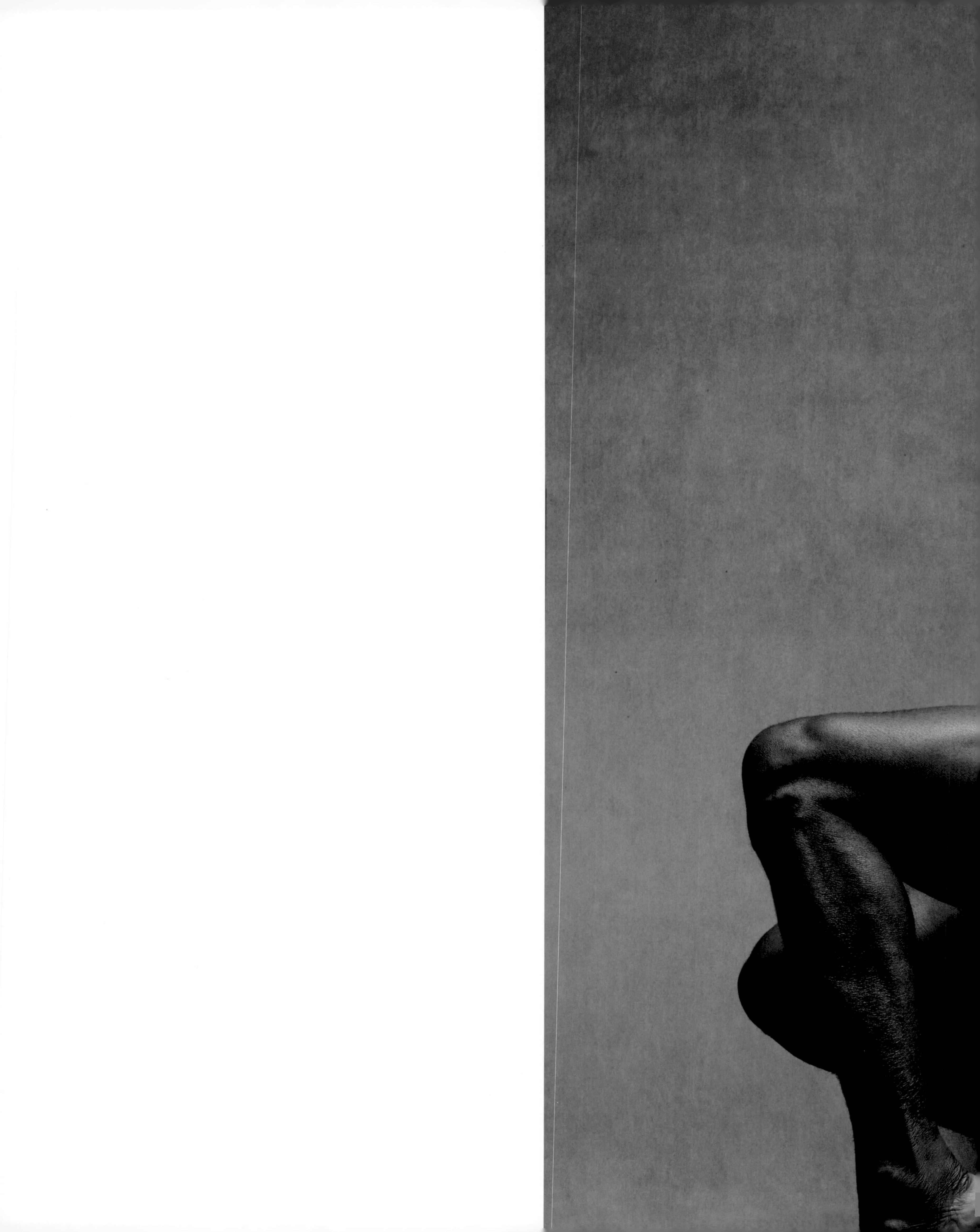

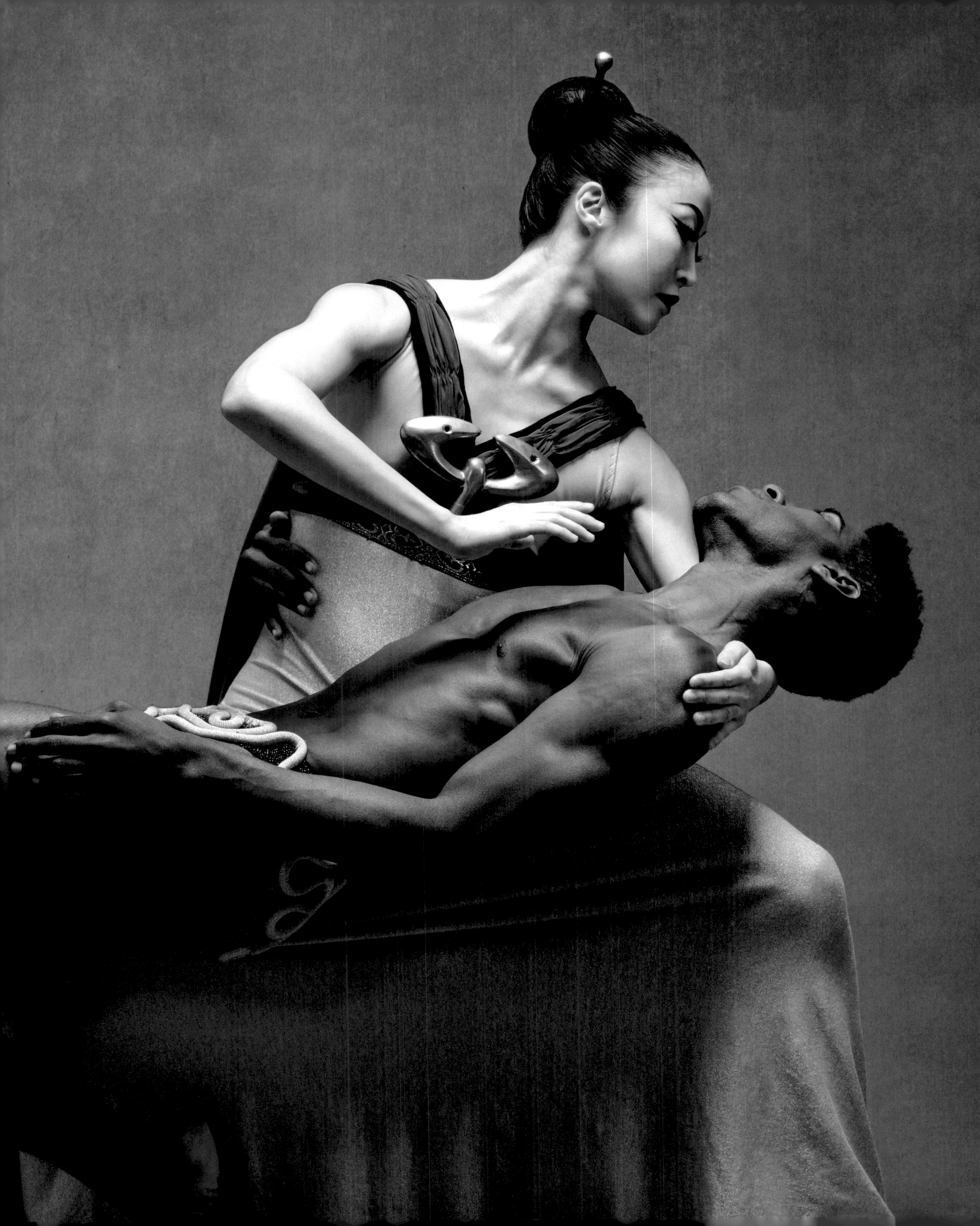

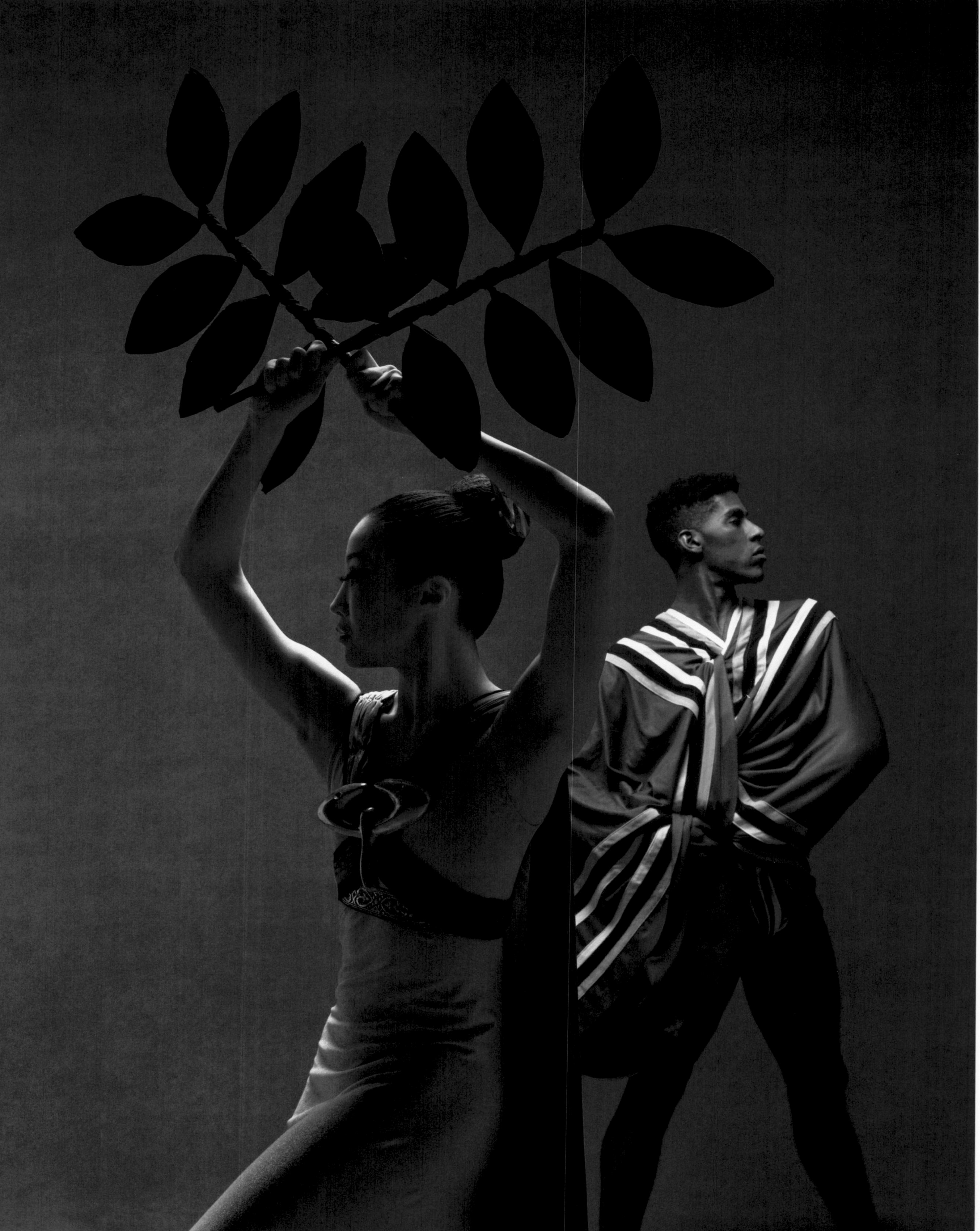

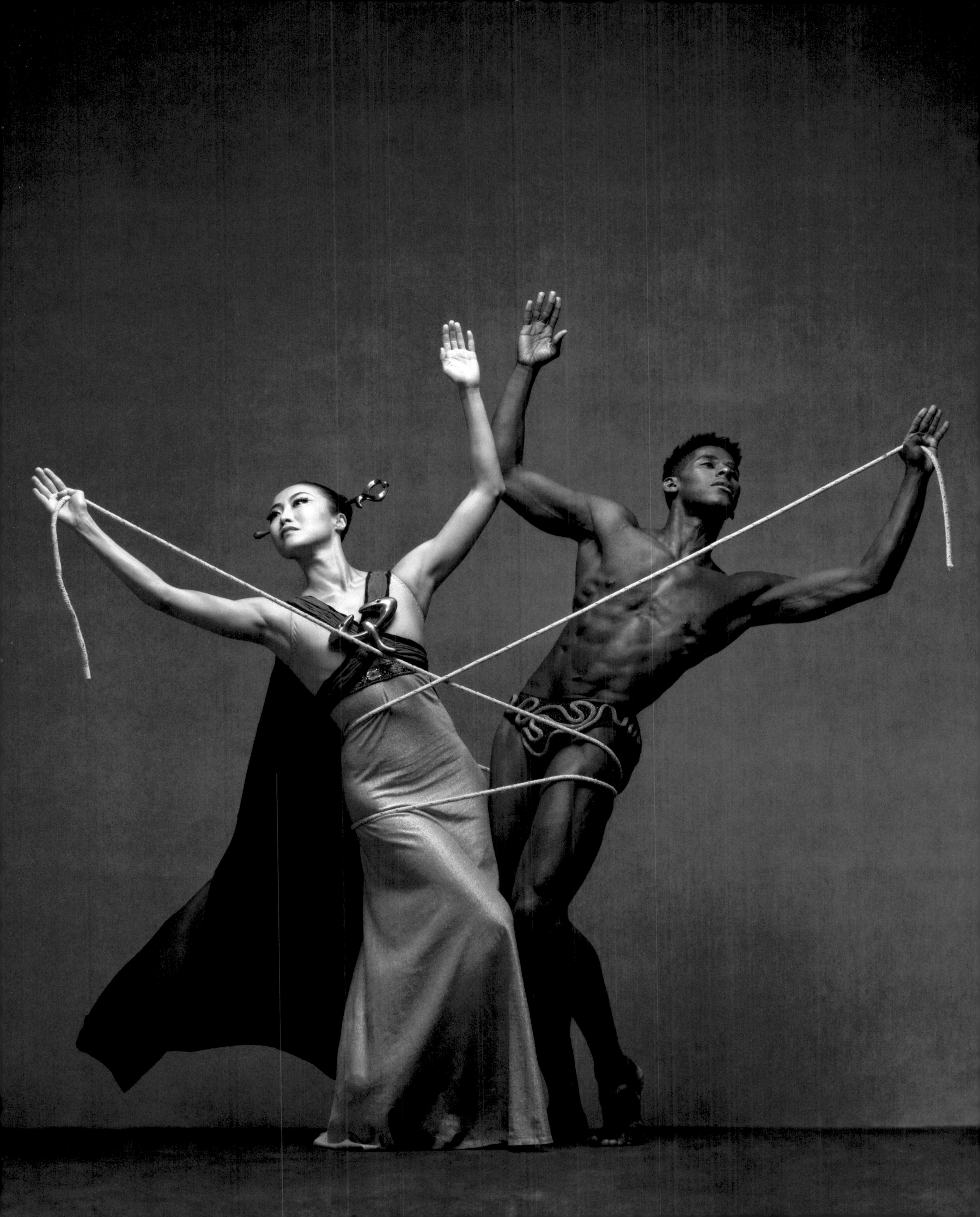

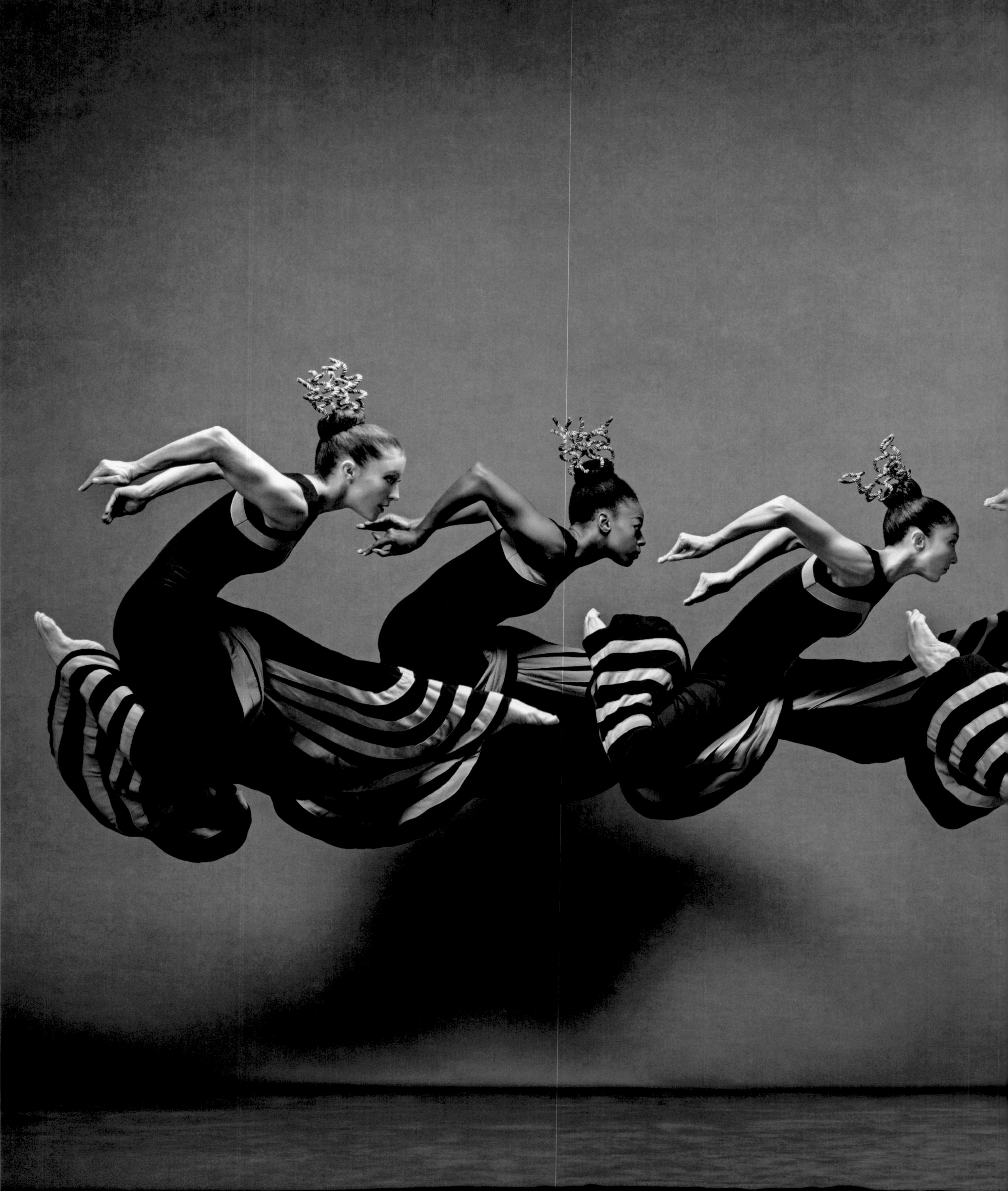

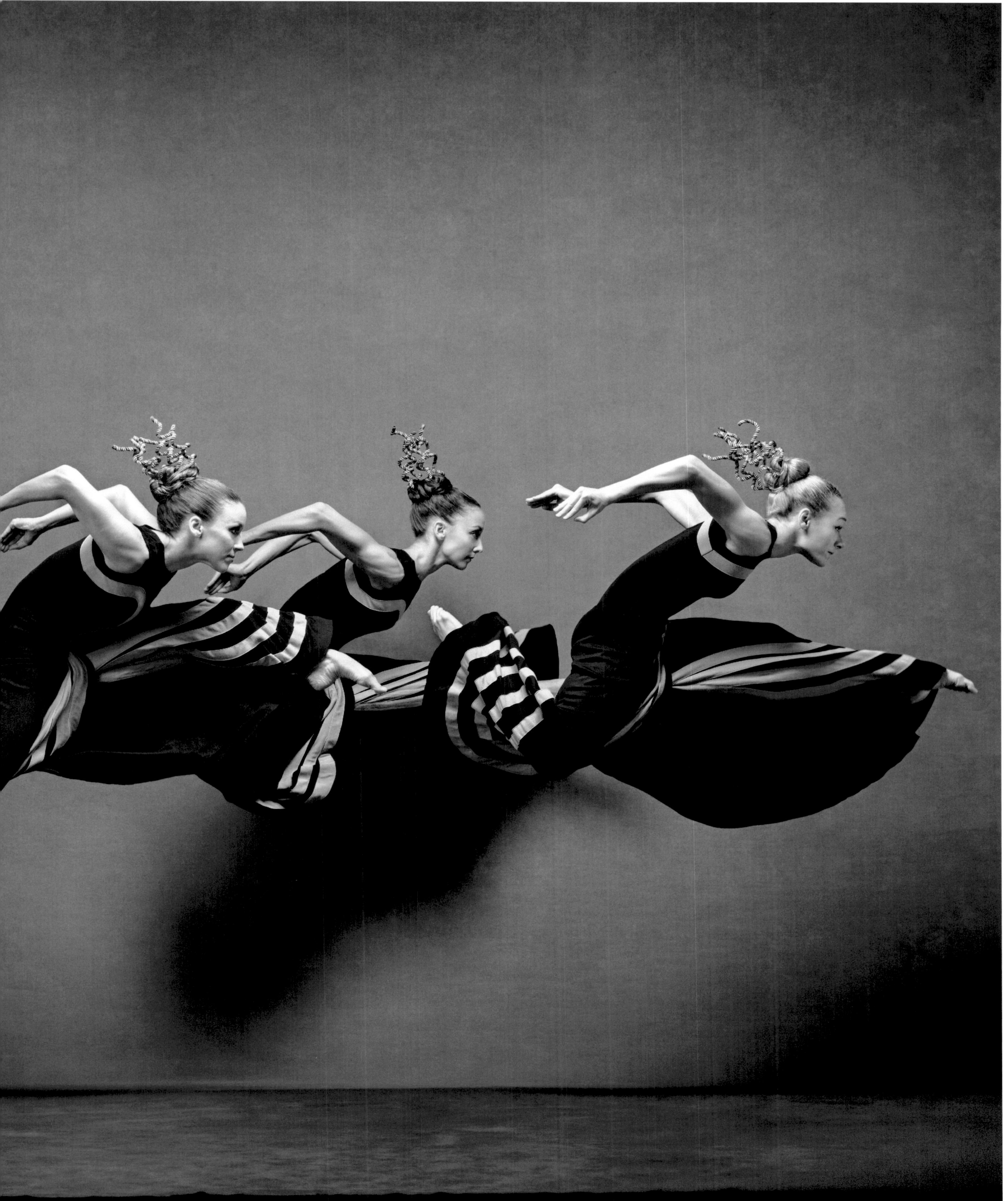

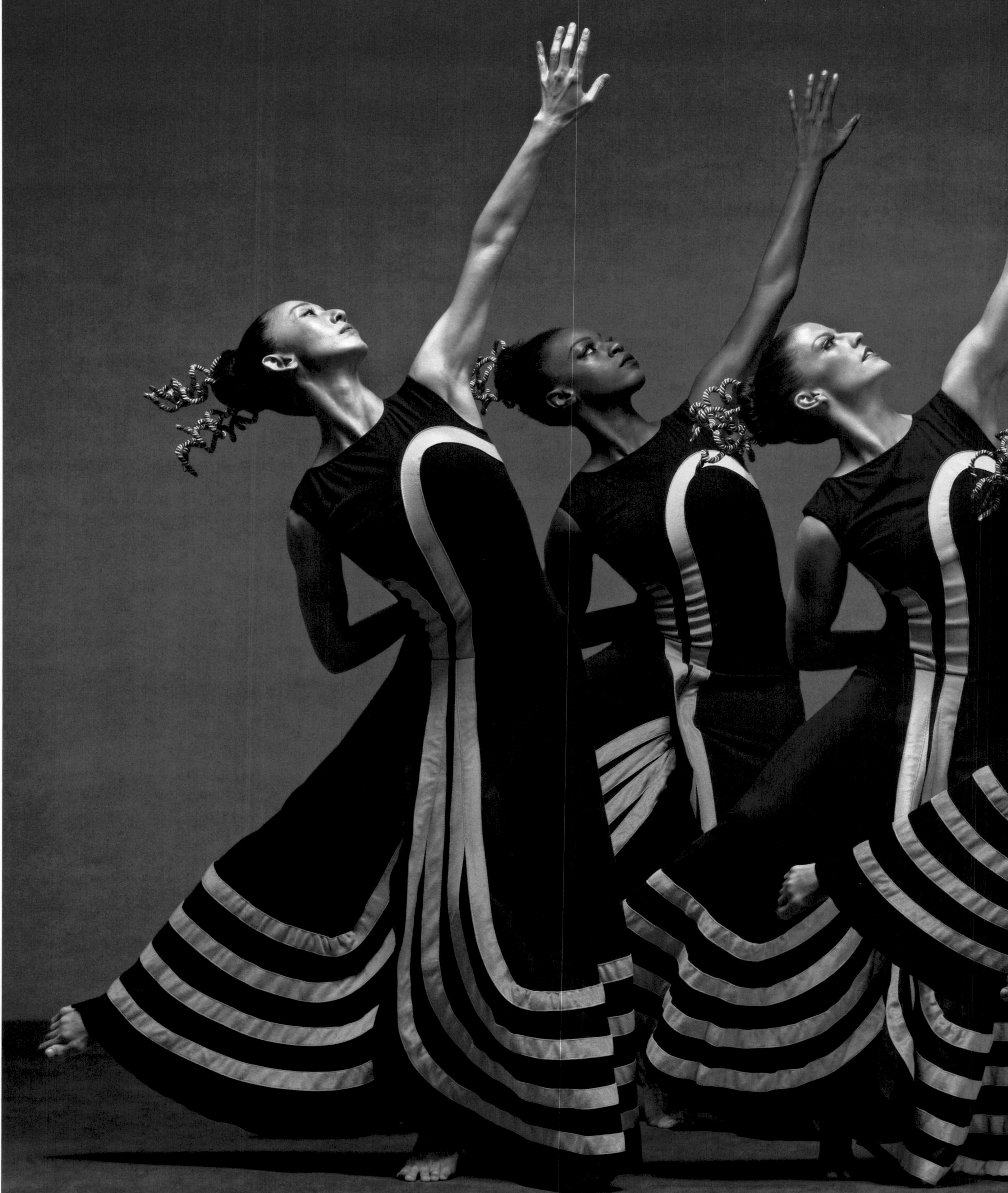

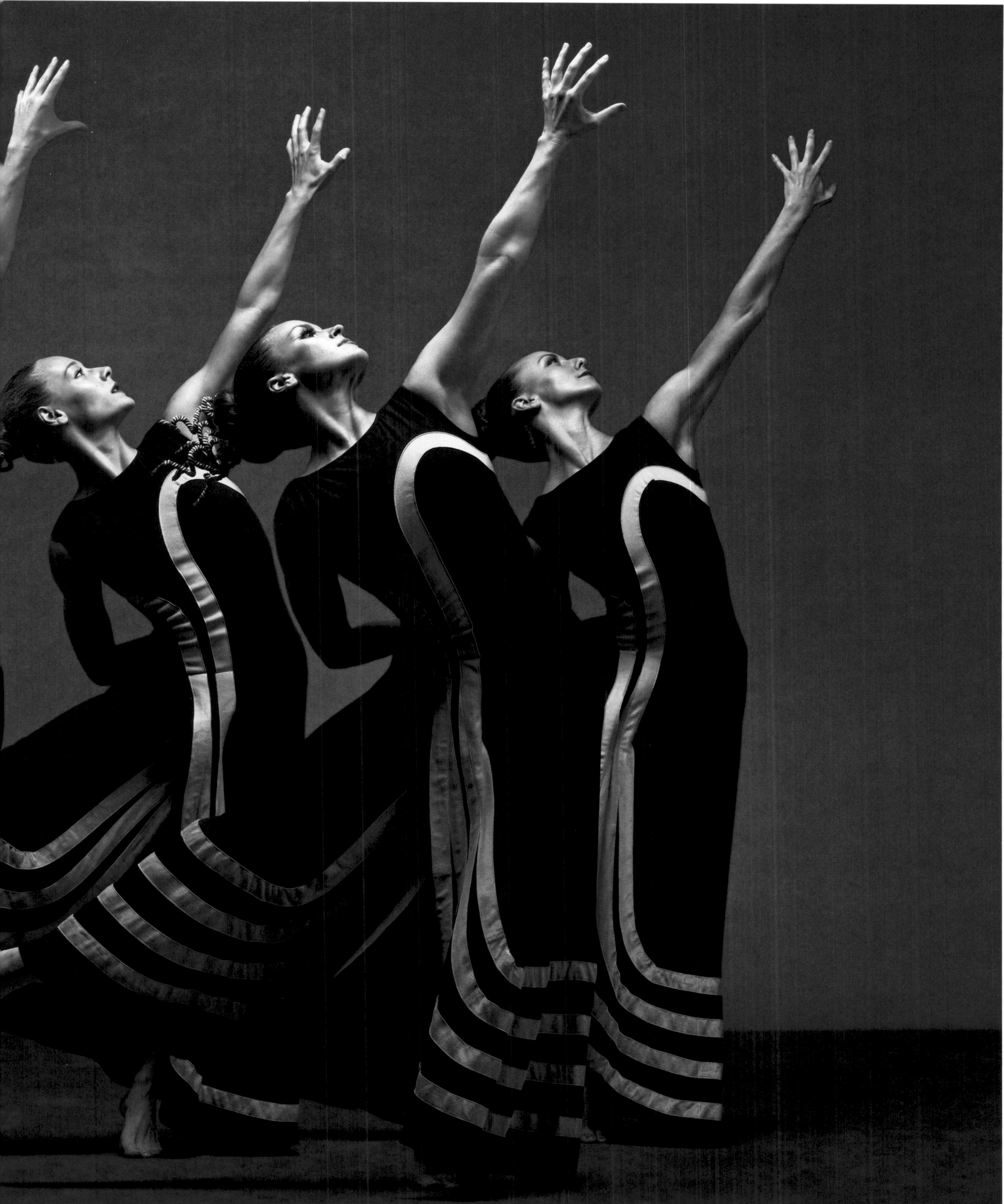

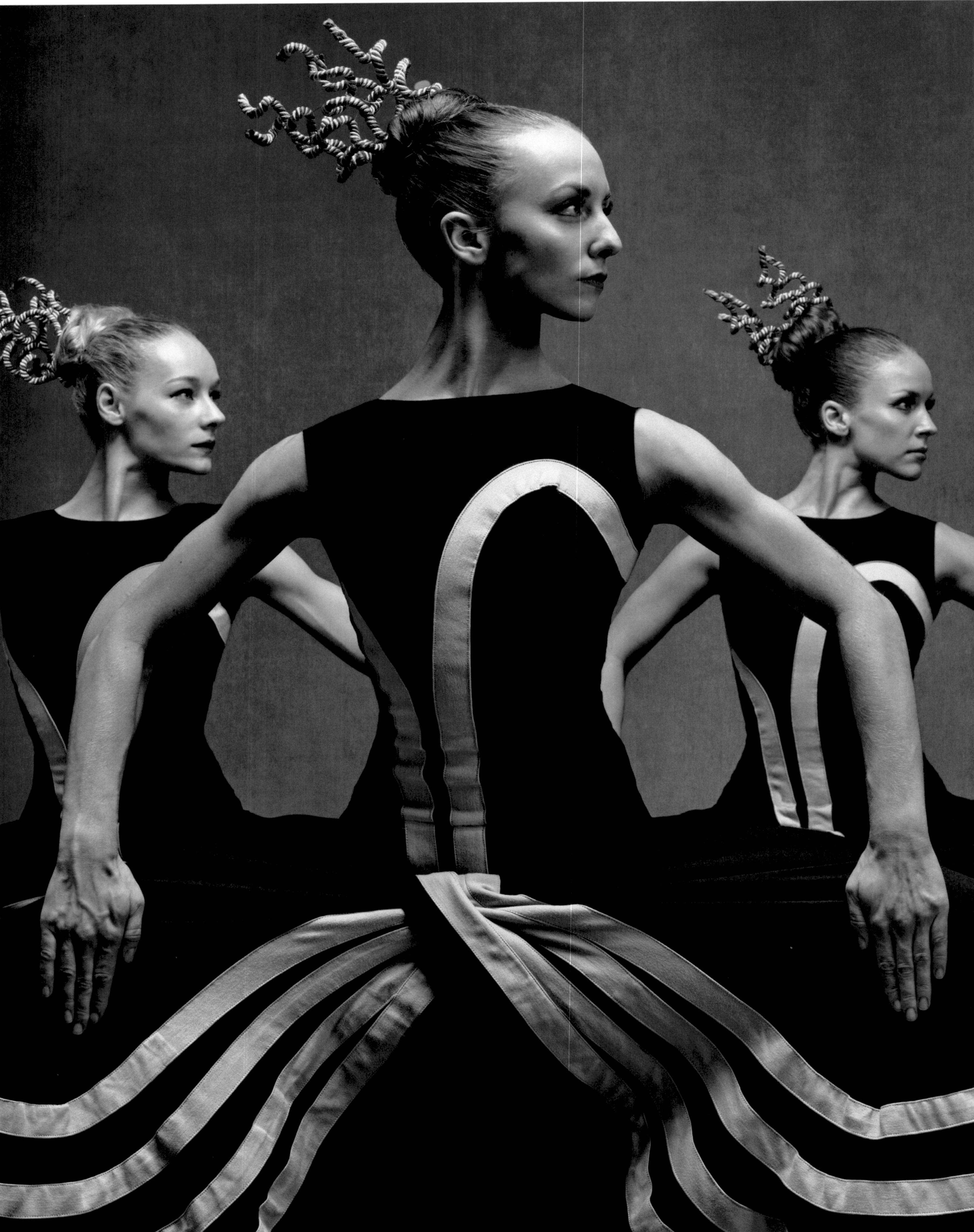

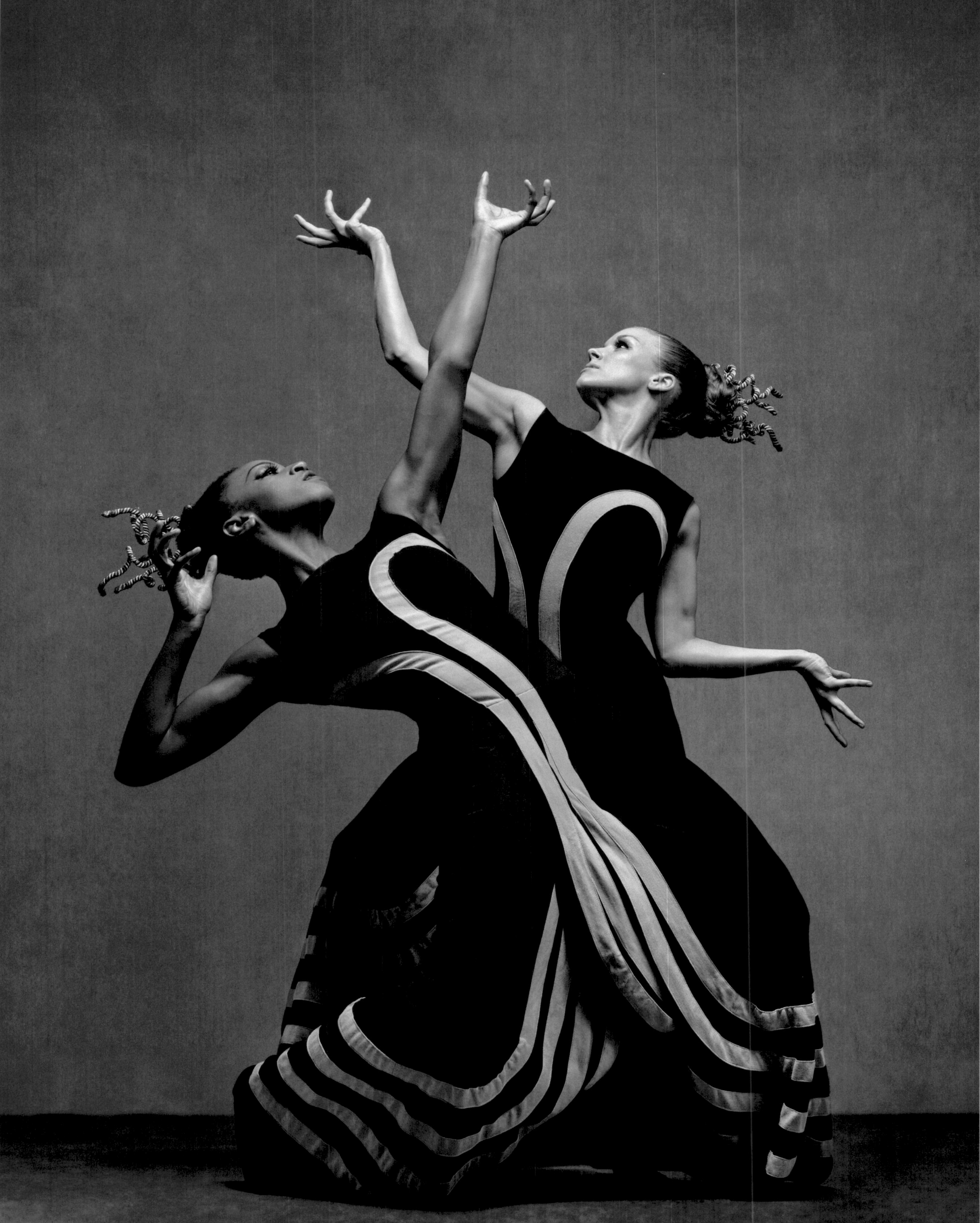

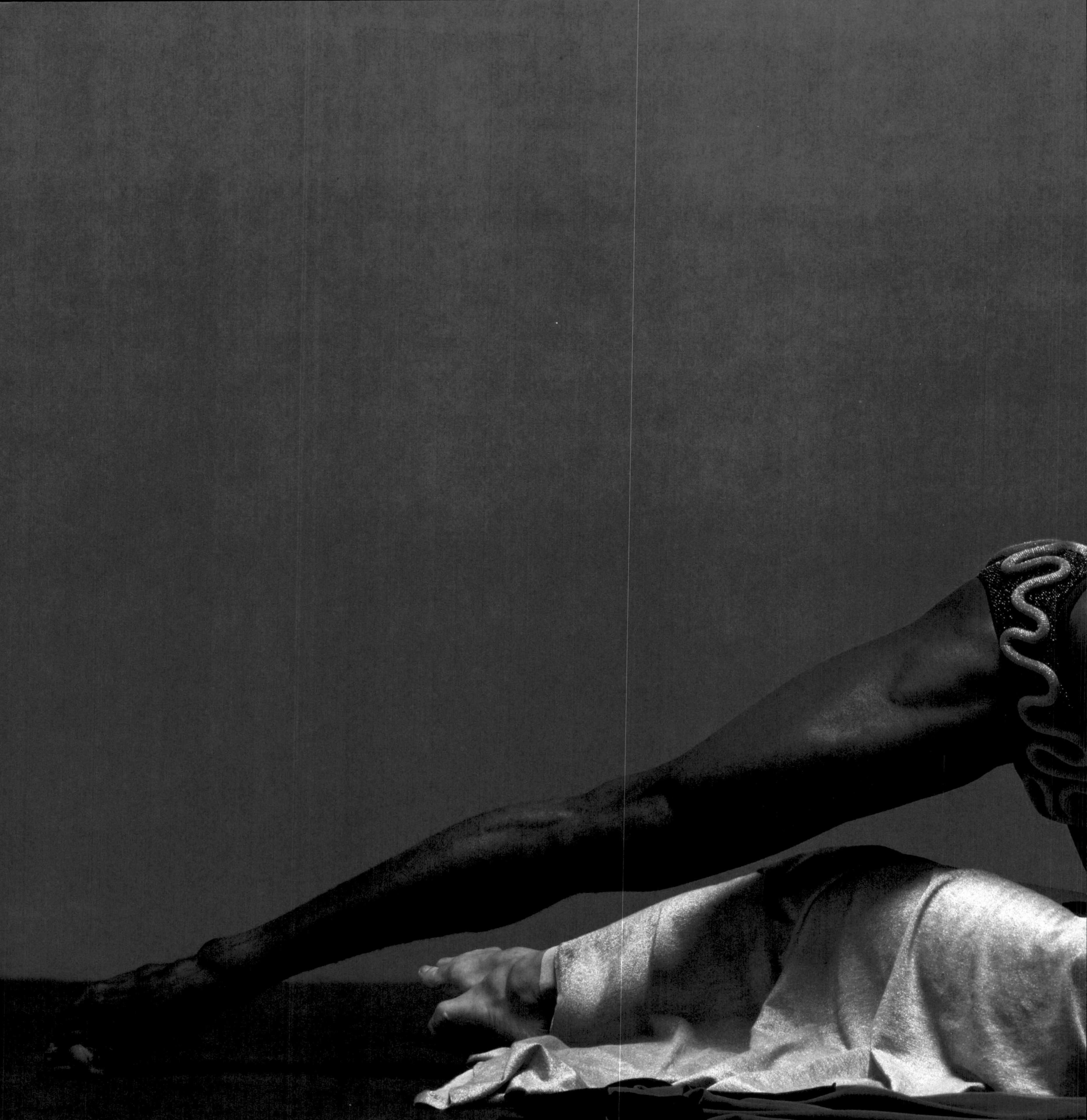

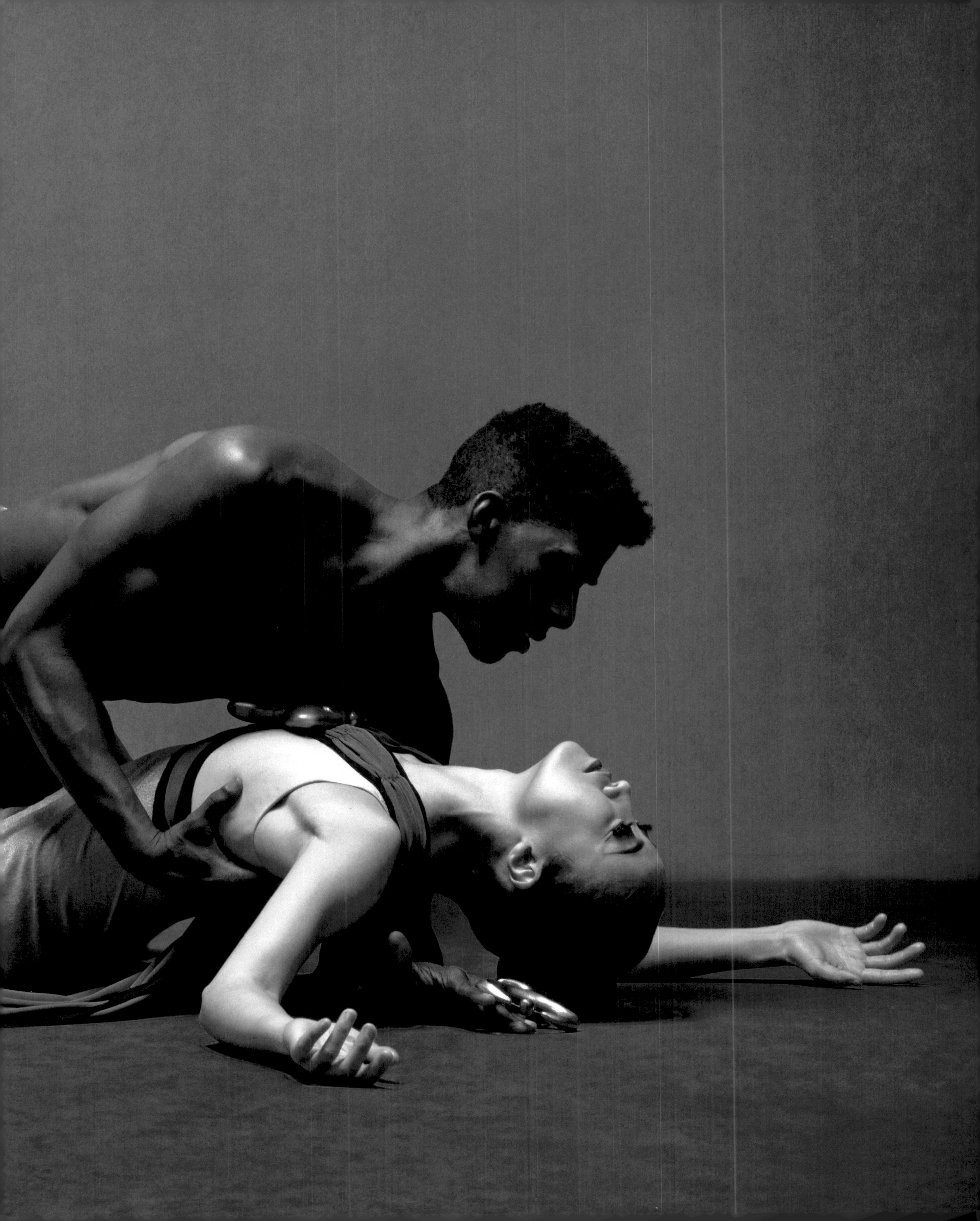

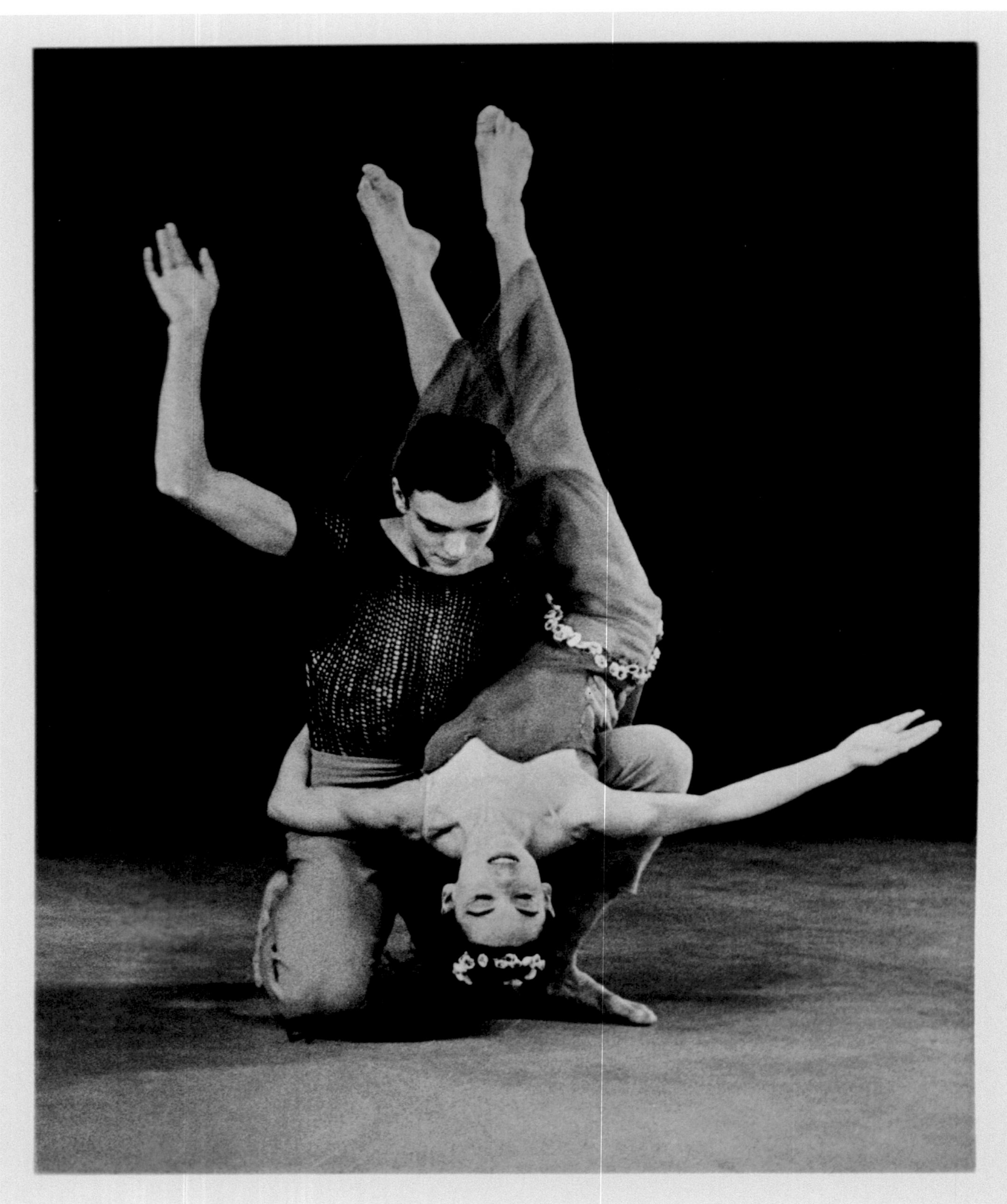

Robert Cohan and Pearl Lang. Photograph by Cris Alexander.

DIVERSION OF ANGELS, 1948

A lyrical paean to three aspects of love.

After a run of dark narrative-based works, Graham reversed course with *Diversion of Angels*, a buoyant, lyrical romp featuring three couples that Graham color-coded in yellow, red, and white to symbolize three aspects of love: capricious young love, passionate romantic love, and deeply devoted mature love. Duets appear out of a kaleidoscope of bold geometric configurations. The women's dresses, designed by Graham, wrap inward at the crotch, an ingenious invention highlighting the dancers' sinuous movement originating at the pelvis. The dancers cartwheel, leap, swoon to the floor, and throw themselves skyward again with abandon. Norman Dello Joio's lyrical score is, like the dance it was commissioned for, a paean to love and mid-century romanticism.

COSTUME DESIGN
Martha Graham

COMPOSER
Norman Dello Joio

Diversion of Angels

COUPLE IN WHITE
Leslie Andrea Williams and Lorenzo Pagano

COUPLE IN RED
Anne O'Donnell Passero and Lloyd Knight

COUPLE IN YELLOW
Laurel Dalley Smith and Jacob Larsen

CHORUS
So Young An, Alessio Crognale-Roberts,
Marzia Memoli, Anne Souder, Richard Villaverde

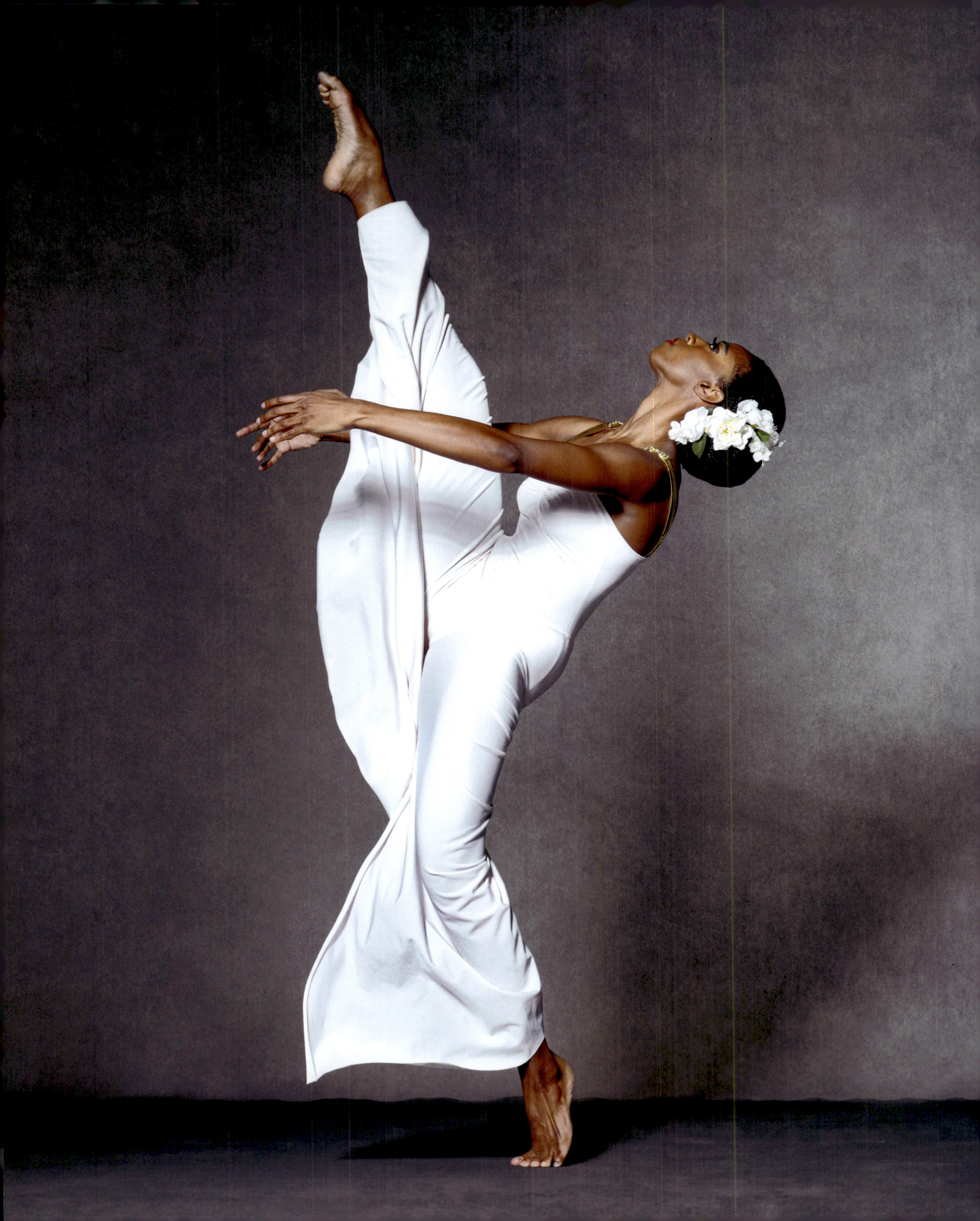

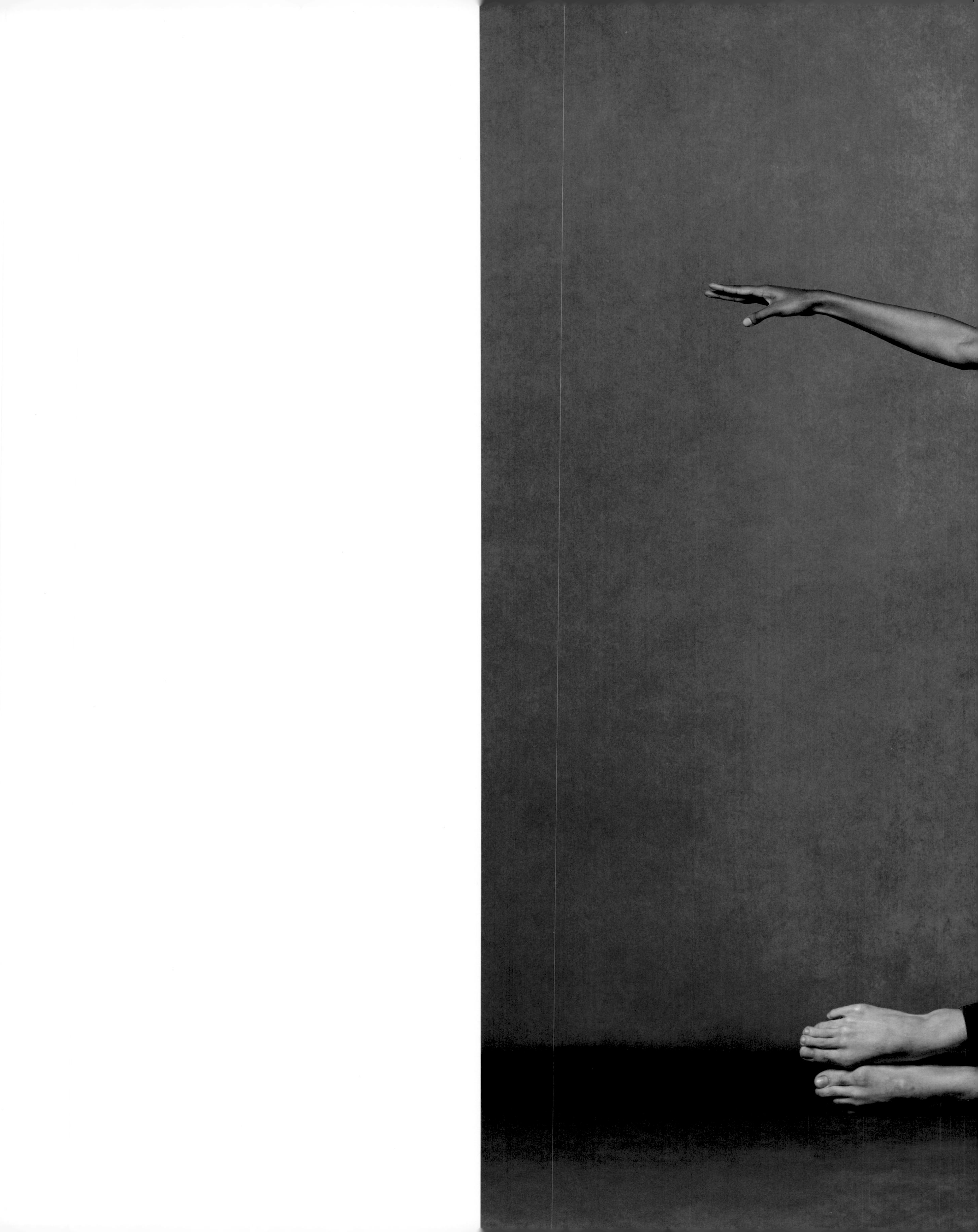

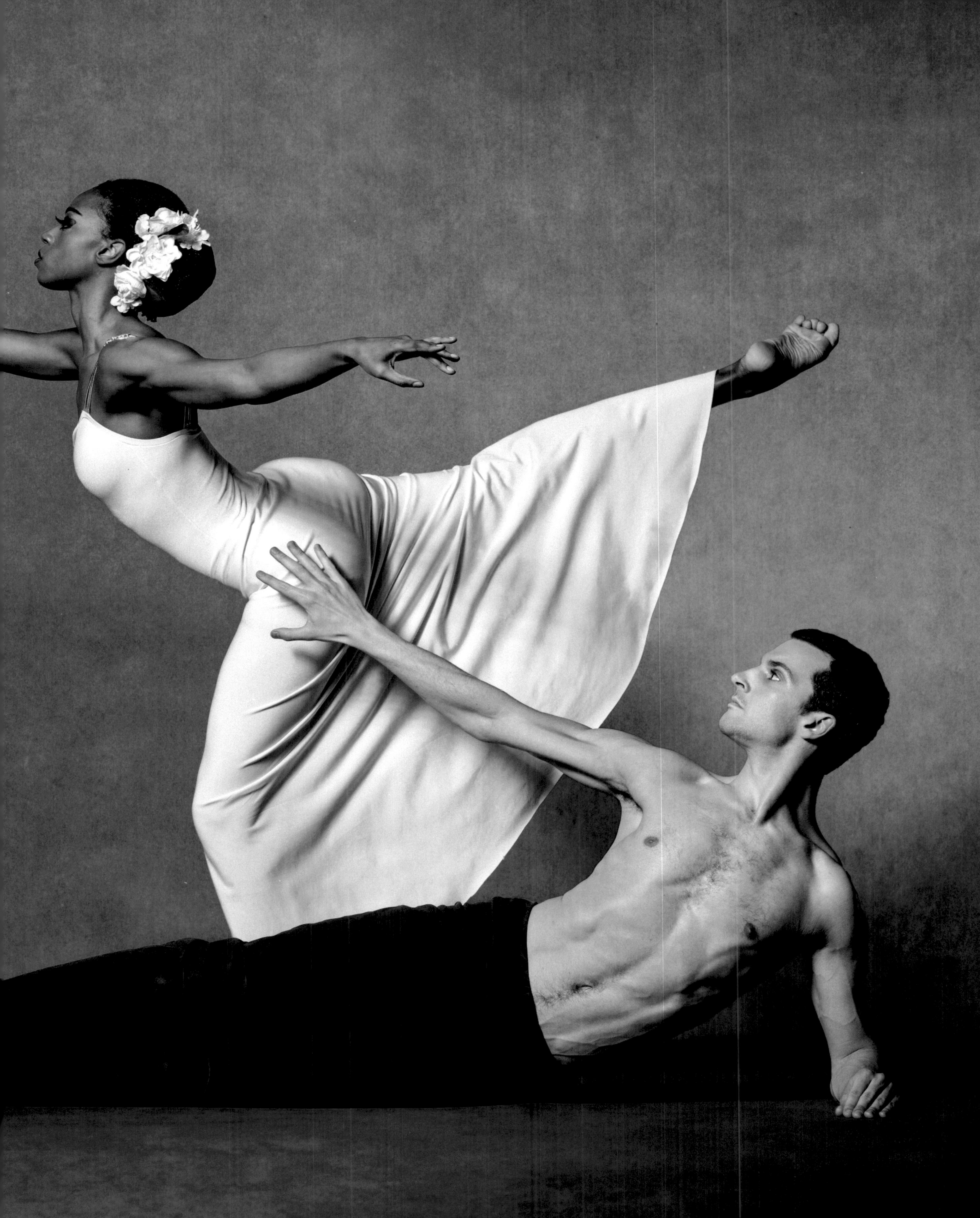

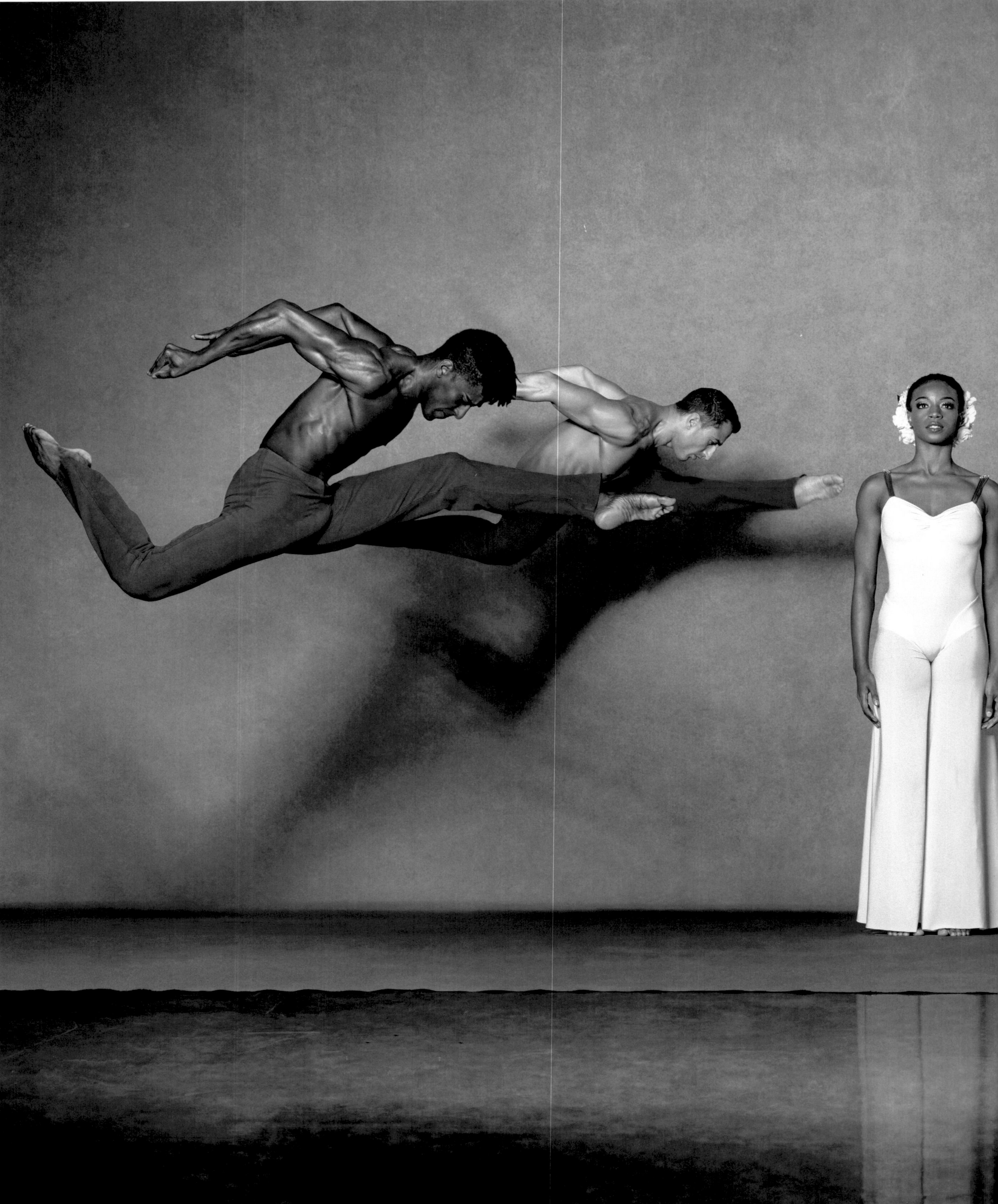

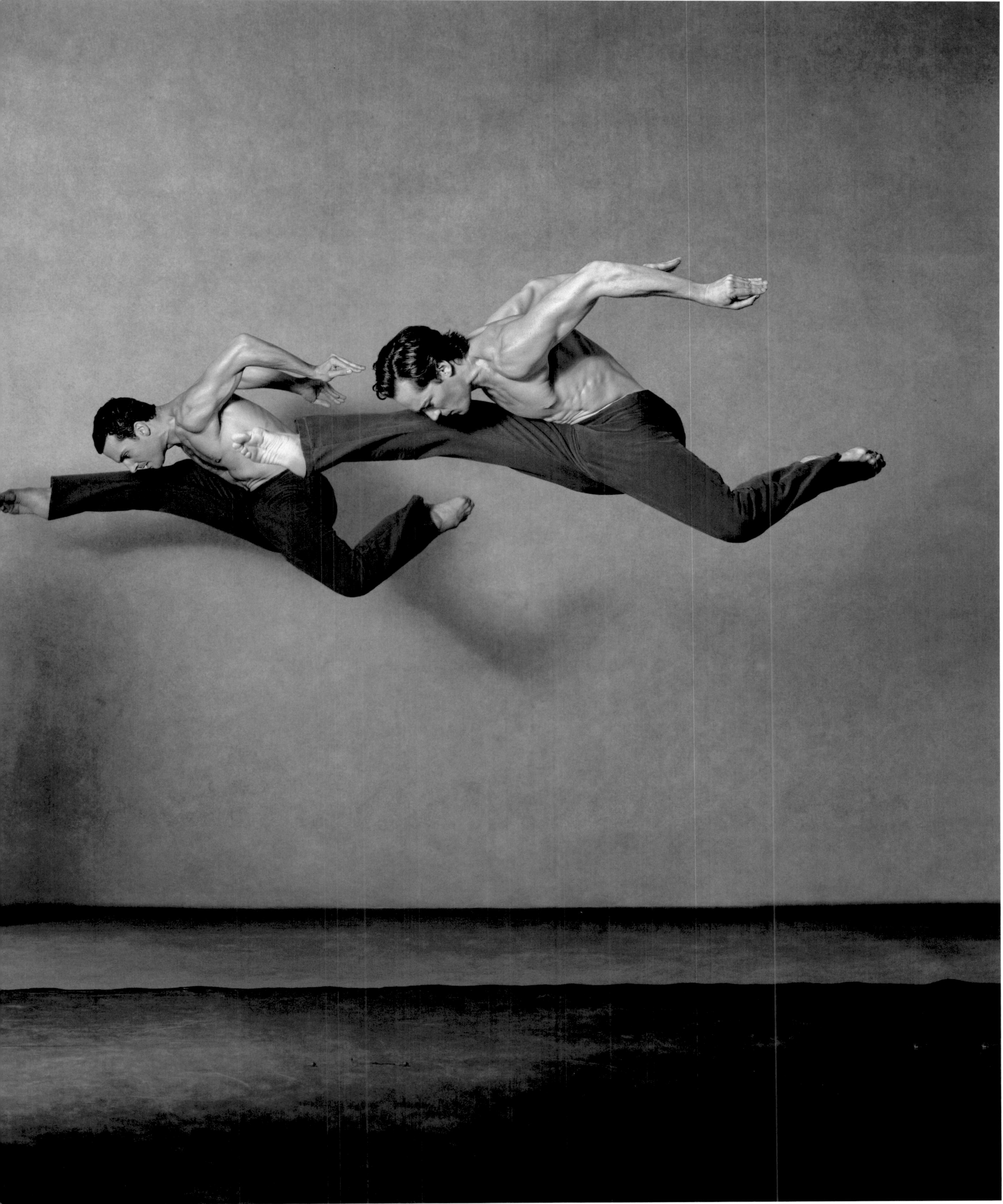

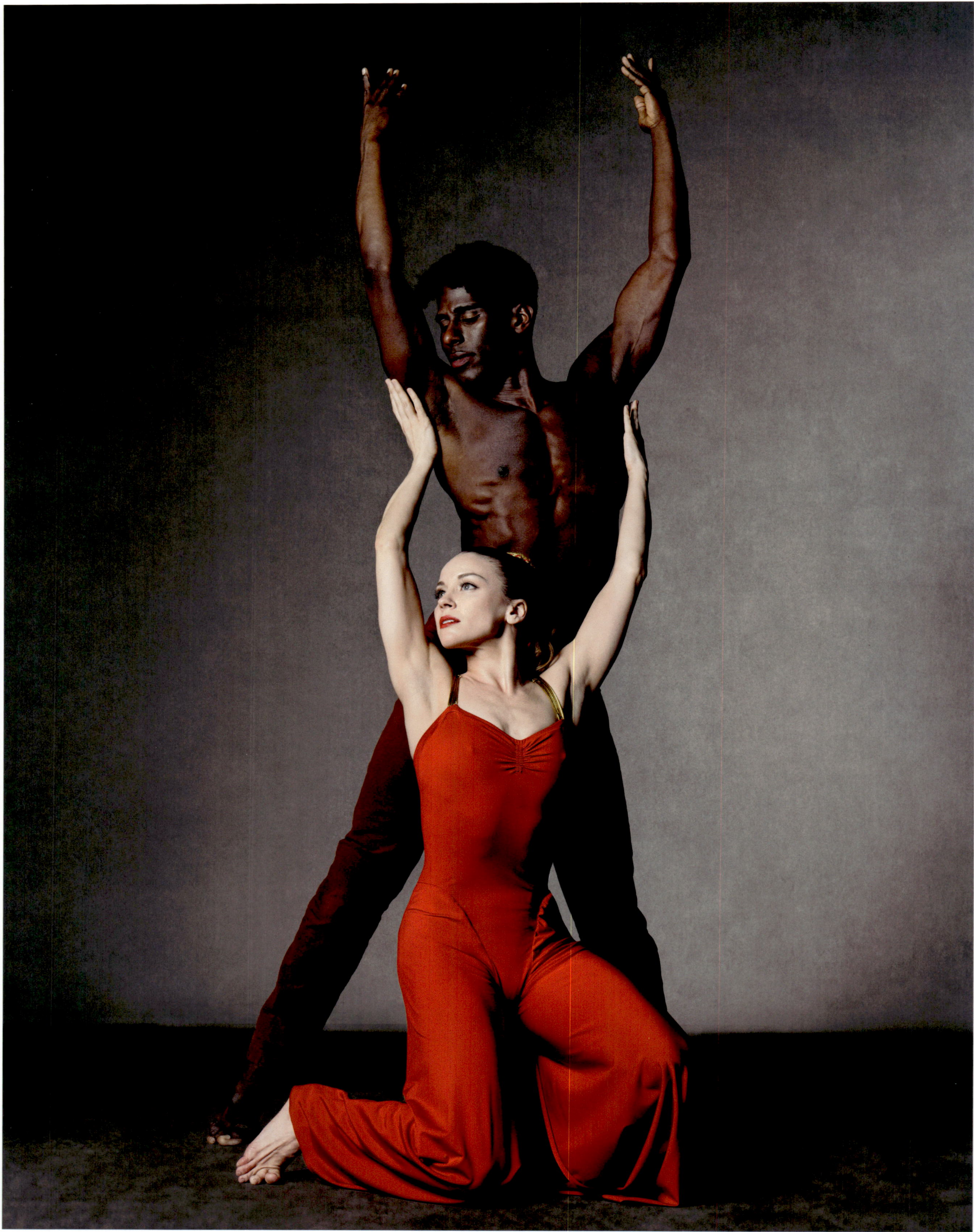

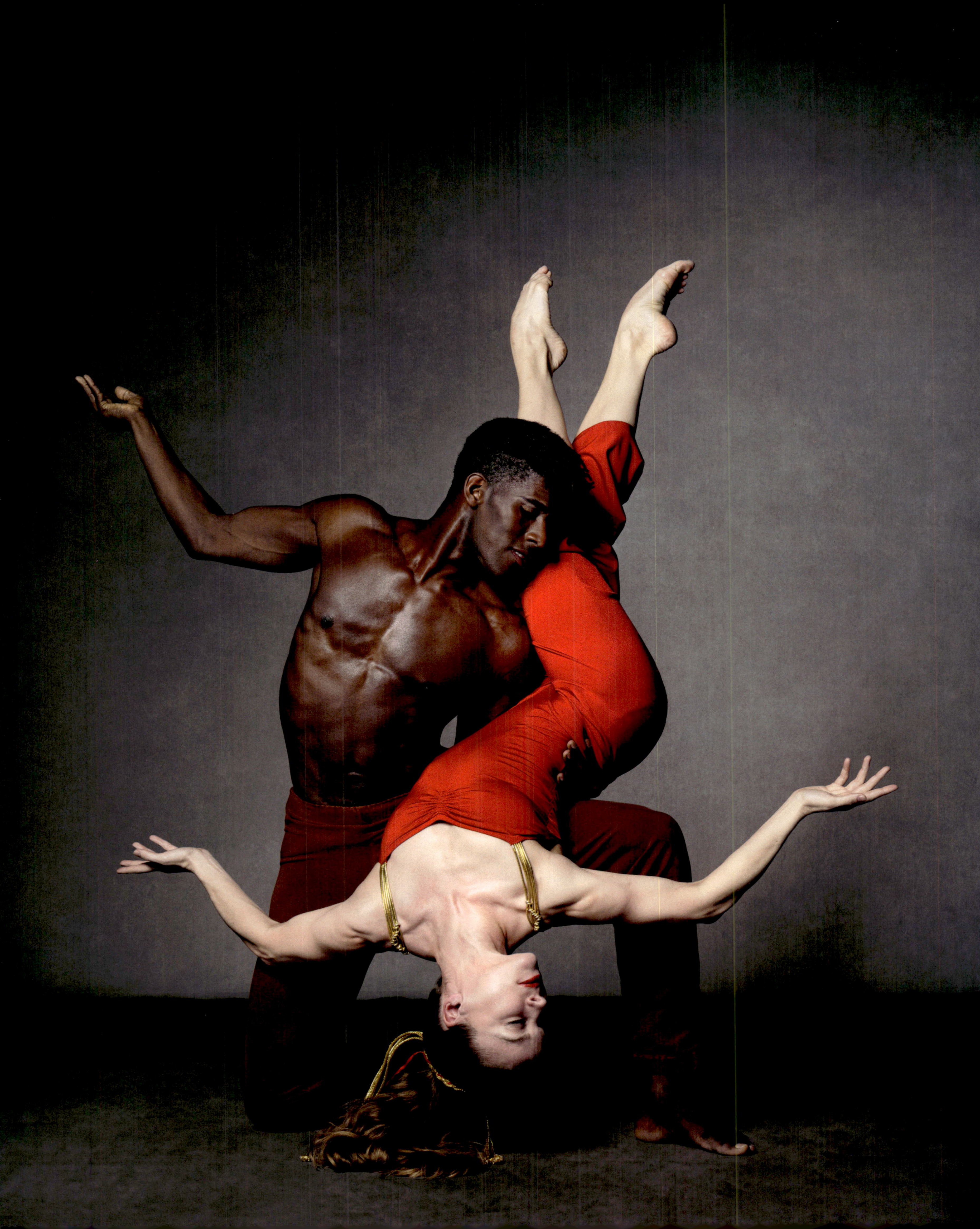

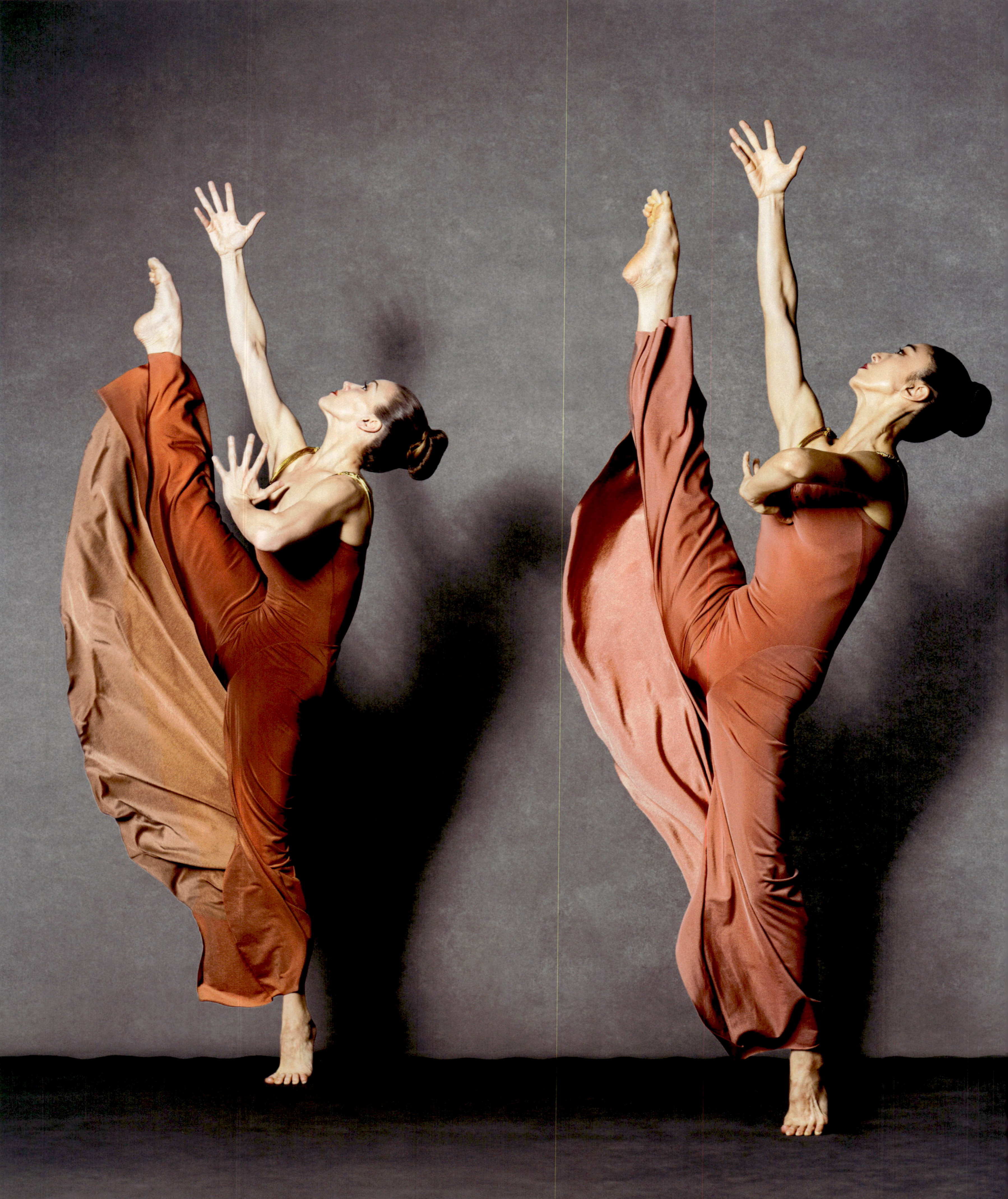

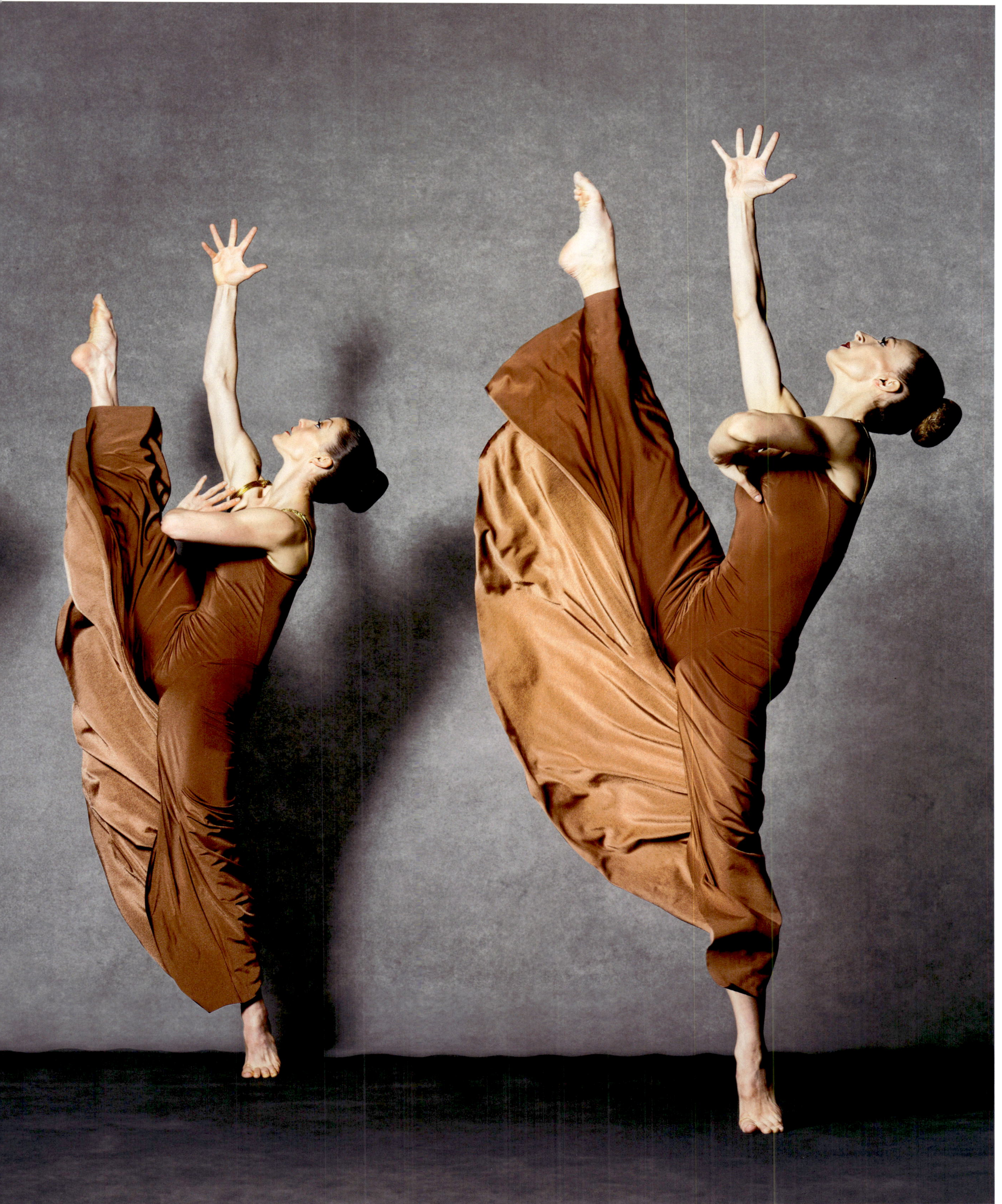

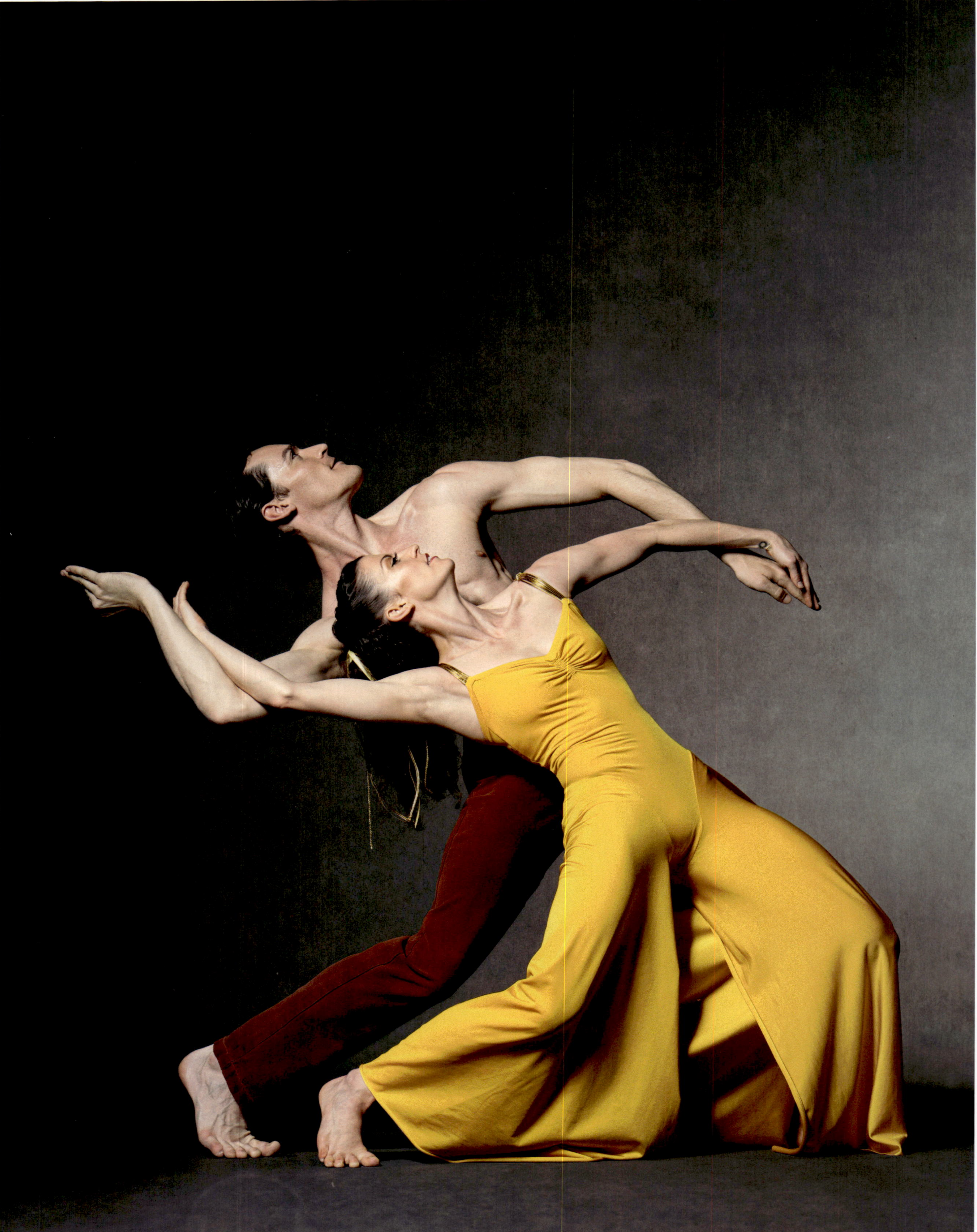

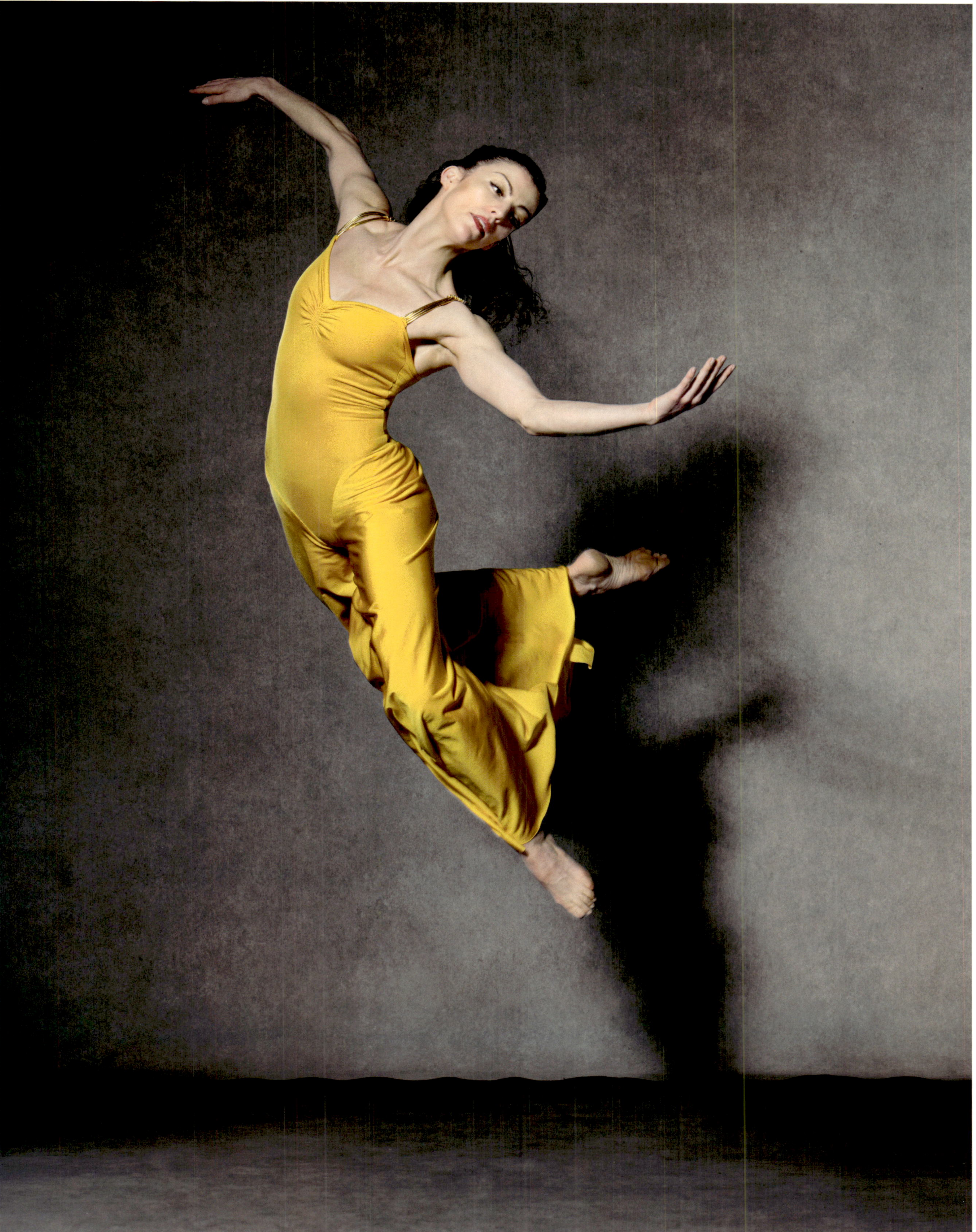

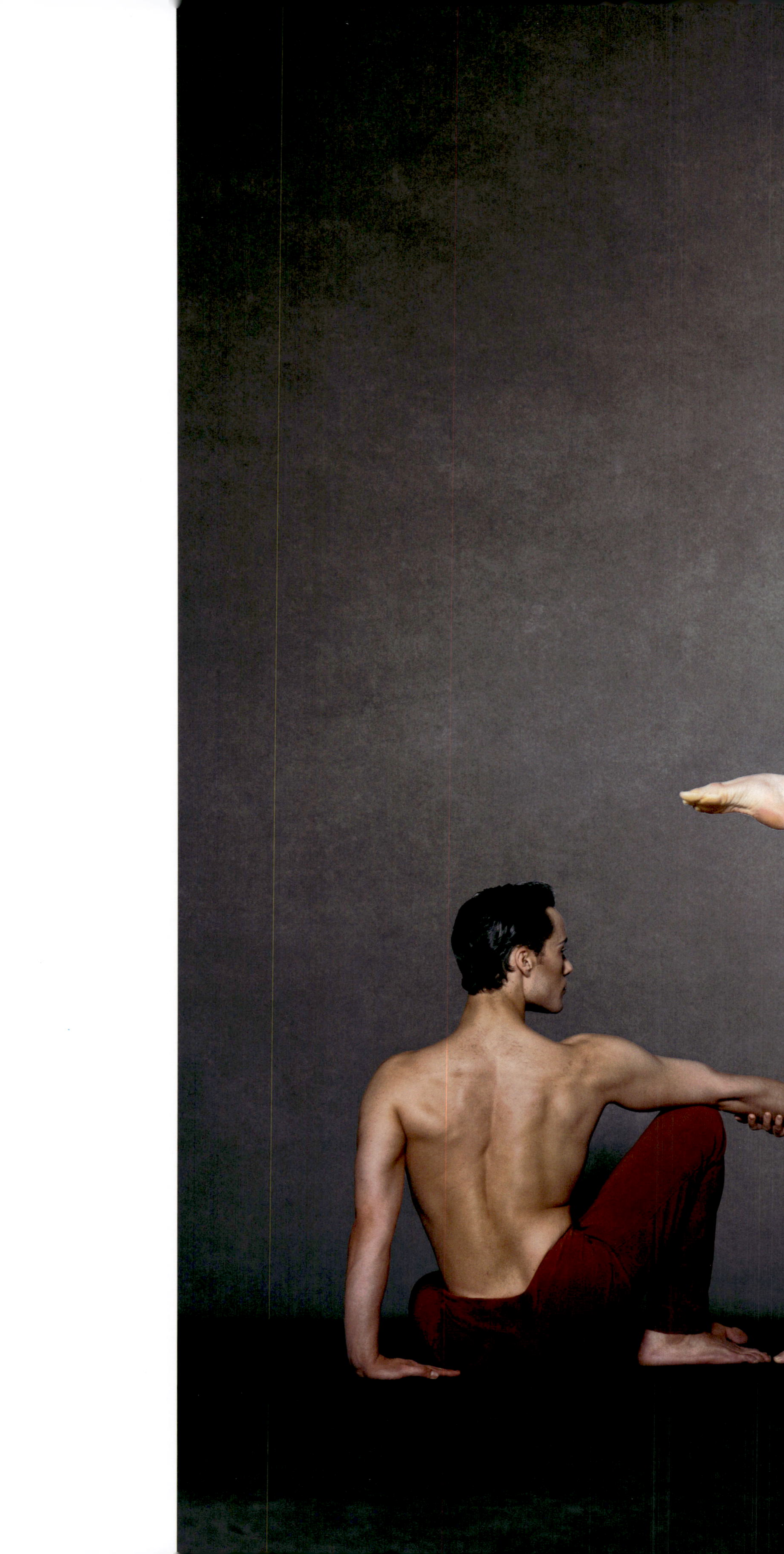

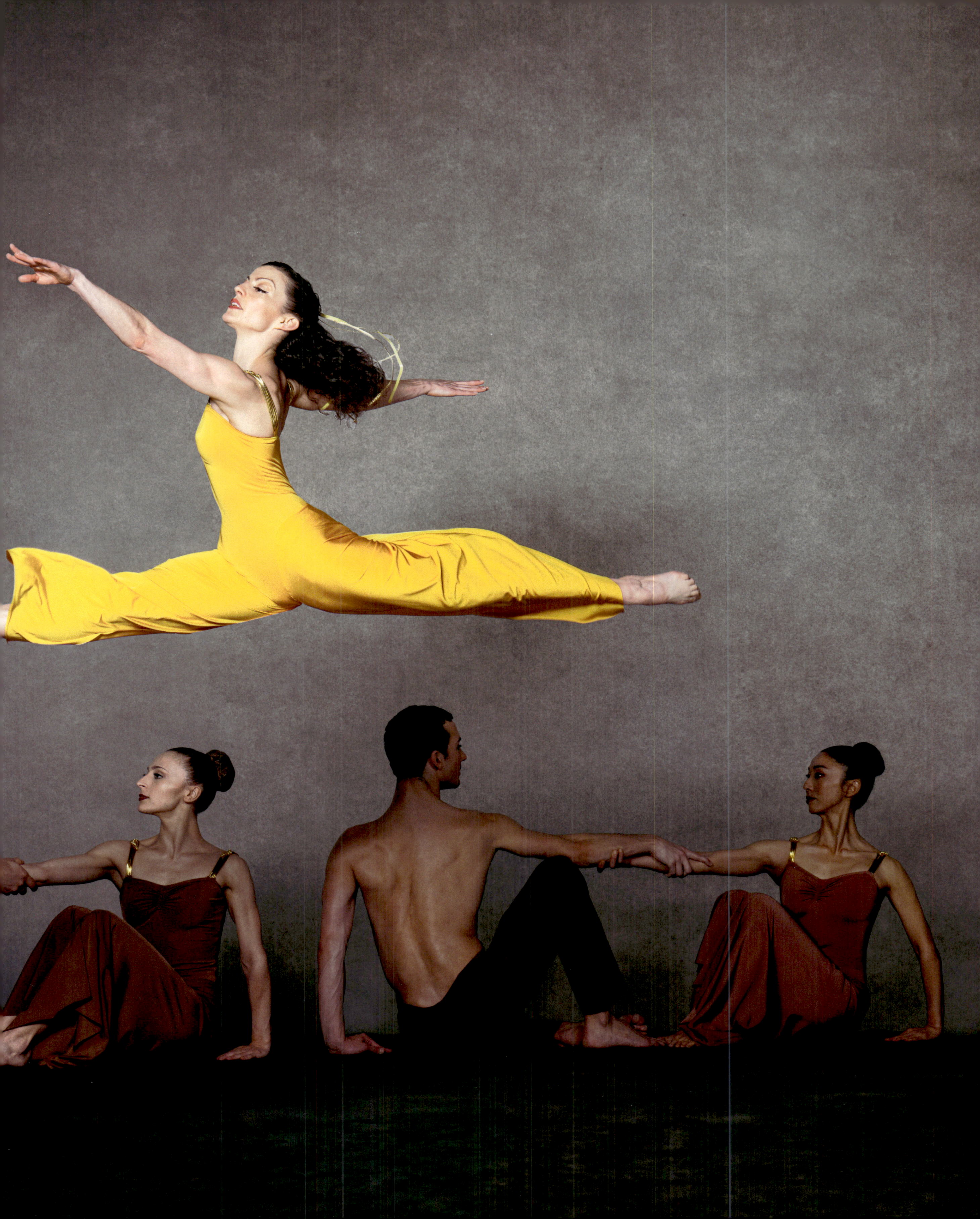

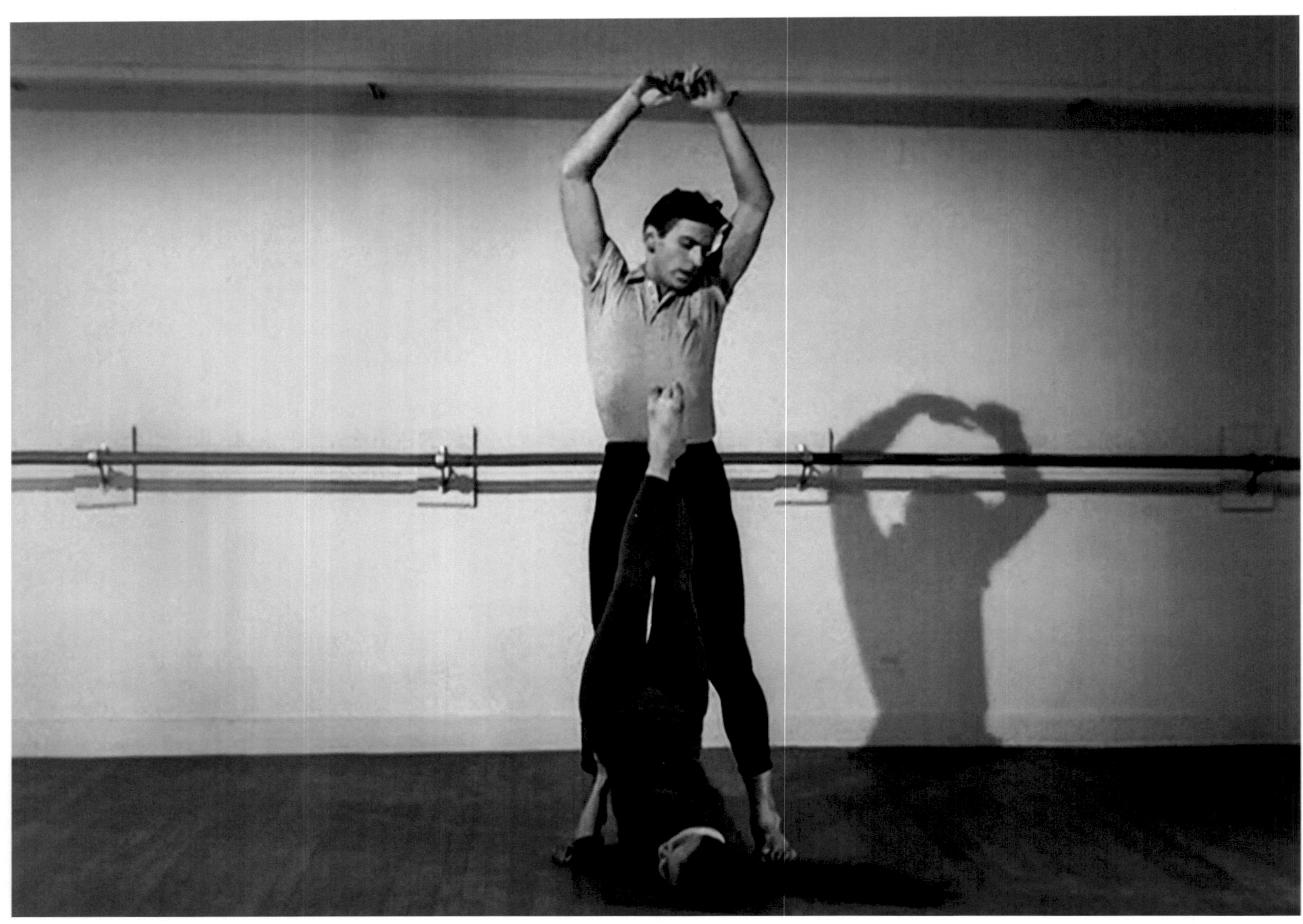

Bertram Ross and Yuriko. Photographer unknown.

MOON DUET FROM "CANTICLE FOR INNOCENT COMEDIANS," 1952

A couple embodies Sun and Moon in a lyrical duet excerpted from the larger work.

Finding inspiration from a poem by Ben Belitt of the same title, Graham cast the five elements of Saint Francis of Assisi with her lead dancers, making for them a series of solos and duets that embodied the Sun, Moon, Stars, Wind, Water, Fire, Earth, and Death. A duet for Brother Sun and Sister Moon has since been excerpted often to showcase Graham at her most gentle and lyrical. Moon moves with scalloped curves as if carving out a path along which the Sun follows close behind, echoing her every gesture. She lies back into his lap and is rocked gently in his cradle. He lifts her in a repeated sweeping motion, drawing circles in the space with her crescent-shaped arms as she lifts both feet and bends her knees, as if gently leaping then floating in air.

SET DESIGN
Frederick Kiesler

COSTUME DESIGN
Martha Graham

COMPOSER
Thomas Ribbink

Moon Duet from
"Canticle for Innocent Comedians"

DANCERS

Jacob Larsen and Anne O'Donnell Passero

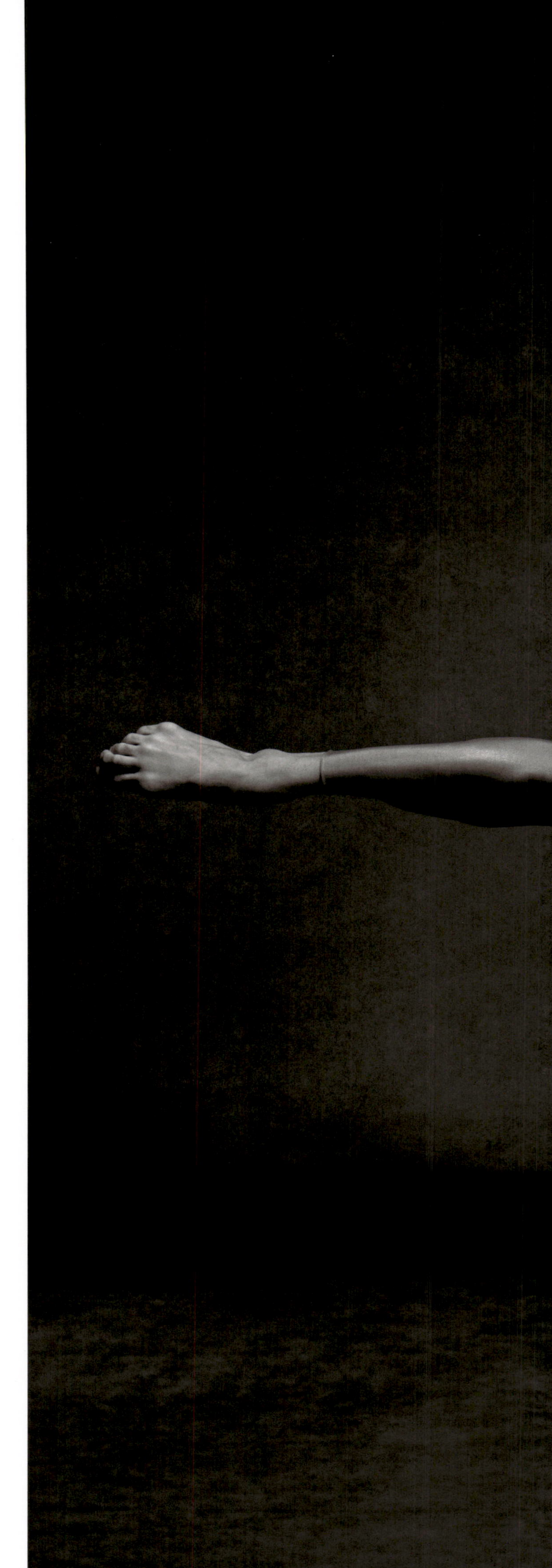

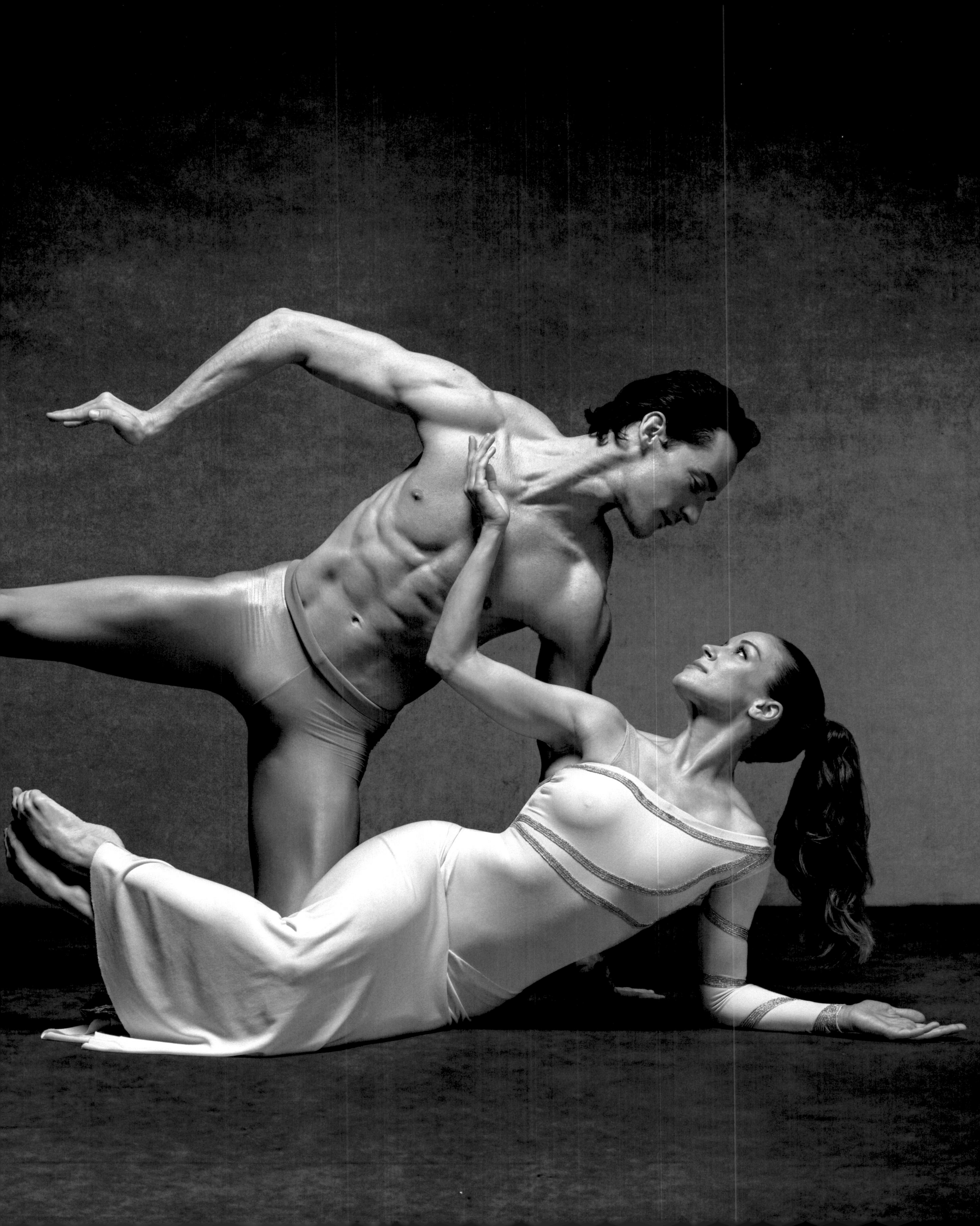

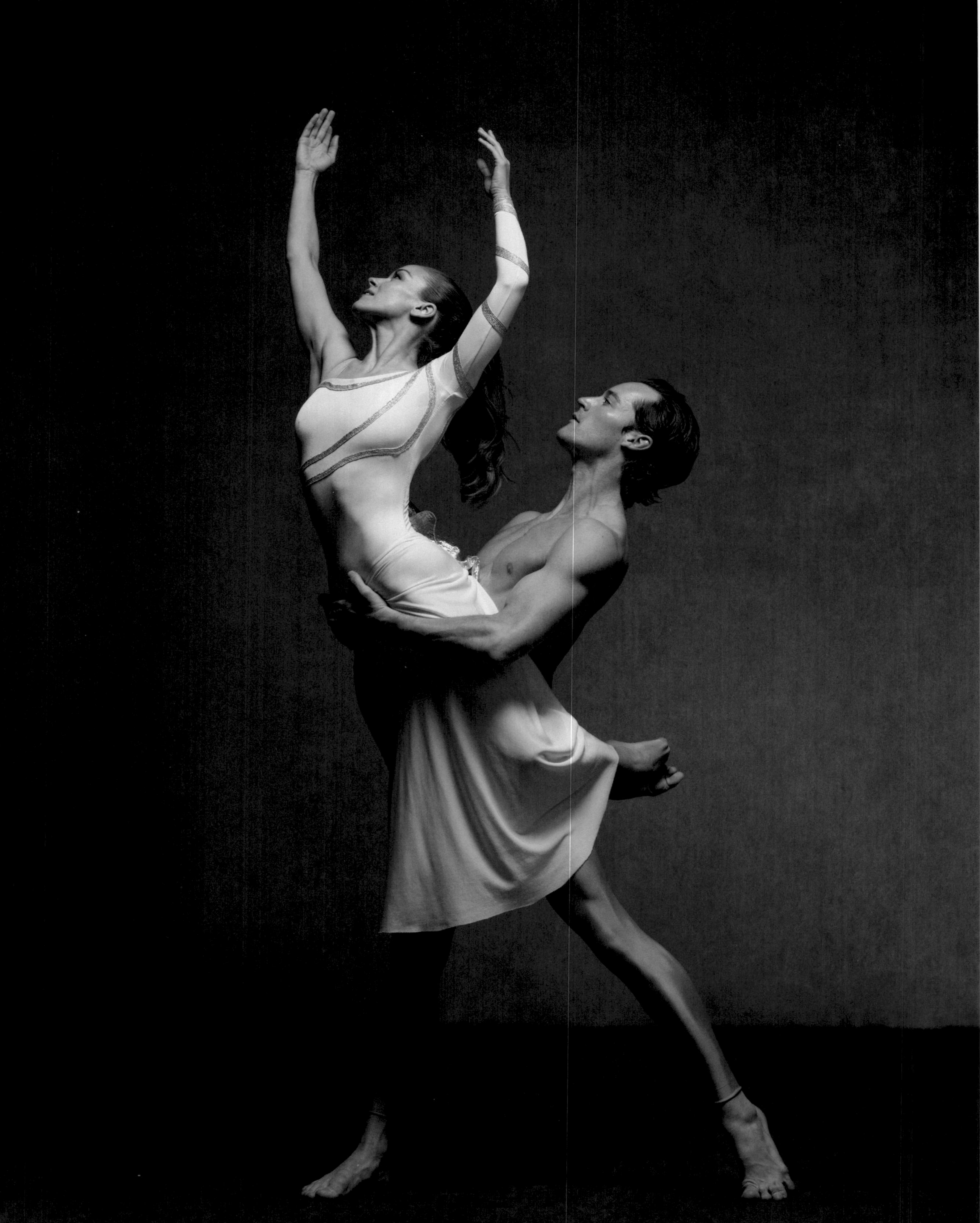

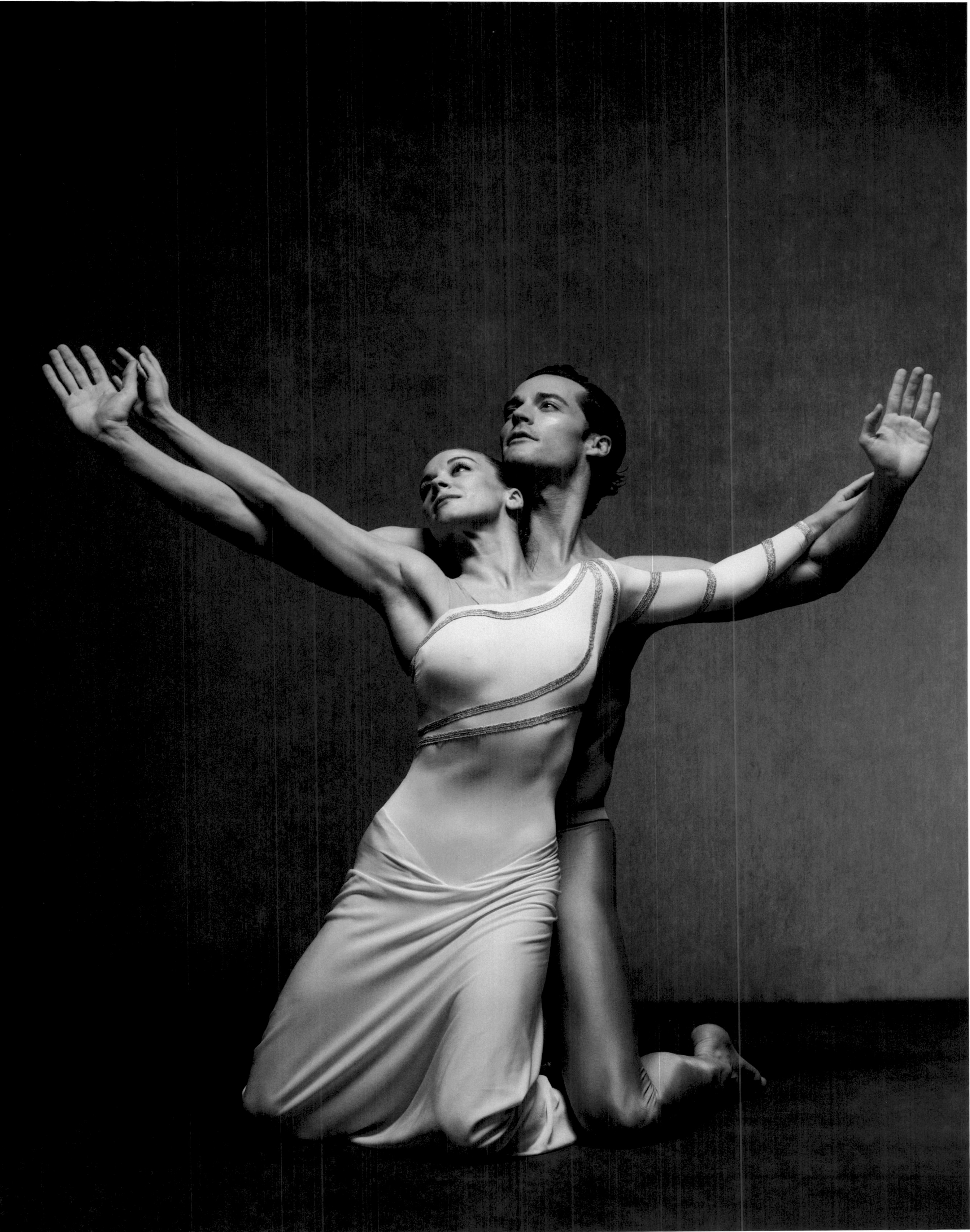

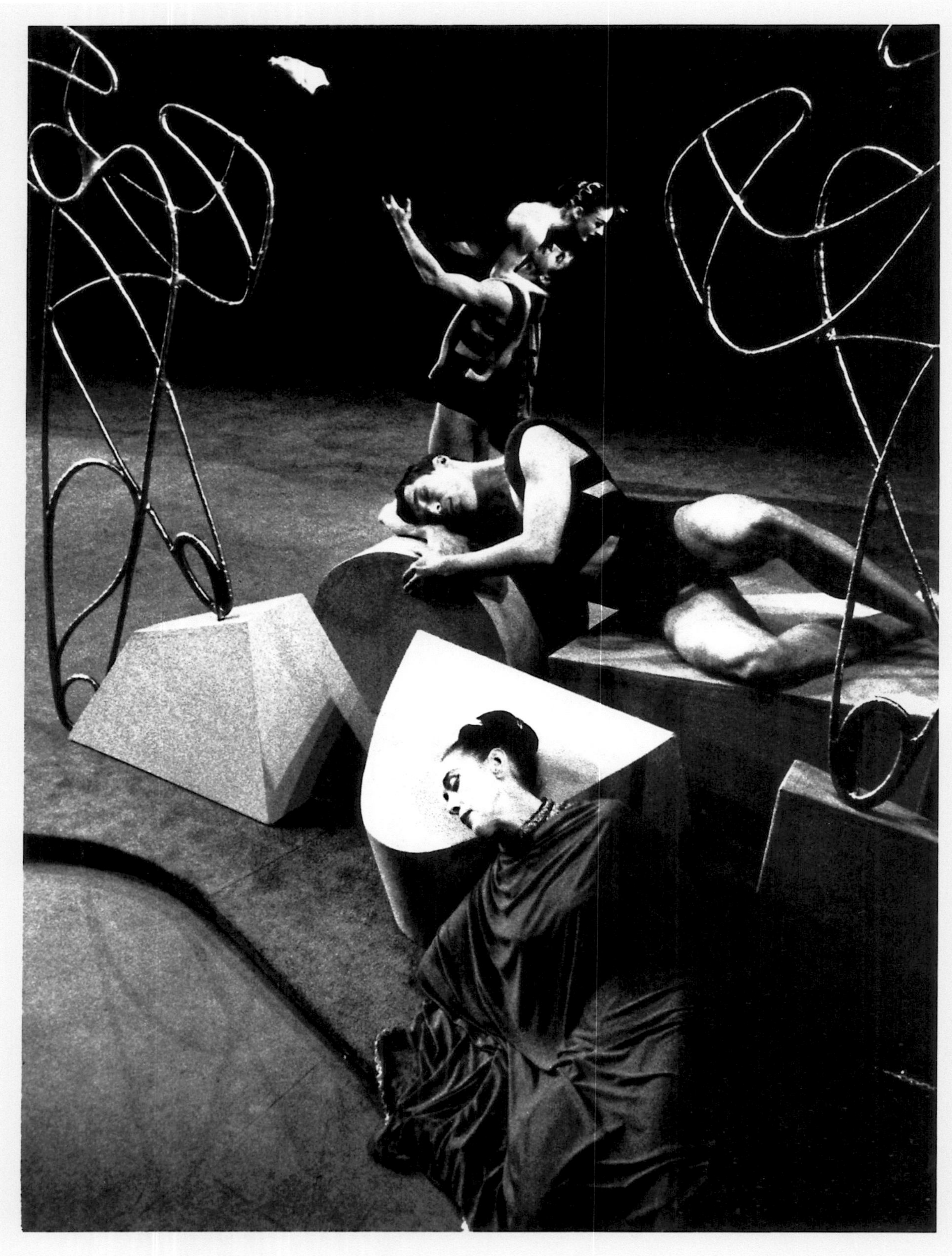

Martha Graham, Paul Taylor, Helen McGehee, and Bertram Ross. Photograph by Burt Glinn.

CLYTEMNESTRA, 1958

An epic danced interpretation of the fall of the House of Atreus.

Graham's only full-evening work is based on events depicted in the *Oresteia* by Aeschylus. She brilliantly upends the chronology of the original to bring us the story retold by Queen Clytemnestra as she argues her final fate with Hades in the Underworld. Defending her own actions, the panoramic spectacle weaves a treacherous tale of murder, revenge, and atonement involving her husband, Agamemnon, and their children Orestes and Electra.

Scenes from her memory play out, frieze-like, across the stage as the dancers portray the harrowing events of the Trojan War and its aftermath: the abduction of beautiful Helen by Paris of Troy; Agamemnon's murder of their daughter, Iphigenia; the destruction of Troy; Clytemnestra's plot to murder Agamemnon; and Orestes's agonizing decision, goaded on by his sister, Electra, to seek revenge on his mother for the murder of their father.

Halim El-Dabh's raw, jagged musical score constantly teases impending tragedy, while Isamu Noguchi's set creates a shifting and evocative architectural frame.

SET DESIGN
Isamu Noguchi

COSTUME DESIGN
Martha Graham,
Helen McGehee, Bertram Ross

COMPOSER
Halim El-Dabh

Clytemnestra

CLYTEMNESTRA
Anne Souder

MESSENGER OF DEATH
Lloyd Knight

NIGHT WATCHMAN
Alessio Crognale-Roberts

ELECTRA
Marzia Memoli

ORESTES
Lloyd Knight

COSTUME DESIGN, NIGHT WATCHMAN
Halston

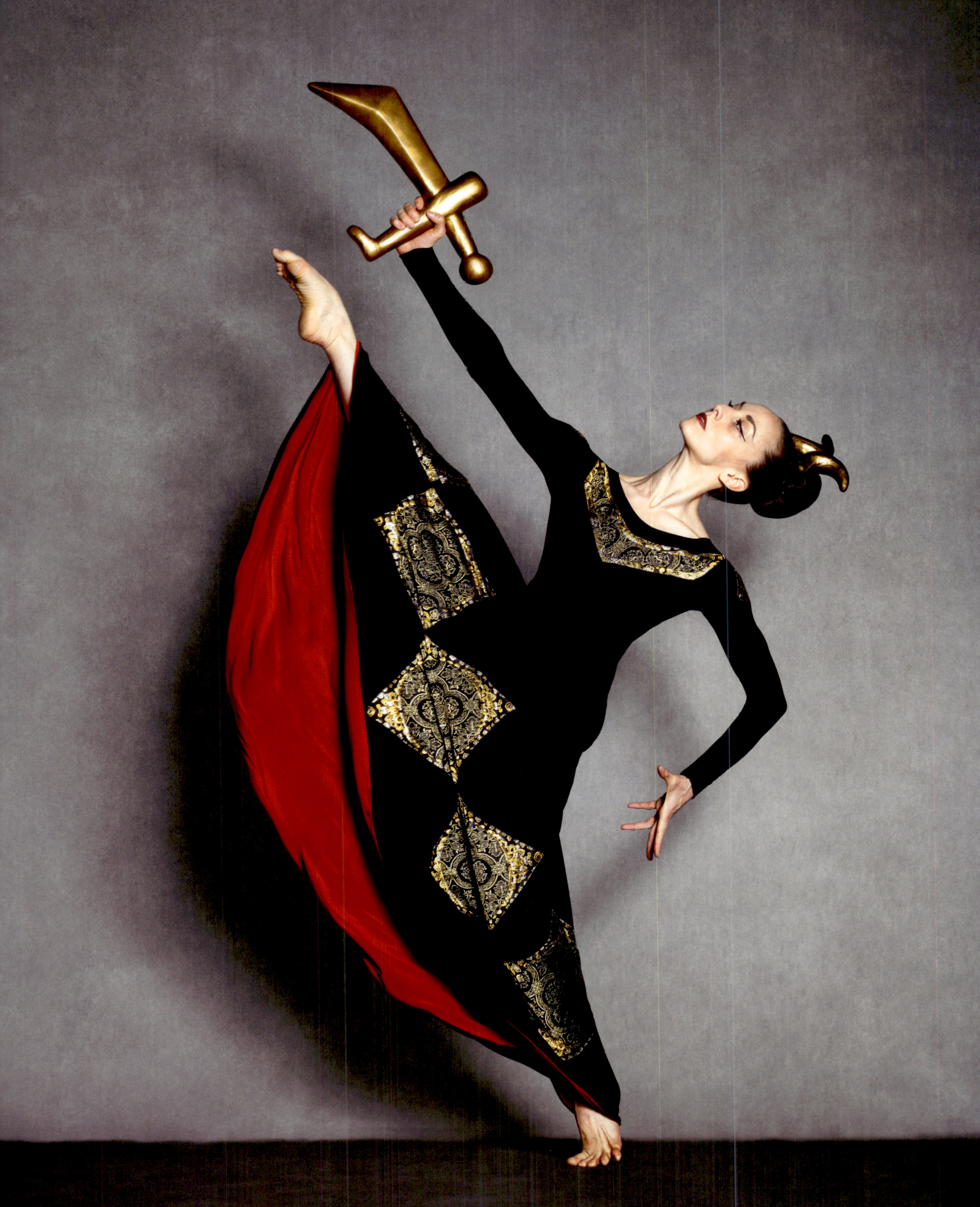

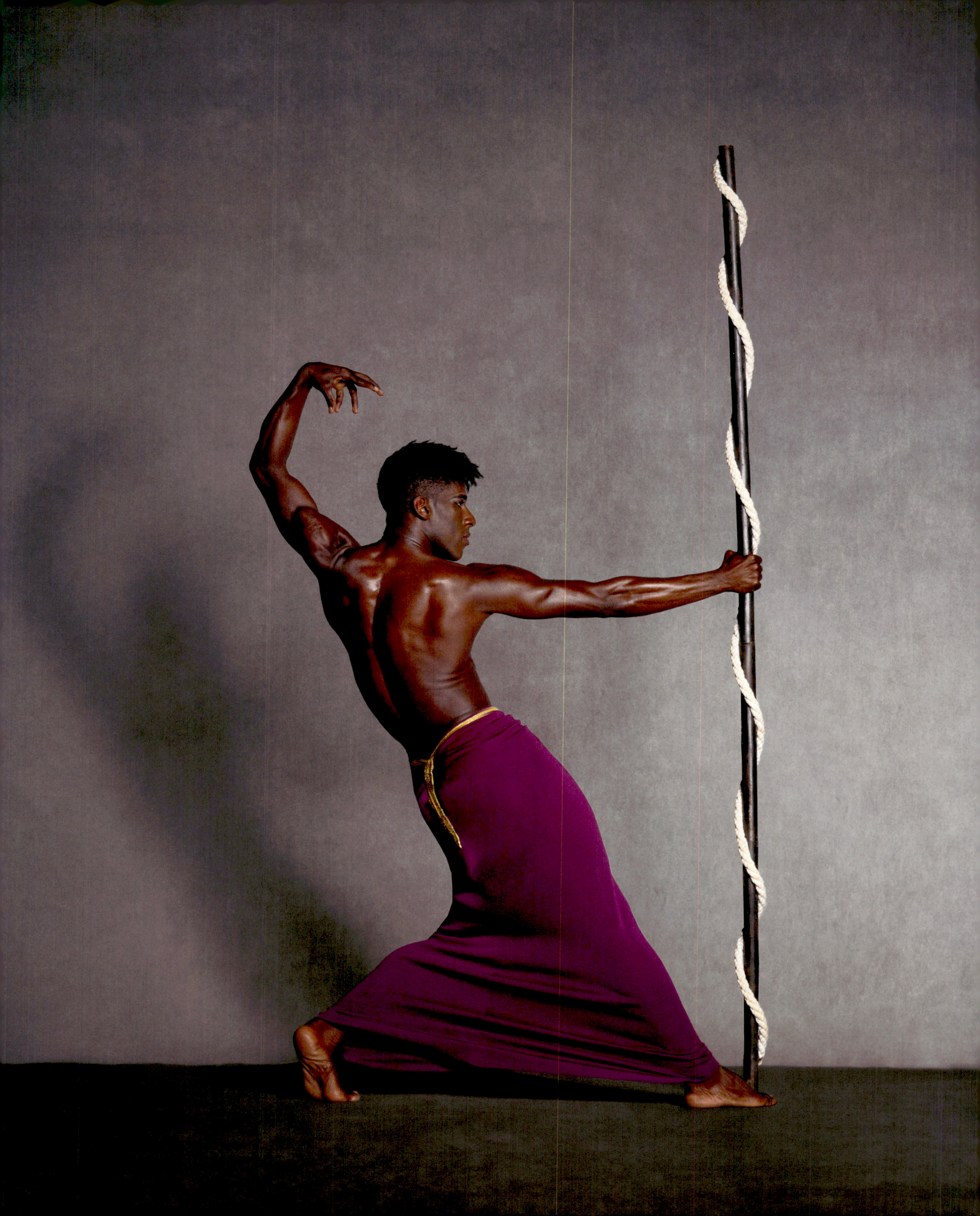

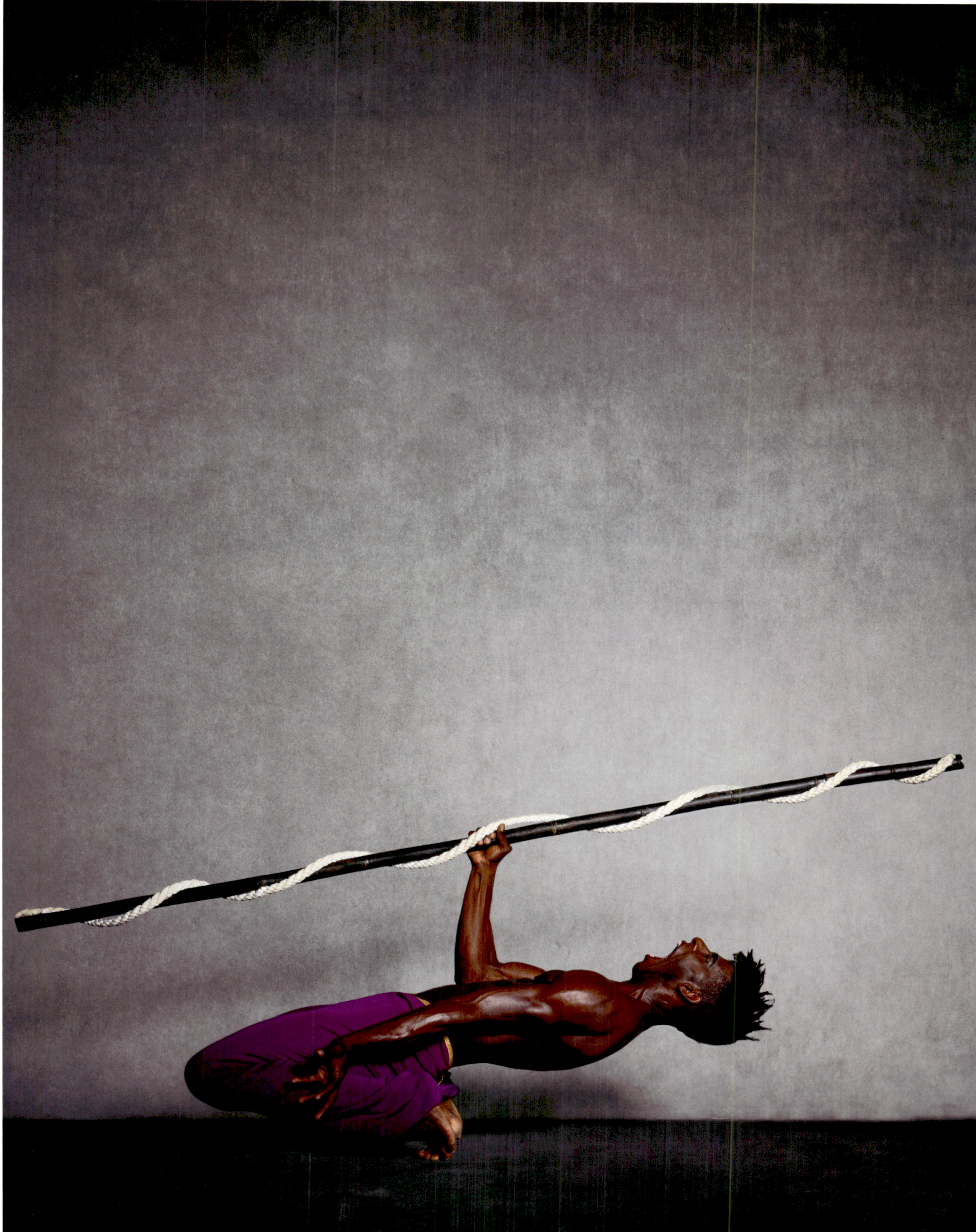

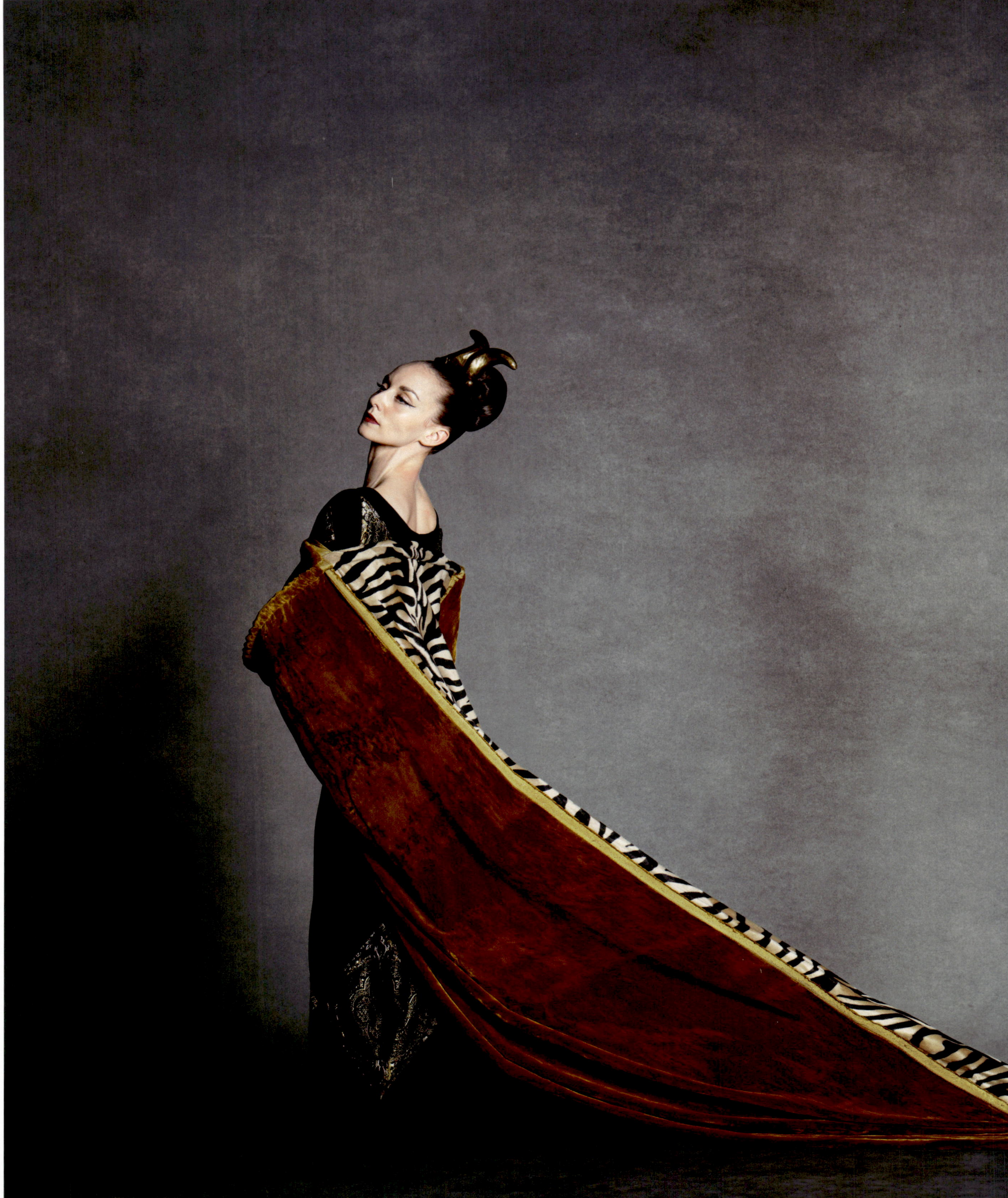

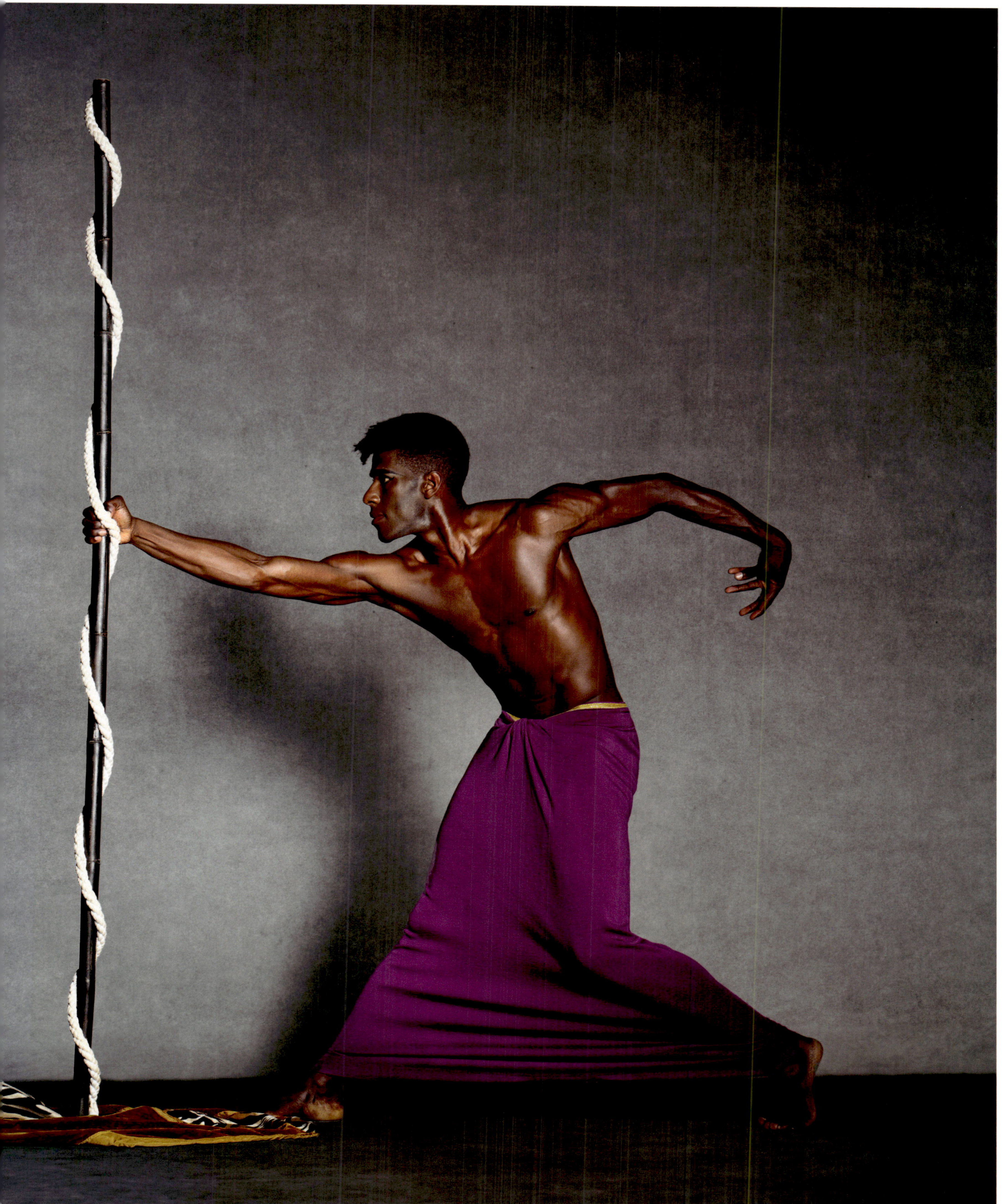

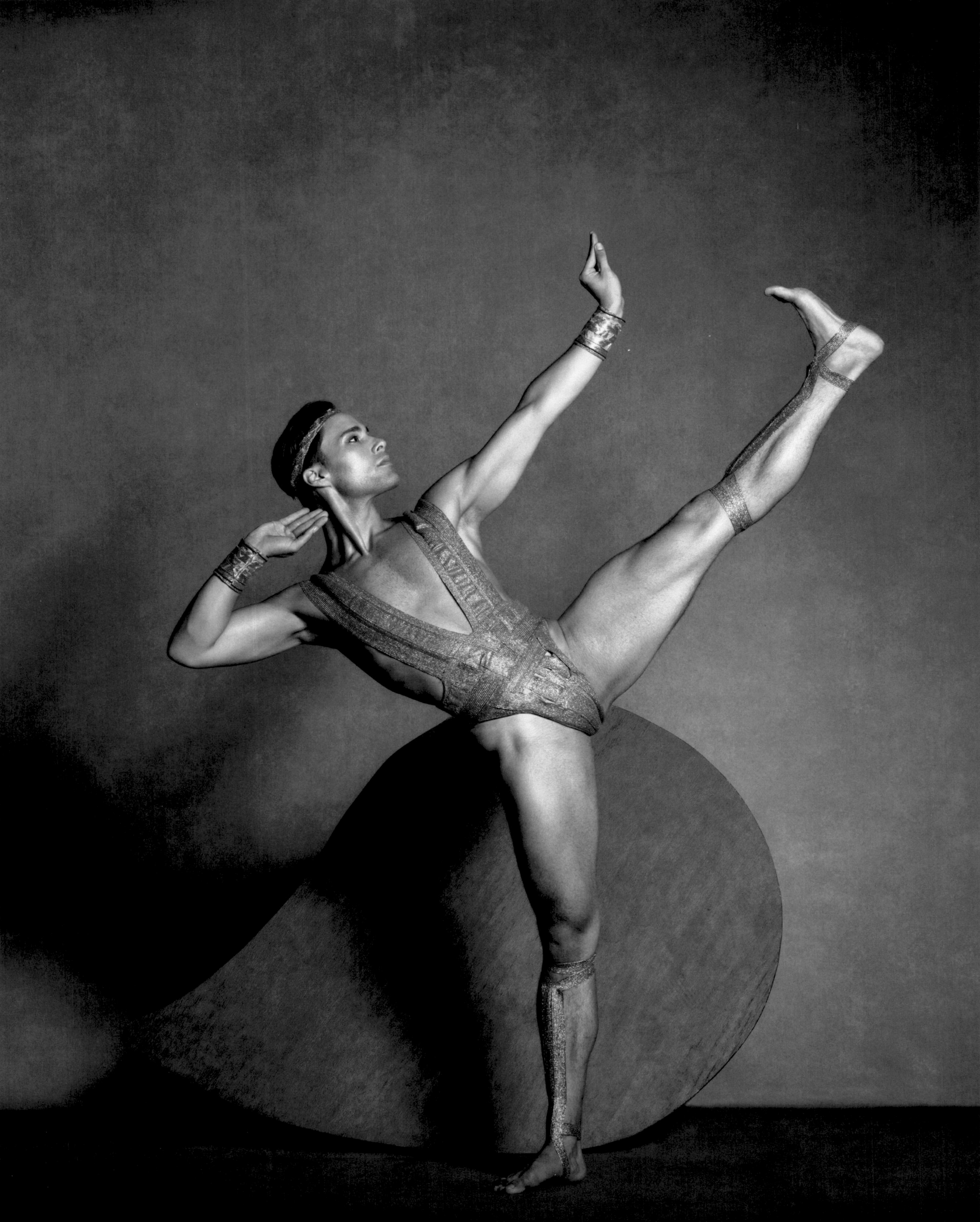

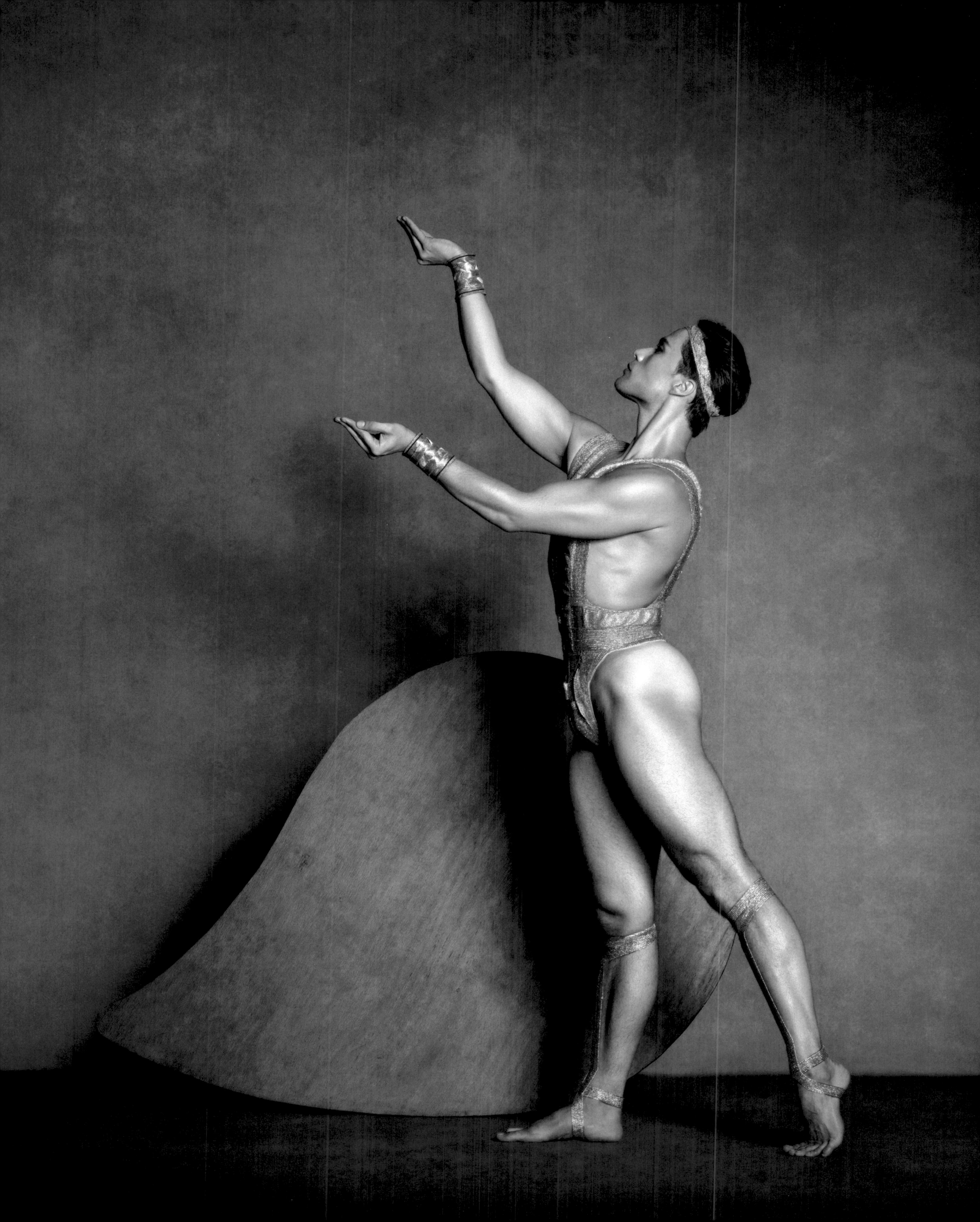

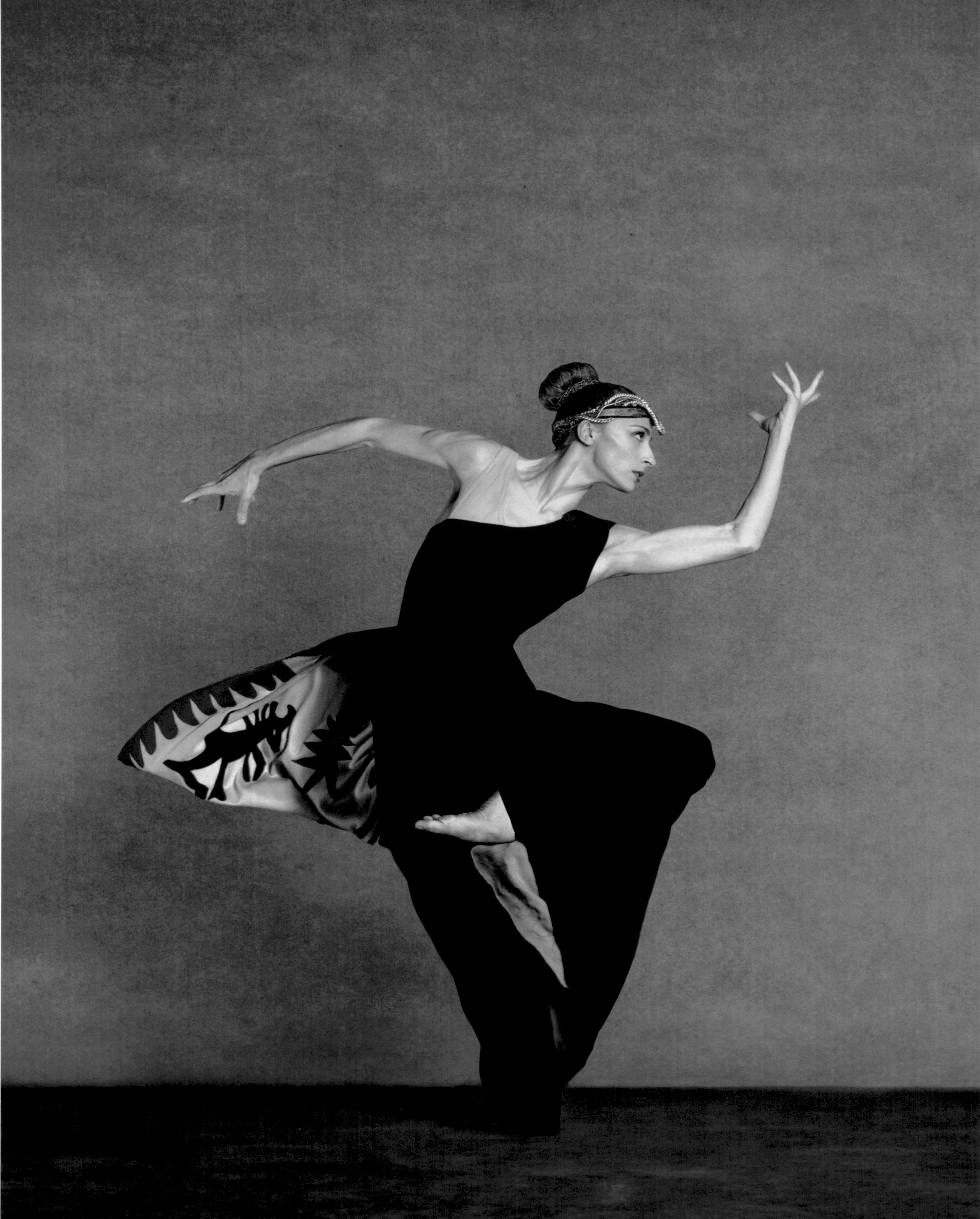

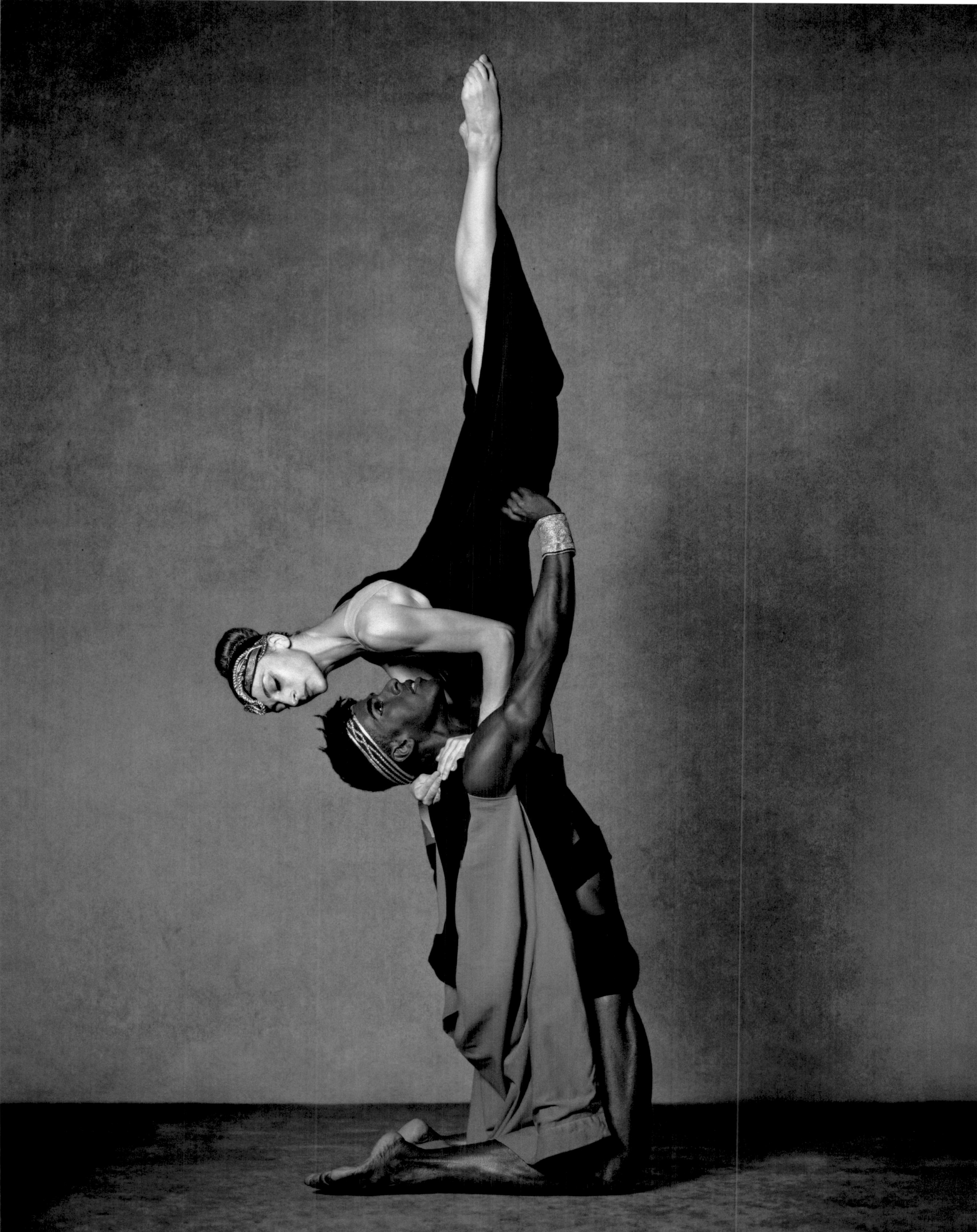

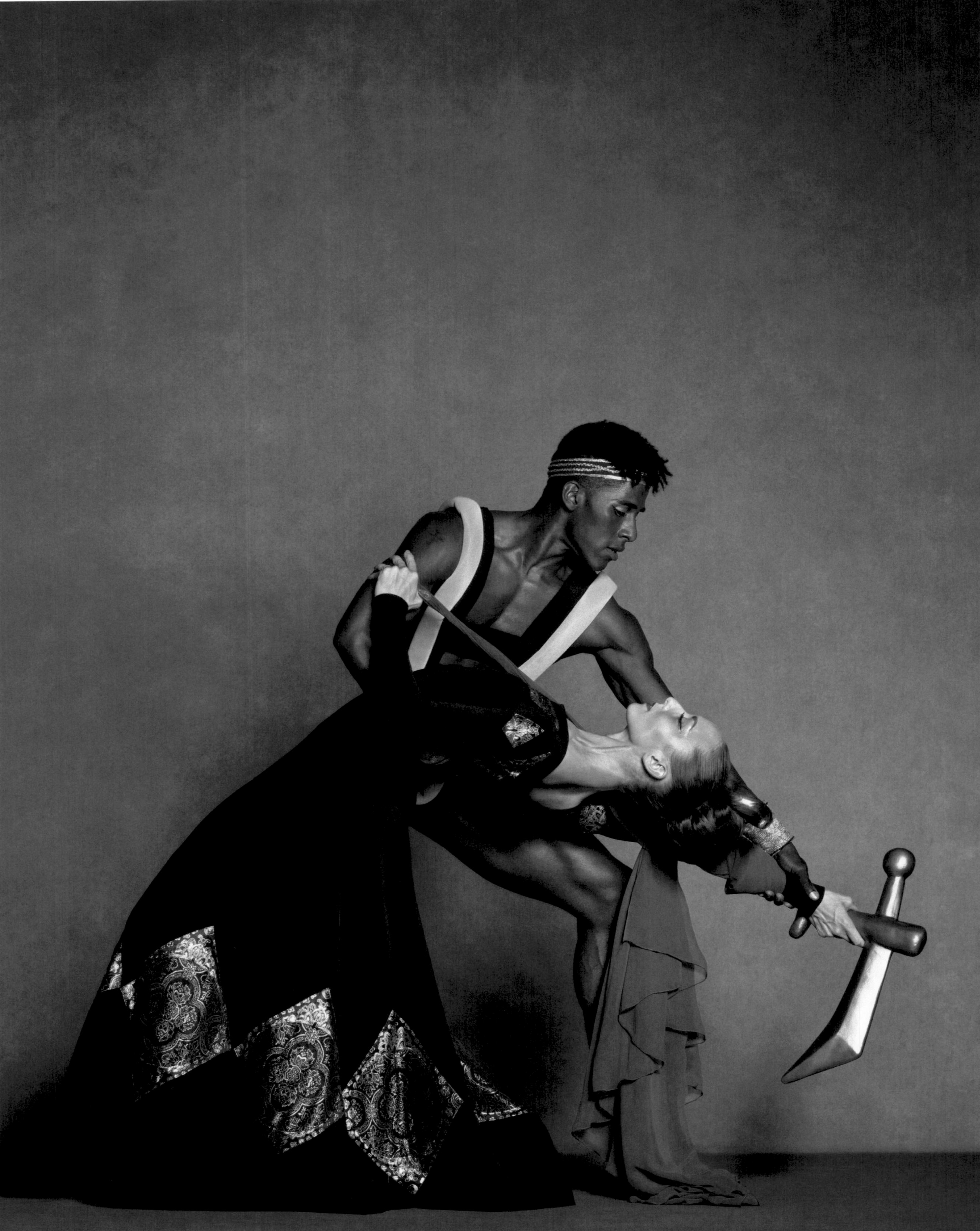

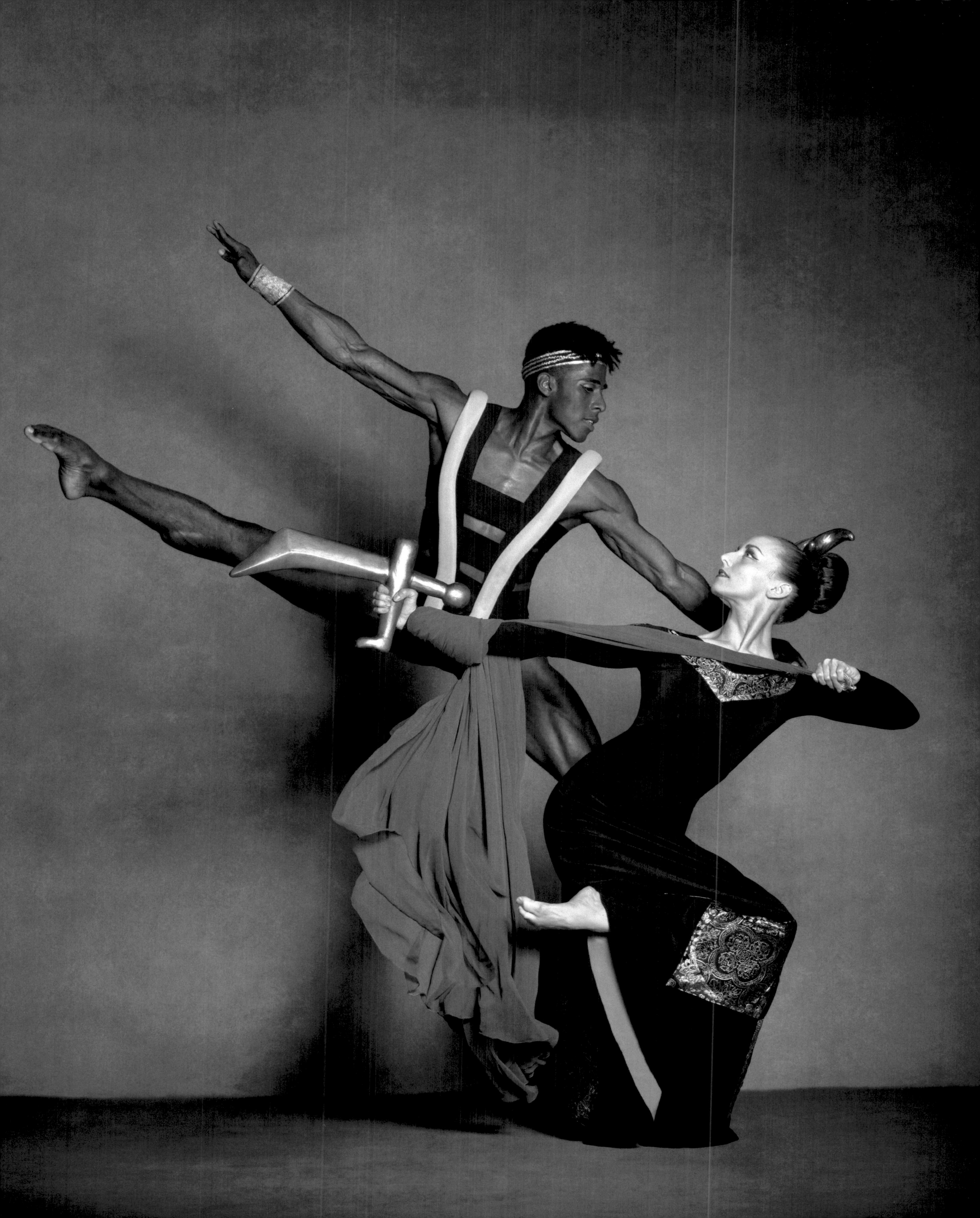

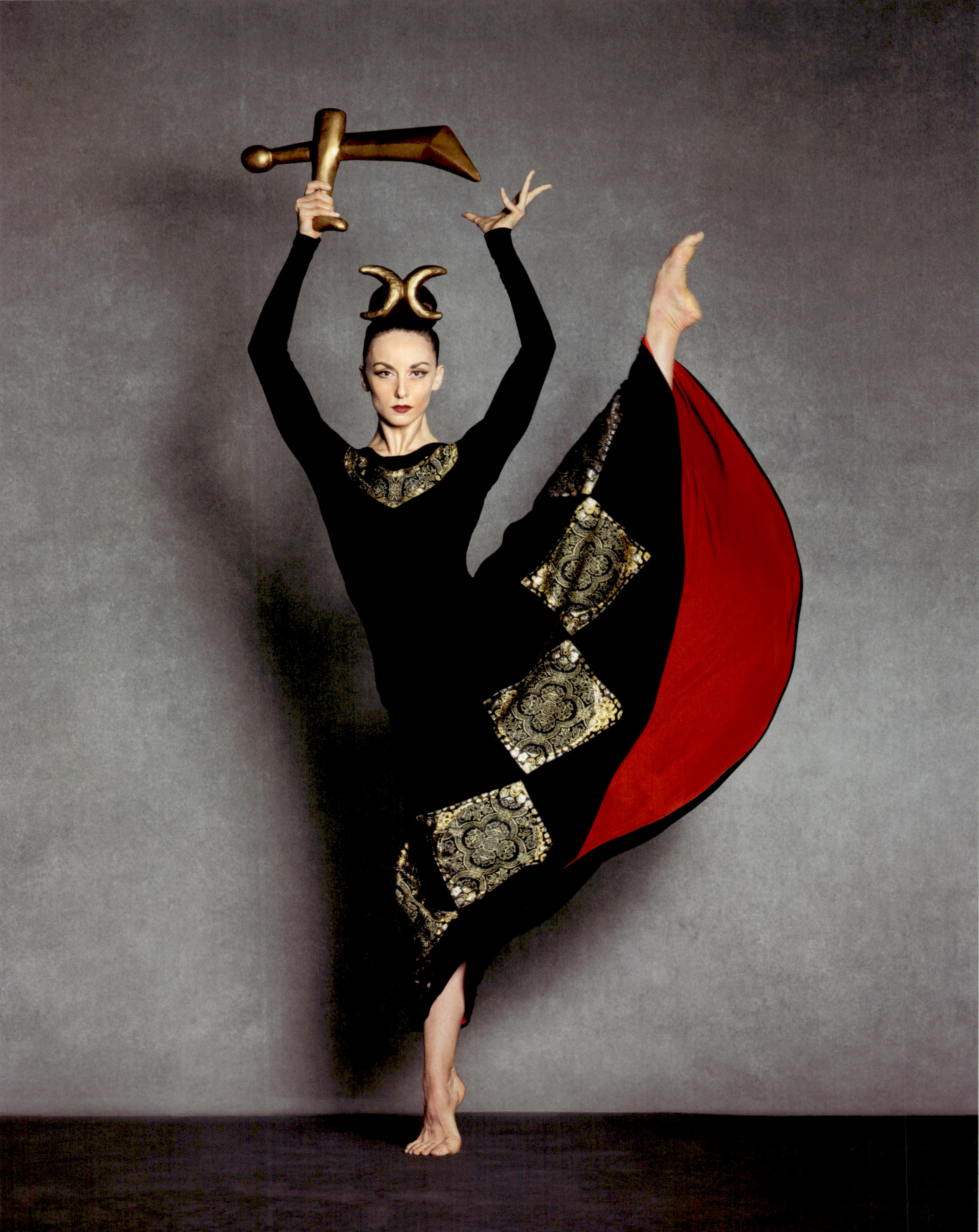

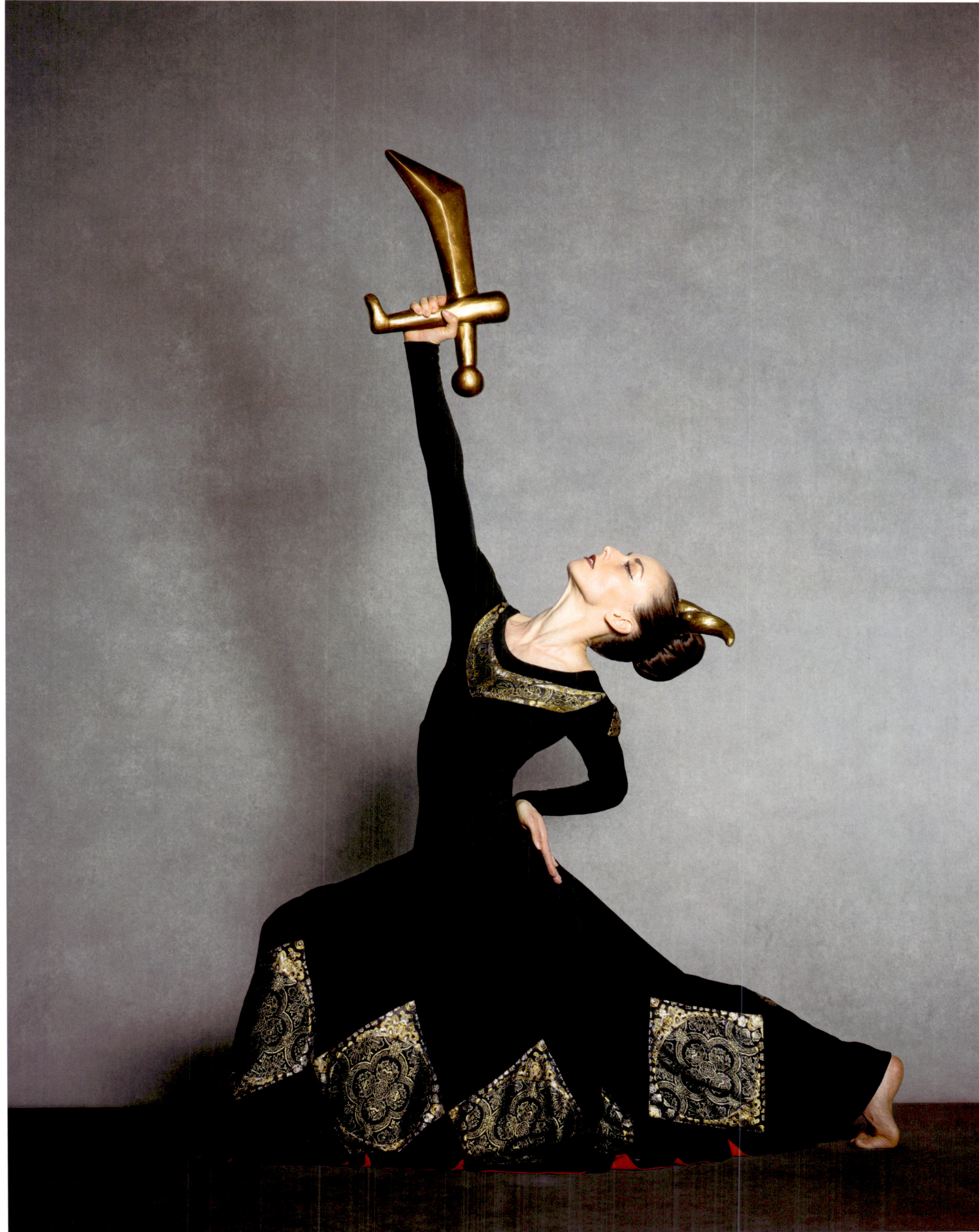

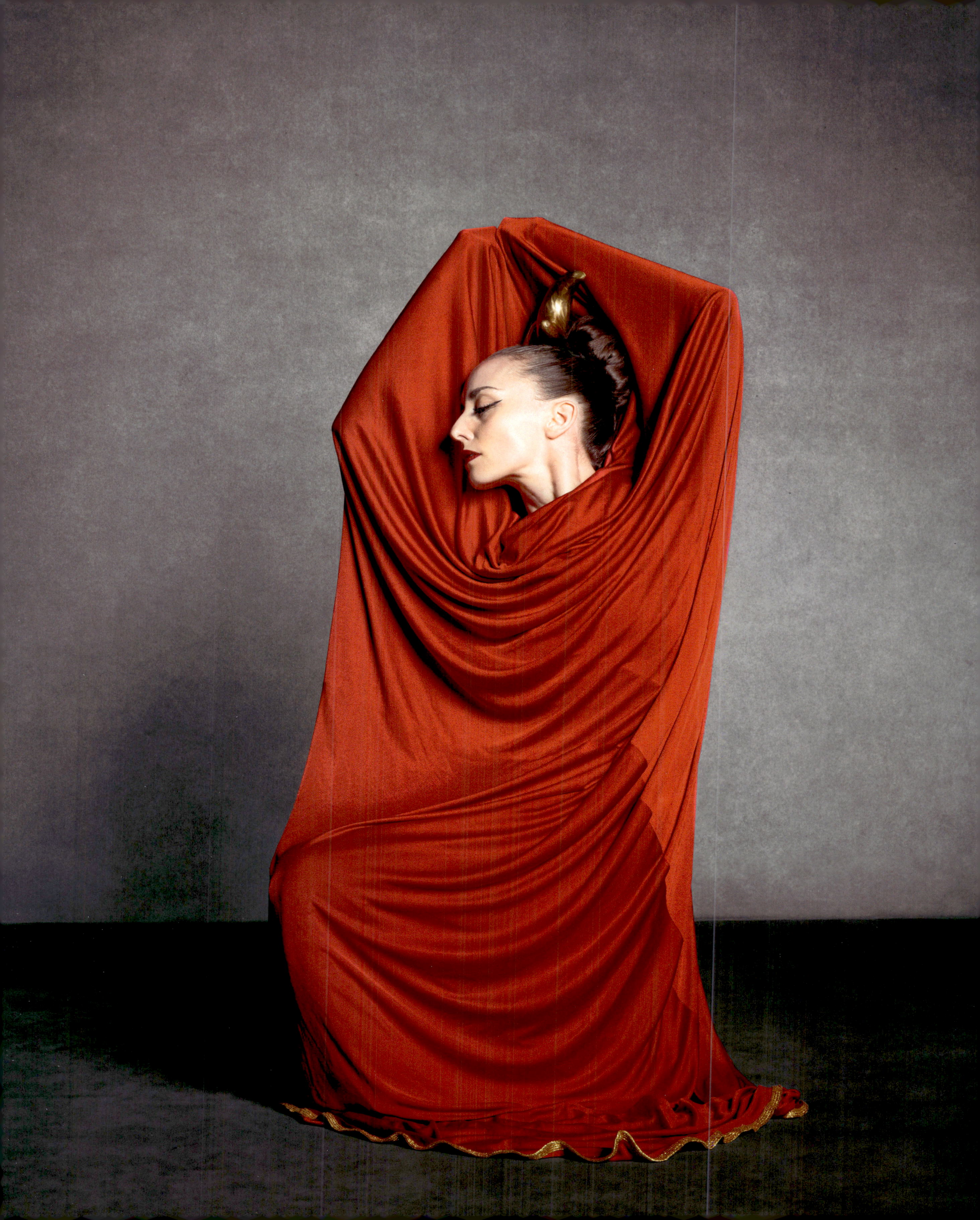

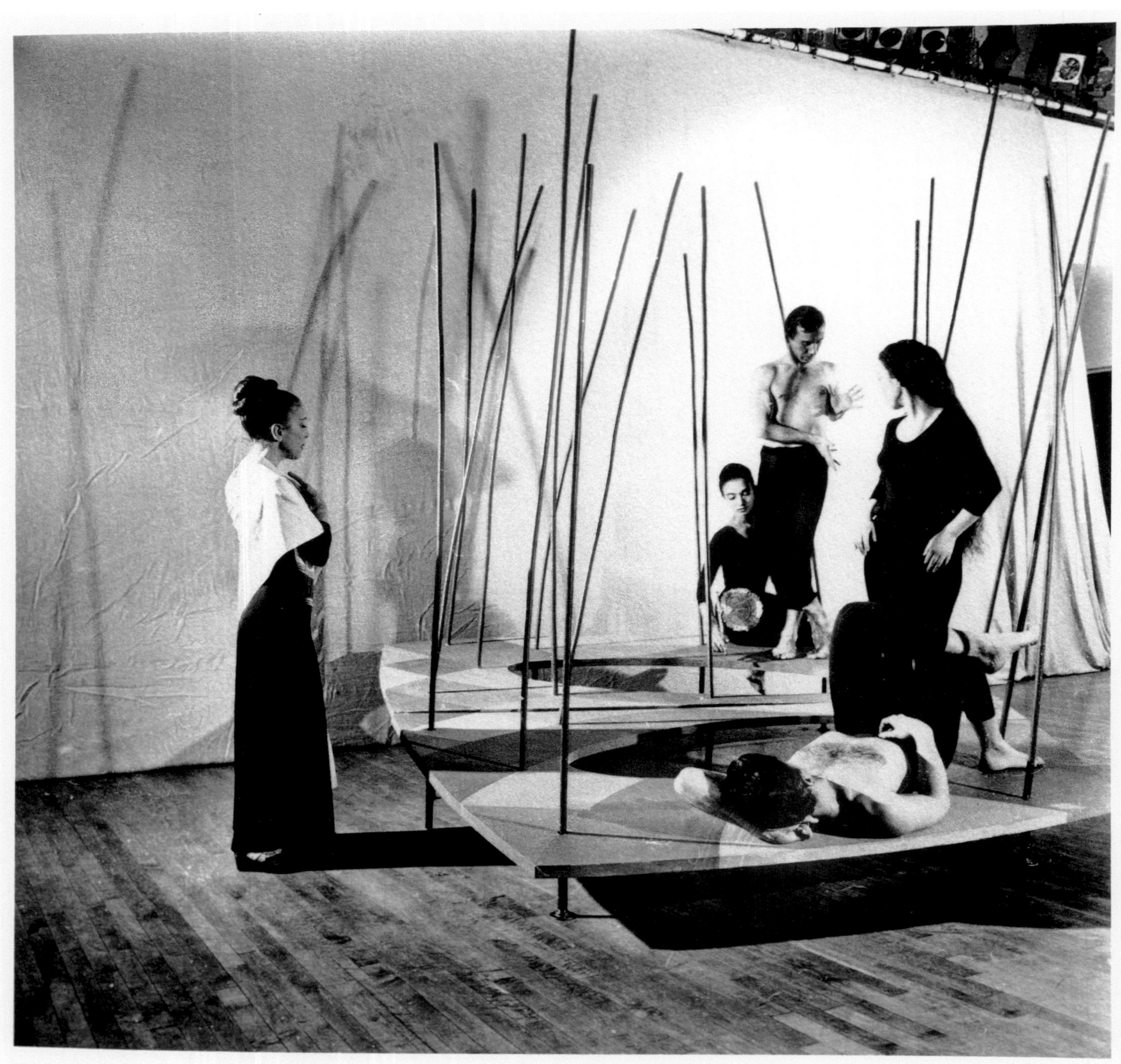

Martha Graham rehearsing *Embattled Garden*. Photograph by Arnold Eagle.

EMBATTLED GARDEN, 1958

Adam and Eve are tempted by
Lilith and the Stranger in a tempestuous
ménage à quatre.

This quartet, danced to a flamboyant musical score by Carlos Surinach, borrows from the Old Testament story of Adam, Eve, the Serpent, known here as the Stranger, and Lilith, a mythological figure from the Hebrew Bible who is theorized to be Adam's first wife.

Caught in a steamy imbroglio, the four figures stalk and slither among the set of tall reeds that characterize Isamu Noguchi's colorfully painted modernist garden. A naive Adam attempts to protect his wife and his domain from the seductive approaches of Lilith and the Stranger, who tempt the innocent couple with their worldly ways. A leggy Lilith beats the air with her fan and mounts Adam's shoulders. The Stranger leaps from his perch on a tree structure and lasciviously taunts both Adam and Eve. Adam eventually rallies to restore his kingdom in a deconsecrated Eden.

SET DESIGN
Isamu Noguchi

COSTUME DESIGN
Martha Graham

COMPOSER
Carlos Surinach

Embattled Garden

ADAM
Alessio Crognale-Roberts

EVE
Anne O'Donnell Passero

LILITH
Natasha Diamond-Walker

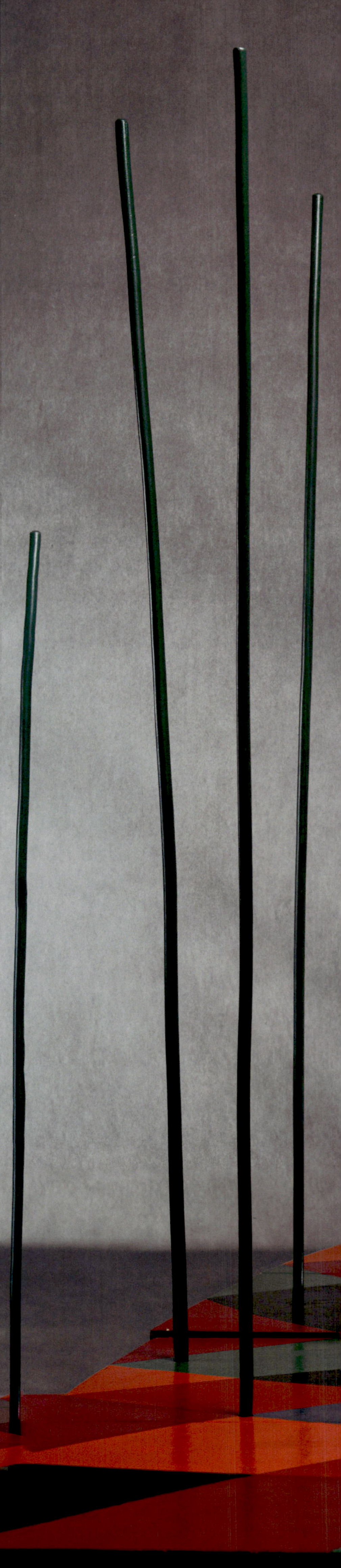

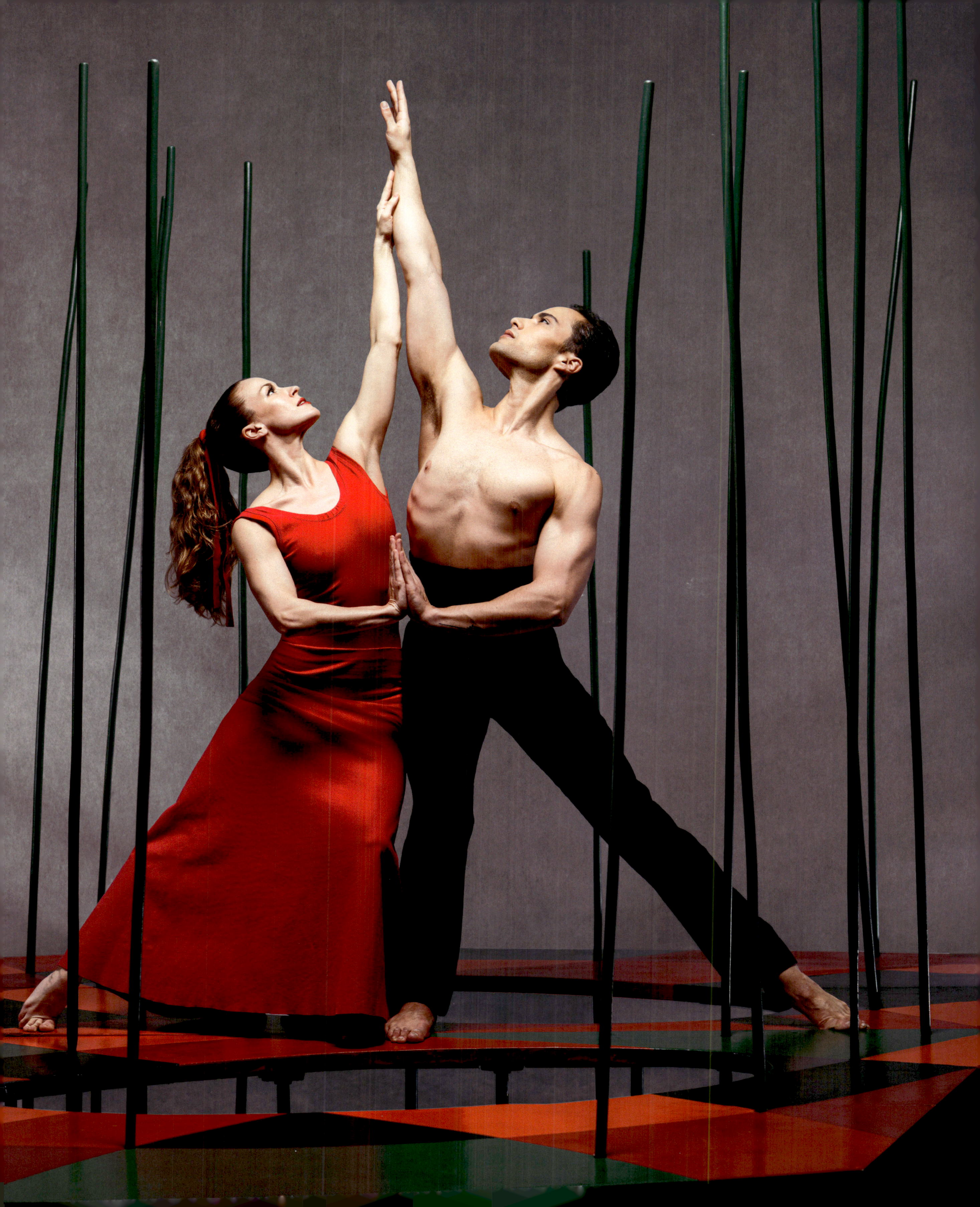

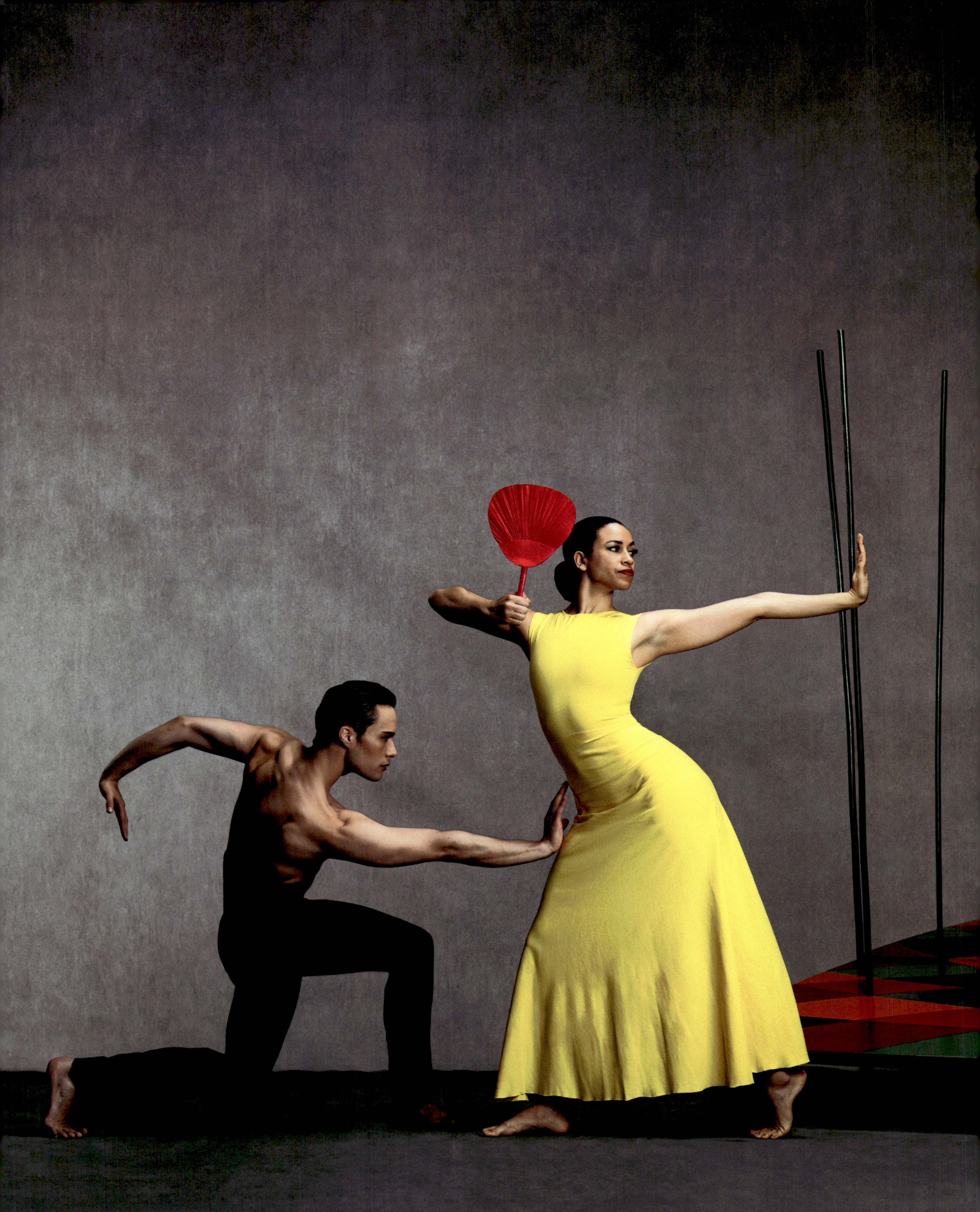

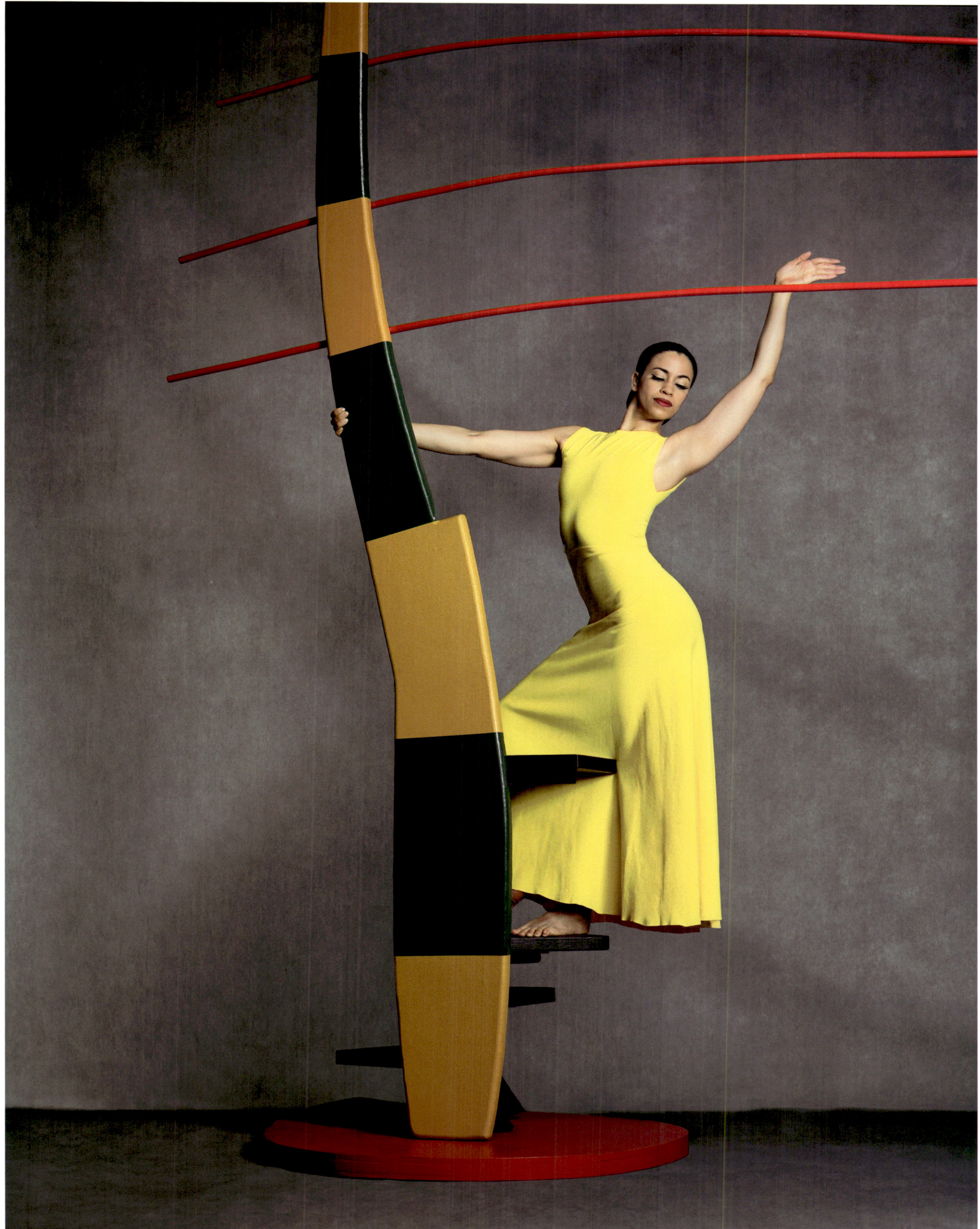

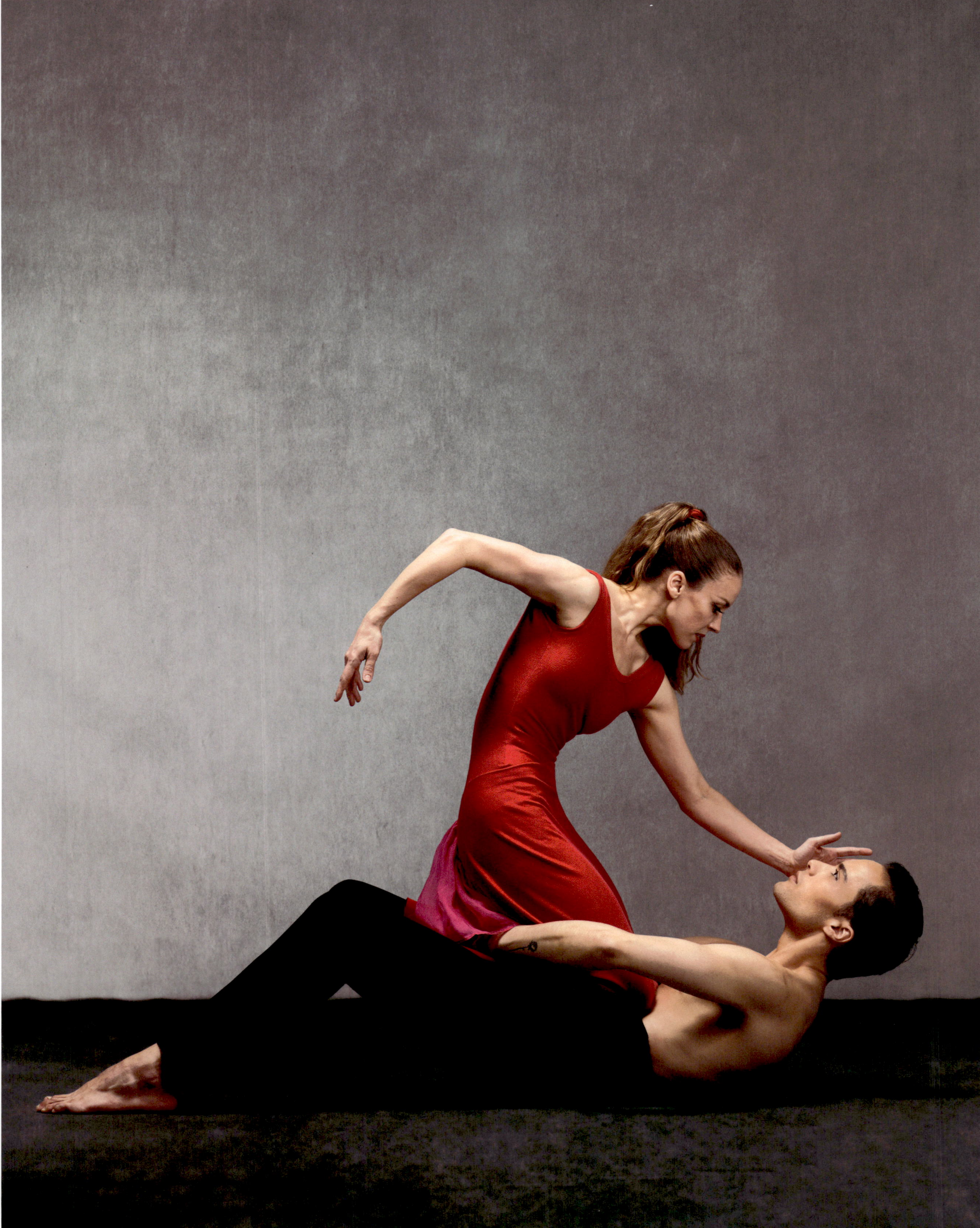

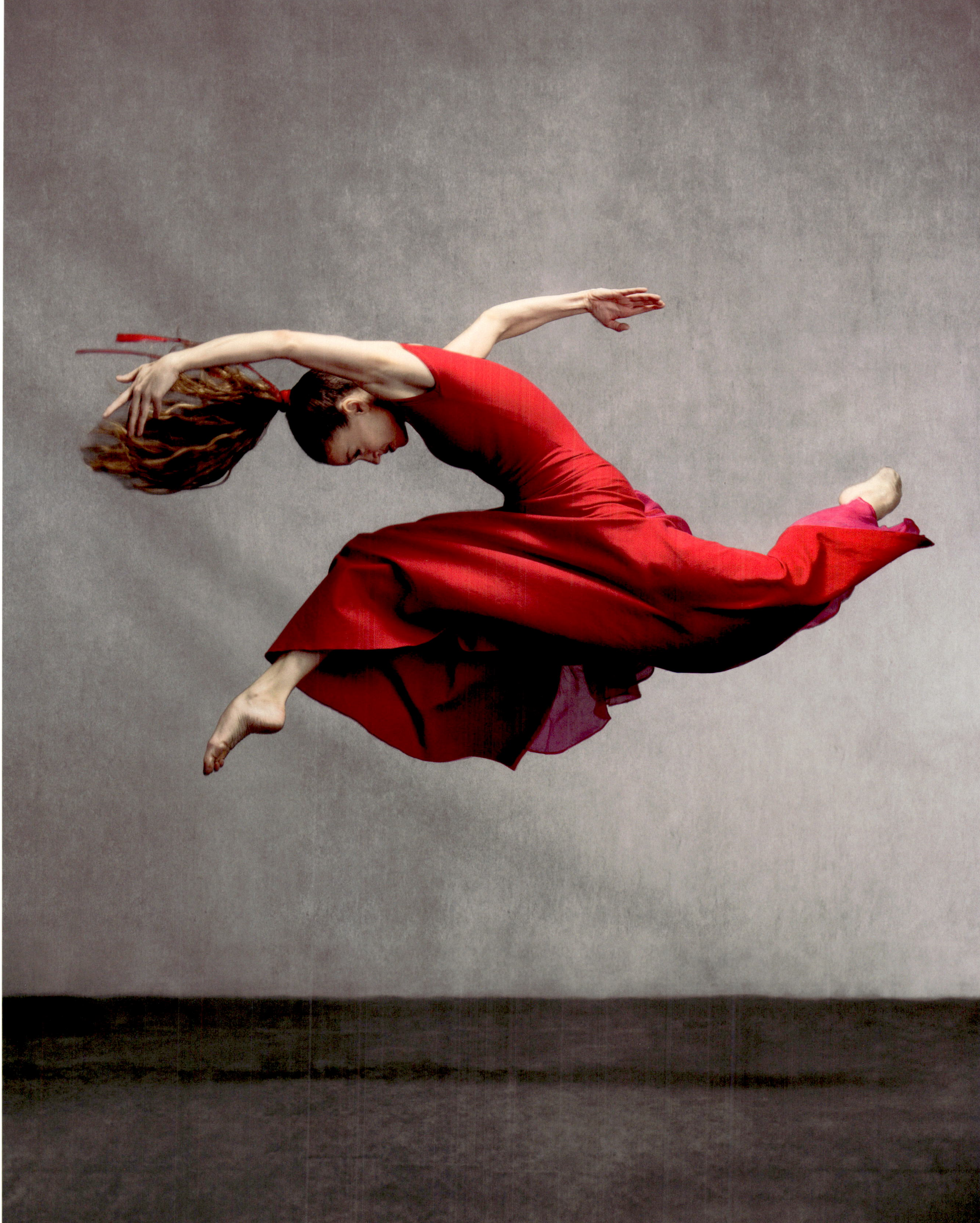

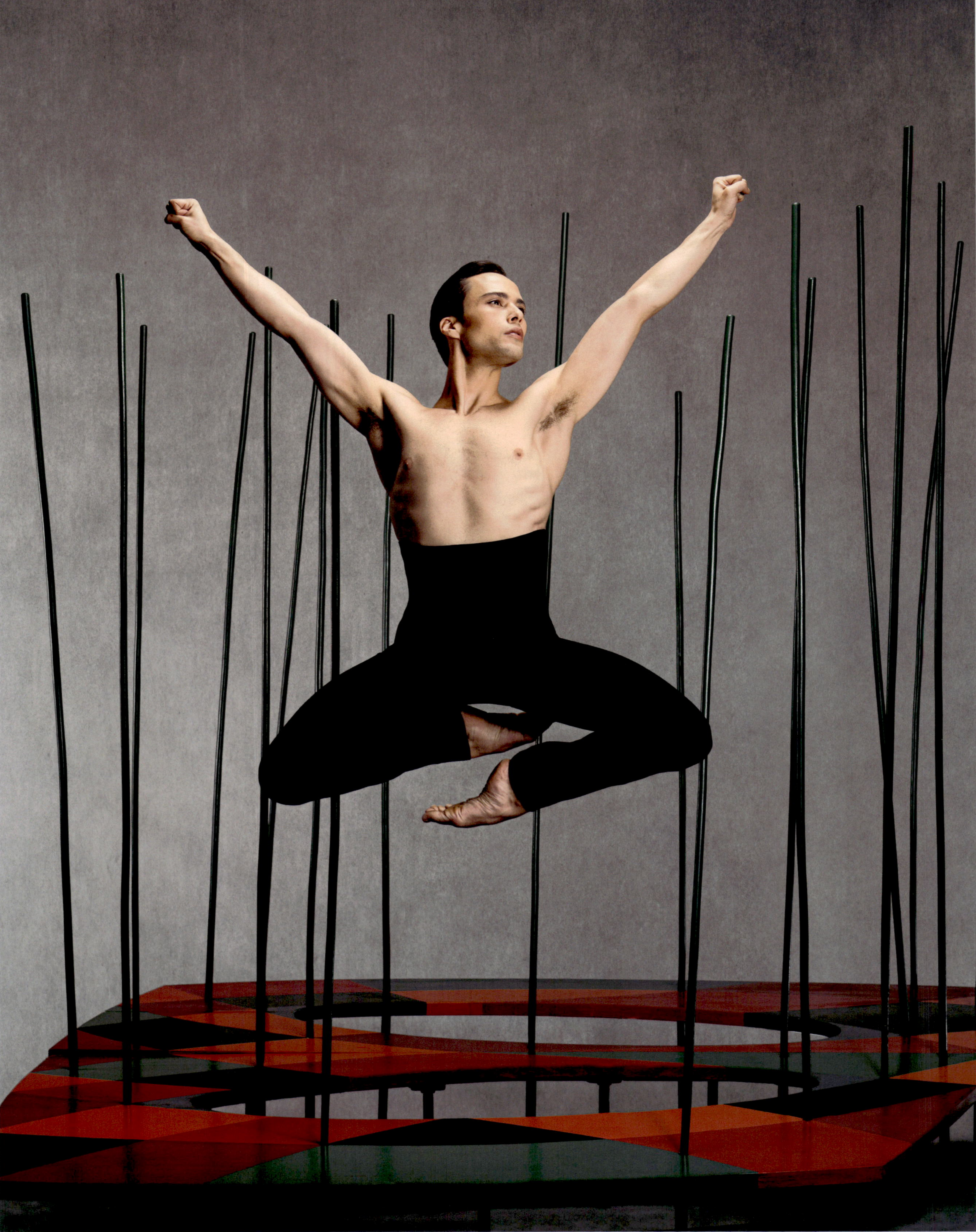

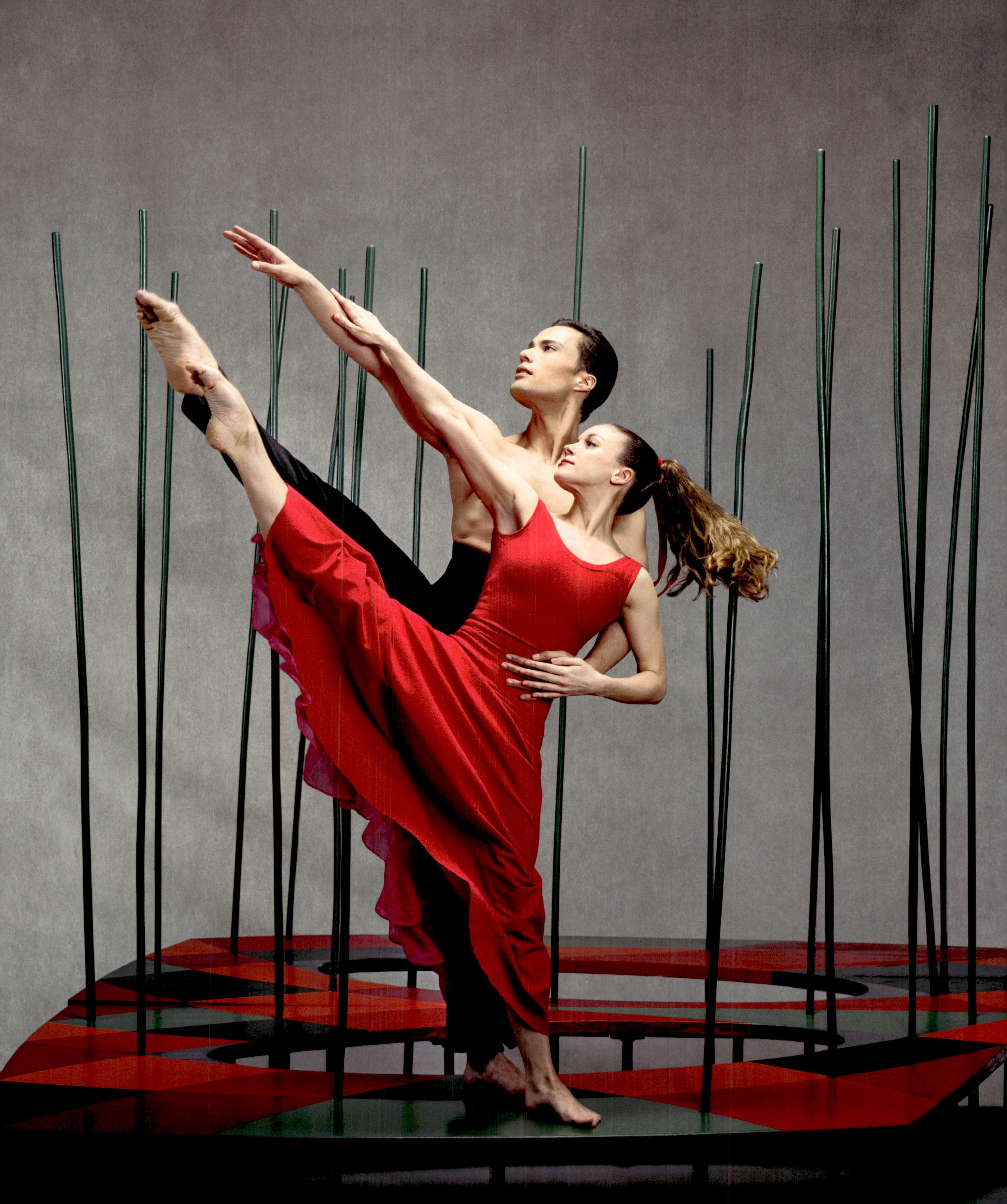

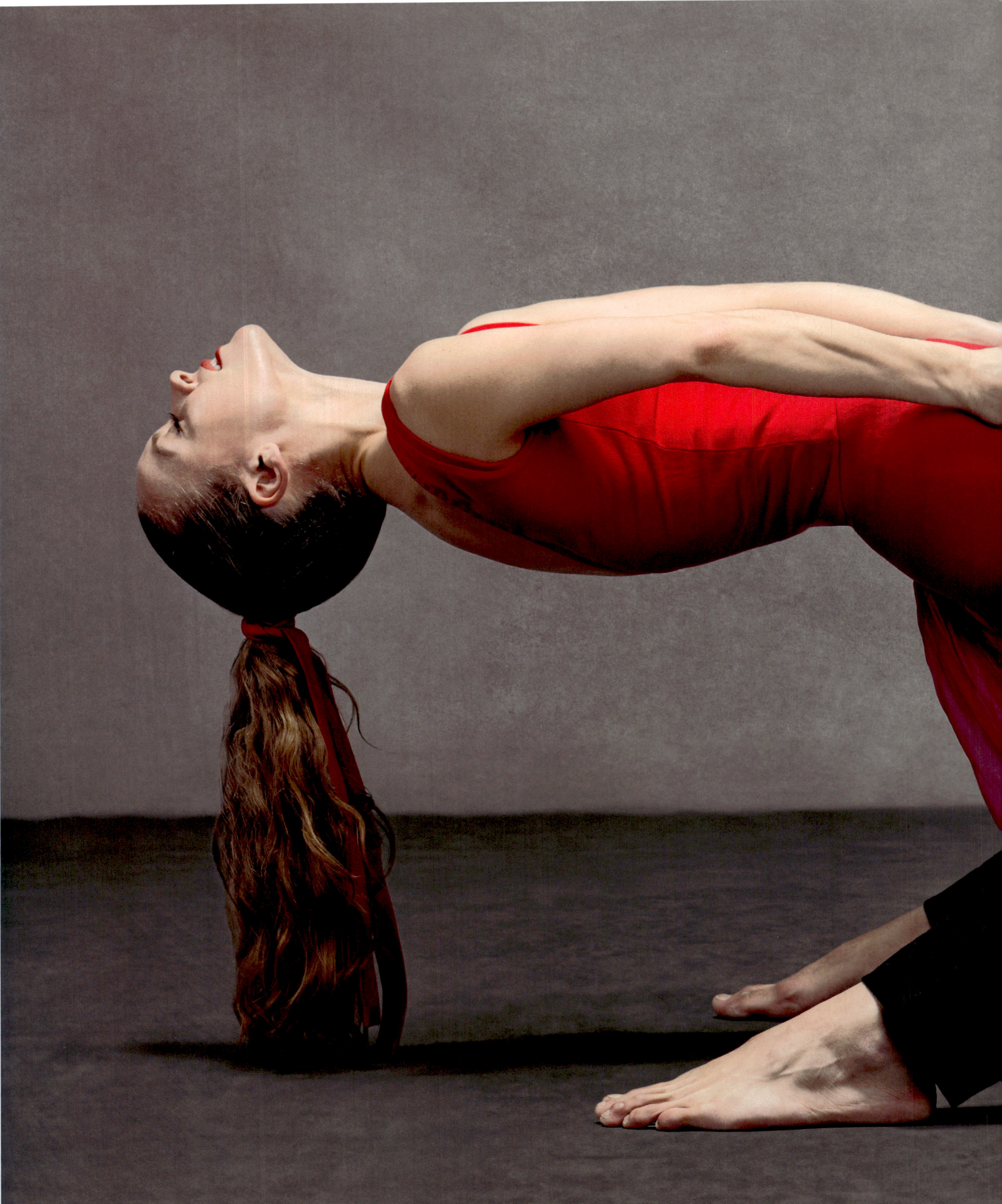

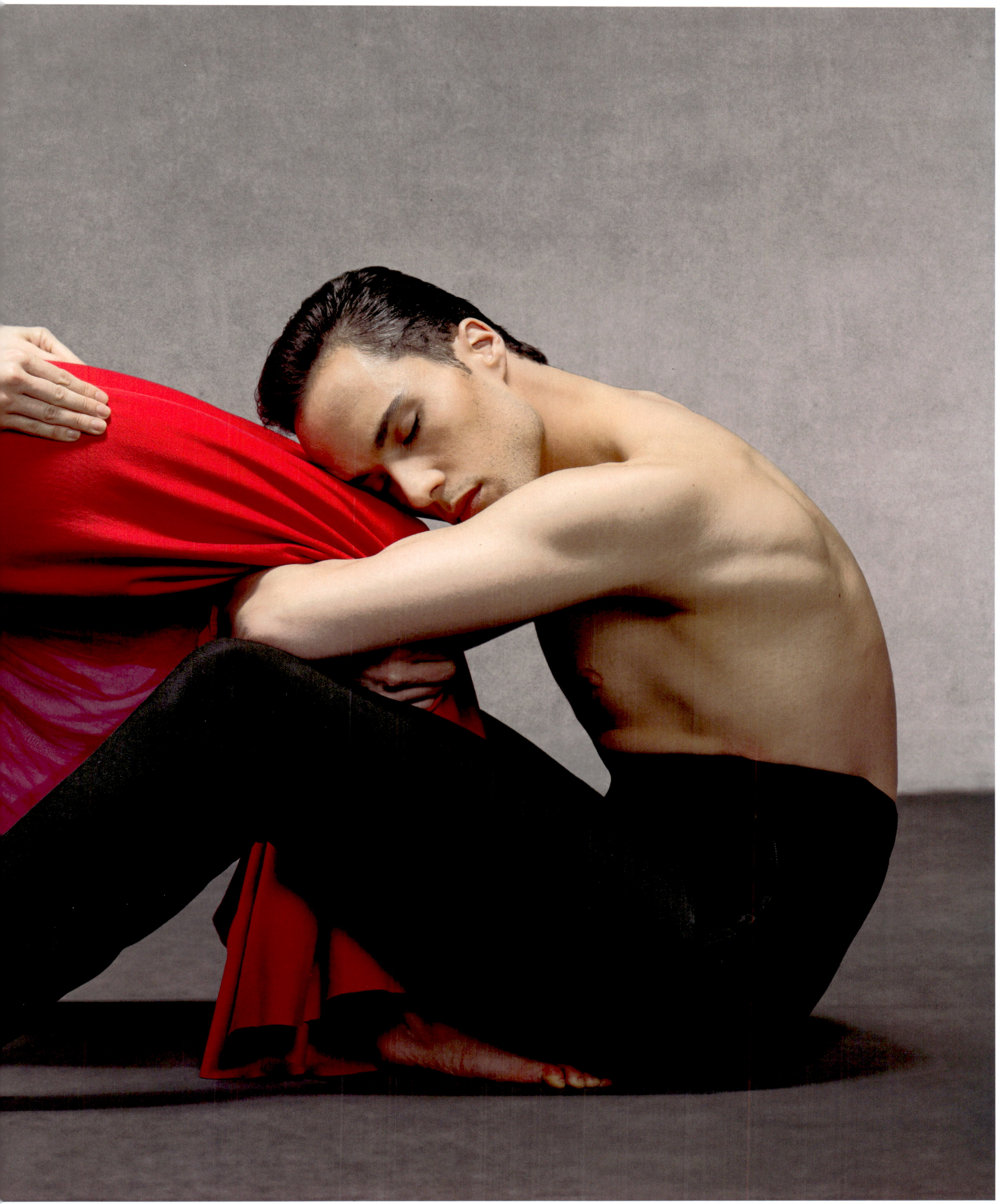

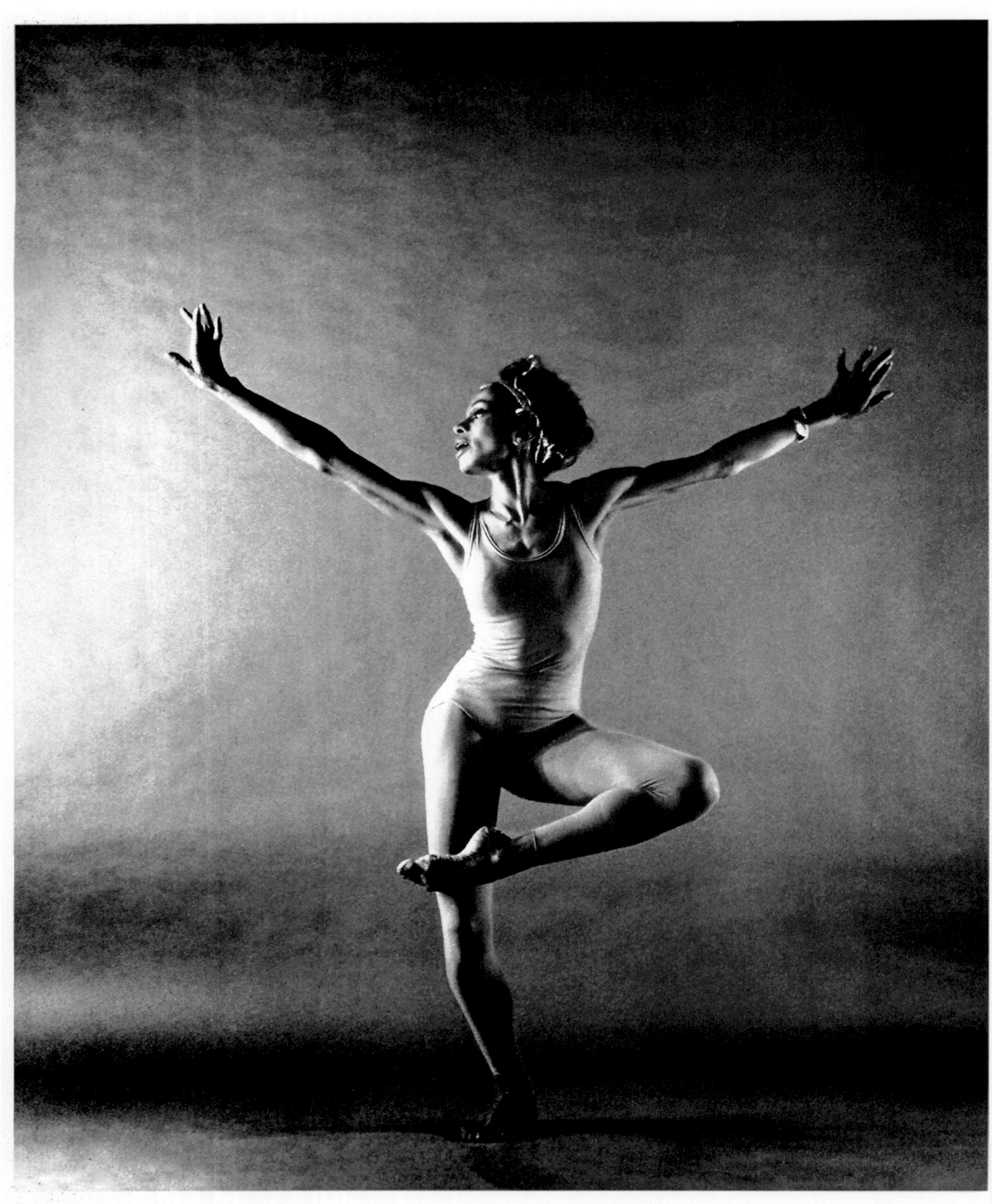

Mary Hinkson. Photograph by Anthony Crickmay.

CIRCE, 1963

Ulysses and his helmsman confront the sorceress Circe and her retinue of enchanted beasts.

The seductive female protagonist of *Circe* hovers on her cloud-like perch and surveys the approach of Ulysses and his helmsman steering their Noguchi-designed vessel as they make their way home in the aftermath of the Trojan War.

As the men come ashore and begin to explore her island domain, Circe transforms them into their animal personae, including a goat, deer, snake, and lion. The helmsman, representing Ulysses's conscience, struggles to protect his master from Circe's seductive charms. Ulysses succumbs at first but is ultimately able to rescue himself from the sorceress's web. He returns to his vessel with his trusty helmsman, and they continue their journey home.

The entire work hovers on the atmospheric music of Alan Hovhaness, whose commissioned score floats like Noguchi's cloud and is populated with mystical-sounding notes.

SET DESIGN
Isamu Noguchi

COSTUME DESIGN
Martha Graham

COMPOSER
Alan Hovhaness

Circe

CIRCE
So Young An

ULYSSES
Lloyd Knight

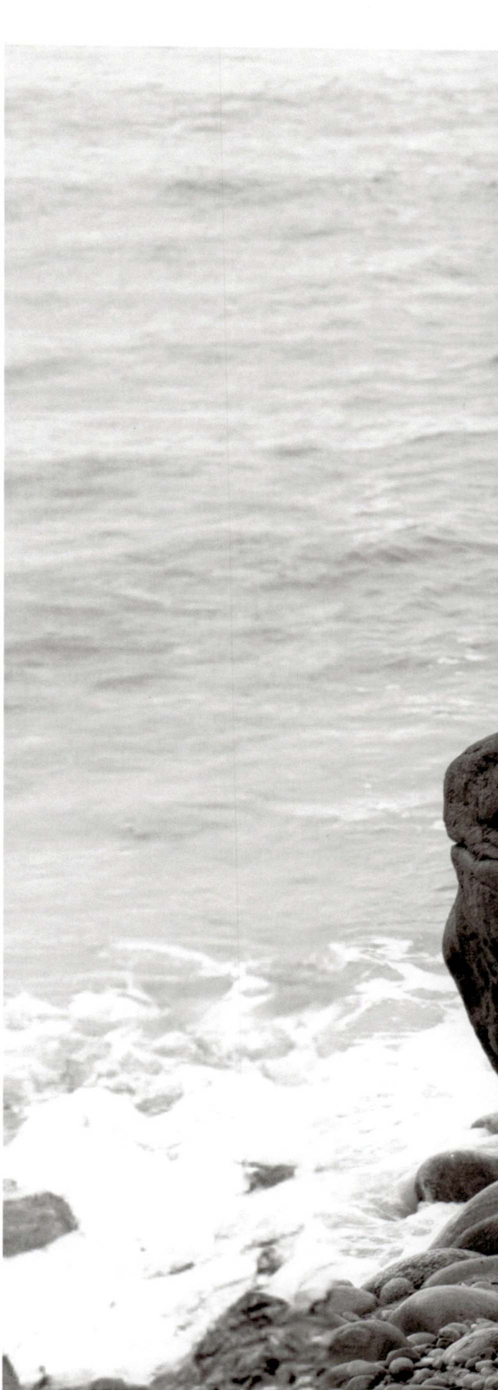

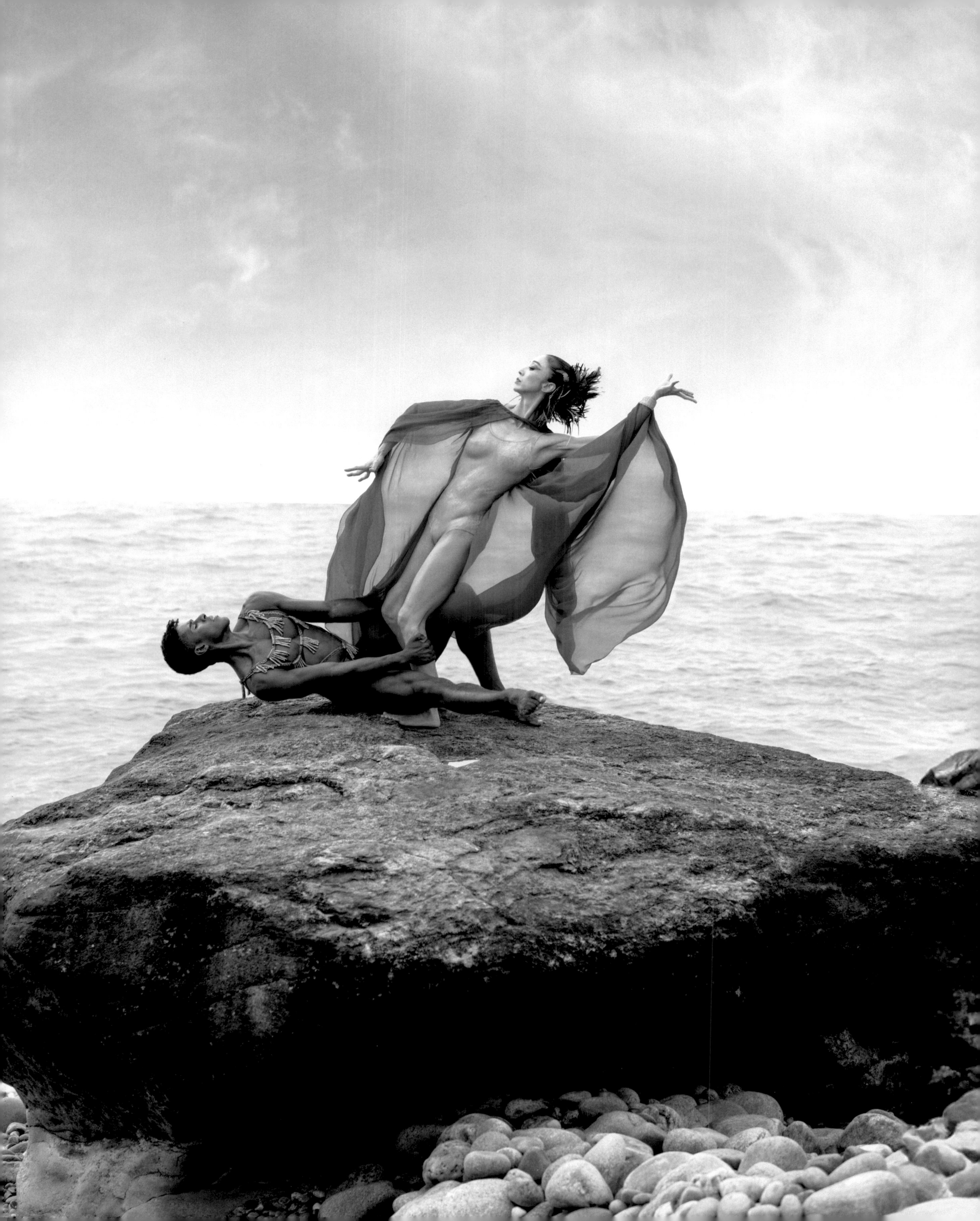

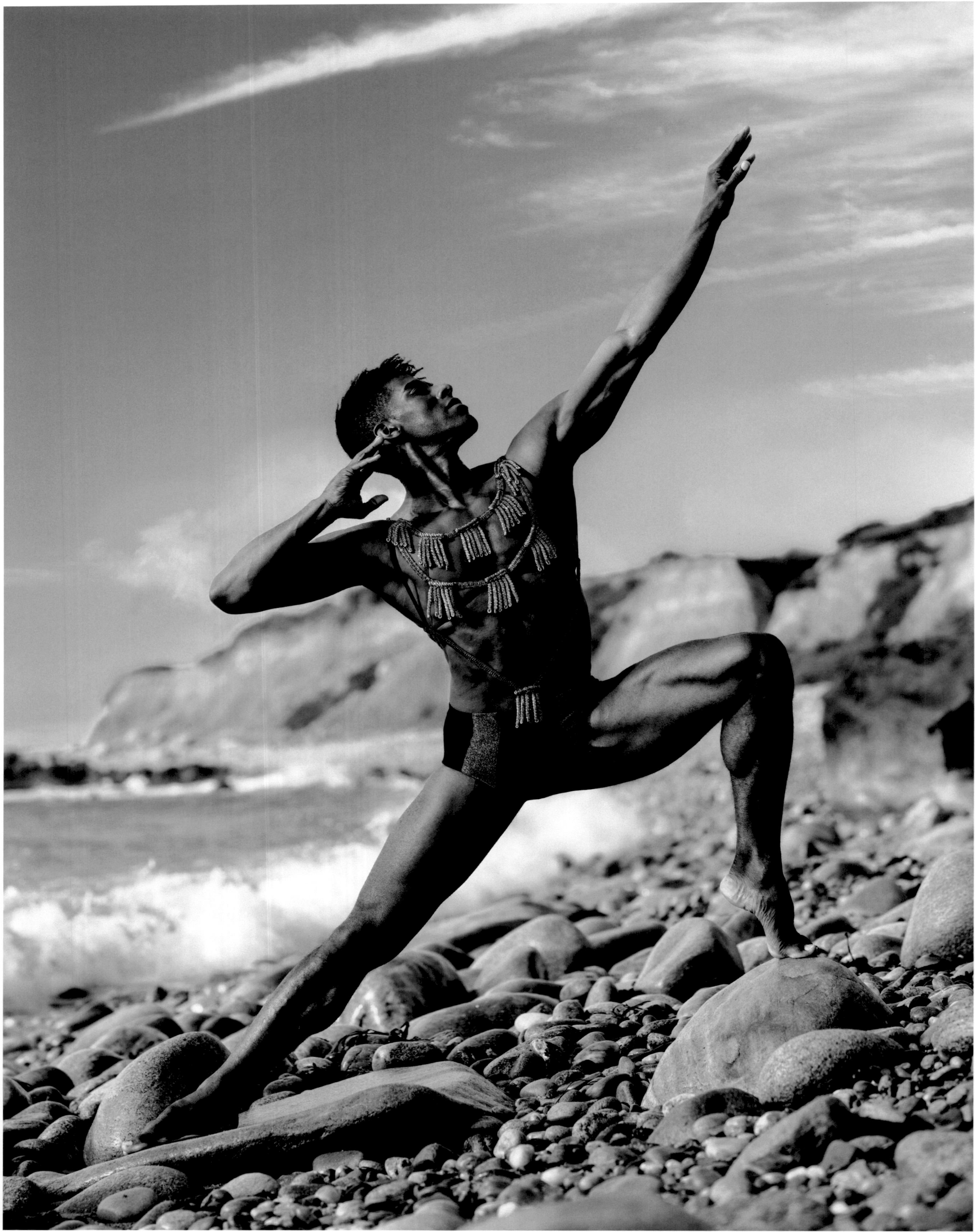

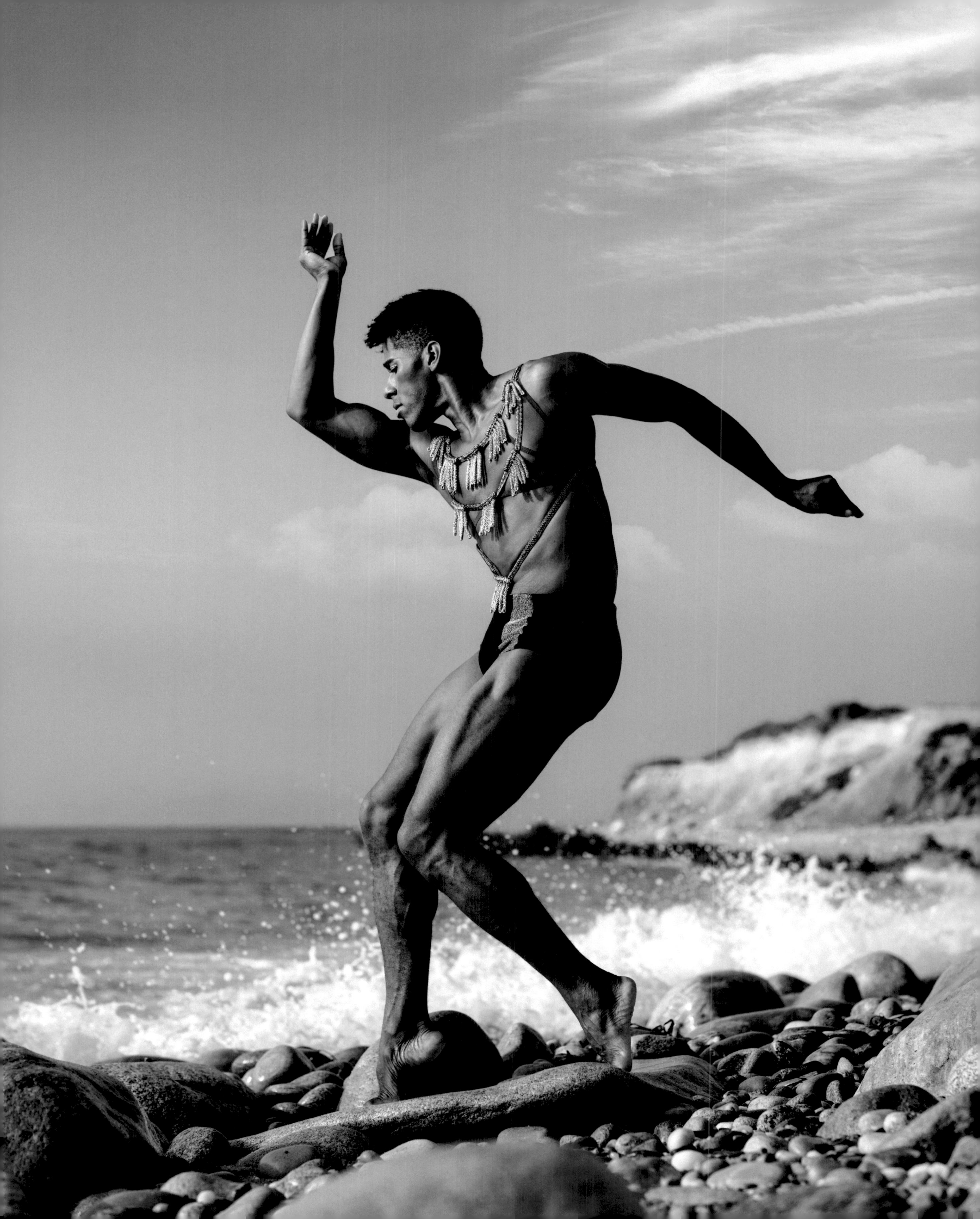

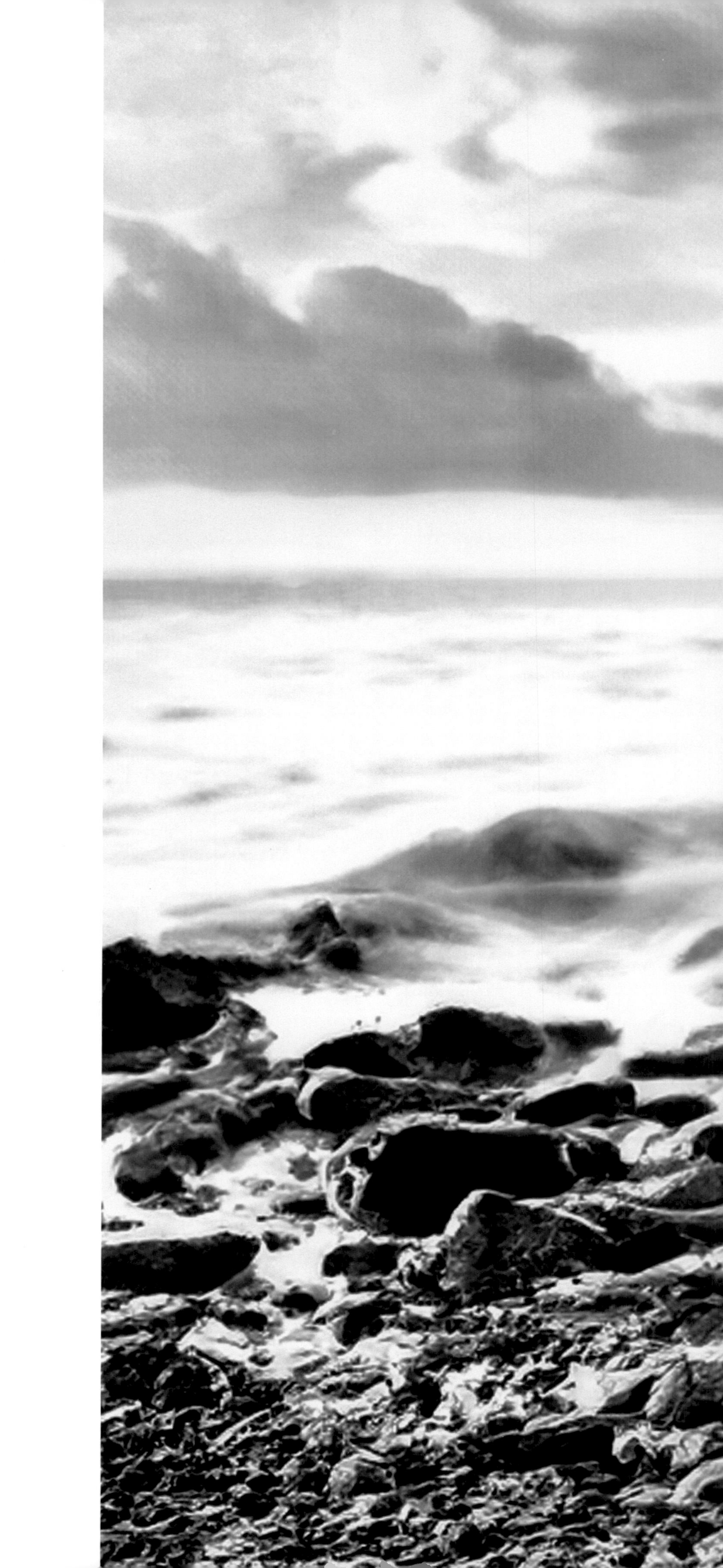

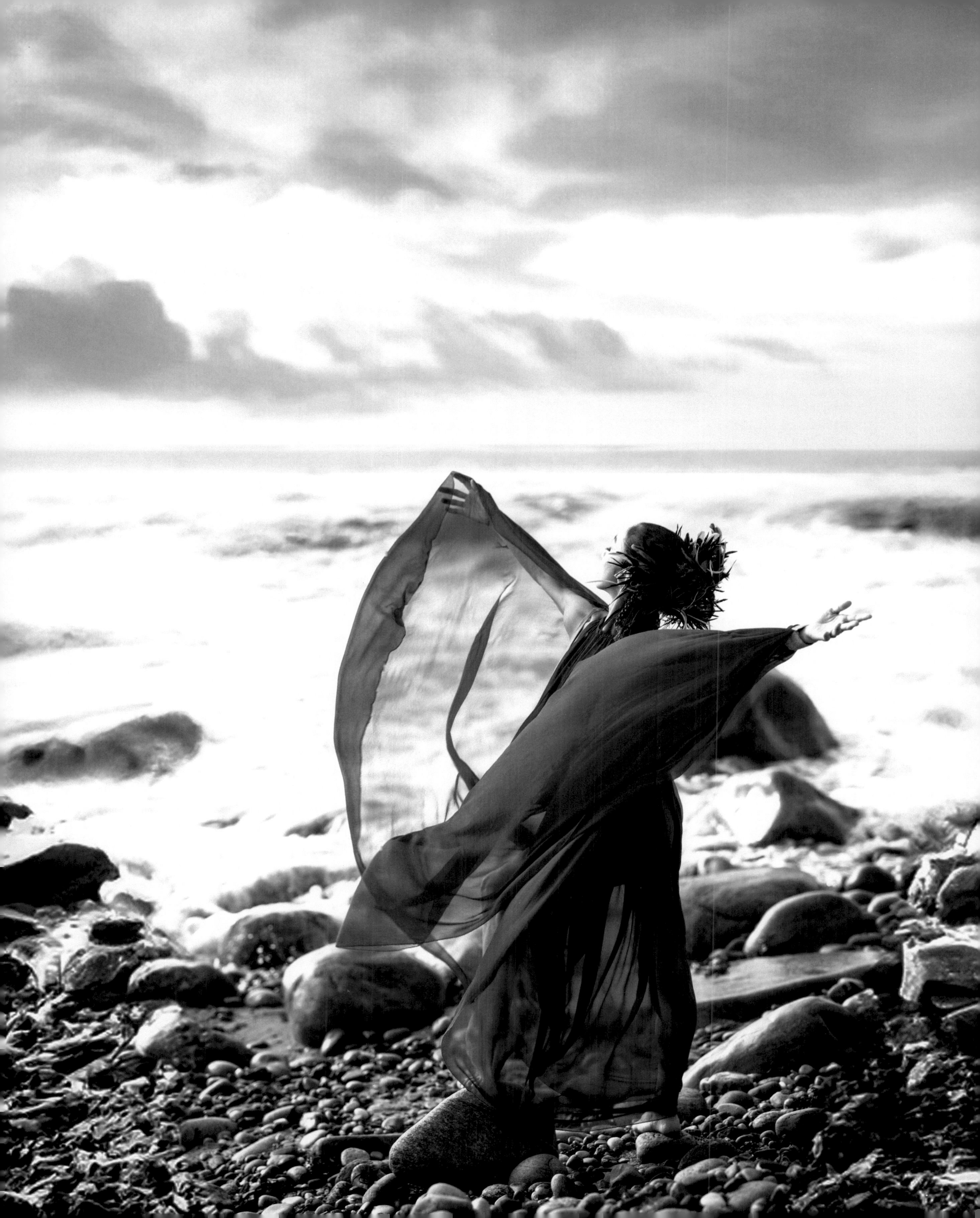

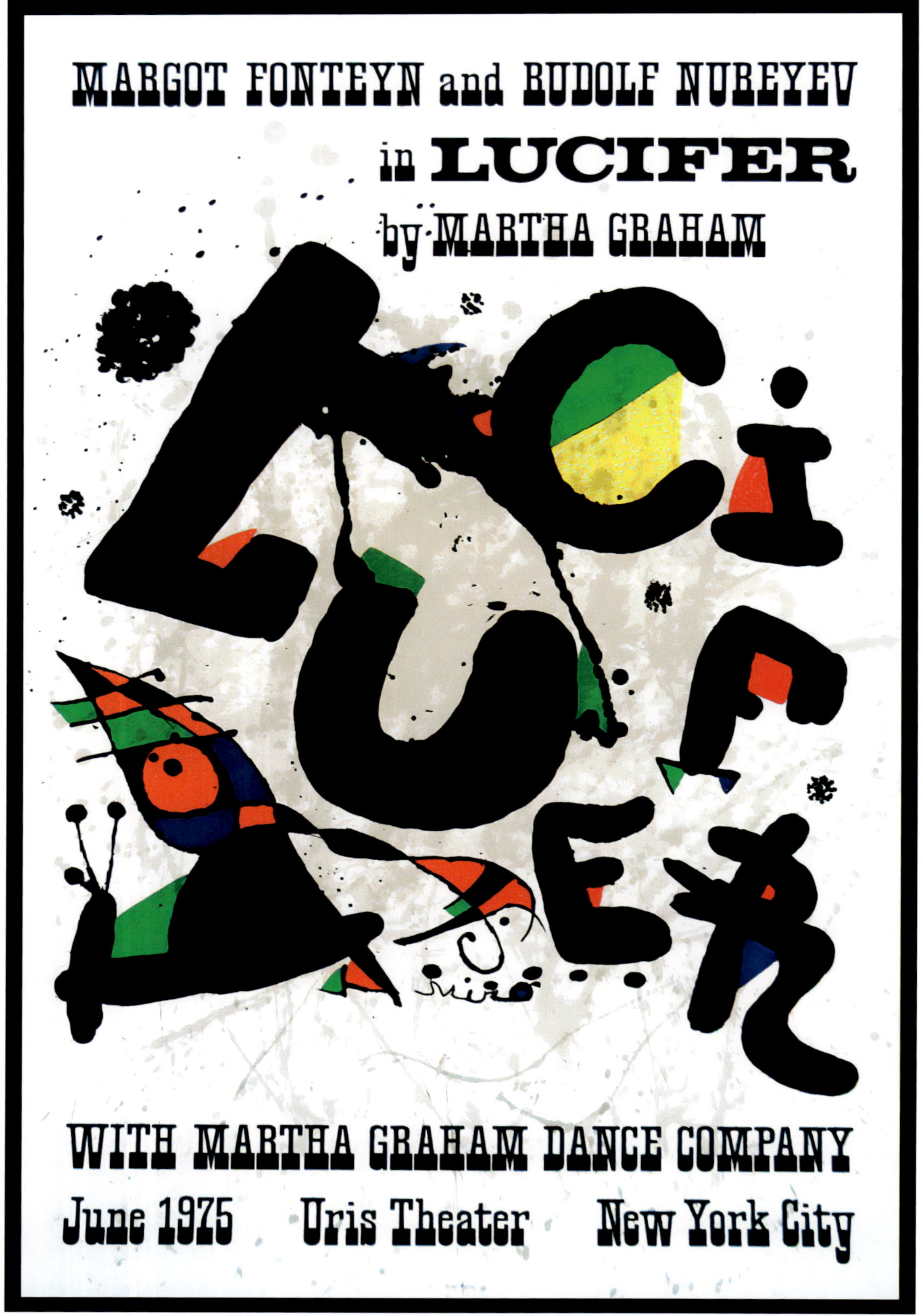

Poster by Joan Miró.

LUCIFER, 1975

God's errant angel wreaks havoc in the underworld.

For *Lucifer*, Graham cast Russian ballet star Rudolf Nureyev as God's fallen angel, whose audacious rebelliousness was not unlike the mischievousness and animal defiance that Graham was drawn to in her favorite guest performer.

Nureyev, performing in an ornately patterned cape and platinum mesh briefs designed for him by Halston, was accompanied by special guest Margot Fonteyn as Night, Lucifer's seductive consort, who surfs onstage on a fabric train. A chorus of barechested, stick-wielding men, led by the Tempter and outfitted in skullcaps and deep blue skirts, threatens to consume Lucifer in a sea of fabric. Lucifer manages to rise from the morass and sweep across the stage, cape flying behind him like wings, to ascend to the top of a craggy gold structure where he communes with Night in a sensual and taunting duet.

SET DESIGN
Leandro Locsin

COSTUME DESIGN
Halston

COMPOSER
Halim El-Dabh

Lucifer

DANCER
Lorenzo Pagano

COSTUME
Halston

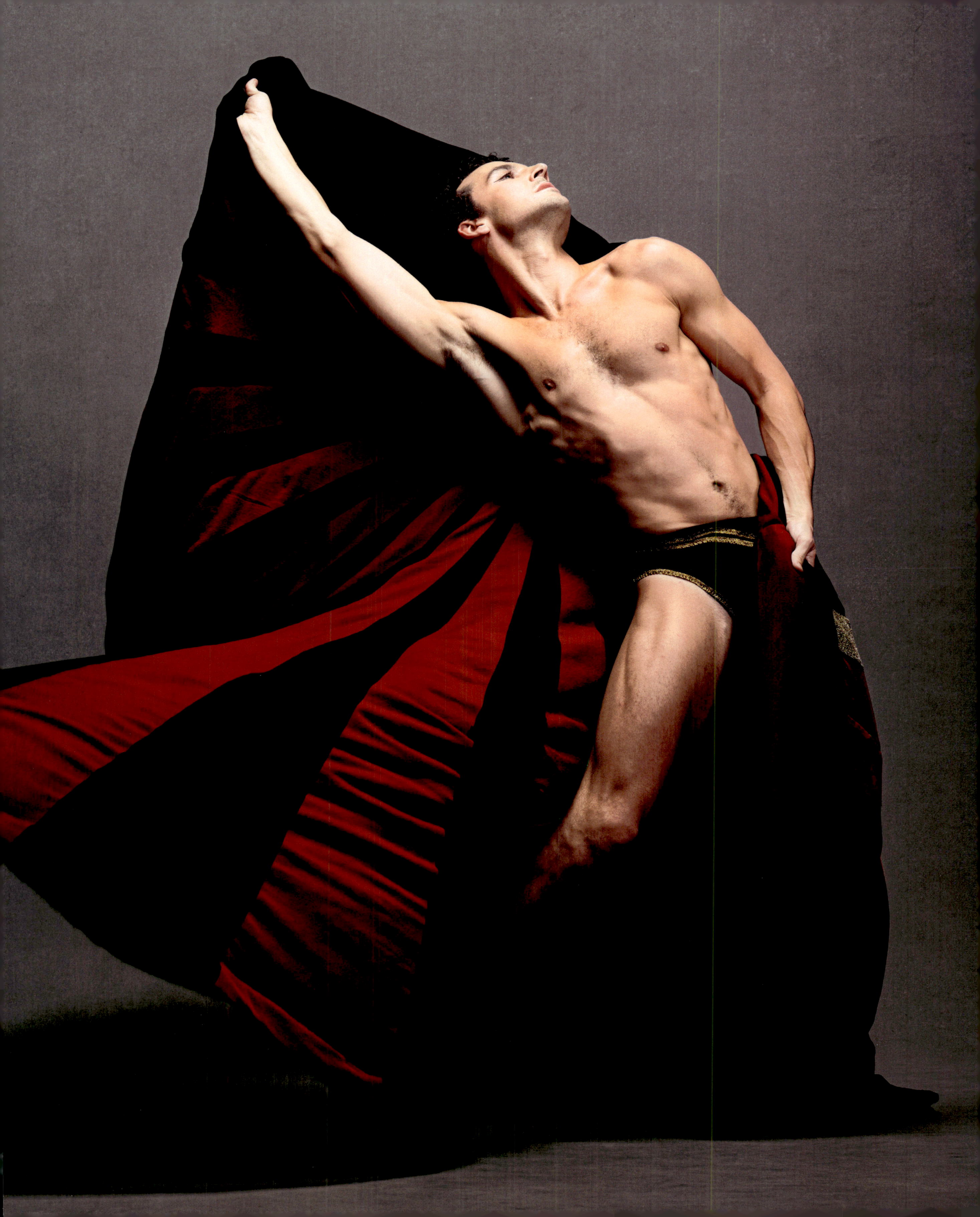

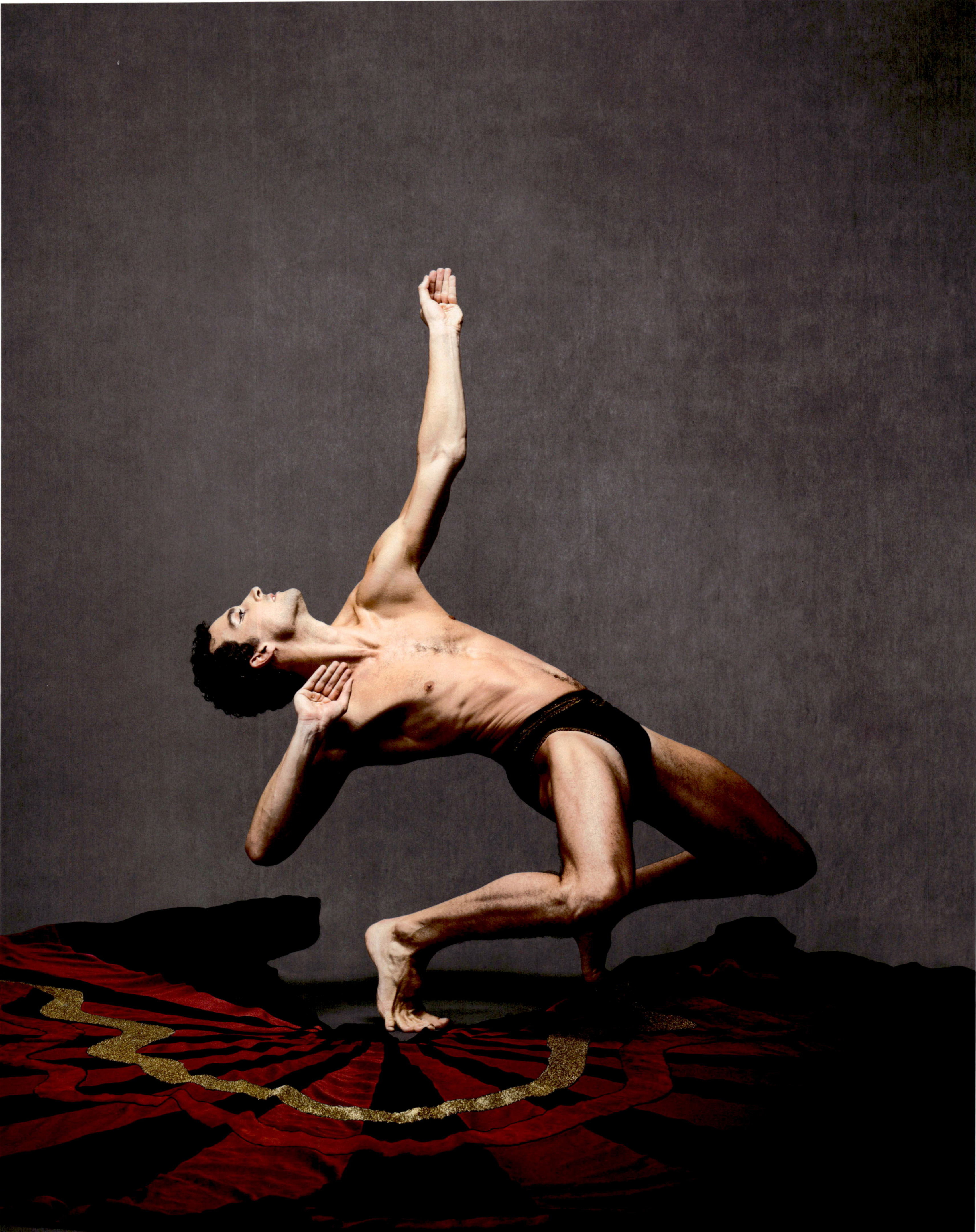

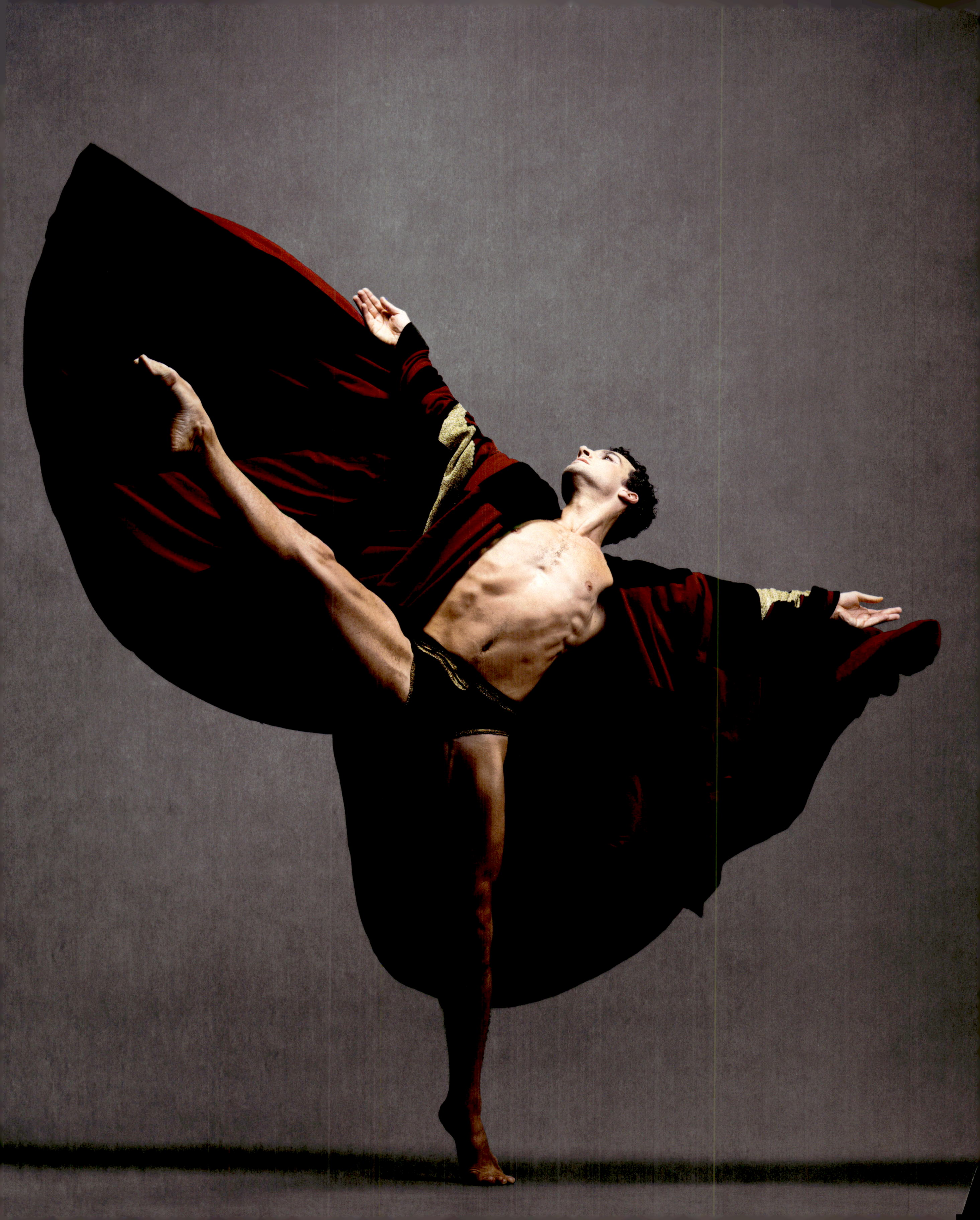

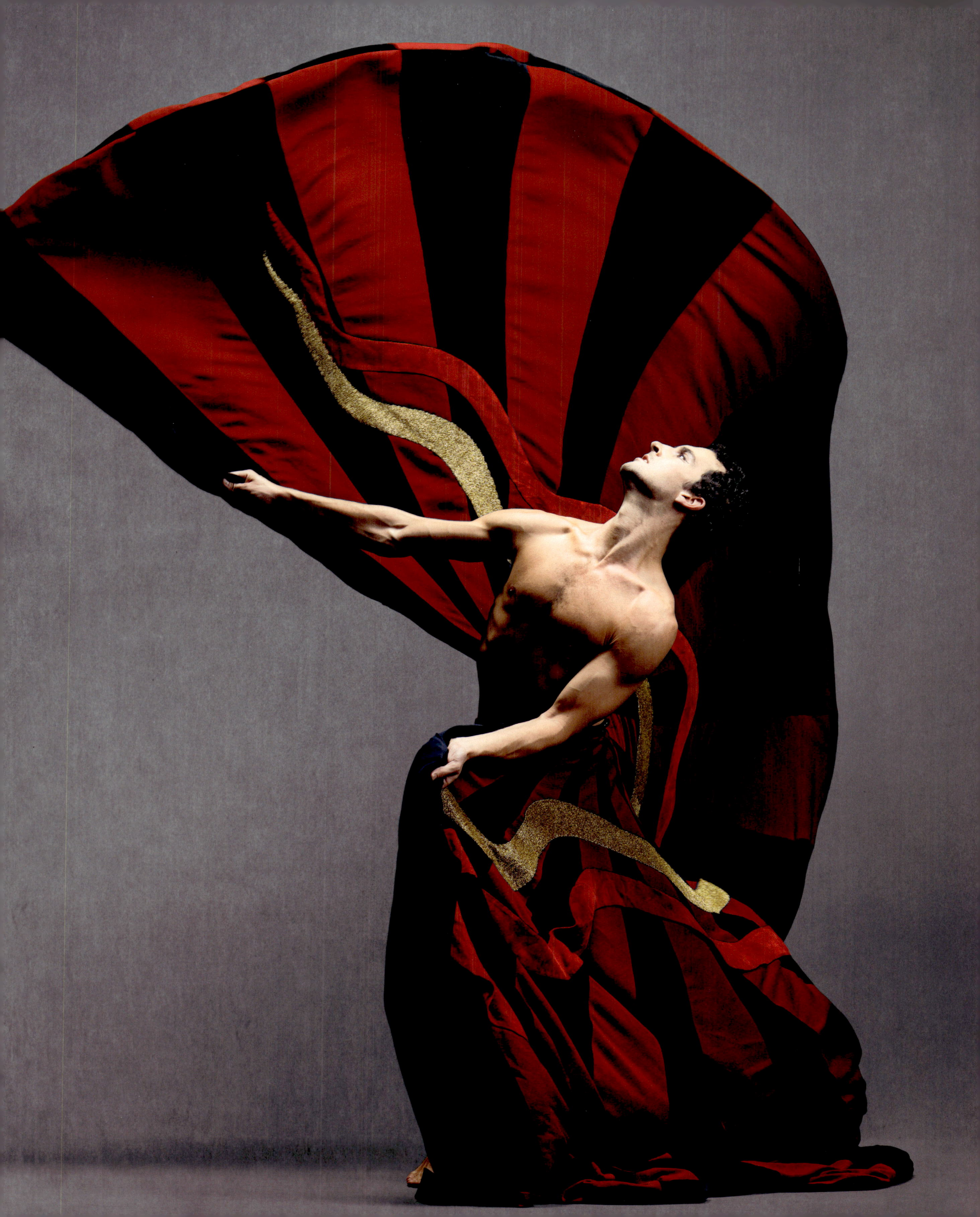

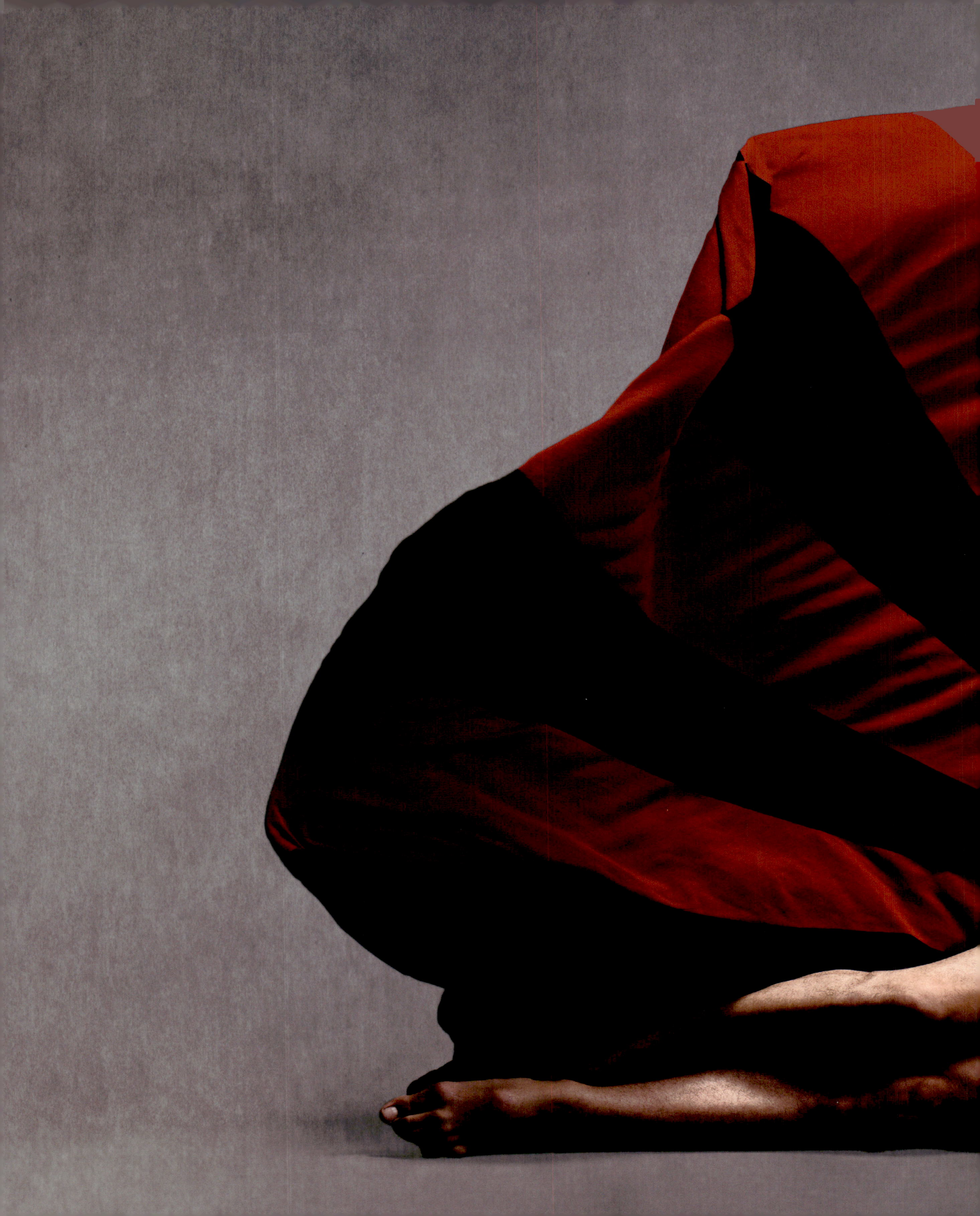

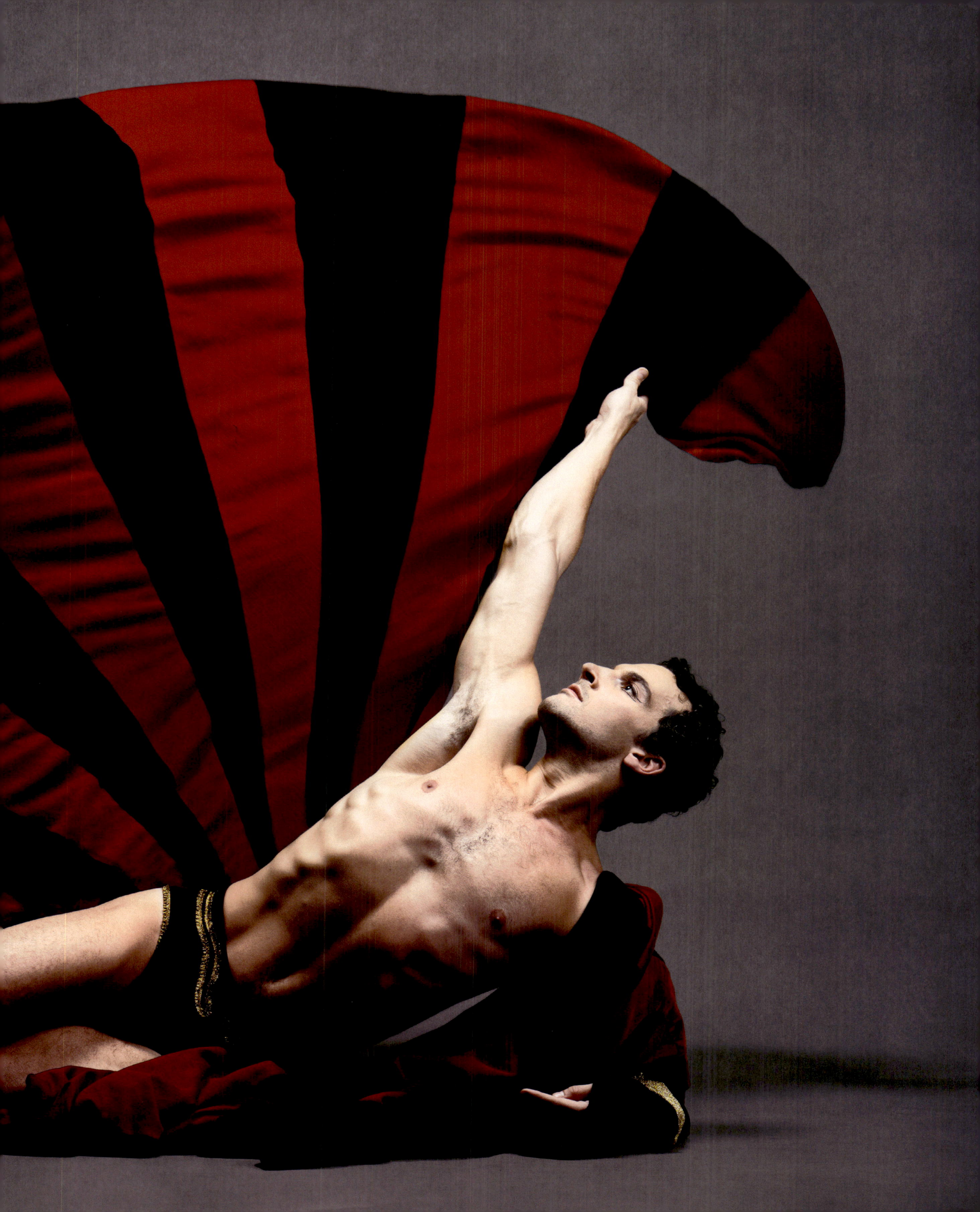

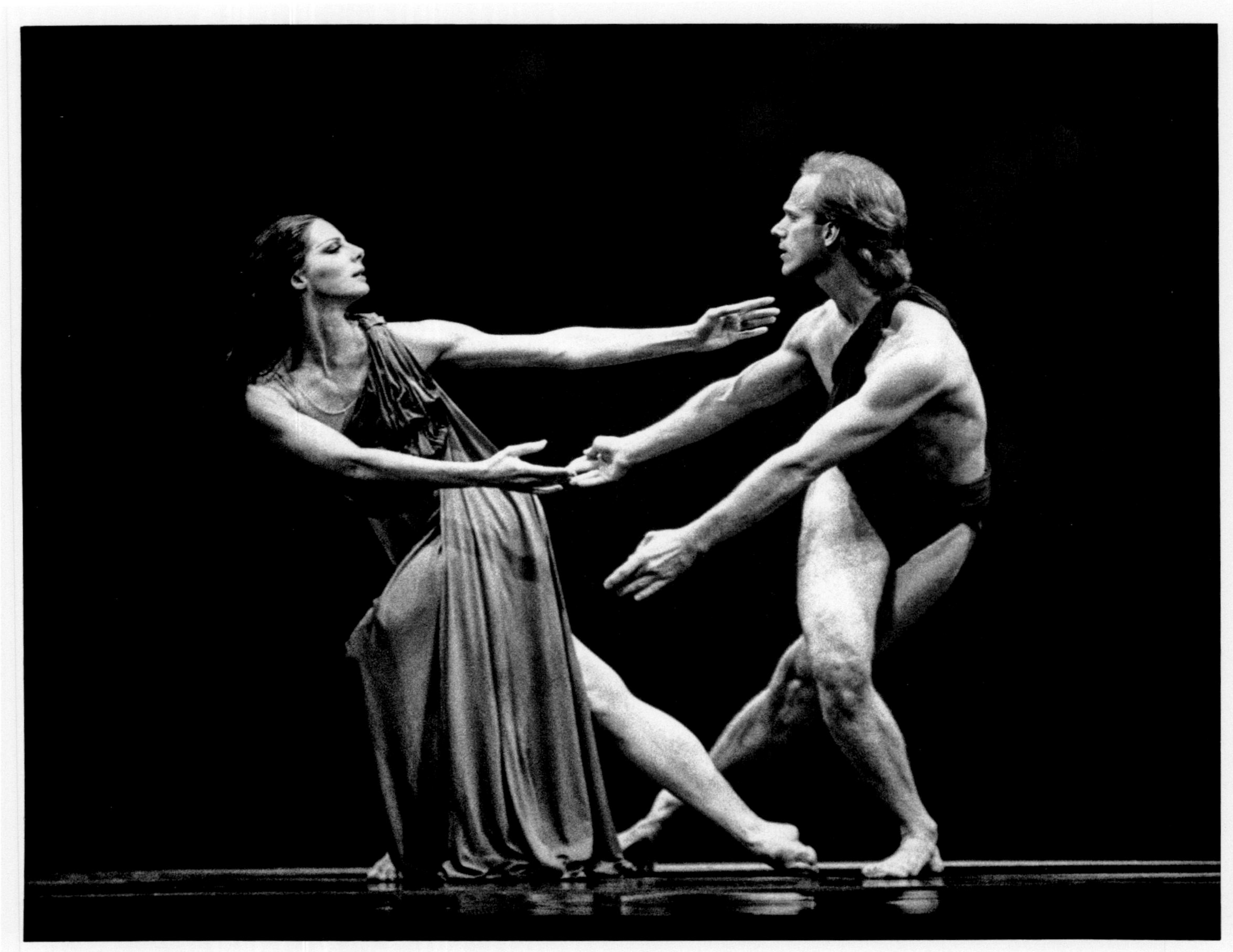

Peggy Lyman and Peter Sparling. Photograph by Sandy Geis.

ACTS OF LIGHT, 1981

A three-part work that celebrates Graham's movement language.

Borrowing for her title a phrase used by Emily Dickinson, Graham stripped her ever-evolving movement vocabulary of narrative or set elements to highlight the sheer physicality and exquisite form of her dancers.

Opening with "Conversation of Lovers," the male dancer enters from the wings, arms opening as if parting the air to carve a path to his lover, who stands alone at center stage. They pursue an exchange of reaches, falls, and lifts, punctuated by pauses evocative of an Etruscan couple guarding their temple of love.

The second section, "Lament," clearly references Graham's iconic solo from 1930, *Lamentation*, and features a female dancer shrouded in a cocoon of white elastic fabric framed by five male acolytes.

Entitled "Ritual to the Sun," the third and final section features the full company of gold-clad dancers, who perform a virtuosic demonstration of the Graham classroom technique.

COSTUME DESIGN
Halston

COMPOSER
Carl Nielsen

"Conversations with Lovers"
from *Acts of Light*

DANCERS
Lloyd Knight and Charlotte Landreau

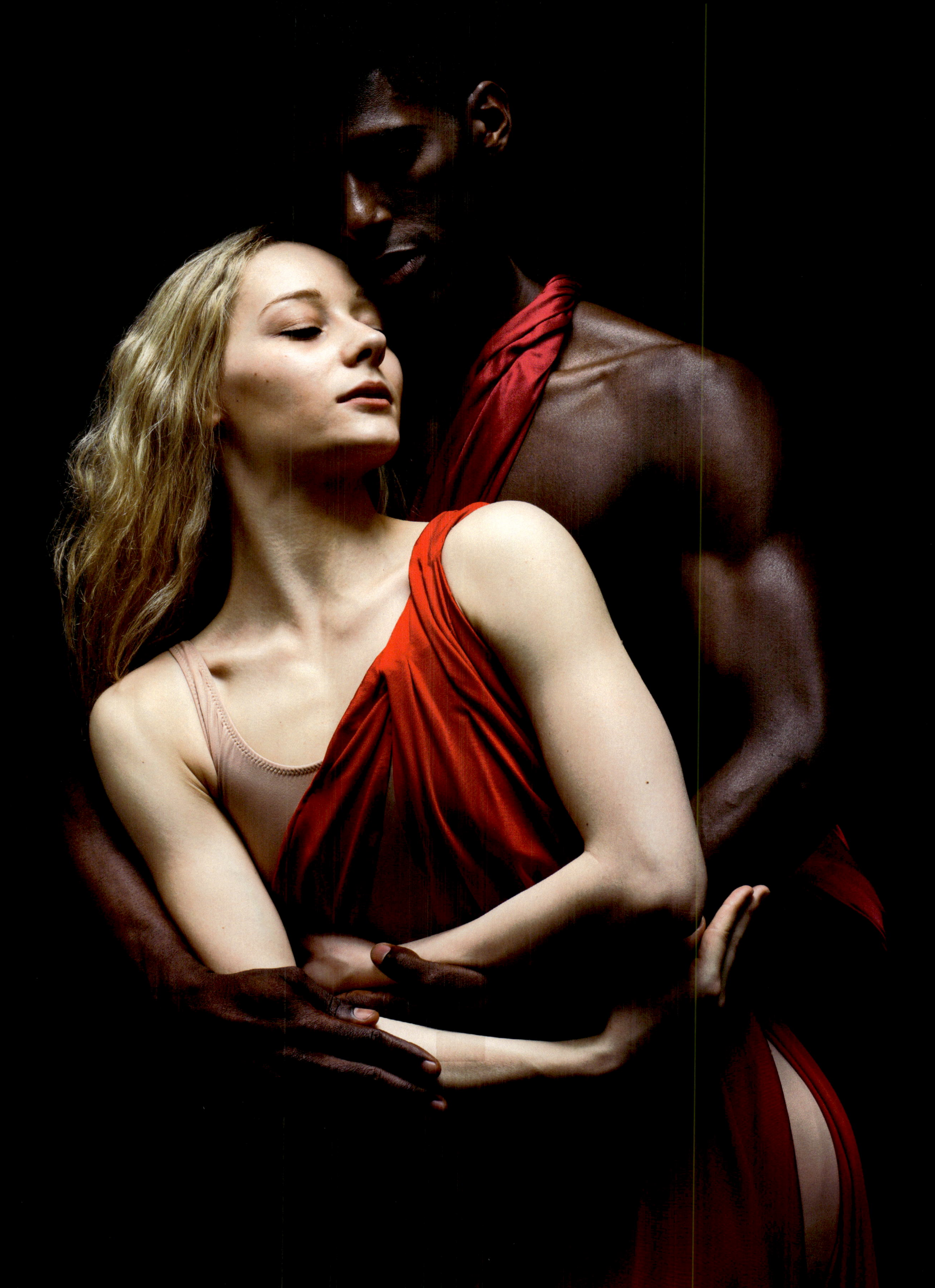

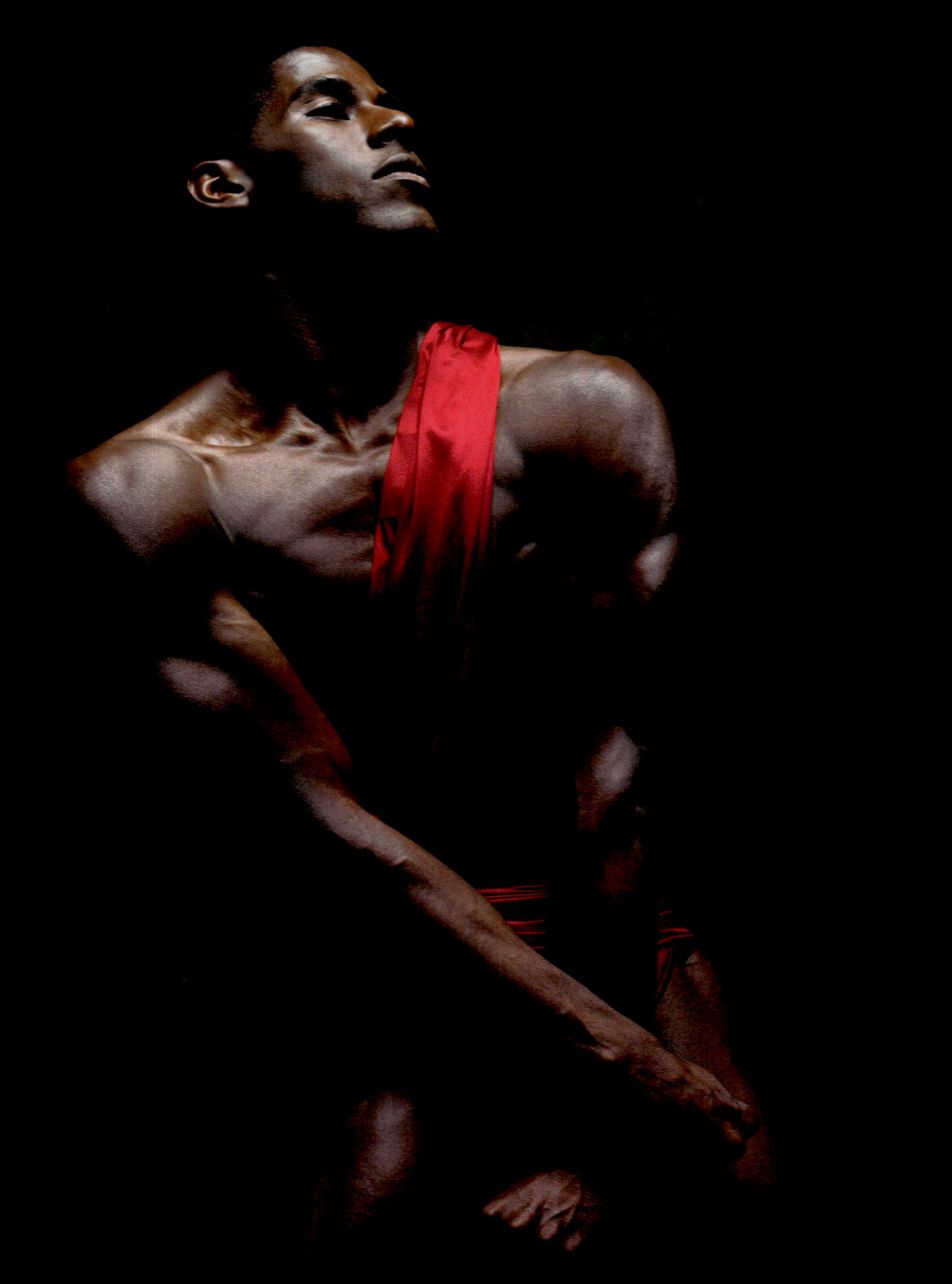

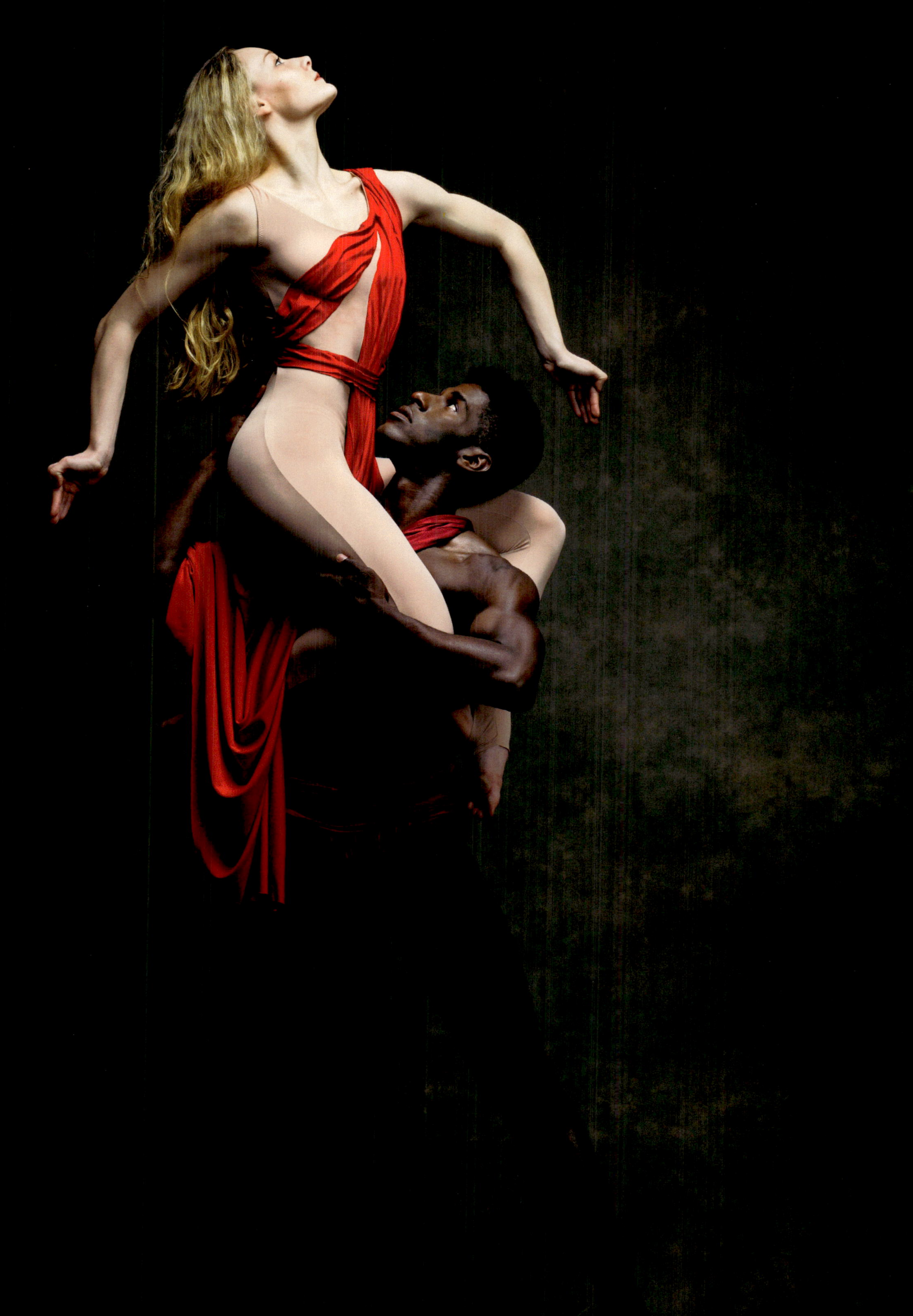

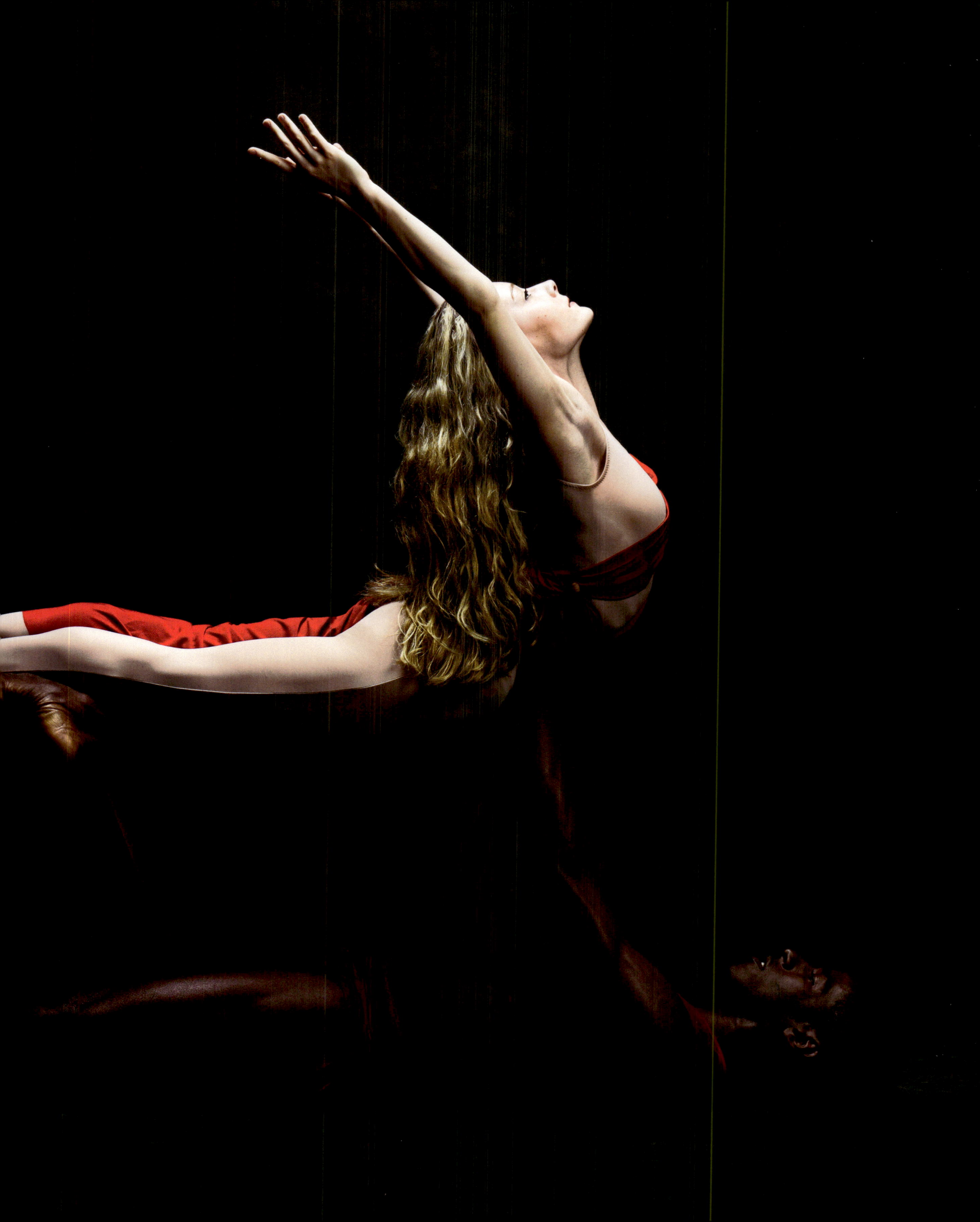

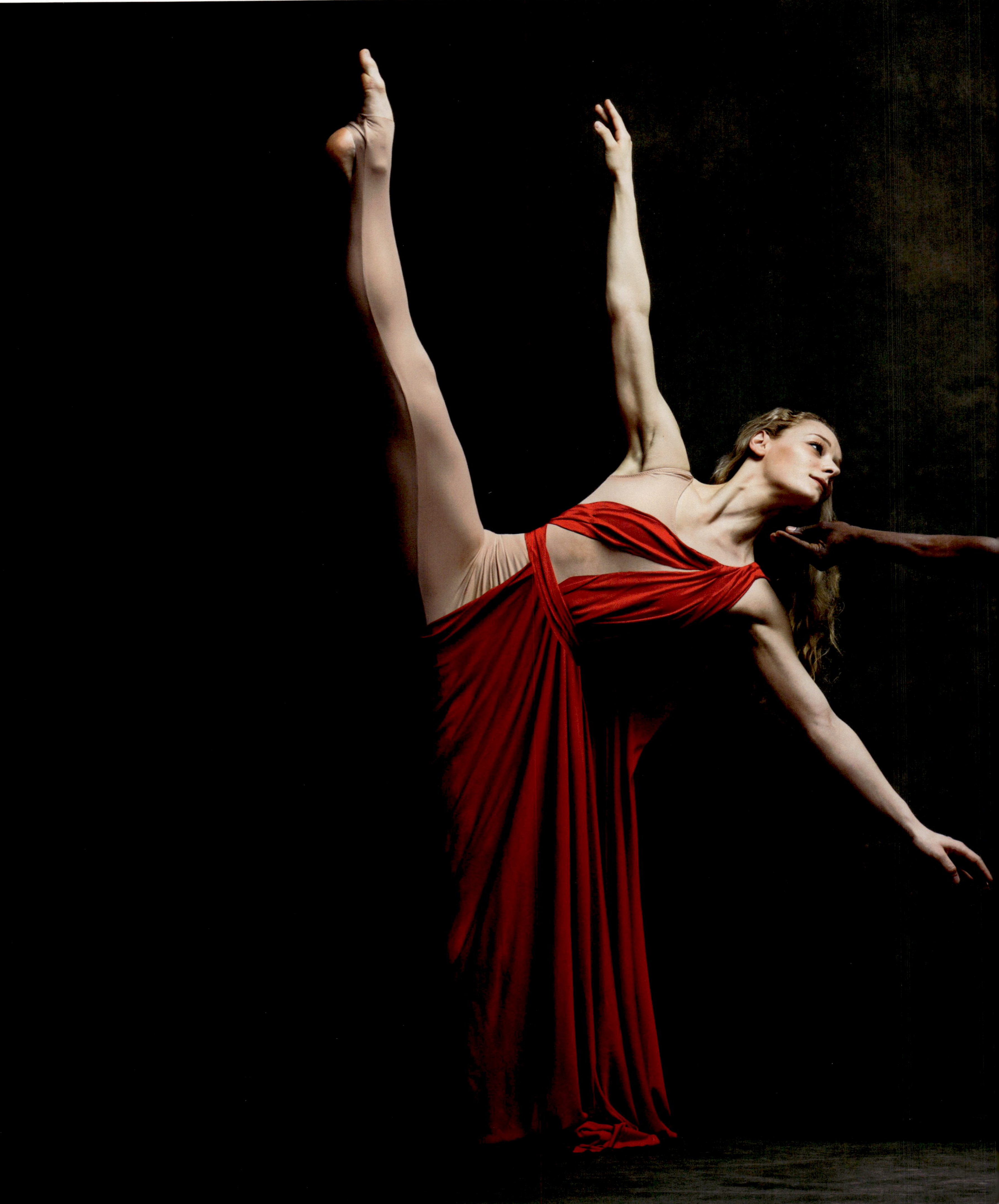

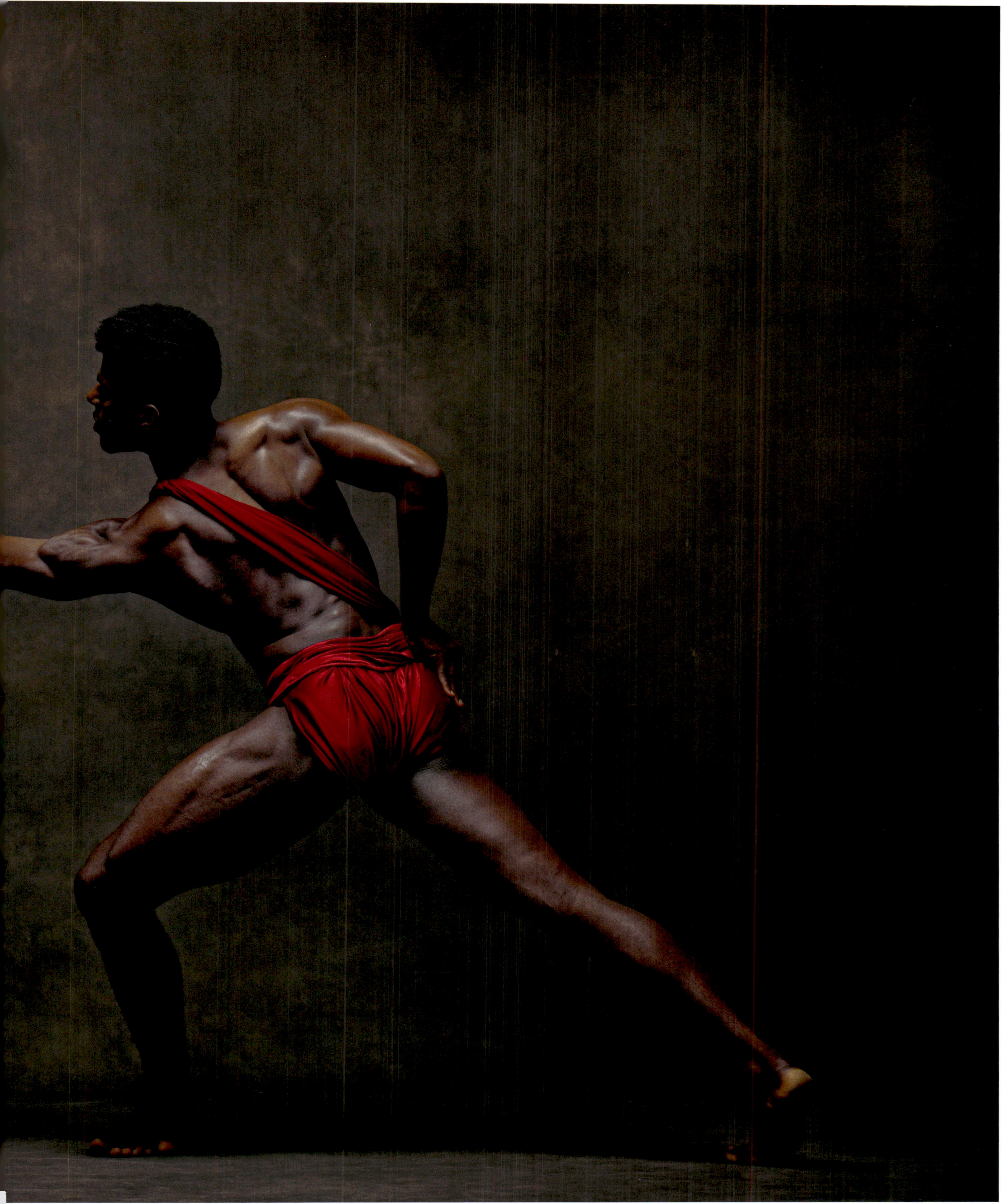

"Lament" from *Acts of Light*

DANCERS

Anne O'Donnell Passero and Jacob Larsen

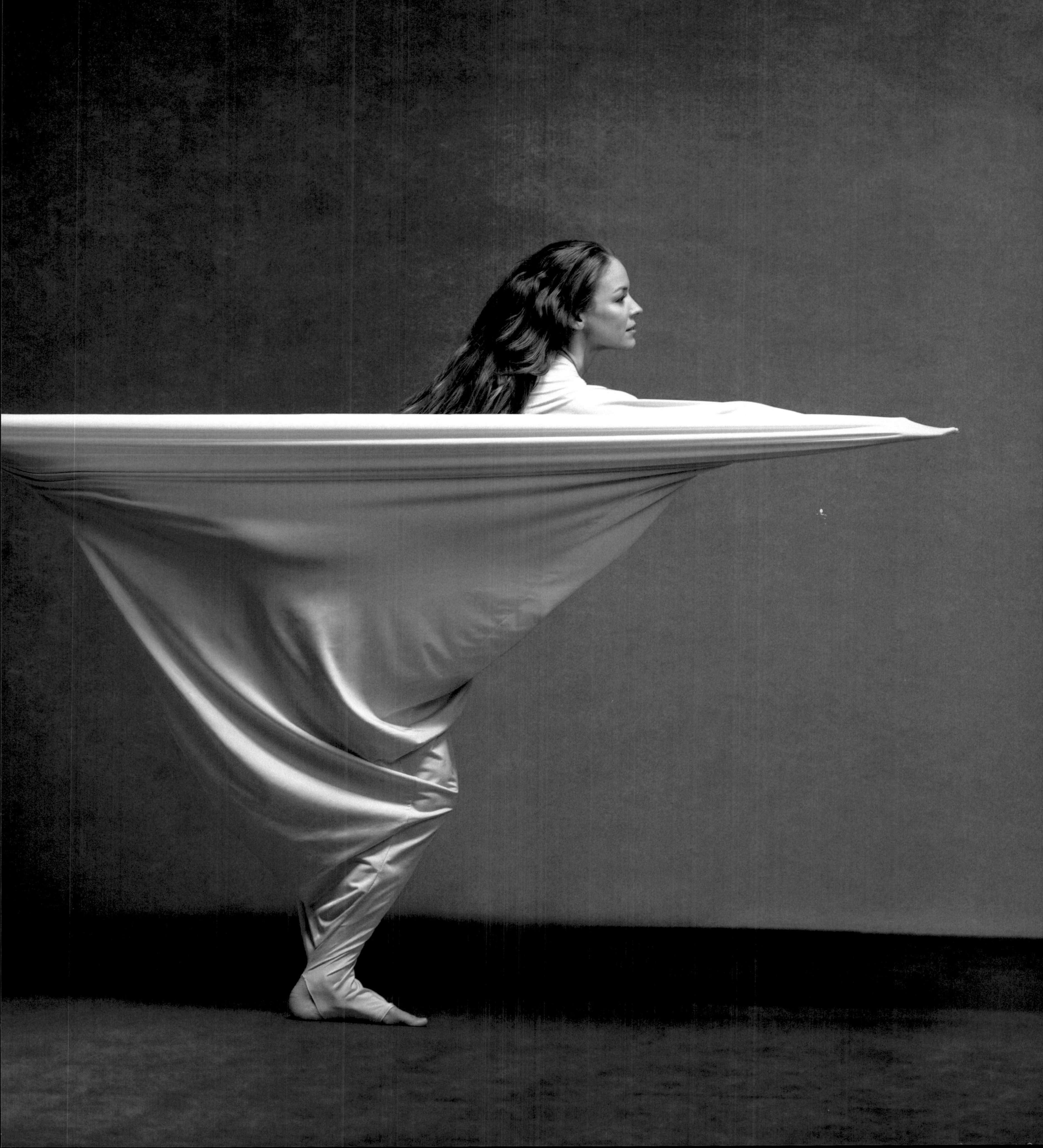

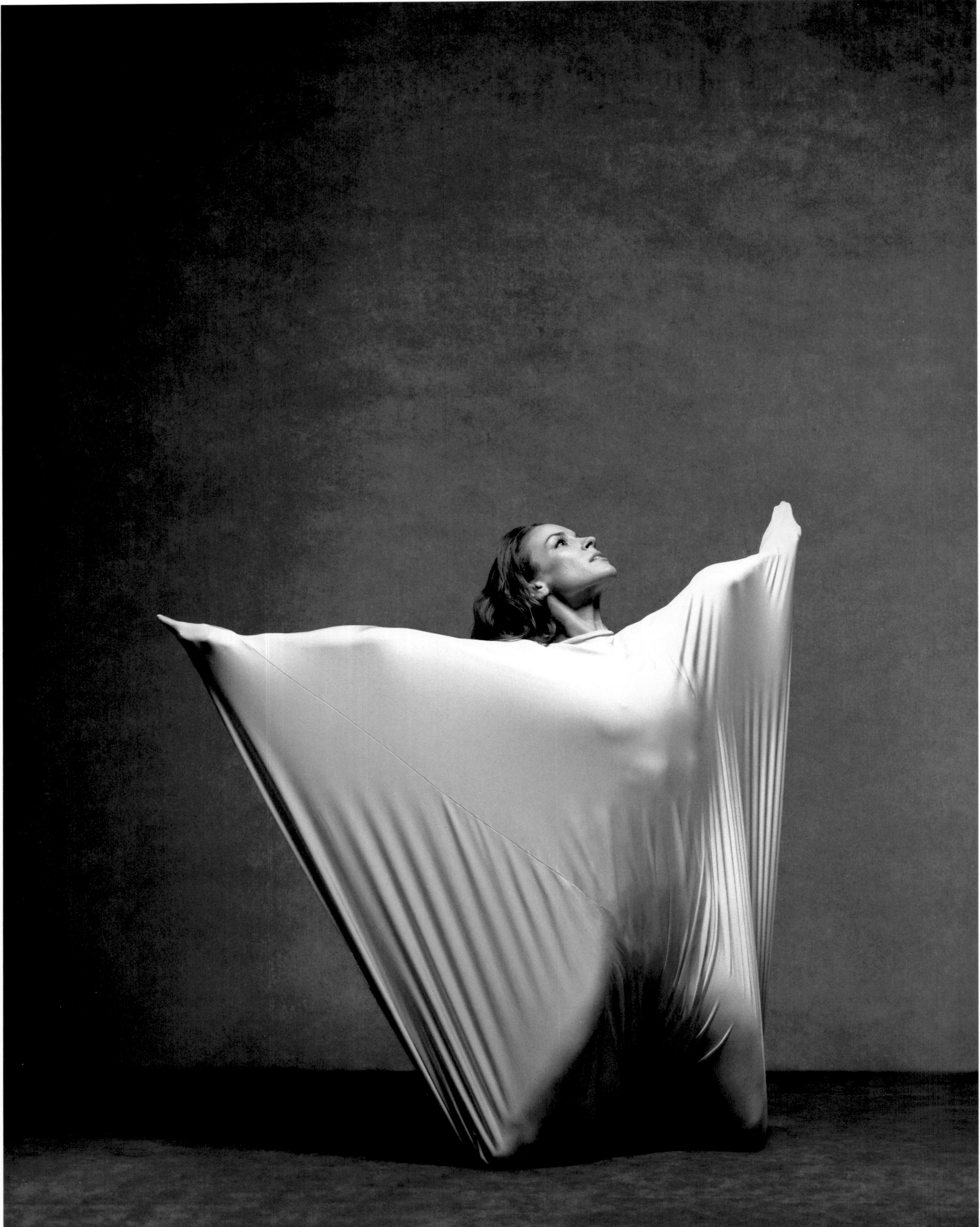

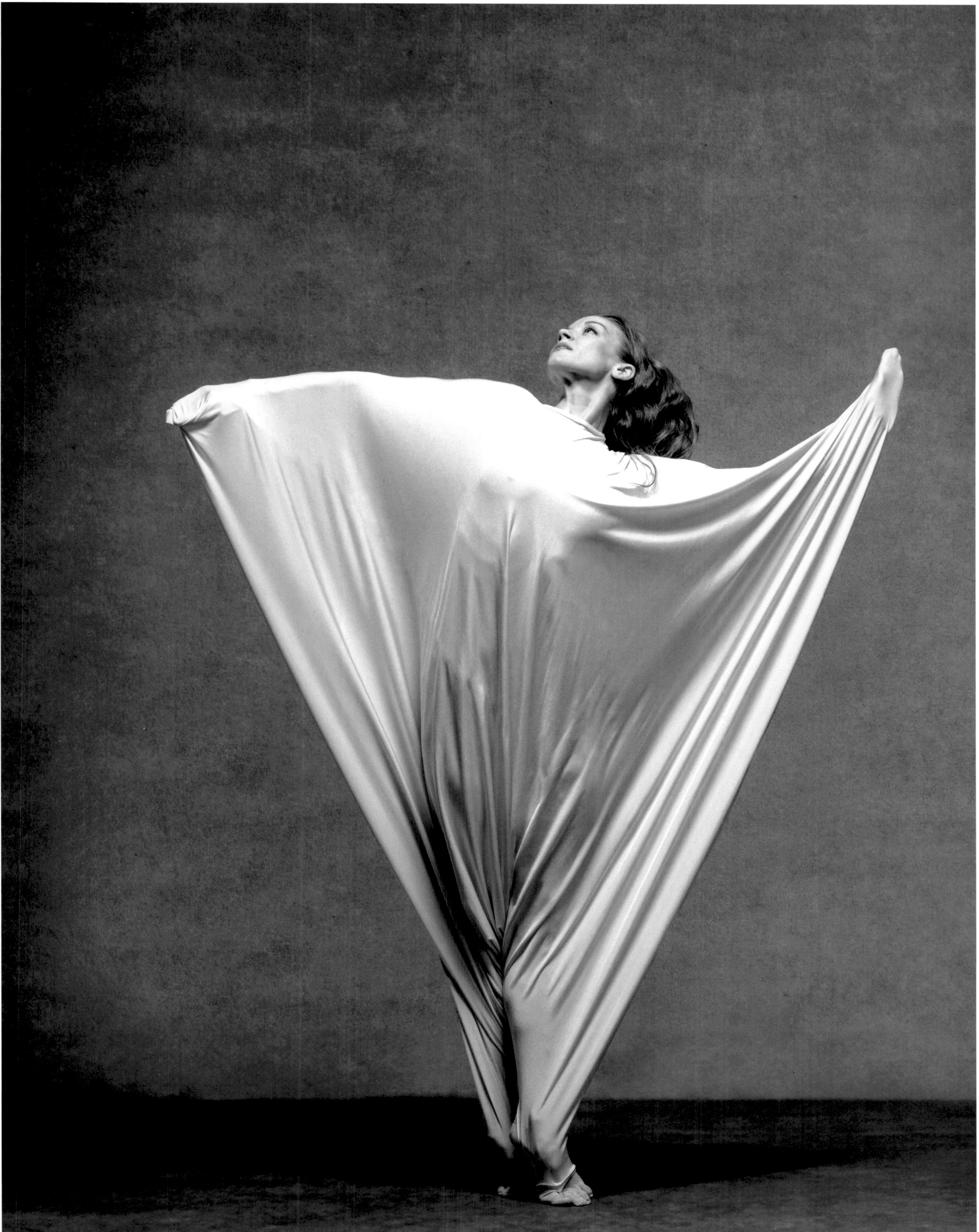

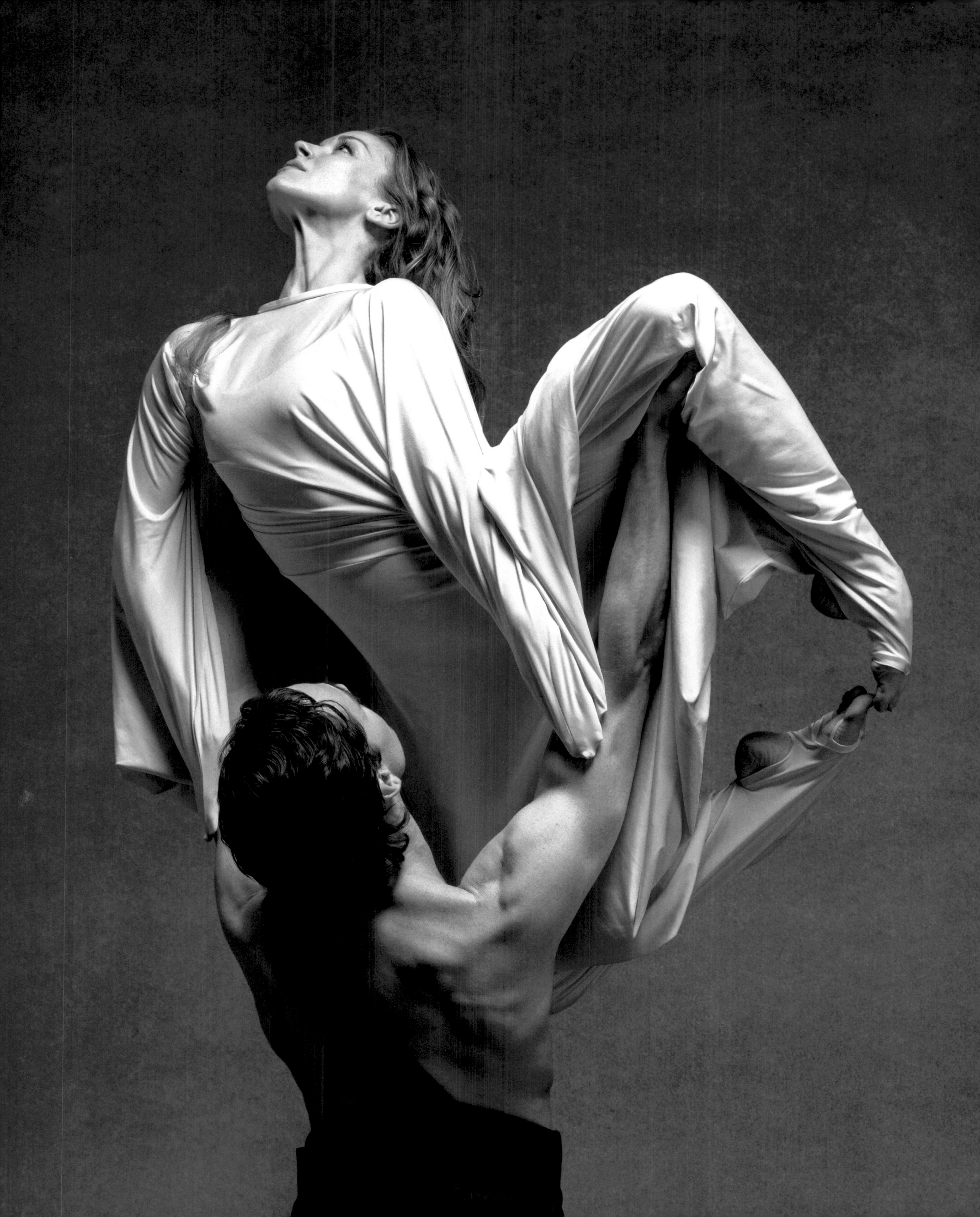

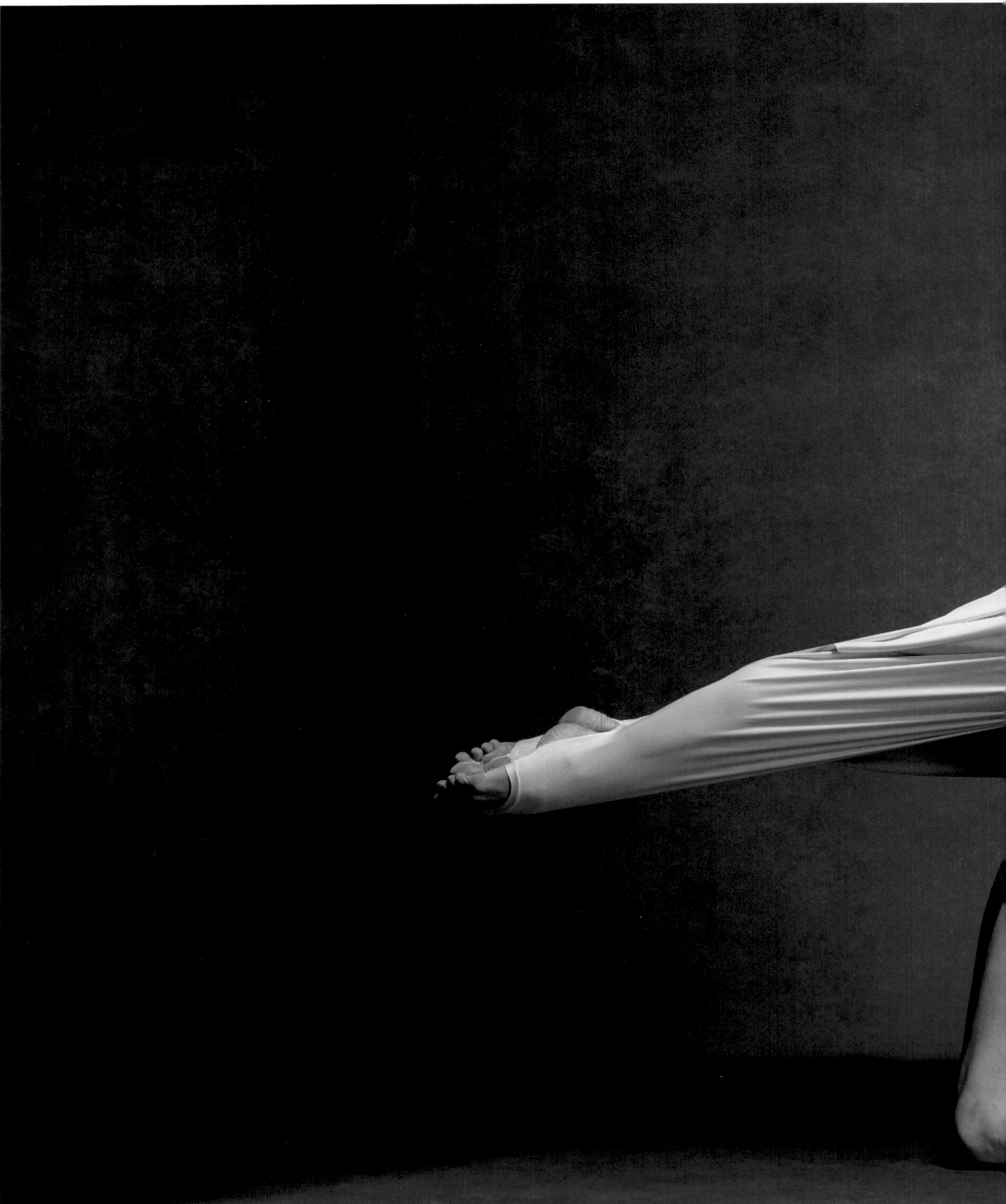

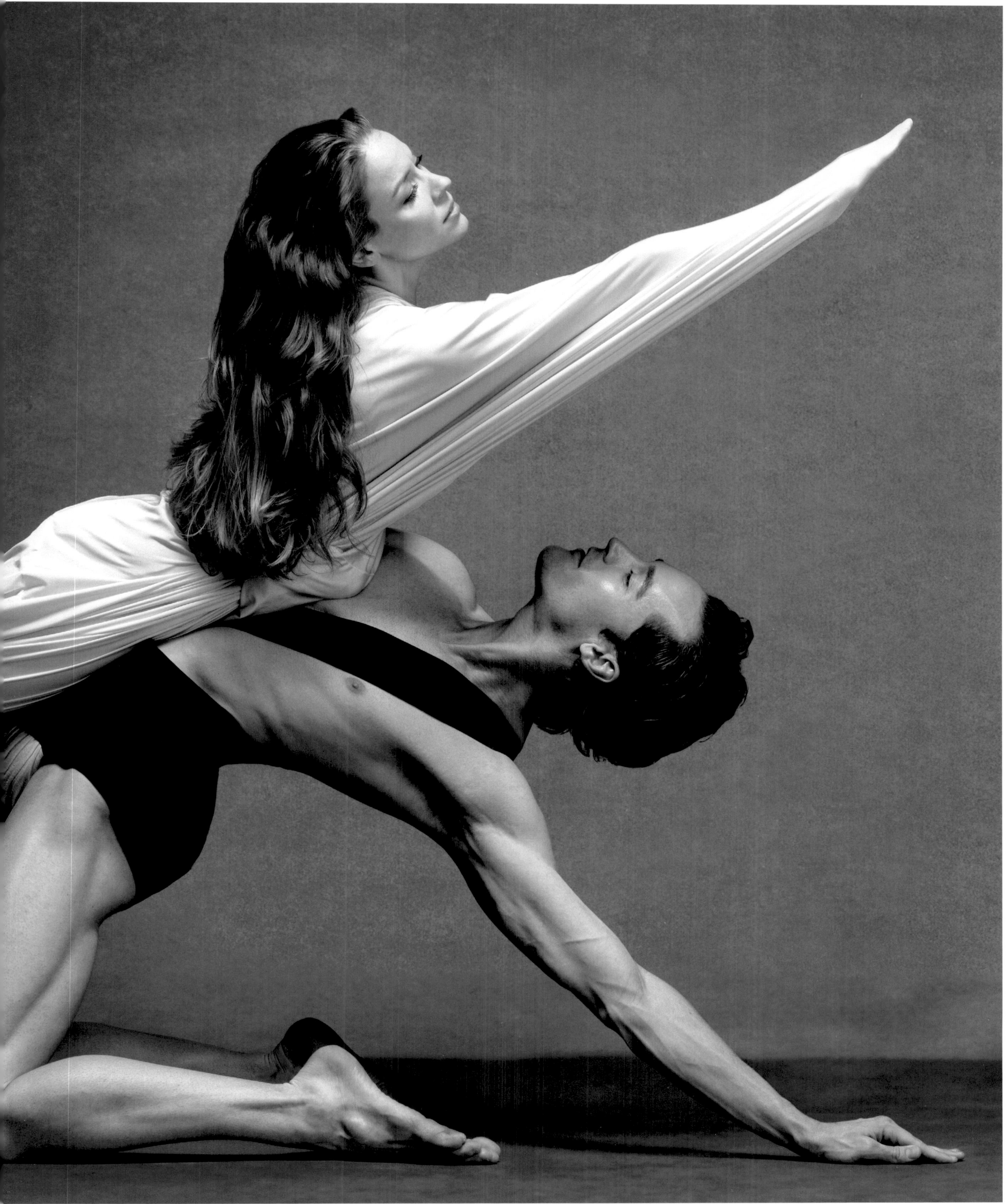

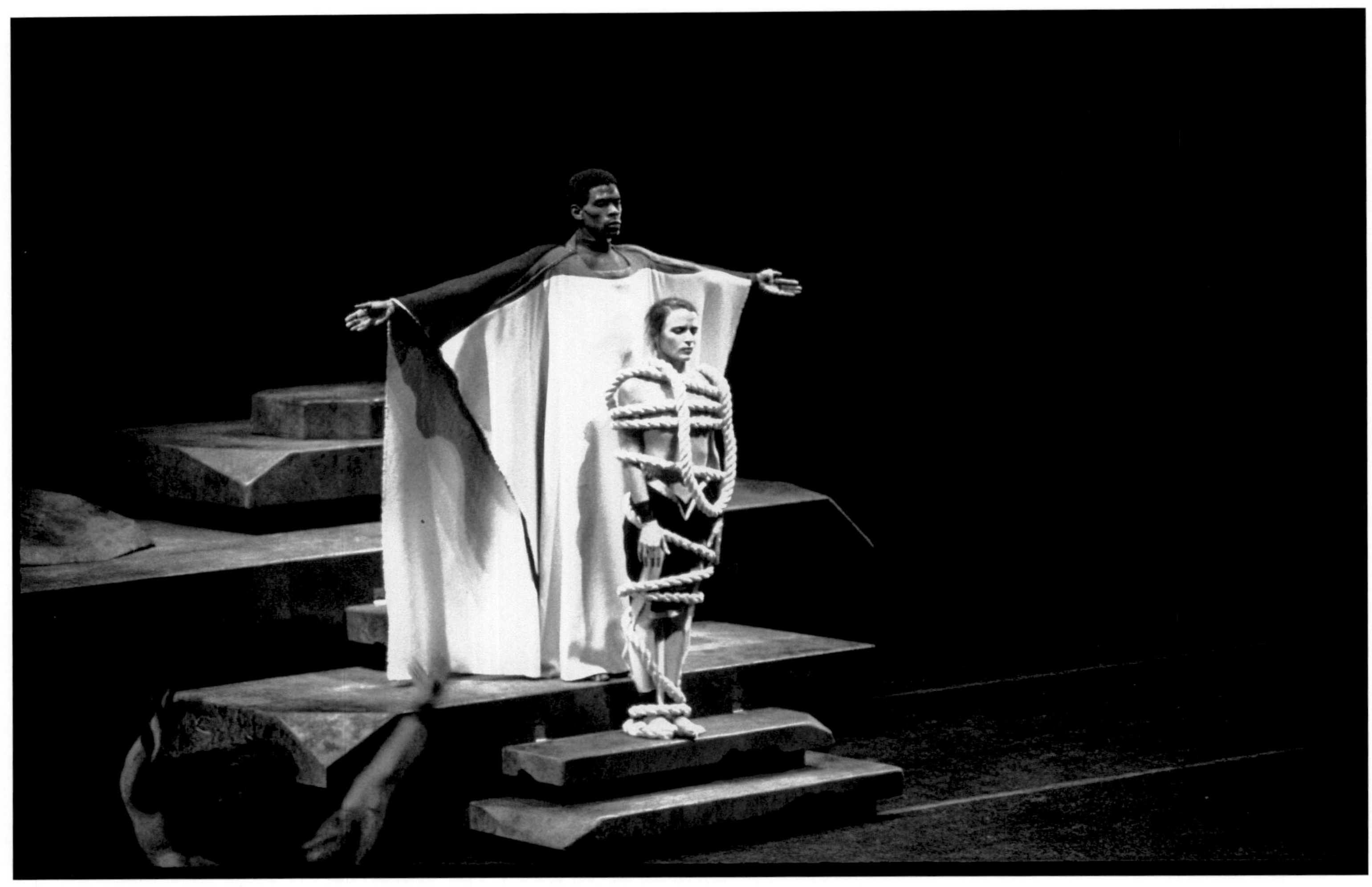

Terese Capucilli as the Chosen One and George White Jr. as the Shaman. Photograph by Martha Swope.

THE RITE OF SPRING, 1984

A tribal community enacts
a seasonal ritual of sacrifice.

Graham first encountered Igor Stravinsky's monumental, revolutionary score when she danced the role of the Chosen One in Léonide Massine's version of *The Rite of Spring* in 1930. Fifty-four years later, she returned to the score to create a full-company masterwork that bookended her long career.

Graham's version of *The Rite of Spring* builds on the concept of a tribal community enacting the seasonal ritual of sacrifice to the gods. The Shaman chooses a virgin, the Chosen One, from among a chorus of women. She is instructed to dance until her death to please the deities. Her grueling ordeal is framed by geometric configurations of the chorus, whose solemn groupings are in sharp contrast with the increasingly ritualized violence between the Shaman and the Chosen One. The Chosen One eventually yields to her doom after a relentless, convulsive solo that levels her repeatedly to the floor. It is a compressed study in Graham's career-long exploration of contract and release, fall and recovery movement.

COSTUME DESIGN
Halston

COMPOSER
Igor Stravinsky

The Rite of Spring

THE CHOSEN ONE
Xin Ying

THE SHAMAN
Alessio Crognale-Roberts

DANCERS
The Company

COSTUME RE-CREATION
Pilar Limosner and Janet Eilber

PROJECTION DESIGN
Paul Lieber

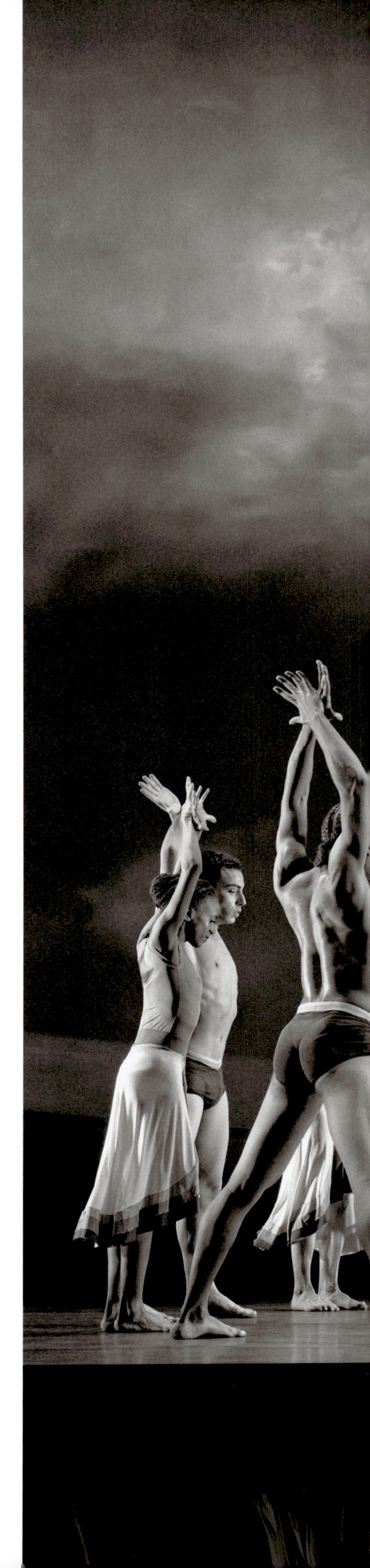

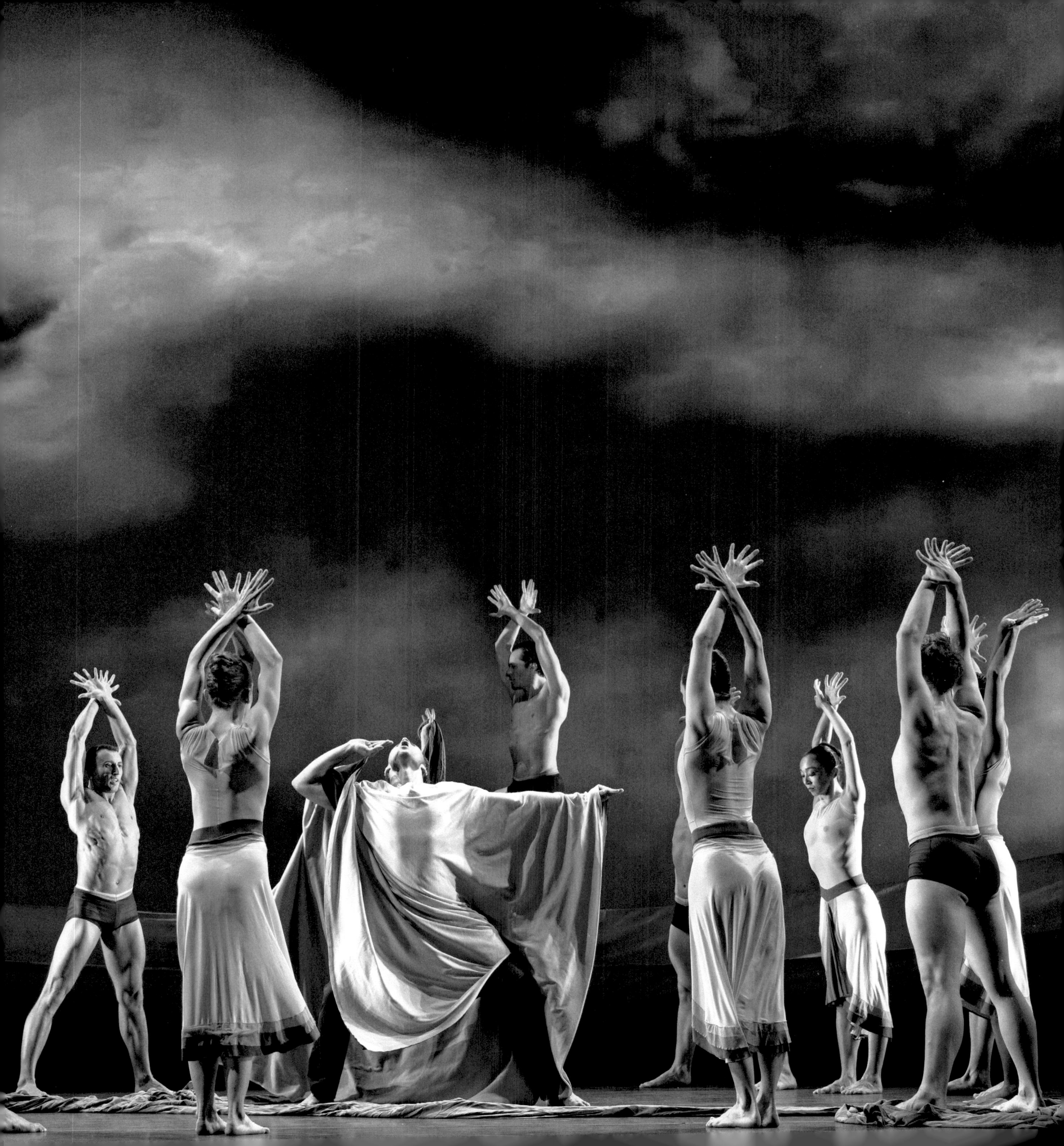

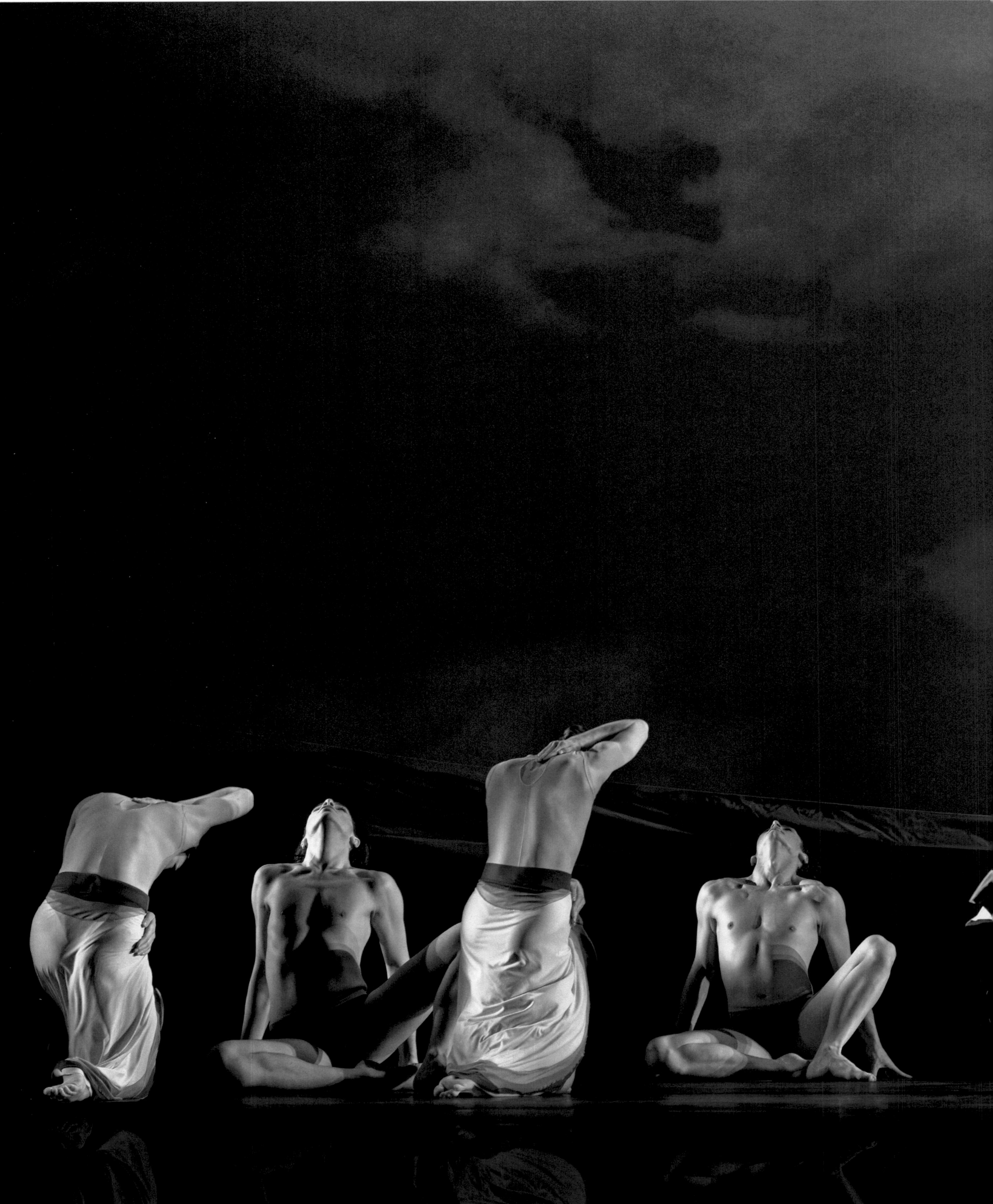

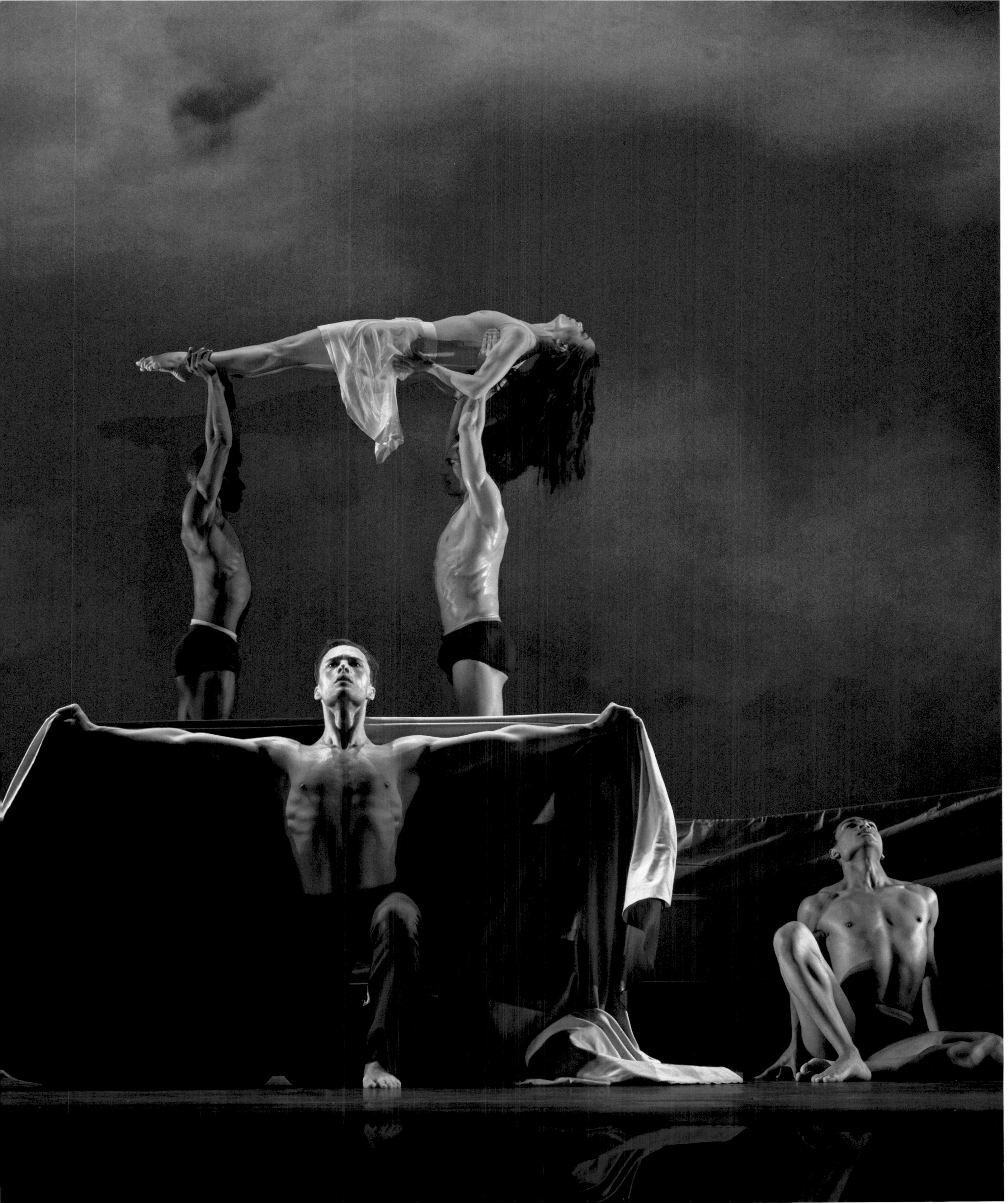

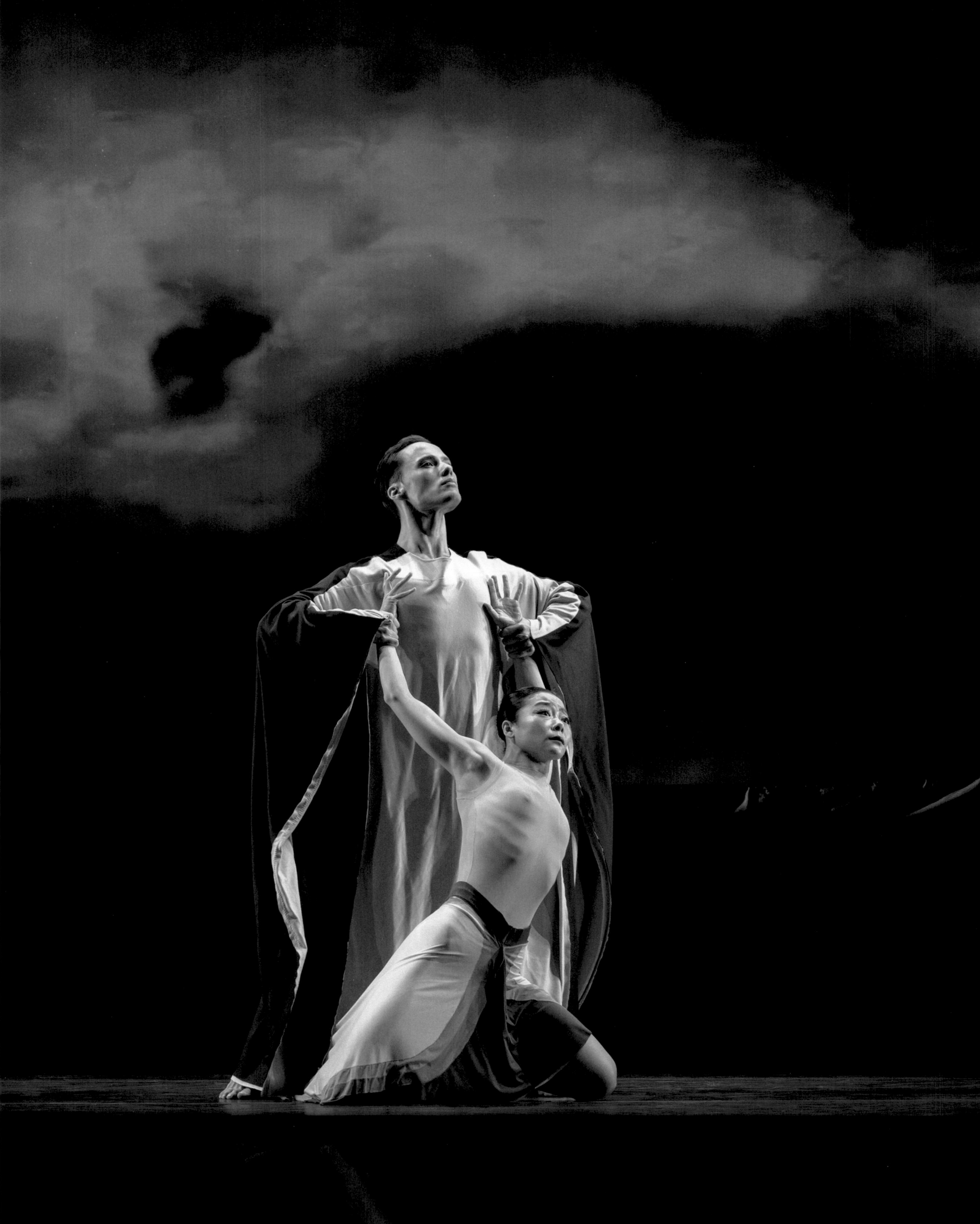

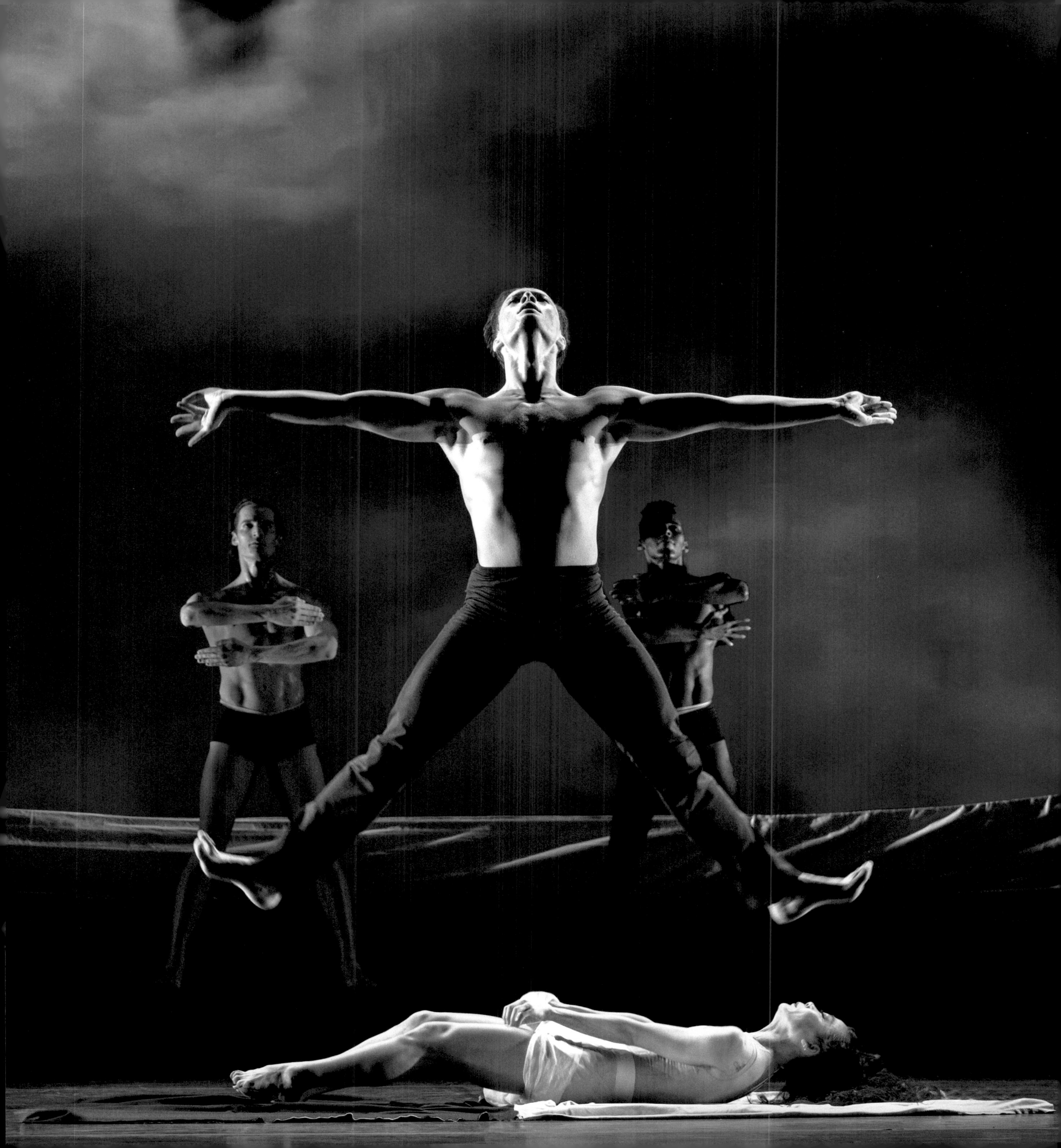

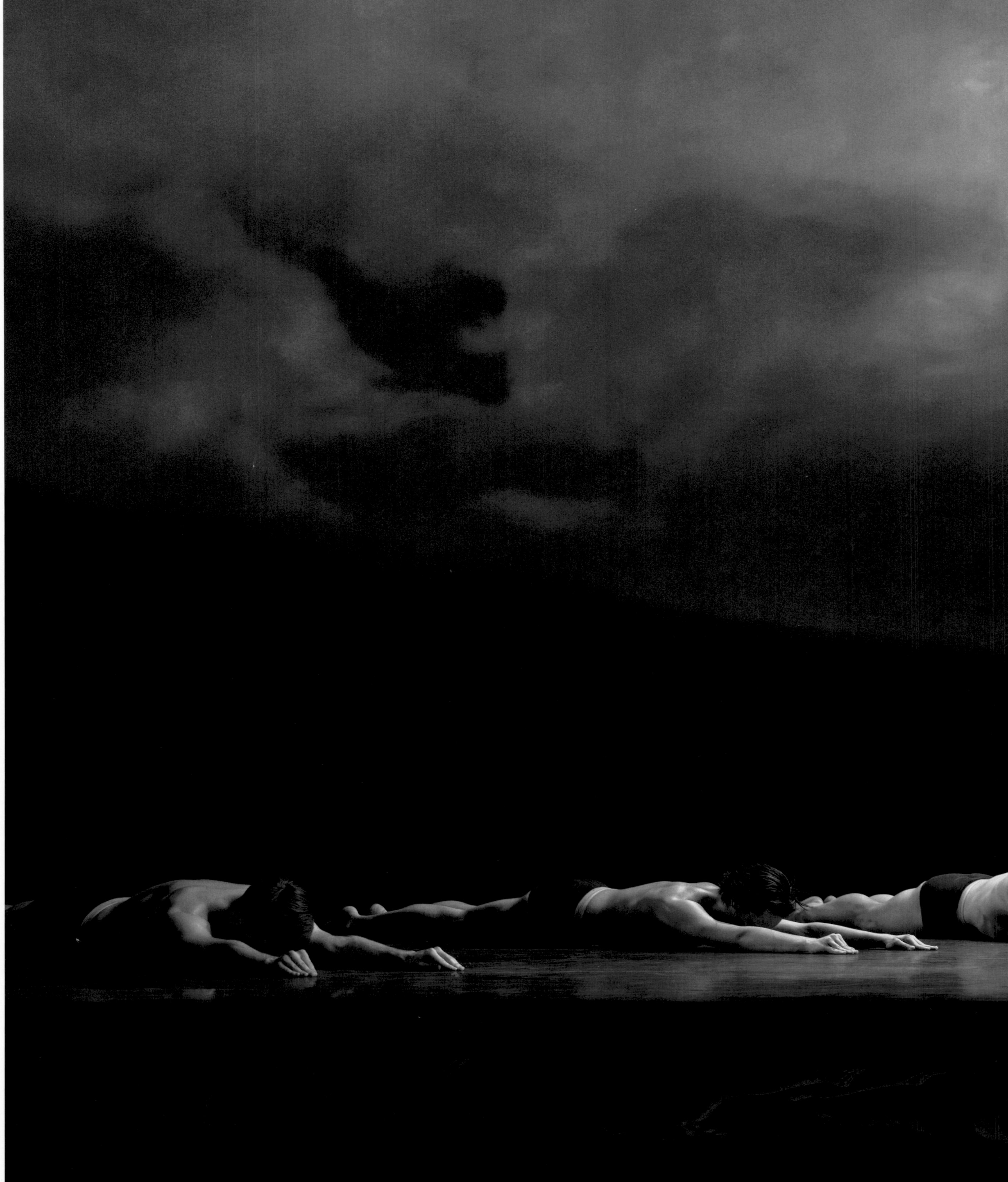

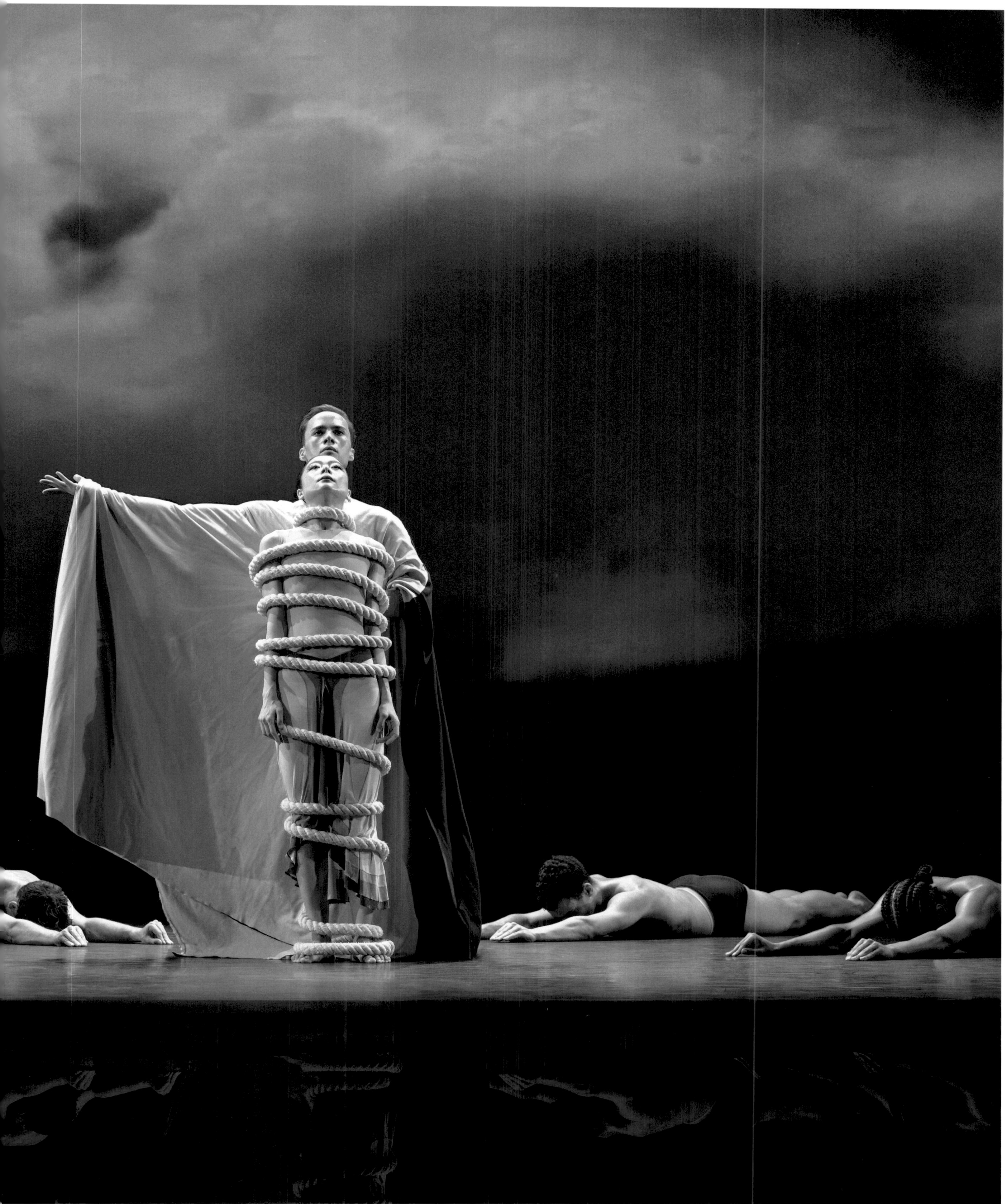

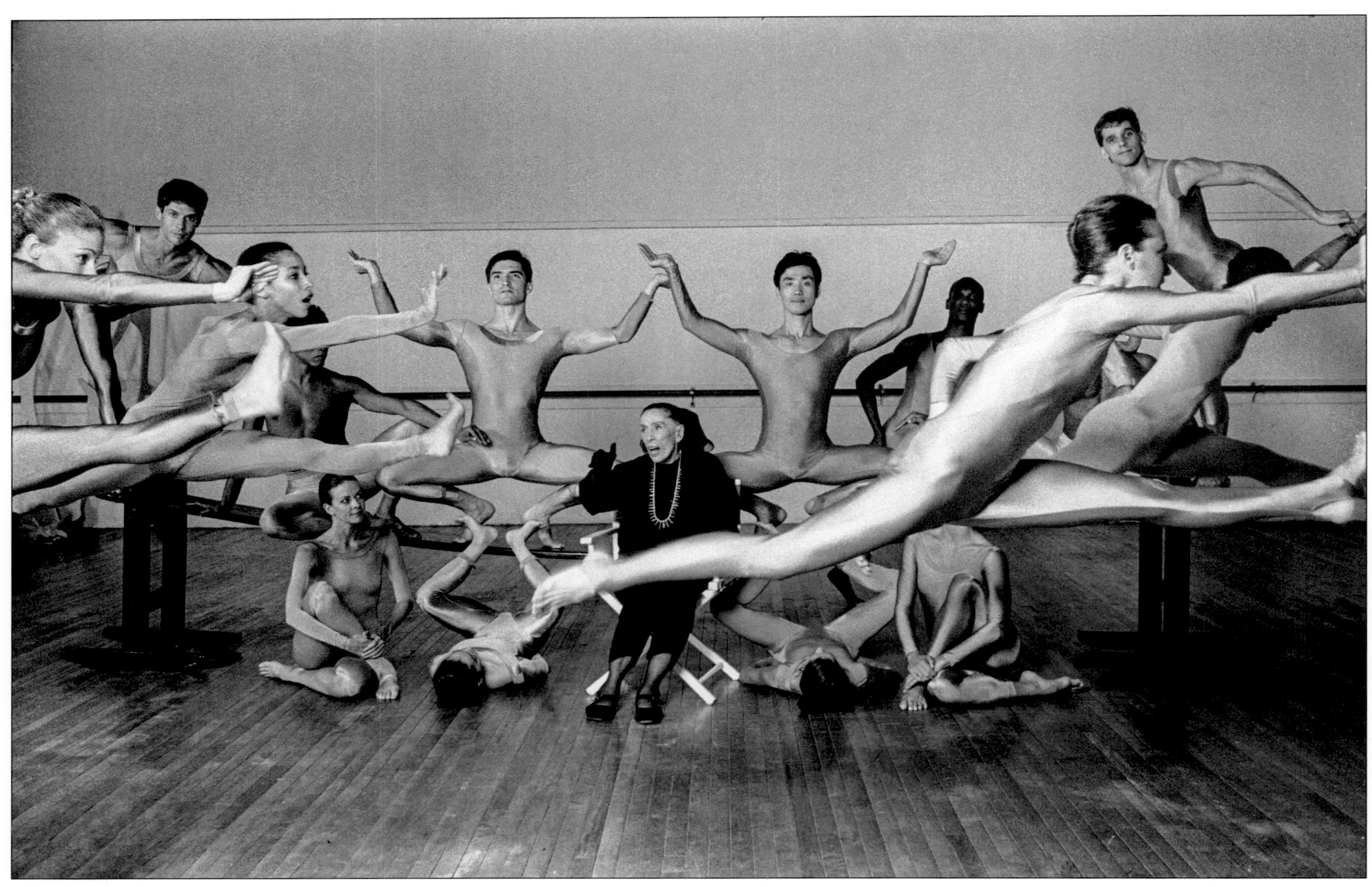

Martha Graham and Company. Photograph by Jim Wilson.

MAPLE LEAF RAG, 1990

A playful send-up of the beleaguered artist.

Graham created this, her last complete work, at the age of ninety-six. *Maple Leaf Rag* opens on a motley assortment of dancers circling, leaping, and bouncing to an ominous repeated chord on the piano. A recording of Graham's voice is heard imploring her one-time pianist and lover, Louis Horst, to play her "the 'Maple Leaf Rag.'" As the Joplin music begins, a solitary woman sits at the center of a long flexible rail in mock agony of the creative process. A witty display of antics follows as dancers invade her space and provide her with lively distractions. A woman enters repeatedly as the voice of creative doom, using a huge circular skirt to slice through the mood. Couples fill the stage with prancing, leaps, cartwheels, and other parodies of classic Graham repertory. As the final work of her long career, Martha looked back and was willing and able to laugh at herself.

SET DESIGN
Martha Graham

COSTUME DESIGN
Calvin Klein

COMPOSER
Scott Joplin

Maple Leaf Rag

DANCERS
So Young An, James Anthony,
Alessio Crognale-Roberts,
Laurel Dalley Smith, Meagan King,
Antonio Leone, Marzia Memoli,
Richard Villaverde

COSTUME RE-CREATION
Karen Young

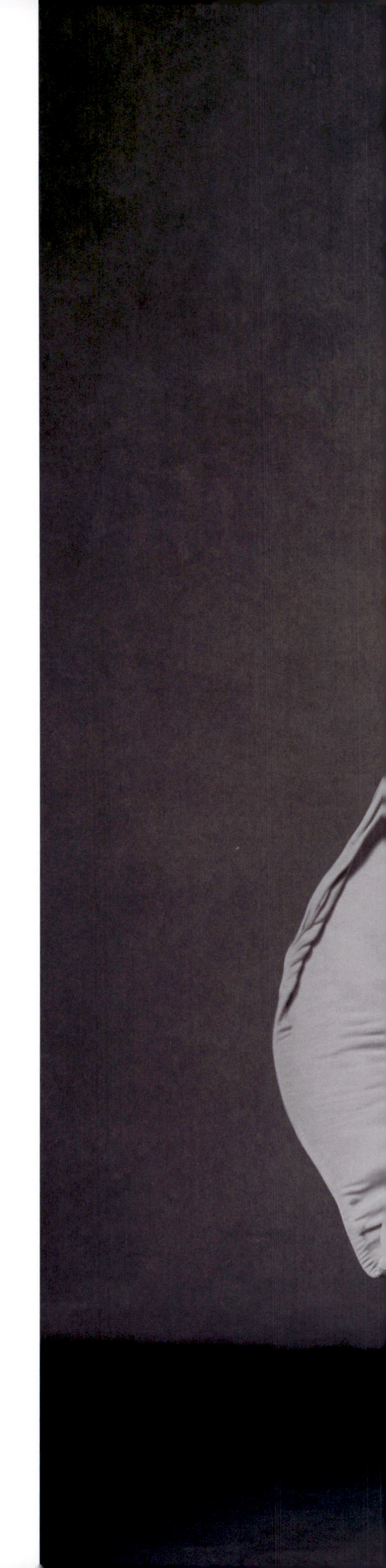

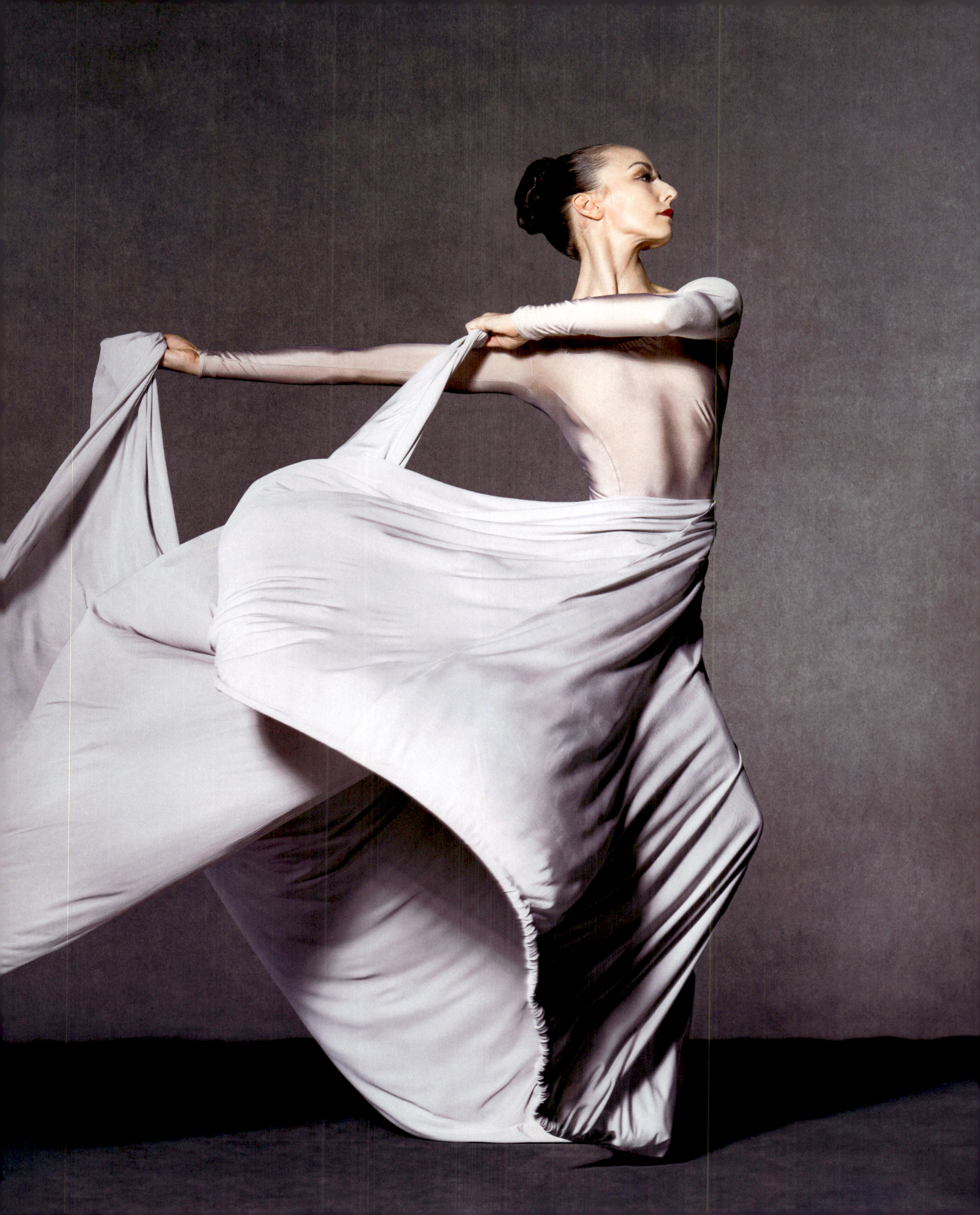

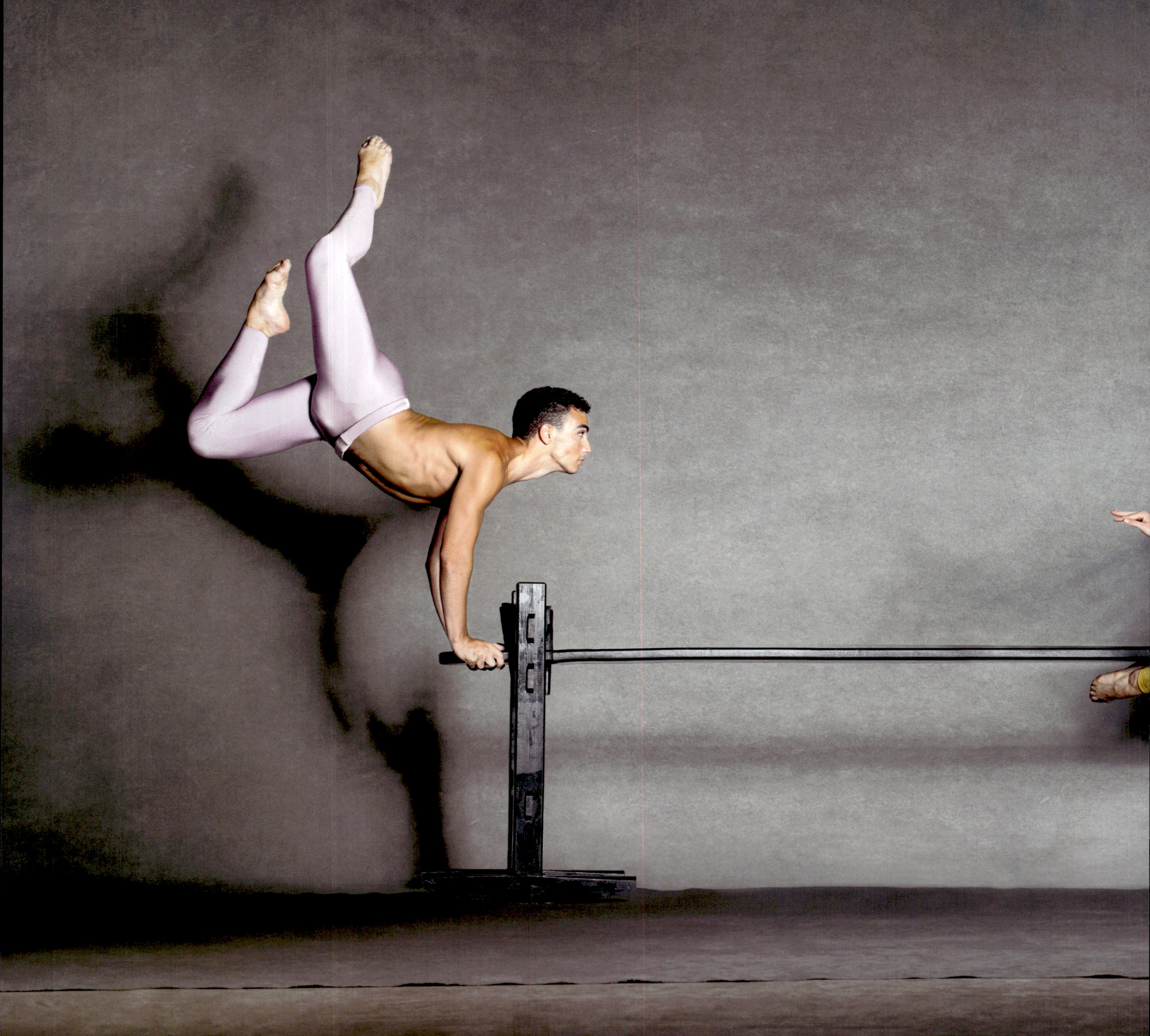

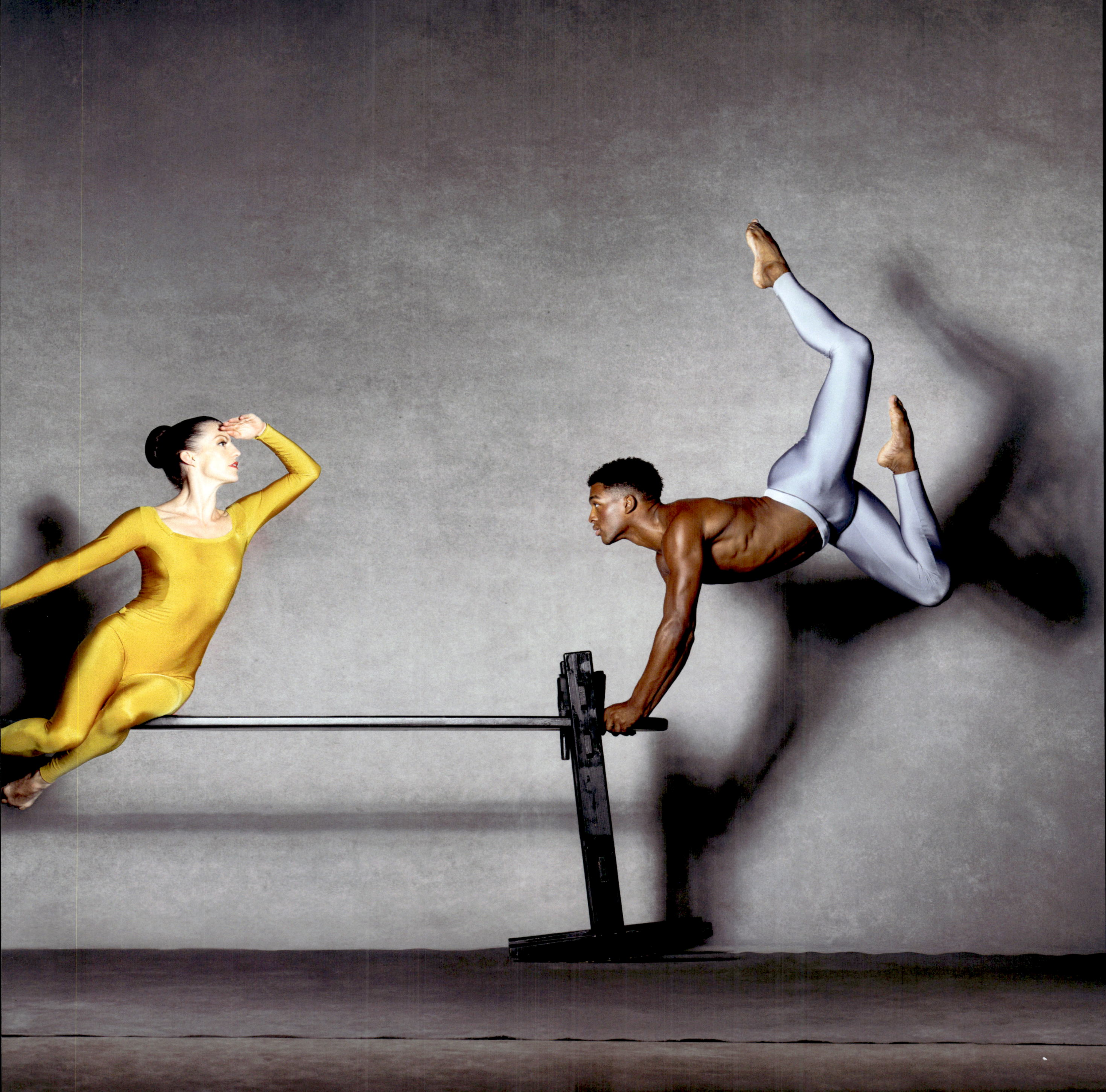

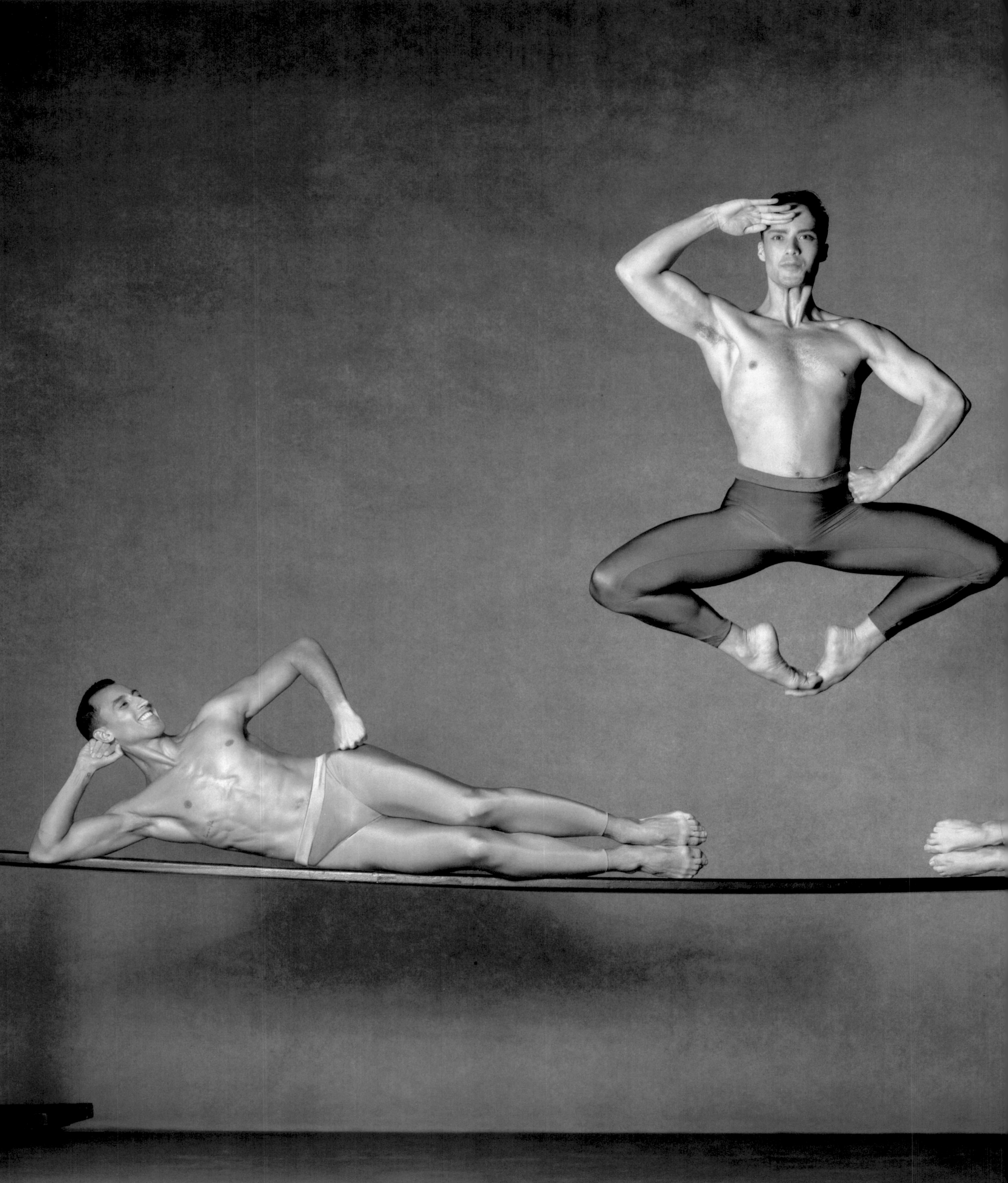

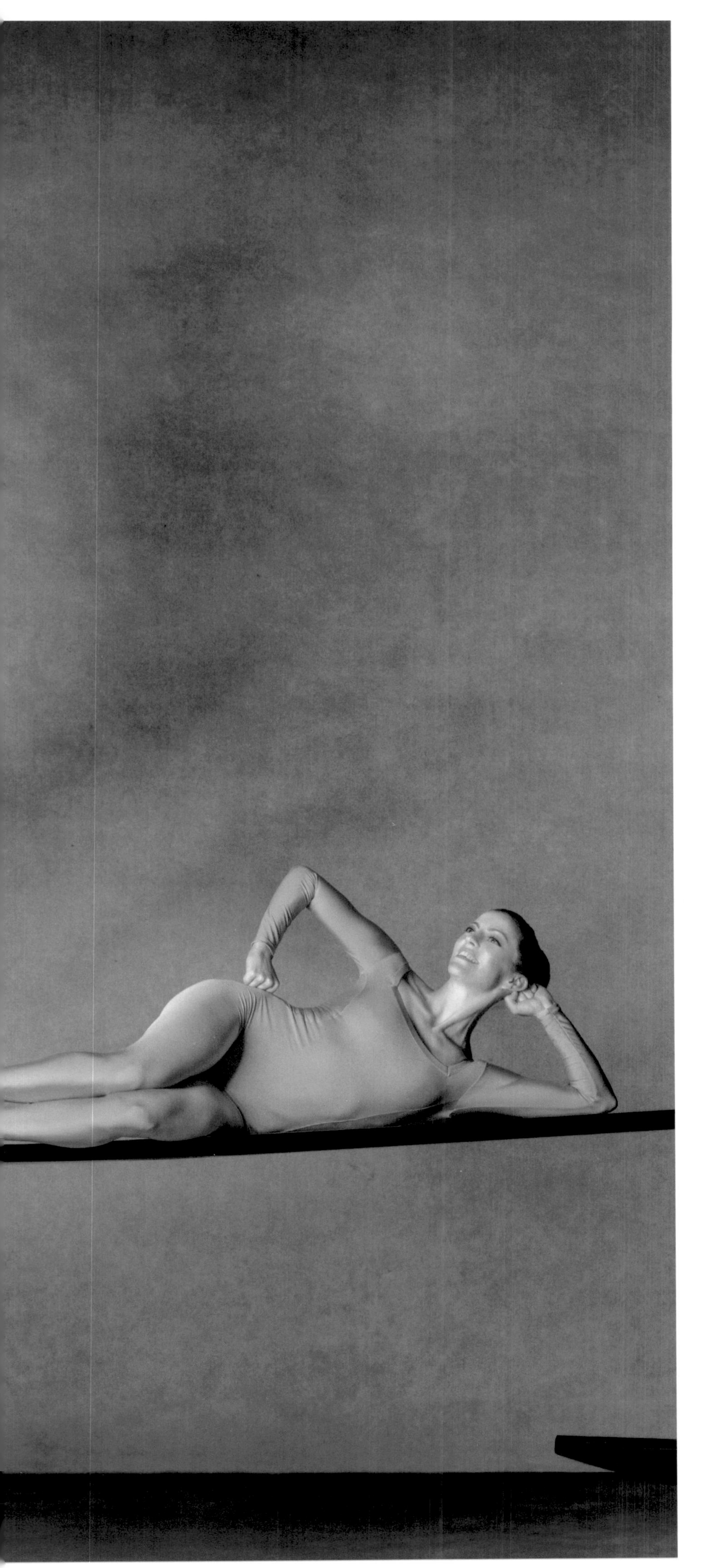

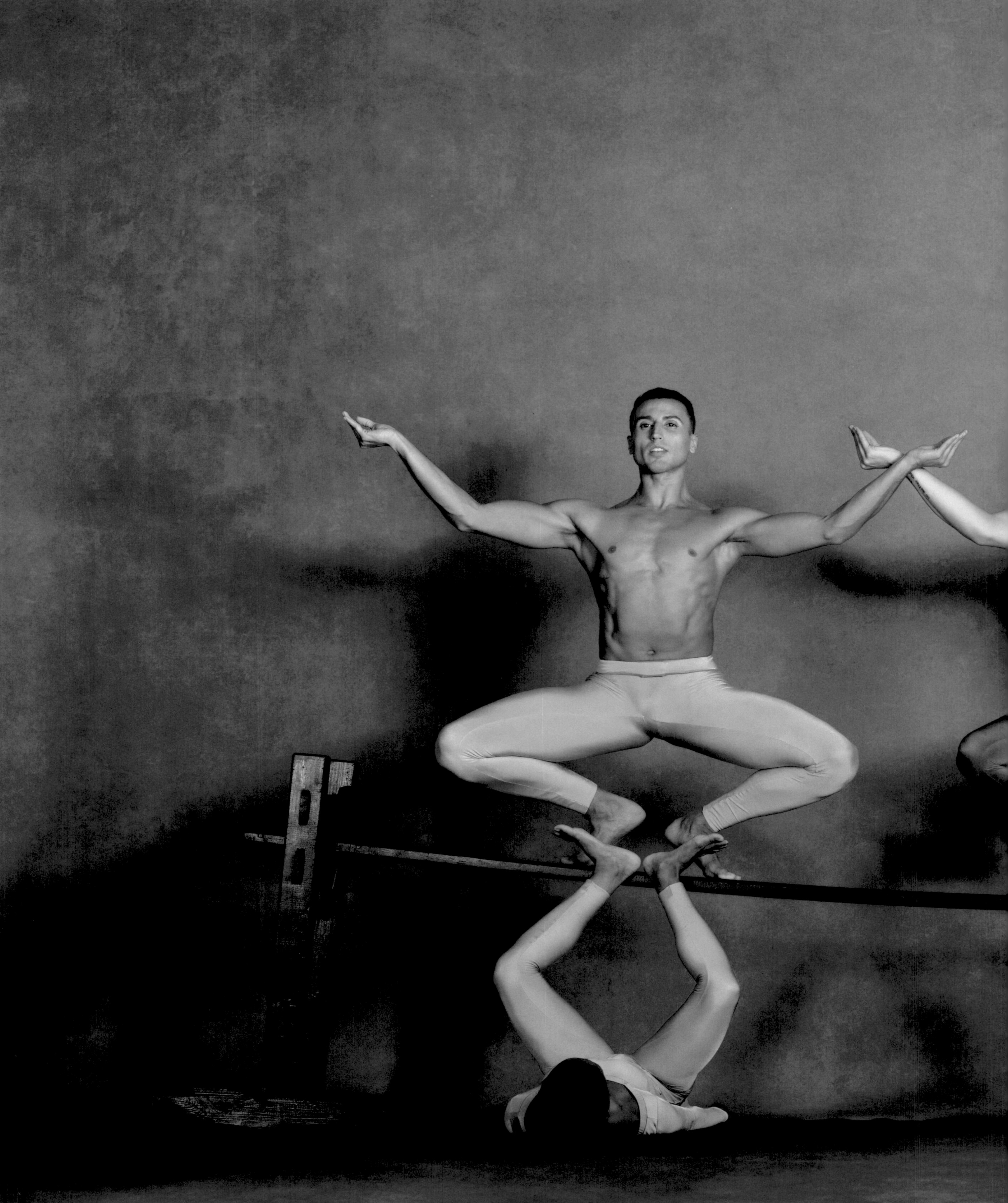

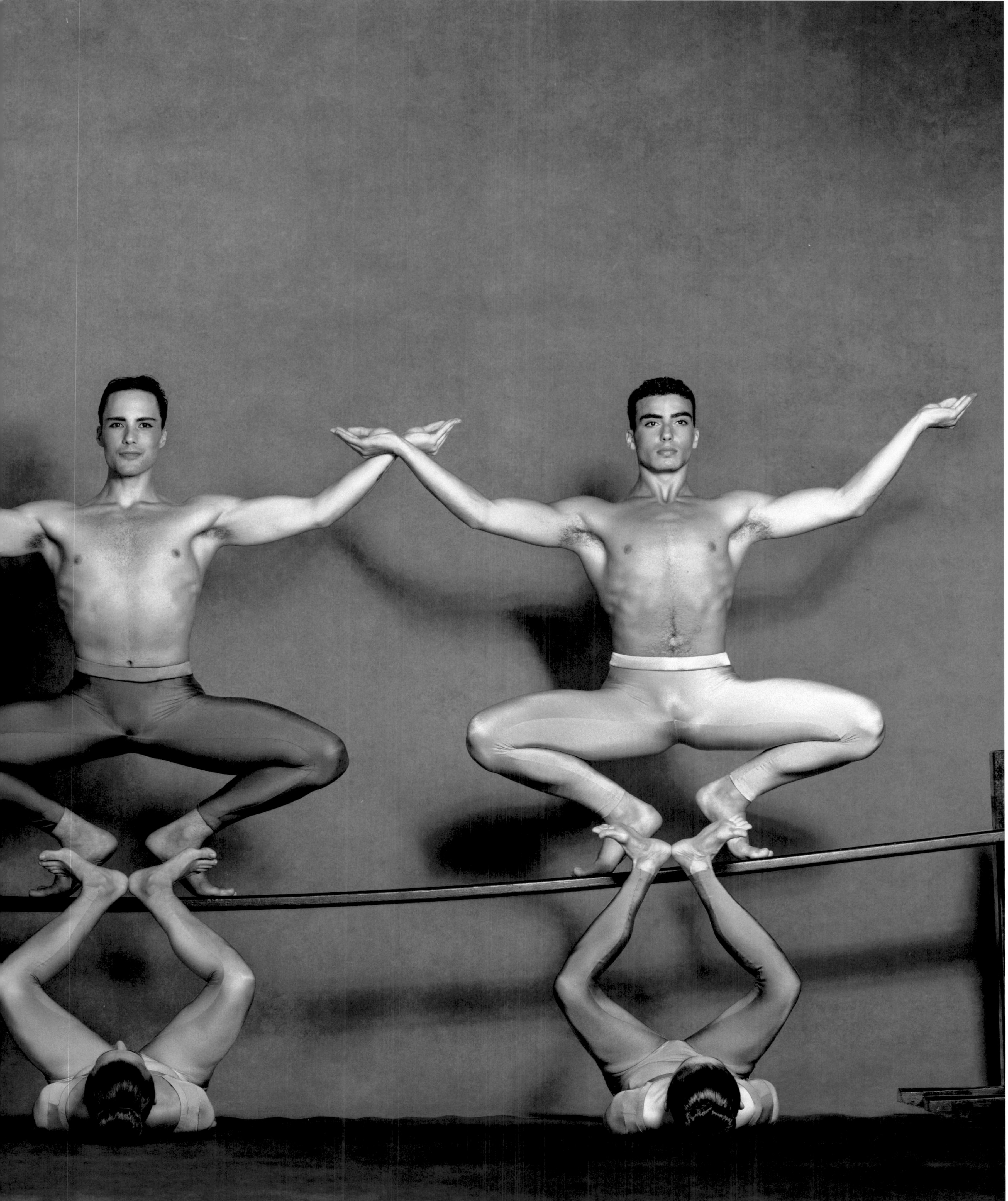

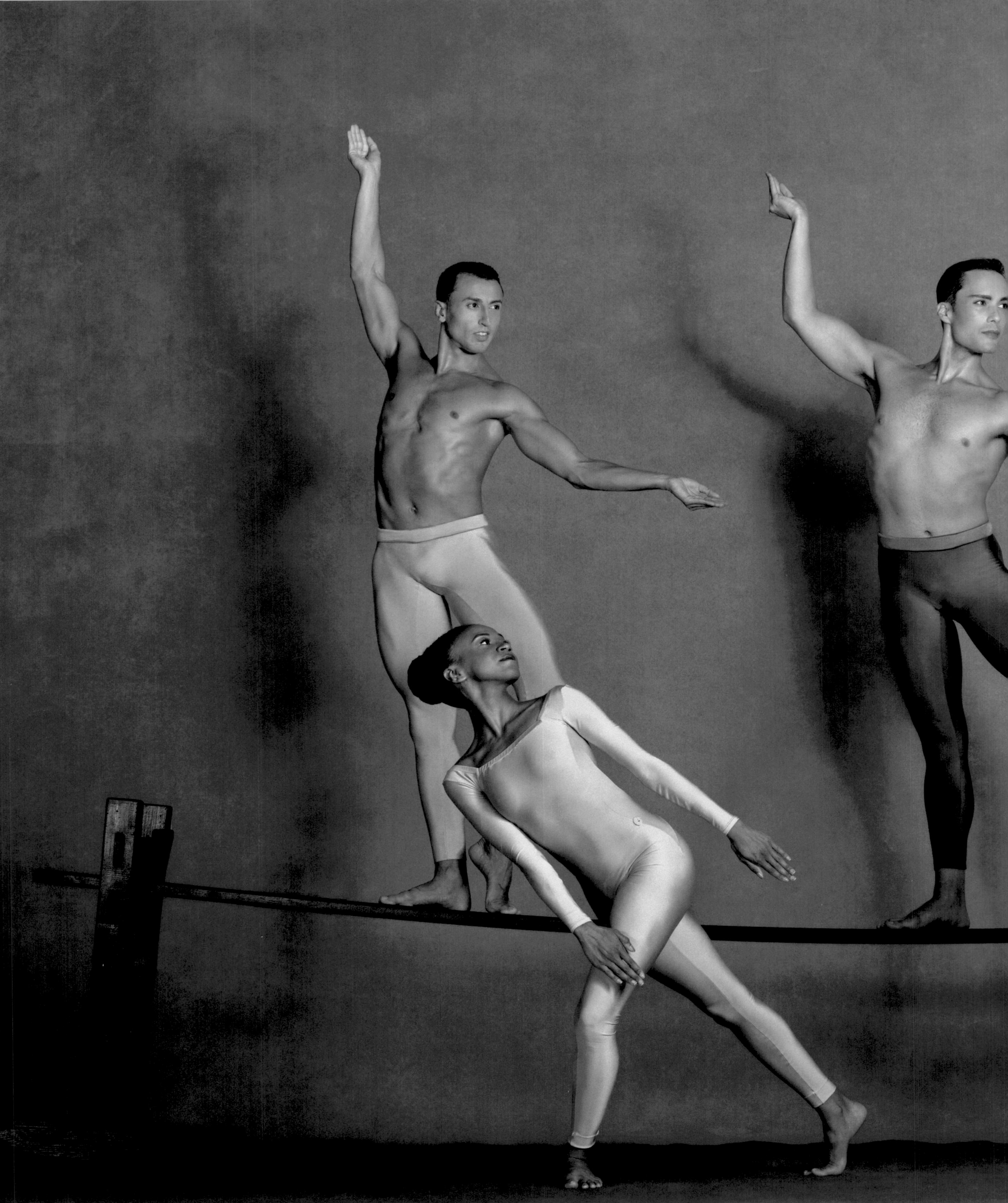

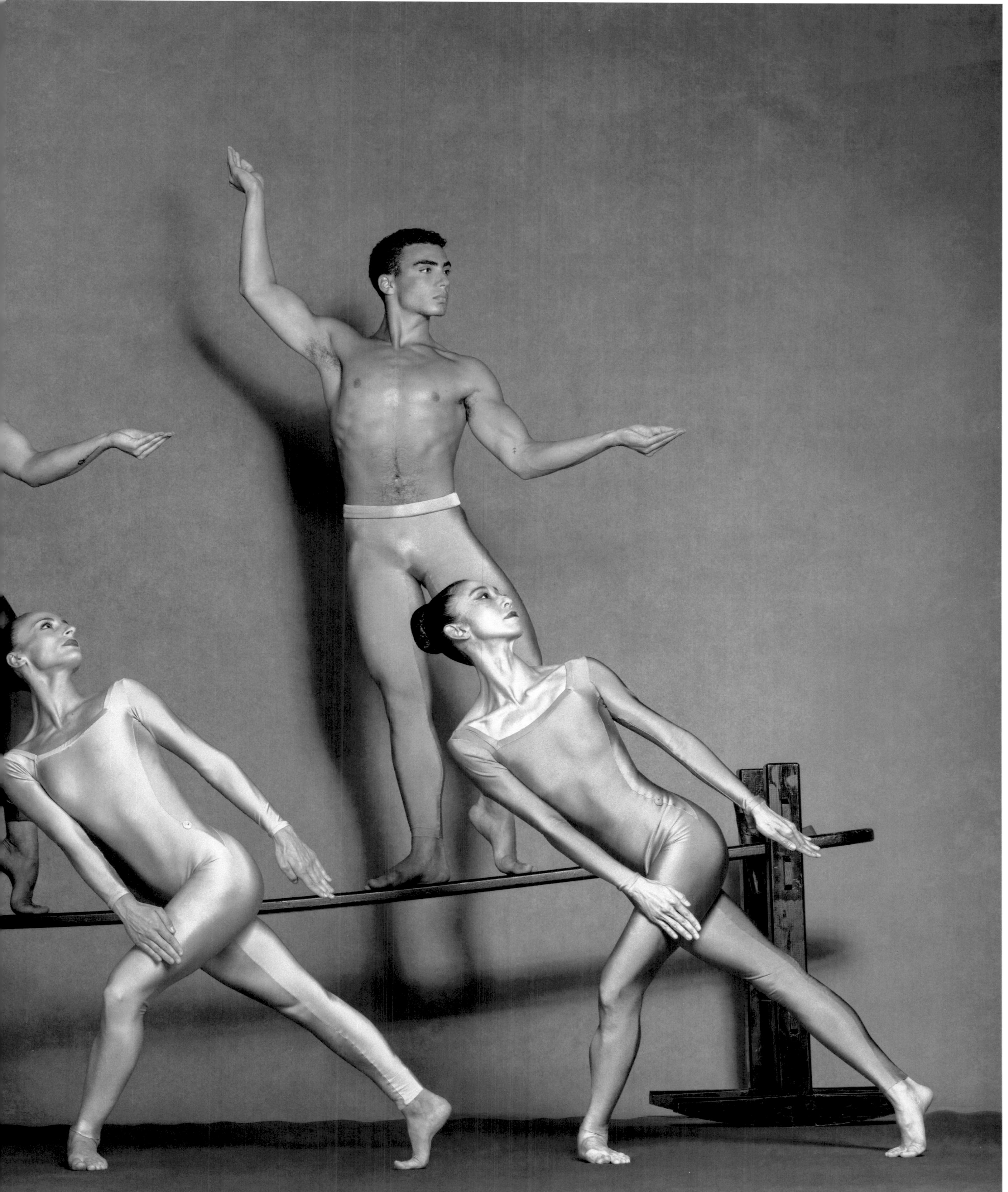

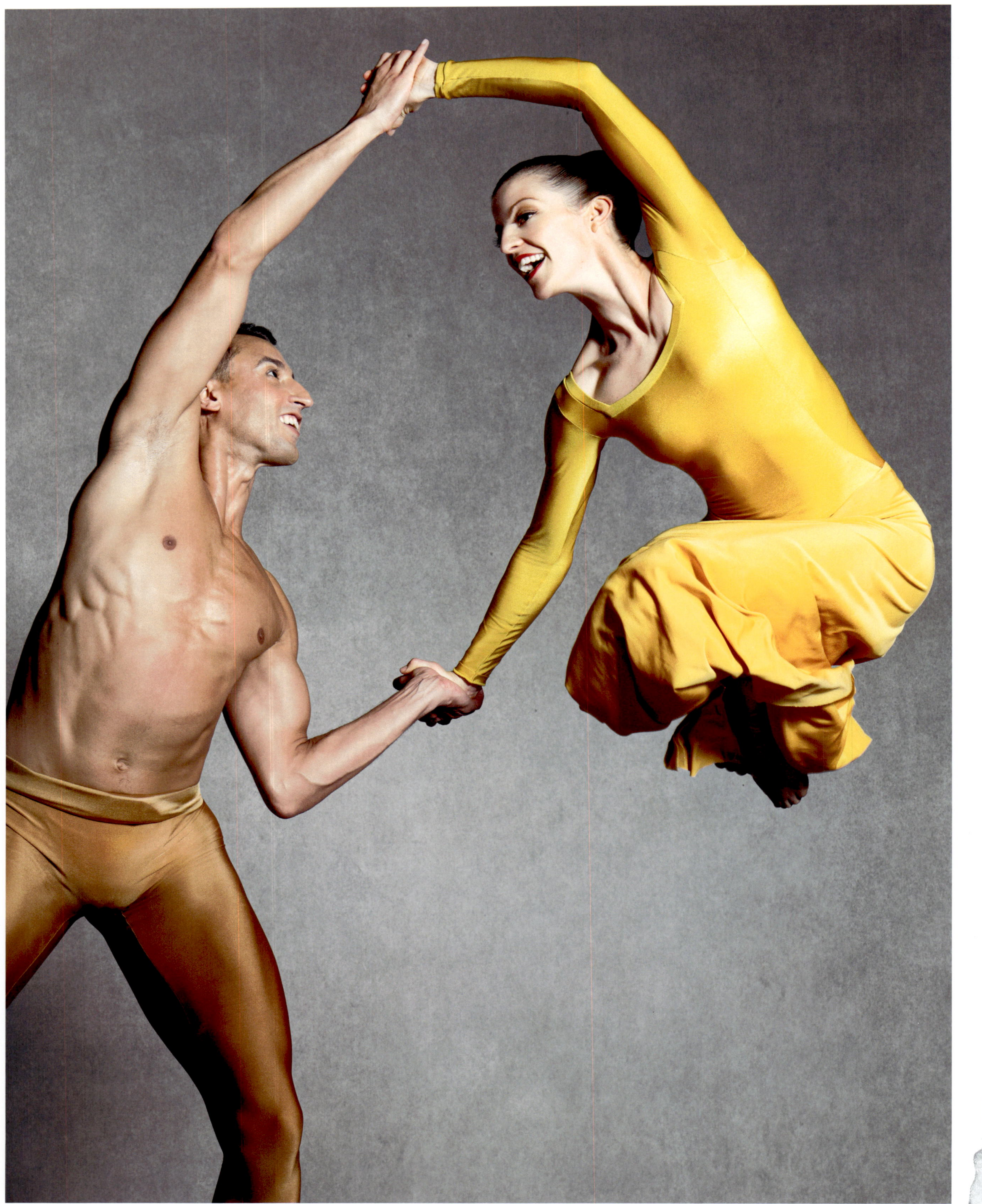

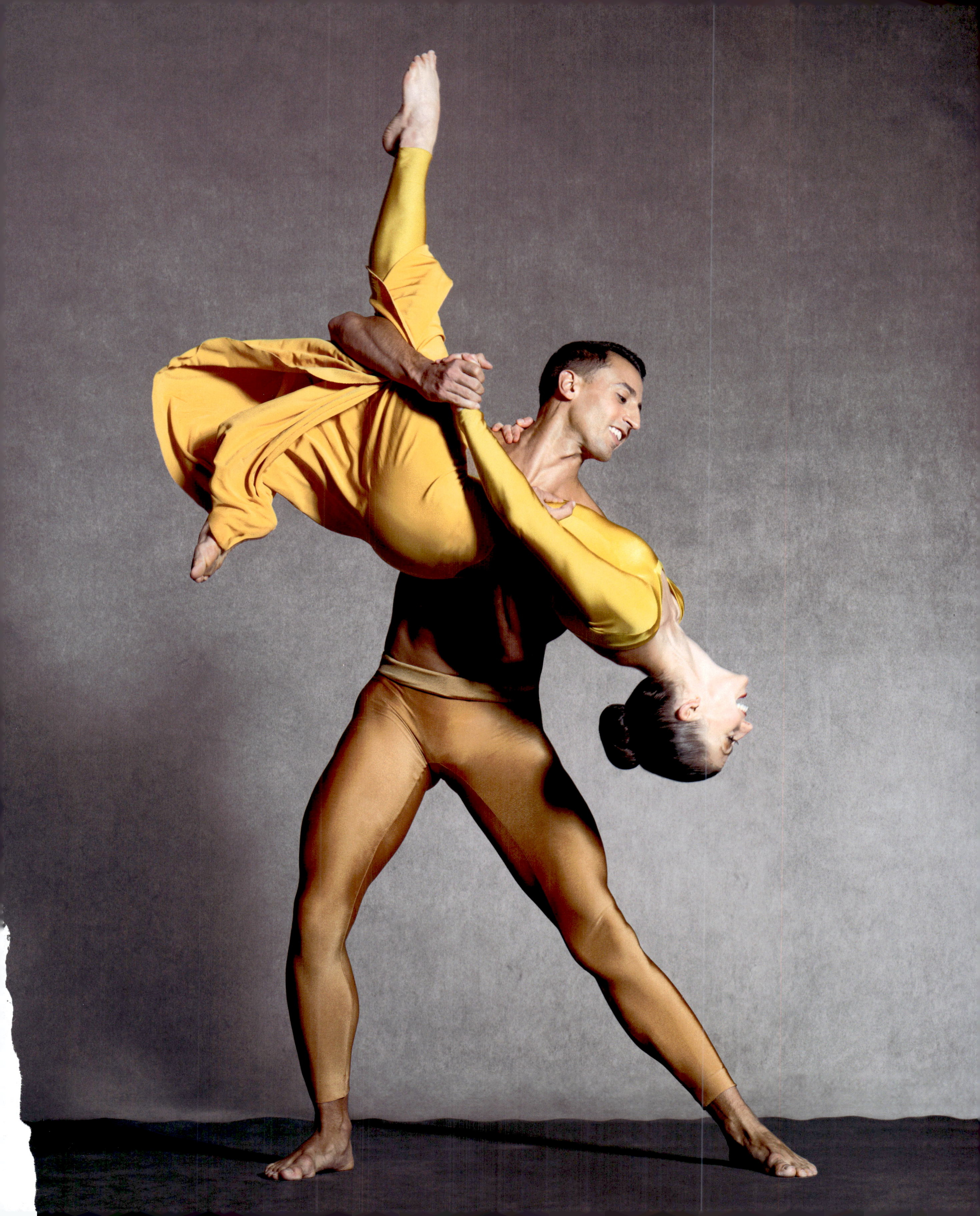

NOGUCHI AND GRAHAM

BONNIE RYCHLAK

Former curator at the Noguchi Museum
and studio assistant to Noguchi

In 1968, Isamu Noguchi explained that his attitude toward making sculpture often came from his work for Martha Graham. Over sixty-odd years, he collaborated with her, making as many as twenty stage sets for her. As he further noted, in the theatre, everything is an illusion. Bigness is a matter of perspective and relationships. The only mechanism that tends to disrupt this dyad is the scale of Graham and her performers.

The first set Noguchi designed for Martha Graham was *Frontier* in 1935. Highly minimal and abstract, it comprised only a stretched rope from the center back of the stage to the upper ends of the proscenium, thereby cutting the stage space into a perspectival delineation. A sense of infinite distance was created. It had within it all the elements of space perception and of volume. Noguchi noted that his interest was to see how his sculpture might exist in the hypothetical space of the theater while creating a living space for human relationships in dance.

Noguchi saw his stage designs as imaginary landscapes. Whether of the American Great Plains or Greek or Hebraic myths, they were sculptural arenas for the dancers. These spaces consisted of stage objects that, at times, directly evinced his sculptures. He often noted that his sculptures were not just sculptures but something like a tool. The objects on the stage had a literal and metaphorical function. This is inimitably illustrated in the dance *Hérodiade* from 1944. The stage objects were extensions of Graham's body, the forms representing the skeleton of her body. In the production, Salome dances before her mirror. What does she see but her own bones? The chair is an appendage of her vertebrae, the clothes rack for the circumscribed bones on which she hung her skin.

"In our work together, it is Martha who comes to me with the idea, the theme, the myth upon which the piece is to be based. She will tell me if she has any special requirements . . . the form is then my projection of these ideas. I always work with a scale model of the stage space in my studio. Within it, I feel at home and am in command. With Martha, there is the wonder of her magic with props. She uses them as extensions of her own anatomy. I conceive of sculpture as a permeation of space. I believe that's how Martha treated it with her body."

However, Noguchi's sets for Graham were sometimes objects to contend with, obstacles and barriers rather than comfortable elements integrated into the dancers' natural movements. As Janet Eilber, a longtime dancer with the Company and its current artistic director, noted, many dancers complained that the Noguchi stage structures created demands and challenges that sometimes tested their endurance. Whether the narrowness of the seat for *Appalachian Spring* or thrones, beds, or chairs with blunt or metal projections, they were painful to sit or lie on for any length of time. Many of the positions needed to be held for several minutes, during

Opposite: Noguchi set for *Dark Meadow*.

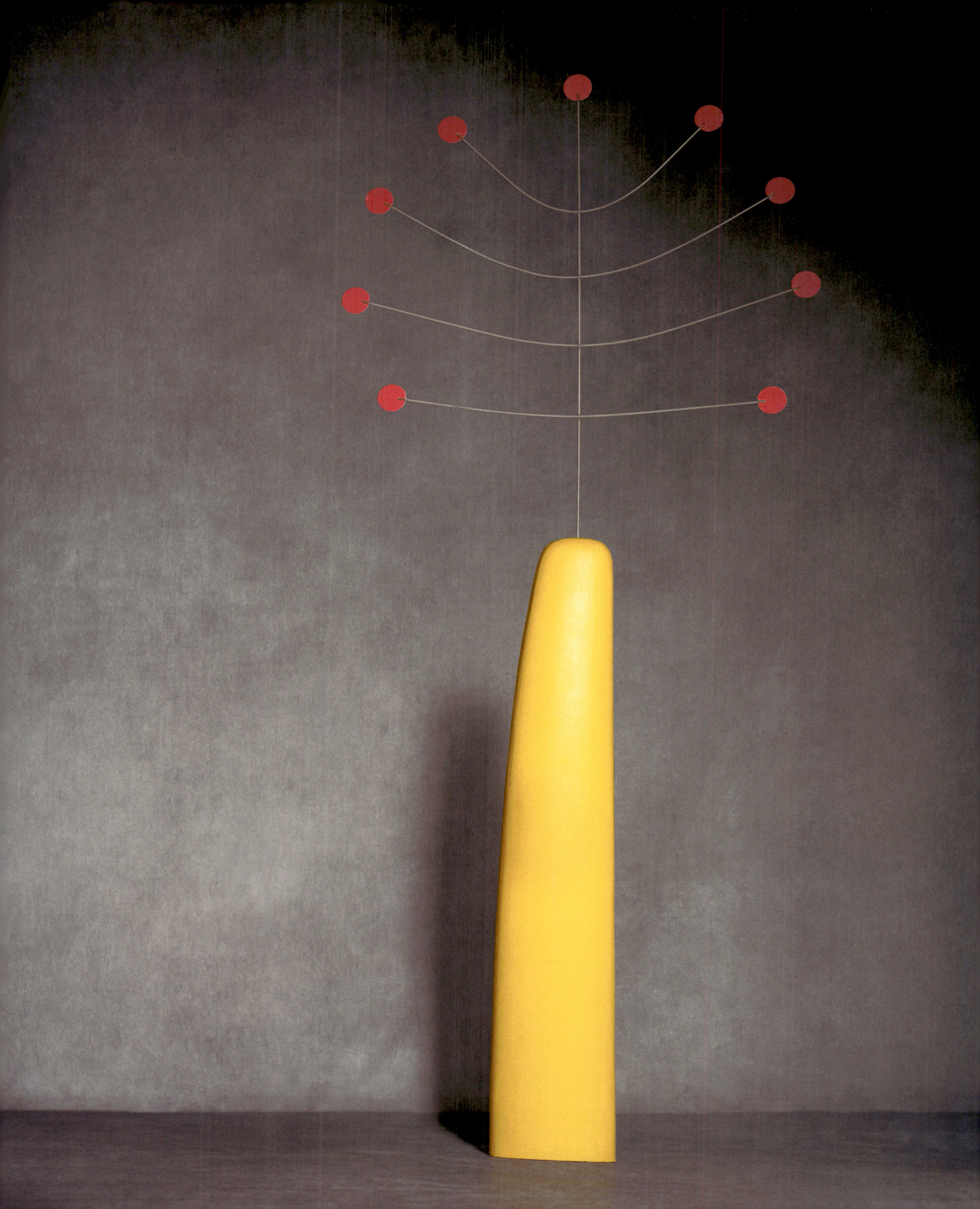

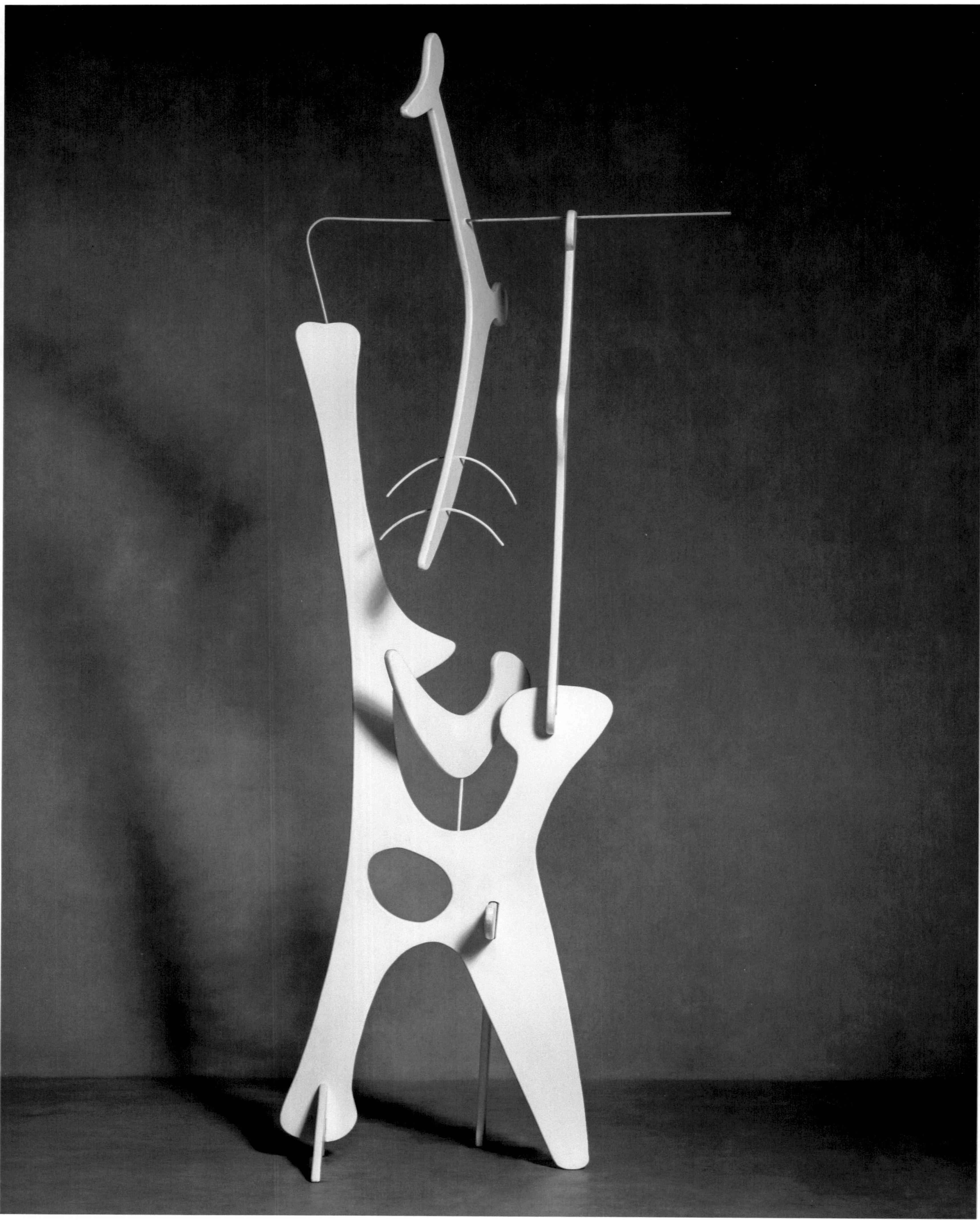

Noguchi set for *Hérodiade*.

which the dancers were required to remain completely phlegmatic. It was believed that Noguchi had knowingly designed his sets for that purpose, not in a sadistic manner but as a method to incite tension, energy, and possibly anger.

On the occasion of an evening honoring Martha Graham at the Dance Collection of the New York Public Library of the Performing Arts at Lincoln Center on November 23, 1973, the program notes indicated that *Cave of the Heart* was Graham's final solo performance. As observed by Robert Horan in an article published in *Dance Index* in 1947, he described Noguchi's low set design, with "personal hazards" low to the floor so that Graham's gaze would remain low, like a preying animal, furtively slinking before her pounce.

Agnes de Mille described Martha Graham's final solo dance in *Cave of the Heart* as a dance of such animal anger and frustration as to defy sense and sensibilities. It evoked disgust, and it was performed as a long pas de bourrée on the knees, including a passage of quivering, carnivorous rage in which Graham would half squat, half kneel, and vibrate the knees in and out like an insect in spasms of evisceration and digestion. And finally, Noguchi's *Spider Dress* encapsulates Graham's transformation into a hungry insect.

The carnality of Graham's dances with Noguchi's designs has been infamous and, in some cases, almost censored. In 1963, *Phaedra*, a dance that was to be sponsored by the State Department for creative export, was considered by some congressmen as bordering on pornographic. Noguchi described the creative process for this dance. He said Graham wanted a bed for Aphrodite and Hippolytus. He made a tall blue-and-black capsule for Hippolytus with small doors that opened to reveal parts of his body. Aphrodite was placed in an immense womb-like structure that opened to reveal a half-naked goddess. She is presented with her legs wide open. On the other hand, she and the structure could have been interpreted as a butterfly leaving her cocoon. However, Graham and Noguchi were never inhibited in their creative visions.

When Noguchi and Graham agreed to collaborate on *Dark Meadow*, Noguchi was working on a large mural commission in Mexico City. The designs for this dance were not specifically of a Mexican aesthetic, but their pronounced and baroque sensibility clearly has elements of a Mexican tenor. Although *Dark Meadow* is part of Martha's Greek cycle, it is more primitive in tone than the myth, Noguchi noted. "The work has to do with a primordial time of the minds. Situations of birth and death and then renewal."

Graham described her relationship with Noguchi thus: "Without Isamu Noguchi, I could have done nothing. He gave me a sense of inhabited, vibrant living space. [Noguchi] always has given me something that lived on stage as another character, as another dancer." Noguchi told Robert Tracy in 1986 that Graham was always having a dialogue with the audience, whereas he, on the other hand, was having a dialogue with the environment and his sculptures in his imaginary landscapes.

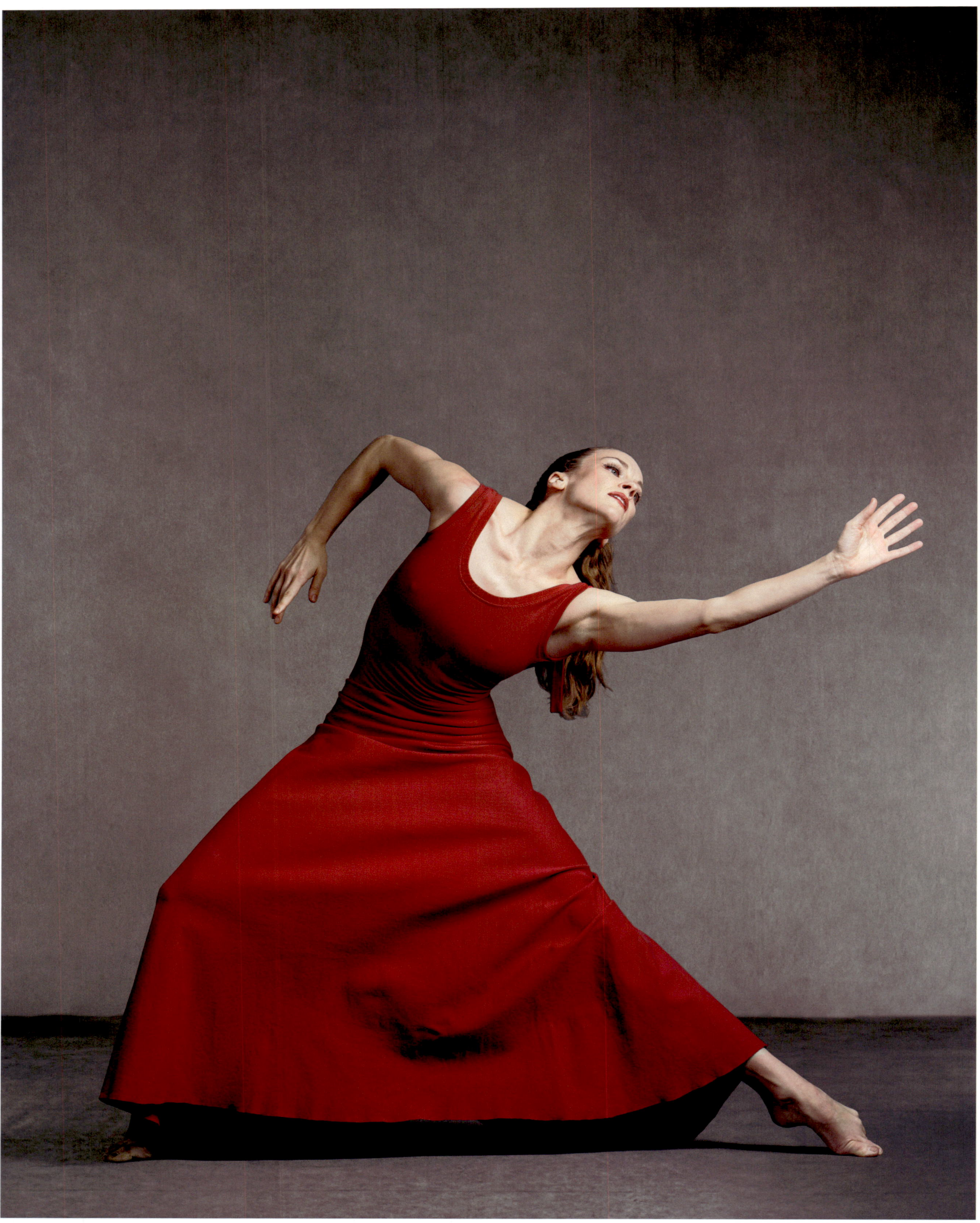

Anne O'Donnell Passero dancing in *Embattled Garden*.

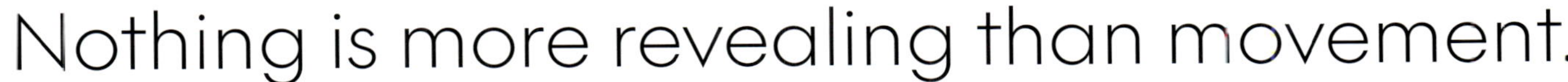

Nothing is more revealing than movement.

—MARTHA GRAHAM

Photographer's Note

DEBORAH ORY

I can remember the first time I saw the Martha Graham Dance Company in Ann Arbor, Michigan, at the Power Center for Performing Arts: I was in high school and studied ballet, but I had never seen modern dance and was certain that I was not going to like it. My mother had tickets, so I was dragged along as her companion. What I saw that evening had a strong impact on my life and would eventually shape much of my career.

The dancers were both beautiful and graceful—like the ballet—but they had a power and intensity to their movement that I hadn't seen before. The women, wearing long stunning dresses, moved with power and force, literally falling to the floor and rising up in a split second, using their hips and pelvises in a sensual—almost sexual—way, and easily leaping through the space. The men moved in angular, sharp, athletic movements. The performance included Halston costumes and Noguchi sets, and I had witnessed something very special and ephemeral. Graham's messages about the human psyche were both raw and emotional.

Within a week I contacted a former Graham principal dancer—Peter Sparling—who was a professor at the University of Michigan, whose class I took, and eventually I became a dance major. An injury later stopped short my dance career, but I stayed close to dance, photographing the rehearsals that I couldn't be in. It was the beginning of my transition to becoming a photographer.

Over the past fifteen years my husband, Ken Browar, and I have been photographing dancers. Ken came to appreciate dance as a fashion photographer and together we've worked with many dancers for our books, but this, our third book, is our first collaboration with a dance company.

Janet Eilber, the Company's artistic director and a former principal dancer for Graham, was one of the first to encourage us when we started photographing dancers. She wrote the introduction for our first book, *The Art of Movement*, and also an essay for our second, *The Style of Movement: Fashion and Dance*. Once we decided to do this book, our first photo session was canceled because of the Covid pandemic, and it felt unclear whether dance would ever return to the stage.

Many of our friends in the Graham Company changed careers or retired as Covid retreated, and new dancers arrived. We had photographed one or two dancers at a time; we hadn't embarked on photographing large groups of dancers. Where would we even have the space to photograph such large groups? As we contemplated how to begin, it felt like there were so many obstacles. The first performance we saw at the end of pandemic was the Graham Company. Russia had invaded Ukraine days before the performance and the Company was performing *Chronicle*, a piece about the tragedy of war. I saw many tears in the audience, and I knew how strongly Graham's messages still resonated, even with a dance created more than eighty years earlier. Energized by the performance, we decided we needed to move forward.

We could never have done this book without the group effort of so many people—from Janet Eilber and LaRue Allen, who encouraged us and gave us their studio space, dancers, and costumes, to the entire dance company—many of whom worked with us on rare days off from tours or after long rehearsals. It is with honesty that I say these photos in the book are the result of everyone coming together with a passion for the art.

I also want to acknowledge the incredible photographers who have come before us and who collaborated with Graham. We've included some of their work in this book—Barbara Morgan, Philippe Halsman, Arnold Eagle, Soichi Sunami, Max Waldman, and many others. We are honored to follow in their footsteps.

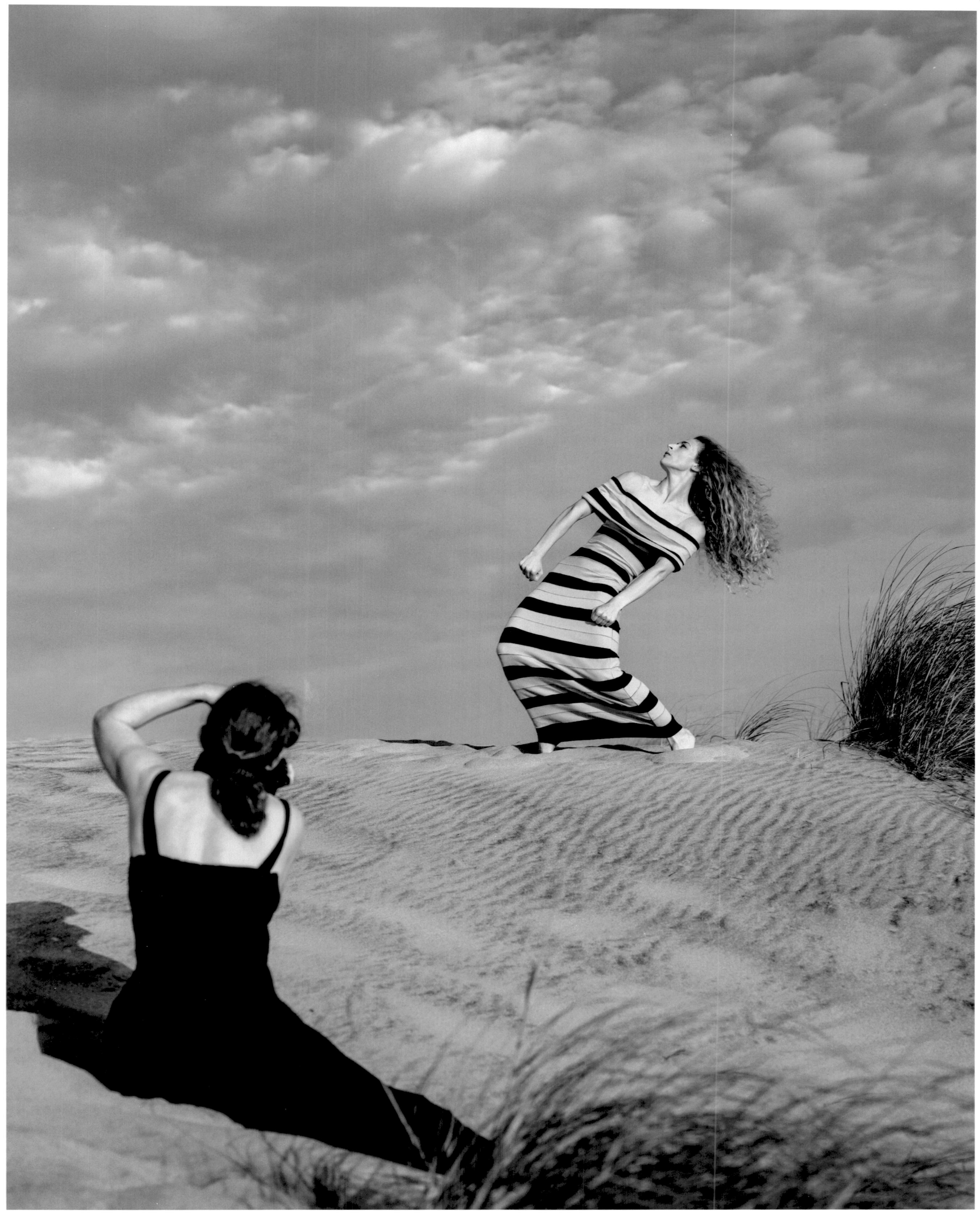

Deborah Ory photographing Marzia Memoli. Photograph by Ken Browar.

Original Casts

Honoring the dancers who first danced these iconic roles.

LAMENTATION
Martha Graham

PRIMITIVE MYSTERIES
Martha Graham, Lillian Shapero, Mary Rivoire, Dorothy Bird, Sydney Brenner, Louise Creston, Matti Haim, Lily Mehlman, Sophie Maslow, Pauline Nelson, May O'Donnell, Lillian Ray, Ethel Rudy, Gertrude Shurr, Anna Sokolow, Joan Woodruff

SATYRIC FESTIVAL SONG
Martha Graham

EKSTASIS
Martha Graham

IMPERIAL GESTURE
Martha Graham

FRONTIER
Martha Graham

CHRONICLE
Martha Graham, Anita Alvarez, Thelma Babbitz, Bonnie Bird, Dorothy Bird, Ethel Butler, Aza Ceskin, Jane Dudley, Frieda Flier, Marie Marchowsky, Sophie Maslow, Marjorie Mazia, May O'Donnell, Kathleen Slagle, Gertrude Shurr, Anna Sokolow, Mildred Wile

DEEP SONG
Martha Graham

EL PENITENTE
Martha Graham, Erick Hawkins, Merce Cunningham

HÉRODIADE
Martha Graham, May O'Donnell

APPALACHIAN SPRING
Martha Graham, Erick Hawkins, May O'Donnell, Merce Cunningham, Marjorie Mazia, Nina Fonaroff, Pearl Lang, Yuriko

CAVE OF THE HEART
Martha Graham, Erick Hawkins, May O'Donnell, Yuriko

DARK MEADOW
Martha Graham, May O'Donnell, Erick Hawkins, Pearl Lang, Natanya Neumann, Marjorie Mazia, David Zellmer, Yuriko, Mark Ryder, Ethel Winter, Douglass Watson

NIGHT JOURNEY
Martha Graham, Erick Hawkins, Mark Ryder, Pearl Lang, Helen McGeHee, Yuriko, Natanya Neumann, Ethel Winter, Joan Skinner

ERRAND INTO THE MAZE
Martha Graham, Mark Ryder

MOON DUET FROM "CANTICLE FOR INNOCENT COMEDIANS"

Yuriko, Bertram Ross

CLYTEMNESTRA

David Wood, Martha Graham, Gene McDonald, Bethany Beardslee, Robert Goss, Ethel Winter, Bertram Ross, Yuriko, Richard Kuch, Dan Wagoner, Helen McGehee, Ellen Siegel, Akiko Kanda, Carol Payne, Ellen Graff, Bette Shaler, Lois Schlossberg, Paul Taylor, Matt Turney, George Nabors

EMBATTLED GARDEN

Yuriko, Bertram Ross, Matt Turney, Glen Tetley

CIRCE

Bertram Ross, Mary Hinkson, Clive Thompson, Robert Powell, Richard Gain, Gene McDonald, Peter Randazzo

LUCIFER

Daniel Maloney, Rudolf Nureyev, Janet Eilber, David Chase, Peter Sparling, Tim Wengerd, Barry Smith, Henry Yu, Ohad Naharin, Elisa Monte, Bonnie Oda Homsey, Jessica Chao

DIVERSION OF ANGELS

Pearl Lang, Helen McGehee, Natanya Neumann, Dorothea Douglas, Joan Skinner, Dorothy Berea, Dale Sehnert, Mark Ryder, Robert Cohan, Stuart Hodes

ACTS OF LIGHT

Yuriko Kimura, Charles Brown, David Hochoy, Jean-Louis Morin, Bert Terborgh, George White Jr., Peggy Lyman, Tim Wengerd, Thea Nerissa Barnes, Jacqulyn Buglisi, Terese Capucilli, Christine Dakin, Donlin Foreman, Judith Garay, Sophie Giovanola, Elisa Monte, Donald Prosch, Jeanne Ruddy, Philip Salvatori, Larry White

THE RITE OF SPRING

Christine Dakin, Terese Capucilli, George White Jr., Larry White, Thea Nerissa Barnes, Joyce Herring, Jaculyn Buglisi, Steve Rooks, David Hochoy, Julian Littleford, Tom Smith, Carol S. Mead, Susan Kikuchi, Judith Garay, Kim Stroud, Jeanne Ruddy, Sophie Giovanola, Ed Zujkowski, Jean Louis Morin, Miguel Moore

MAPLE LEAF RAG

Kathy Buccellato, Terese Capucilli, Laura Horvath, Miki Orihara, Daniela Stasi, Camille Brown, Joyce Herring, Theresa Maldonado, Maxine Sherman, Kim Stroud, Denise Vale, Myra Woodruff, Floyd Flynn, Mario Camacho, Peter London, Pascal Rioult, Tancredo Tavares, Young-Ha Yoo, Lyndon Branaugh, Kenneth Topping, Duane Cyrus

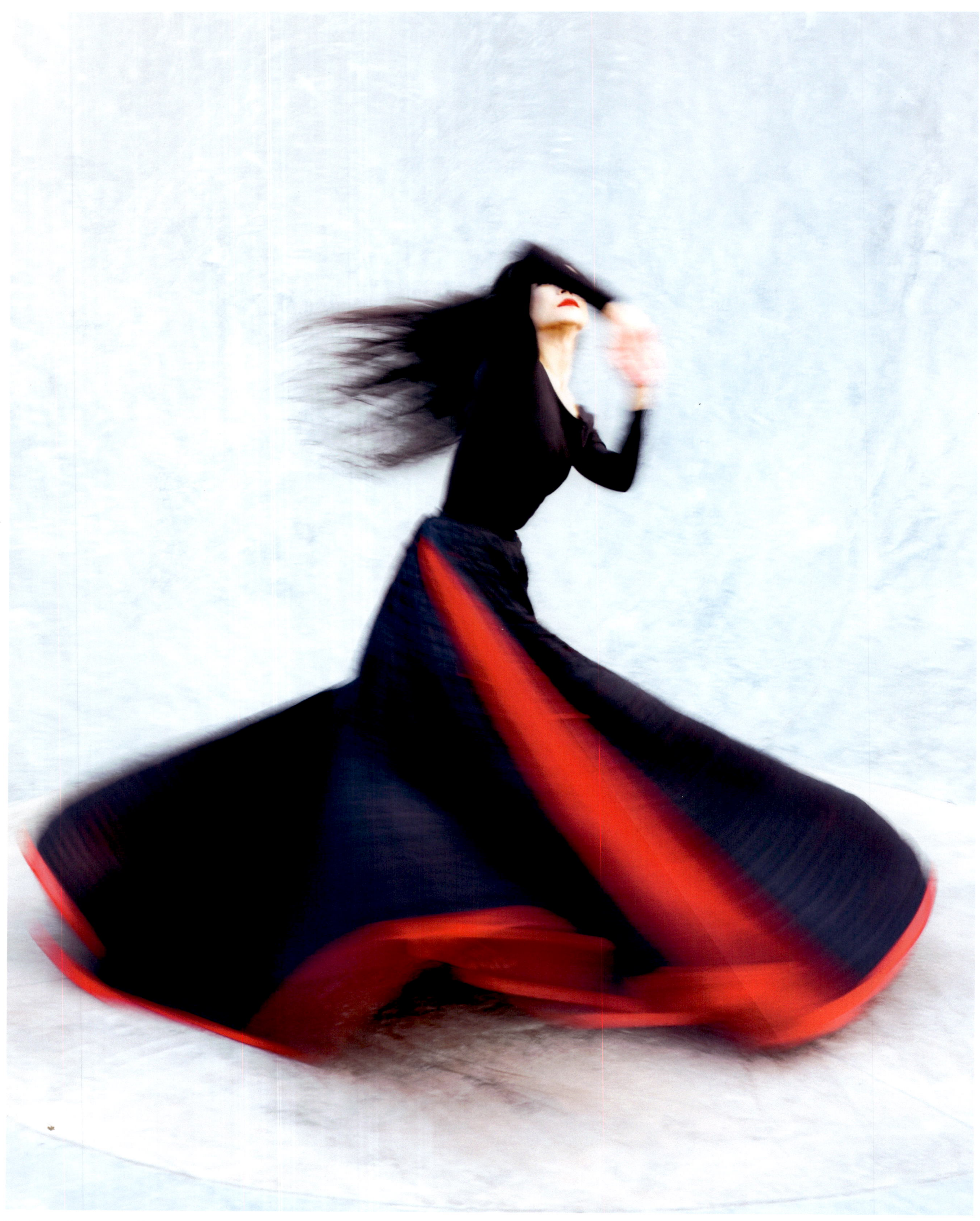

Xin Ying dancing in *Chronicle*.

Acknowledgments

Many individuals deserve our gratitude for giving their time to this project. We'll start with Janet Eilber, who has supported us since we started photographing dancers years ago and has been by our side with every detail in this book. LaRue Allen, Joyce Herring, Simona Ferrara, and the entire team at the Martha Graham Dance Company who spent countless hours on this book. Becky Koh, who edited both this book and *The Art of Movement* and without whom this would not have been possible—and also thank you to Katie Benezra and the staff at Black Dog & Leventhal. Peter Sparling, my very first Graham teacher, who wrote the text and was always there to give advice. Bonnie Rychlak, sharing her love of Graham and Noguchi in her essay. Xin Ying, the stunning dancer on our cover. Lloyd Knight, who was the first dancer we ever photographed together and who shared his talent and inspiration through the entire project. Hooman Majd, our dear friend and fantastic writer who was there every step of the way to advise.

We would also like to thank:

AGMA, Neil Baldwin, Tom Biondo, Josef Blazer from Blazing Editions, Mariola Briales, Matt and Nancy Browar, Jeff Dunas, Simon Elliot, Corey Field, Michael Grecco, Genie Guenard from the UCLA Library Special Collections, John and Jeri Heiden from Smog Design, Luis Hernandez, Rita Jules, Jeff Korchek, Caleb Krieg, Robyn Lange, Lloyd Mayor, Miko McGinty, Virginie Mécène, Fred Midgley, Chloe Morrell, Lauren Mosier, Linda Murray from the New York Public Library for the Performing Arts, the Noguchi Museum, Sarah Oliphant, Jenna Ory, Sarah Ory, Monica Ramirez-Montagut from the Parrish Museum, Ben Schultz, Melanie Scranton, Philippa Serlin, Ivan Shaw, Melissa Sherwood, Stephanie Shin, Jon Slesinger from Fotocare, Denise Vale, Simon Van Booy, Merry Varr Franey from Blazing Editions, Elizabeth Waterman, Elise Weisbach, and Karen Young.

And to all the dancers who gave their time, energy, and artistry:

So Young An, James Anthony, Ane Arrieta, PeiJu Chien-Pott, Alessio Crognale-Roberts, Laurel Dalley Smith, Natasha Diamond-Walker, Anne O'Donnell Passero, Meagan King, Lloyd Knight, Charlotte Landreau, Jacob Larsen, Antonio Leone, Devin Loh, Marzia Memoli, Amanda Moreira, Lorenzo Pagano, Kate Reyes, Anne Souder, Richard Villaverde, Leslie Andrea Williams, and Xin Ying.

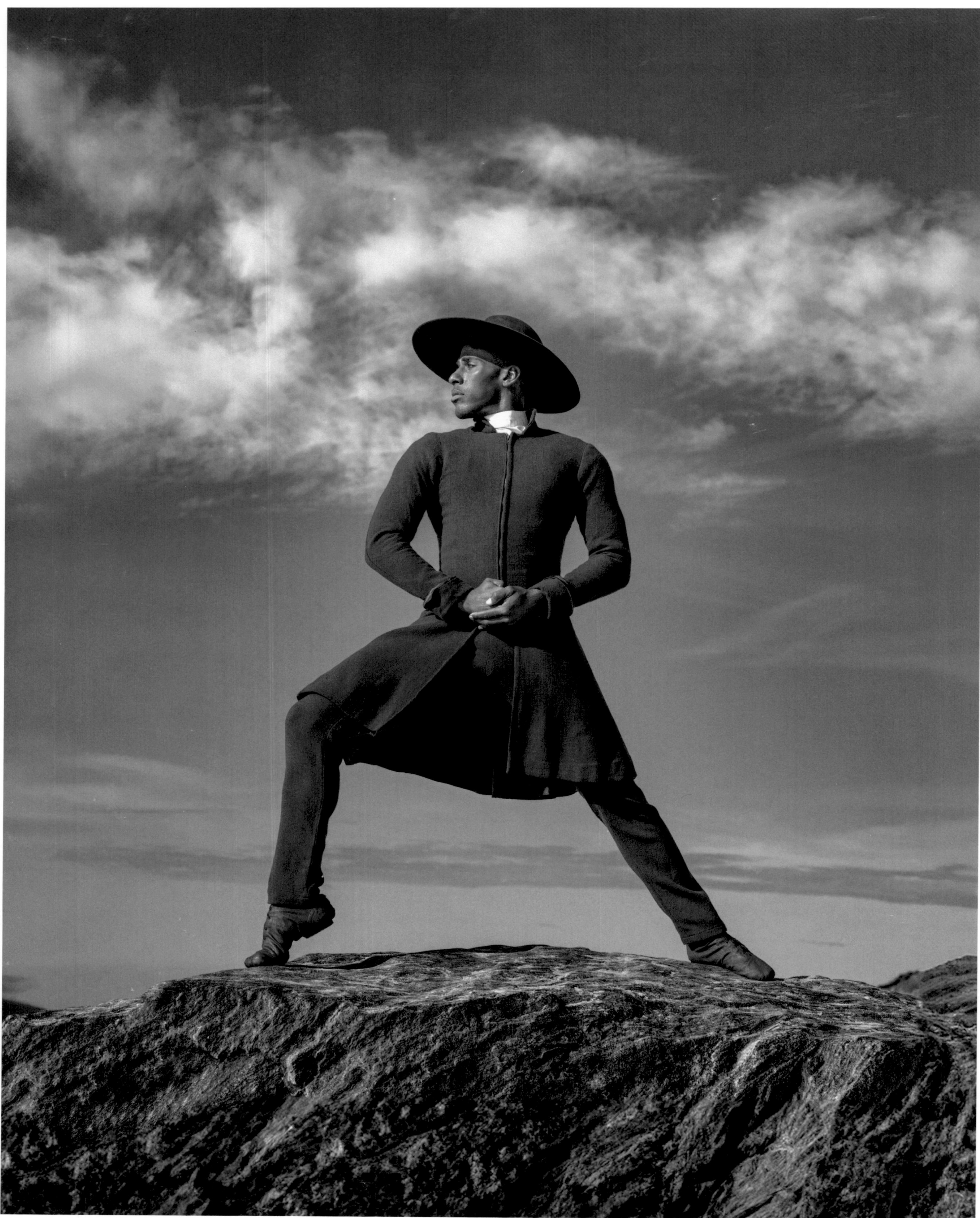

Lloyd Knight dancing in *Appalachian Spring*.

Dancers are the messengers of the gods.

—MARTHA GRAHAM

Black Dog & Leventhal Publishers
Hachette Book Group
1290 Avenue of the Americas, New York, NY 10104
www.blackdogandleventhal.com
BlackDogandLeventhal @BDLev
Author website: www.nycdanceproject.com Author Instagram: @nycdanceproject

First Edition: October 2025

Published by Black Dog & Leventhal Publishers, an imprint of Hachette Book Group, Inc. The Black Dog & Leventhal Publishers name and logo are trademarks of Hachette Book Group, Inc.

Black Dog & Leventhal books may be purchased in bulk for business, educational, or promotional use. For more information, please contact your local bookseller or the Hachette Book Group Special Markets Department at Special.Markets@hbgusa.com.

The publisher is not responsible for websites (or their content) that are not owned by the publisher.

All photographs used with permission of the Martha Graham Resources. Additional credits: Cris Alexander: *Diversion of Angels*. Courtesy of the Martha Graham Resources. Anthony Crickmay: *Circe*. © Anthony Crickmay/Victoria and Albert Museum, London. Philippe Halsman: *Cave of the Heart*, *Dark Meadow*, *Night Journey*. Philippe Halsman/Magnum. Joan Miró poster: *Lucifer*. © Successió Miró/Artists Rights Society (ARS), New York/ADAGP, Paris 2024. Barbara Morgan photographs: *Lamentations*, *Primitive Mysteries*, *Imperial Gesture*, *Deep Song*, and *El Penitente*. Courtesy Barbara and Williard Morgan photographs and papers/UCLA Library Special Collections. Martha Swope: *The Rite of Spring*. © NYPL. Soichi Sunami: *Ekstasis*. Courtesy of the Martha Graham Resources. Max Waldman photographs: *Frontier*, *Errand into the Maze*. © Max Waldman, USA. All rights reserved. Andy Warhol illustration: *Satyric Festival Song*. © 2024 The Andy Warhol Foundation for the Visual Arts, Inc./Licensed by Artists Rights Society (ARS), New York. Jim Wilson: *Maple Leaf Rag*. Jim Wilson/NY Times/Redux.

Print book jacket and interior design by Miko McGinty Inc.

Library of Congress Cataloging-in-Publication Data

Names: Browar, Ken, author. | Ory, Deborah, author.
Title: Martha Graham Dance Company 100 years / Ken Browar and Deborah Ory, NYC Dance Project ; Text by Peter Sparling.
Other titles: Martha Graham Dance Company one hundred years
Description: New York : Black Dog & Leventhal, [2025] |
Summary: "This is the exclusive 100-year anniversary celebration of the Martha Graham Dance Company, America's oldest company and one of the most popular and esteemed dance companies in the world. This book offers exclusive access to the current company as well as pieces of archival material" —Provided by publisher.
Identifiers: LCCN 2024036357 (print) | LCCN 2024036358 (ebook) | ISBN 9780762487448 (hardcover) | ISBN 9780762487455 (ebook)
Subjects: LCSH: Martha Graham Center for Contemporary Dance—History. | Graham, Martha. | Modern dance.
Classification: LCC GV1786.M37 B76 2025 (print) | LCC GV1786.M37 (ebook) | DDC 792.809—dc23/eng/20240812
LC record available at https://lccn.loc.gov/2024036357
LC ebook record available at https://lccn.loc.gov/2024036358

ISBNs: 978-0-7624-8744-8 (hardcover); 978-0-7624-8745-5 (ebook)

Printed in China

IM

10 9 8 7 6 5 4 3 2 1